Dyslexia in Context

Dyslexia in Context

Research, Policy and Practice

Edited by

GAVIN REID,
University of Edinburgh

ANGELA J. FAWCETT,
University of Sheffield

W

WHURR PUBLISHERS
LONDON AND PHILADELPHIA

©2004 Whurr Publishers

First published 2004 by
Whurr Publishers Ltd
19b Compton Terrace, London N1 2UN, England and
325 Chestnut Street, Philadelphia PA 19106, USA

British Library Cataloguing in Publication data
A catalogue record for this book is available from the British Library.

ISBN 186156 42 6 0

Printed and bound in the UK by Athenaeum Press Limited, Gateshead, Tyne & Wear.

Contents

Contributors

Bodil Andersson. Speech and language pathologist with a broad experience of reading and writing issues, ranging from the hospital sphere and language pre-school work to adult education and user organization work. She is also member of the editorial board of the *Journal of the Swedish Dyslexia Association.* She has a strong interest in assistive technology and is also engaged in software development for people with reading and writing difficulties.

Virginia W. Berninger. A professor of educational psychology, Director of the NICHD-funded Multidisciplinary Learning Disabilities Center, and Co-Director of the Brain, Education, and Technology Center at the University of Washington. Her research involves developing methods to assess and treat reading and writing disabilities, focusing particularly on nature–nurture interactions within systems models. The Psychological Corporation has kindly sponsored her presentation.

Jane Browning. Executive Director at the Learning Disabilities Association of America and former Executive Director of the President's Committee on Mental Retardation, a position she held under the Clinton Administration. She organized an international PCMR conference on poverty and disability at the City University of New York Graduate Center.

Vinita Chhabra. A Research Scientist within the Child Development and Behaviour branch of the National Institute for Child Health and Human Development (NICHD). She serves as the NICHD liaison to joint educational activities with the National Institute for Literacy and the Department of Education and assists with adolescent/family literacy initiatives at the NICHD. Vinita has worked at the NICHD Yale Center for Learning and Attention on reading disabilities research. Vinita also served as a research scientist in support of the National Reading Panel.

Steve Chinn. Principal and founder of Mark College, Somerset, UK, a secondary school for dyslexic boys. Chair of the BDA International Conference in 1994. He has written widely on mathematics and dyslexia and lectures worldwide.

Victoria Crivelli. Senior Specialist Teacher for ICT and Resources, Teaching and Training, for Worcestershire Support Services. Chair of the British Dyslexia Association's Computer Committee (BDACC). She has specialized in dyslexia and learning difficulties for 20 years, working with all age groups, including adult education, and is the author of a variety of works.

Margaret Crombie. Support for Learning Manager for the Highland Council Education, Culture and Sport Service. She is author of a number of books and articles on dyslexia and has researched the effects of dyslexia on the learning of a foreign language in school. She has also investigated how dyslexia manifests itself at the early stages of a child's life and how early intervention can help children showing signs of difficulties.

Pamela Deponio. Starting her career as a classroom and later support for learning teacher, Pamela is currently a lecturer in the Moray House School of Education at the University of Edinburgh where she teaches on undergraduate courses and is programme organizer for postgraduate courses in Education Support.

Angela Fawcett. Senior research fellow and lecturer in the department of psychology at the University of Sheffield. Her theoretical research on dyslexia with Roderick Nicolson fed into the construction of best-selling screening tests for dyslexia. She is chair of the 2004 British Dyslexia Association International Conference, and editor of *Dyslexia: an International Journal of Research and Practice.*

Anne Henderson. Educational consultant and dyslexia specialist, affiliated to the dyslexia unit at University College Wales, Bangor, and also a BEAM mathematics consultant. She taught dyslexic students for 30 years, focusing for 15 years on the difficulties they experience with mathematics, and has written four books on dyslexia and mathematics.

Mike Johnson. Leader, Centre for Inclusive Education and SEN, Institute of Education, Manchester Metropolitan University. Mike was a primary school teacher and educational psychologist before his career in teacher education, and has directed projects for the EU in Lithuania, Estonia and Kyrgystan and in the UK for the DfES, QCA, RSPCA and the British Epilepsy Association.

Deborah Knight. Assistant professor, University of Delaware, teaching courses about struggling readers, reading methods, and the psychology of reading. Research interests include reading disabilities, especially dyslexia; phonological and orthographic processing; early intervention; decoding in adults; and the linguistic and cognitive aspects of reading comprehension.

Geoff Lindsay. Professor of educational psychology and special educational needs at the University of Warwick, and Director of the Centre for Educational Development, Appraisal and Research. He is a chartered educational psychologist.

Neil Mackay. Previously Senior Teacher/SENCO in a comprehensive school and now an independent consultant and trainer, Neil originated the phrase and concept 'dyslexia friendly schools'. He works in Europe and Hong Kong on teacher training initiatives and with the BDA and LEAs in the UK to spearhead dyslexia-friendly schools initiatives.

David McLaughlin. An educational and occupational psychologist, as well as the Professional Director of the Adult Dyslexia and Skills Development Centre, London. He is a Visiting Professor in the Department of Psychology at the University of Buckingham. David is principal author of *Adult Dyslexia: Assessment, Counselling and Training* by McLaughlin et al. (Whurr, 1994) and *The Adult Dyslexic: Interventions and Outcomes* by McLaughlin et al. (Whurr, 2002).

Roderick Nicolson. Professor in Cognitive Psychology and Head of Department at the University of Sheffield. Chair of the British Dyslexia Association International Conference (2001). Following an interest in learning, his dyslexia research with Angela Fawcett has influenced both theory (via their automatization deficit and cerebellar deficit hypotheses) and practice (via their dyslexia screening tests). They have published over 100 refereed articles and book contributions, together with over 100 conference presentations, including keynote speeches at several international conferences on dyslexia.

Lindsay Peer. Education Director and Deputy Chief Executive of the British Dyslexia Association for 10 years until 2003. She is a consultant, lecturer and author and works widely with issues related to children and adults.

John Rack. Head of Research at the Dyslexia Institute. His interests have included children's collaborative learning with computers in primary classrooms, early reading development, applied questions about the effectiveness of intervention and the important role of phonological processing skills in dyslexia. He contributes to decisions on policy within the DI and at government level and is currently serving on a DfES working party on assessments for dyslexia in higher education.

Gavin Reid. Senior lecturer in educational studies at the Moray House School of Education, University of Edinburgh. He is an experienced teacher, educational psychologist, university lecturer and researcher who has written and edited course books for teacher training in the field of dyslexia and literacy. He has also co-developed screening tests to identify literacy and other specific difficulties. He is a member of the BDA Accreditation Board and a director of The Red Rose School for dyslexic children in St Anne's, Lancashire.

G. Reid Lyon. A research psychologist and the Chief of the Child Development and Behaviour Branch at the National Institute of Child Health and Human Development (NICHD) within the National Institutes of Health (NIH), Dr Lyon has served on the faculties of the University of Alabama-Birmingham, Northwestern University, and the University of Vermont and is the author and co-author of over 120 journal articles and book chapters addressing learning and reading development in children. Dr Lyon also currently serves as an advisor to President George W. Bush on child development and education research.

Sally E. Shaywitz. Professor of Pediatrics at the Yale University School of Medicine, where she co-directs the NICHD-Yale Center for the Study of Learning and Attention, Dr Shaywitz is the author of *Overcoming Dyslexia: A New and Complete Science-Based Program for Reading Problems at any Level* published by Alfred A. Knopf in 2003. Dr Shaywitz was elected to membership in the Institute of Medicine of the National Academy of Sciences and served on the National Reading Panel and on the Committee to Prevent Reading Difficulties in Young Children of the National Research Council.

Linda Siegel. Currently Associate Dean of Graduate Programs and Research and a professor in the Department of Educational Psychology and Special Education at the University of British Columbia in Vancouver, British Columbia, Canada, Linda Siegel holds the Dorothy C. Lam Chair in Special Education. She has conducted research in learning disabilities, language and cognitive development, the role of psychoeducational assessment in the identification of learning disabilities, bilingualism, premature and high-risk infants, and the early identification of learning disabilities. She has been the editor of the *International Journal of Behavioural Development* and the Associate Editor of *Child Development.*

Ian Smythe. A private consultant on dyslexia working world-wide with governments and non-governmental organizations, Ian obtained his PhD on 'Cognitive factors underlying reading and spelling difficulties: a cross-linguistic study' from the University of Surrey. He is the main editor of the *International Book on Dyslexia* published by Wiley.

John Stein. Fellow and tutor in medicine at Magdalen College, Oxford, since 1970. He has carried out a great deal of research on visual guidance of eye and limb movements in neurological patients and dyslexics. He has put forward the hypothesis that children's reading problems result from impaired visuomotor and auditory processing, which is caused by abnormal development of large nerve cells in the brain (magnocellular neurones).

Robert Sweet. Professional Staff Member for the Committee on Education and the Workforce within the US House of Representatives. In this role, he focuses on improving reading instruction in the United States. He was the primary author of the Reading First Legislation. For twenty years Mr Sweet served as a high school teacher, educational textbook salesman, and teacher trainer for McGraw Hill and Holt Rinehart and Winston. In 1981 he joined the Reagan Administration and held positions at the US Department of Education, the National Institute for Education, and the White House. Under President George H.W. Bush he was Administrator for Juvenile Justice, and Associate Director for the Children's Bureau at the US Department of Health and Human Services.

Moira Thomson. Principal Teacher, Learning Support and Special Educational Needs at Broughton High School, Edinburgh; also Development Officer, City of Edinburgh Education (where responsibilities include supporting dyslexia); Associate Tutor, Scottish Network for Able Pupils and Associate Assessor, Her Majesty's Inspectors of Education. Co-authored City of Edinburgh's Framework of Support for dyslexic pupils at the secondary stage. Recently published the City of Edinburgh's Guidelines for Special Assessment Arrangements. She pioneered laptop use by dyslexic learners.

Aryan Van der Leij. Previously a school psychologist and gaining his PhD in severe reading disabilities in 1983, he became Professor of Special Education in 1984, from 1999 at the University of Amsterdam. He is Vice-chairman of the Dutch Dyslexia Programme (1998–2010), a university consortium running longitudinal studies with children at risk of dyslexia (aged 0–10 years), four prevention studies (5-year-olds) and a genetic study. He supervises the Amsterdam longitudinal study and is national co-ordinator of the intervention studies. Further research programmes include arithmetic, basic cognitive processes in LD, LD and brain functioning, and social-emotional problems, with senior researchers Peter de Jong, Theo van Leeuwen, Helma Koomen and Victor van Daal, 10 PhD students and two postdocs. He is head of the Department of Educational Sciences of the University of Amsterdam.

Glenn Young. An adult with learning disabilities/dyslexia that were not diagnosed until the age of 30. He has worked in several capacities in the US federal government, focusing on the area of adults with learning disabilities. He has also provided direct technical assistance to a number of states on learning disability issues, and has hosted several major conferences dealing with learning disabilities.

Introduction

We feel privileged, as editors of this book, to have had the opportunity to collaborate with contributors all of whom are researchers and practitioners of high standing in the field of dyslexia, internationally recognized for their achievements. They contributed to this conference book despite the many demands on their time, thus indicating their belief in the value of this project. We would like to thank them for their contributions, which we know will be well received by the attendees at the conference and, indeed, by all involved in the field of dyslexia throughout the world.

This publication, like the conference, has an international flavour with contributions from Europe, the US and the UK. The contributors have endeavoured to place their chapters within a contemporary and relevant context, and we have recognized the importance of ensuring that contributions are completely 'up to date'.

The book is divided into three sections – research, policy and practice. Each of the sections is preceded by an editors' introduction to set the scene for the section and to outline some of the key points that may be of interest to readers.

We hope that this publication will satisfy the need for current information on dyslexia, will help to fuel and inform the debate, and will offer guidance on practice. Ultimately it aims to benefit all children and adults with dyslexia, helping them to develop their full potential in education, in the workplace and in life.

Gavin Reid
Angela Fawcett

CHAPTER 1

An overview of developments in dyslexia

GAVIN REID, ANGELA J. FAWCETT

One of the strongest views to emerge from the BDA International Conference in 2001 was that there is a need for consensus. There was, and still is, a growing awareness of the many and often disparate strands of thought that in some way affect children and adults with dyslexia as well as teachers, parents, researchers and other professionals involved in the field. Nicolson (2001: 22) suggested that, whereas outstanding progress had been made in the years since 1990, there is an 'emerging consensus that a broader framework is needed for causal explanations and for diagnostic aids [for dyslexia]'. He also suggested that this consensus should enable the sciences – neuroscience, cognitive science and learning theory and their application to education – to come together with policy and government. He took the view that a coherent strategy is required, characterized by partnerships, 'kite marking' and multi-disciplinary, multi-perspective projects aimed at redefining the field of dyslexia.

Although only a few years have passed since this was written it is interesting to reflect how the field of dyslexia has in fact moved since the turn of the twenty-first century, in terms of the direction of research in the sciences, the policies of governments and the practice of teachers. This is the context for this chapter, which aims to identify and discuss the advances in dyslexia, to provide reflective comment on the way ahead, and to introduce and relate these comments to the subsequent chapters of this book.

The chapter will be divided into sections corresponding with the main themes of this book – research, policy and practice, with research addressed by Angela Fawcett and policy and practice by Gavin Reid. Some of the points made are expanded in subsequent chapters as this book intends to reflect the current state of the field of dyslexia, the developments, insights and innovations.

Research

It is encouraging to note a change in emphasis in publications. In 2003 they placed research in dyslexia within a broader framework, bringing in a range of interdisciplinary perspectives.

If we consider the state of play for each of the main theories in turn, it should be clear that significant progress has been made in each. There is an emerging synergy between these theoretical developments, leading to a more satisfactory explanation of the symptoms of dyslexia than the individual theories on their own. It would be premature to describe an emerging consensus but one of the most striking aspects of recent developments has been an acknowledgement of the need to consider a range of theories in order to understand the causes of dyslexia. This has been coupled with an awareness of the complexity of dyslexia and the need to consider co-morbidity between different and frequently overlapping developmental disorders.

Naturally, this interdisciplinary approach is still in its infancy, which means that there are issues still to be resolved, limiting the firm conclusions that can be drawn. For example, there is a need to ensure that research groups share their methodologies, because even simple changes to the research design can significantly affect the outcomes found. Moreover, there is a need to ensure that subjects are drawn from an ecologically valid school-based sample so that results can be generalized. It would hardly be surprising if subjects diagnosed on the basis of their language skills showed severe phonological deficits, children referred via a vision clinic showed visual impairment, or children diagnosed as clumsy showed cerebellar deficits. There is no substitute for pooling our techniques and working with groups diagnosed as dyslexic on the basis of their literacy symptoms, and preserving the criterion of normal IQ, in order to check for commonalities and differences and relative impairments.

It is important for research purposes to maintain the distinction between dyslexic children and those with more generalized difficulties. Interestingly, recent research has demonstrated that, although all children with reading difficulties can be characterized by phonological difficulties, static cerebellar tests can differentiate between dyslexic children and other children with reading difficulties (Fawcett et al., 2001). Here, of course, we should bear in mind Morton and Frith's (1995) levels of explanation, understanding that different theories may be applied at the cognitive, behavioural or brain-based level. Thus, phonology and speed of processing may be seen as symptoms of the dyslexic deficit, whereas the magnocellular and cerebellar deficit are at the brain-based level.

Fawcett and Nicolson often illustrate their talks with the Hindu story that describes four blind men and an elephant, each identifying something different by touch, whether it be the tail as a rope, the side as a wall, and so on. As our understanding of the different facets of dyslexia develops, it becomes clear that the theories are by no means incompatible and that each strand is worthy of further investigation to enrich our knowledge base. Our ultimate aim must be to link from the brain to behaviour, to allow a more sophisticated diagnostic system based on the specific difficulties each child encounters.

The phonological deficit

This has remained the dominant hypothesis in dyslexia since the early 1980s and readers should need little introduction to the area, which has been a particularly fruitful one for research. Phonological awareness is a meta-linguistic skill involving knowledge about the sounds that make up words, which has been consistently found to be impaired in children with dyslexia, at both the syllable and the phoneme level. There is no doubt that children and adults with dyslexia suffer from phonological deficits (as do other poor readers). The research base here was recently enriched by recognition of the role of speed of processing, which has added another dimension to phonological research, through the double deficit hypothesis (for an excellent series of reviews see Wolf, 2001), which dominated the 2001 conference. This links in with the findings of the National Reading Panel (2000), which recognized the importance of fluency in reading development (see Chapter 15 of this book).

The recent work that has most strongly captured our imagination focuses on risk factors in families with dyslexia (see, for example, Chapter 3 in this volume), studies from Lyytinen's lab (Lyytinen et al., 2001), and the work of Snowling and colleagues in the UK (Snowling et al., 2003). It is particularly encouraging to note Snowling's interactive model of reading development in which problems in establishing a phonological pathway in dyslexic families may be compensated for at an early stage by children who have strong language skills. This has strong implications for early identification and support, and suggests that genetic endowment can be overcome in interaction with a supportive environment.

Some of the most interesting recent work emerging from this field includes a series of studies that have considered potential overlaps between the theories of dyslexia. Ramus (2003) has presented a series of tests of phonological, motion sensitivity and cerebellar function to adults and children with dyslexia, in order to establish the proportions within their panels showing each type of deficit. Wimmer has adopted a similar approach, but in this case he has compared dyslexic and ADHD children with controls. Most exciting of all, in our view, are the brain-based studies that explain phonological difficulties in terms of other theories, including the work of Berninger and her colleagues (see Chapter 5 in this volume).

In our view, investigation of the links between the theories and between brain and behaviour is clearly the way forward.

The magnocellular deficit

One of the most striking aspects of research in dyslexia in the last few years has been a considerable upsurge in interest in the magnocellular deficit hypothesis. Although the area remains controversial, the concept of a pan-sensory deficit in auditory visual and kinaesthetic processing is now being consistently researched, after many years of neglect by all but a few, reflected in debate between protagonists and those who disputed the theories (for example, Skottun and Parke, 1999). Stein suggests that the mechanism by which the magnocellular deficit impacts on reading relates to the role of stability in fixation and the need for saccadic eye movements in reading. Wobbliness in the magnocellular system means that the order of the words may blur and become unstable, which Stein suggests causes the difficulties in reading in dyslexia. In research over many years, Stein has suggested that binocular instability is a prime cause of reading deficit, which can be remedied by occluding one eye for those children with unstable fixation (Stein, 2001). Stein's group compared motion sensitivity with reading and spelling ability in groups of adults and children – good, average and poor readers. Strong correlations were found with reading and even higher ones with their spelling ability across the range of ability (Talcott et al., 2003). Despite solid research from Stein's group, however, the relationship between deficits in the magnocellular system and reading was not transparent.

In current research, the role of the visual magnocellular system in reading, which remained a puzzle to many, is becoming more clearly defined. Some interesting research from Chase and his colleagues (2003) suggests that colour is critical in reading, with red light selectively suppressing the magnocellular pathway, but facilitating the parvocellular pathway. However, although this provides a plausible mechanism for the involvement of the magnocellular system, evidence on the incidence of magnocellular deficits in dyslexia remains mixed. Interestingly enough, moreover, although Sperling et al. (2003) found evidence of magnocellular deficits, this correlated negatively with phonological deficits in their group, with the children with greatest phonological impairment showing magnocellular performance in the normal range. Thus it is not clear whether or not a visual magnocellular deficit explains the known phonological deficits, although auditory magnocellular deficits seem more clearly linked. This is an area of intense research activity, with the investigation of the role of magnocellular deficits in early reading a priority.

The cerebellar deficit

The emergence of new evidence from mainstream cognitive neuroscience on the role of the cerebellum in language suggested that the cerebellar deficit hypothesis could provide a parsimonious explanation for the range of problems suffered by children with dyslexia. This was proposed by Nicolson and Fawcett, based on their early work on automatization and primitive skills. This suggested that any viable theory of dyslexia must be able to account for deficits in balance, speed and phonology, which characterized the performance of between 80% and 90% of the Sheffield dyslexia research panel. In the 2001 book, a full report was given of the research leading to the cerebellar deficit hypothesis, including converging evidence from brain and behaviour (for a review see Nicolson et al., 2001).

One of the key questions raised by those who challenge the cerebellar deficit hypothesis has been why patients with cerebellar damage do not show reading deficits. Naturally, we would expect differences between a normally developing system that receives an unexpected insult (such as a tumour) and a system that develops abnormally from the start. However, recent research demonstrates just such an impairment (see the work of Scott et al., 2001, and Moretti et al., 2002, on the role of the cerebellum in reading).

There is now little doubt that cerebellar function is mildly disturbed in some dyslexics. This is evident from studies both of brain and of behaviour in different groups of children and adults with dyslexia. Balance and gait deficits linked to the cerebellum have been found in children with dyslexia in Norway (Moe-Nilssen et al., 2003) using an accelerometer to measure posture more accurately. There has been a series of studies of eye-blink conditioning, which is known to be mediated by the cerebellum, showing impairments in dyslexia (Coffin and Boegle, 2000; Nicolson et al., 2002). A study by Rae et al. (2002) used imaging to show cerebellar symmetry in dyslexics but not controls. Rae et al. argued that the relationship of cerebellar asymmetry to phonological decoding ability and handedness, together with their previous finding of altered metabolite ratios in the cerebellum of dyslexics, suggest alterations in the neurological organization of the cerebellum, which relate to phonological decoding skills, in addition to motor skills and handedness. Further, individuals with dyslexia could be distinguished from controls based on the volume of the right anterior lobe of the cerebellum (Eckert et al., 2003). These findings provide an explanatory mechanism for the phonological deficits in dyslexia (see Chapters 2 and 5 in this volume).

Nevertheless, as the cerebellum receives a heavy magnocellular input and itself contains magnocells, evidence for cerebellar involvement could be taken as further evidence for the hypothesis that impaired magnocellular development underlies dyslexics' problems. Moreover, the work of Wimmer and colleagues argues that cerebellar deficits are attributable to co-morbidity with ADHD (Raberger and Wimmer, 2003).

The way forward

Currently, the status of the three main theories of dyslexia is arguably less clear-cut than it seemed in 2001. In our view, we are moving towards finding the final pieces of information that will help us to understand the enigma of dyslexia. There is a consensus that we need to consider different theories and begin to address issues such as co-morbidity. This is currently fuelling research into dyslexia and related difficulties. No one would be surprised if this approach were driven by researchers convinced that their own theories are correct, but regardless of the motivation behind their co-operation, it is a step towards establishing the truth. This inevitably makes research more complicated, because naturally enough, complex designs are more difficult to interpret than simple designs. However, this is a healthy state for research and for science, encouraging researchers to challenge the accepted wisdom and to focus on some of the more interesting questions in dyslexia. Further research is needed to untangle the relative contribution of these deficits and to reach a consensus in the area. In the process, a series of neglected areas is emerging for consideration, including learning (Nicolson and Fawcett, 2000; Vicari, 2003) and aspects of attention in different modalities (Facoetti et al., 2003; Moores et al., 2003). This has the potential to unravel some of the issues in the complex area of sustained and switching attention, and allows us to differentiate between children with simple problems in attention related to their dyslexia, and those who would be diagnosed as ADHD.

It would be naïve to assume that we are even nearing a theoretical consensus but, in attempting to answer some of the important questions that have arisen in dyslexia over the past few years, we are moving the field forward and expanding our knowledge of dyslexia substantially. It seems plausible that we may eventually identify a range of sub-types in dyslexia, perhaps through their 'brain signatures' with some deficit in learning at the sensory or the central processing level that affects different aspects of performance depending on the individual strengths and weaknesses of the child in interaction with their environment. These research findings inform our understanding of dyslexia and feed naturally into the areas of policy and practice below.

Policy and practice

One of the most salient aspects in relation to policy is its relationship with practice. There have been some outstanding examples of the linking of policy and practice in recent years involving, particularly, the development of dedicated resources for intervention and professional development courses at all levels linked to policy initiatives.

The major policy initiatives that have impacted on practice in the last few years include the following: the government reports on dyslexia in the Republic of Ireland and Northern Ireland; the revised Code of Practice in England and Wales and the Support for Learning legislation in Scotland, as well as the number of government and collaborative funded projects in the UK and Europe.

Europe

In Europe there has been a sprinkling of government initiatives in dyslexia but the potential for the new, larger Europe, and the need in particular for East European countries to make real progress in policy and practice in dyslexia, are very real challenges. These challenges, however, are firmly in the sights of many, and in October 2002 the British Dyslexia Association (BDA) and the European Dyslexia Association (EDA) combined their respective dyslexia campaigns to hold the first co-ordinated European-wide dyslexia awareness campaign. The EDA has also been involved in East–West projects that intend to promote the profile and the impact of dyslexia throughout Europe. Moreover, in October 2003 the EDA held its first all-European International conference in Budapest. These initiatives will in fact heighten the awareness of dyslexia in many 'new' European countries and already there have been vigorous campaigns arising from recently formed associations, such as the North Cyprus Dyslexia Association (personal communication, 2002), which have involved direct contact with high-ranking government officials.

Northern Ireland and the Republic of Ireland

There has been a recent trend for governments and agencies initiating working groups in dyslexia and other specific learning difficulties to try to establish the state of the field, the research and the shortcomings in current arrangements. This is highly commendable and inevitably will have an impact on practice. One example is that of Northern Ireland, whose *Report of the Task-group on Dyslexia* was published in April 2002 (Department of Education Northern Ireland, 2002). In the foreword to the report, the Minister for Education stated that 'when the North–South Ministerial Council was established, special education was an immediate priority for both our Education Departments, and we decided that dyslexia and autism should be the areas for first attention'. The Minister went on to say that the report

> highlights very real concerns and challenges for all of us in education, particularly the need for training for classroom teachers in recognising where children have, or may have, dyslexia, and in putting in place the means to address their difficulties – and, most importantly, to ensure that the obstacle which their difficulties presents in accessing the rest of the curriculum is minimised. Equally, these are challenges for further and higher education, for employers and for society, because dyslexia is not a condition that disappears with maturity. (Department of Education Northern Ireland, 2002)

This report acknowledged the need for early intervention, that dyslexia occurred across a spectrum from mild to severe and that intervention should be in place to meet this range of needs. The report also recommended that further research was needed on the most appropriate forms of intervention as a matter of urgency in the post-primary level.

The report also suggested that consideration should be given by the Department of Education to the dyslexia training component of Initial Teacher Education courses with a view to offering students the opportunity to gain accredited training. The task group report also recommended the development of further guidance materials for circulation to schools and parents such as a 'good practice guide', which included a CD-ROM.

It is also interesting to note, given the theme of consensus and collaboration mentioned earlier in this chapter, that the report recommended that there 'should be an informed partnership between the teachers, outside support agencies, parents and pupils helping to maintain a consistency of approach'.

One of the important developments in relation to practice is the view that dyslexia is no longer exclusively within the domain of 'specialists'. There has been an increase in training needs across all sectors, involving all levels of teachers and not just those with a specific remit for special needs. It is interesting to note, therefore, that the Northern Ireland report suggested that 'all teachers are responsible for recognising the early signs of dyslexic difficulties and pupil underachievement.' At the same time the expertise built up by many over the years should not be wasted. The report indicated that there should therefore be a teacher or teachers available within the school who, with a greater level of expertise, can advise teachers regarding those pupils with a moderate degree of dyslexic difficulty and who can facilitate further advice and resources from support services when necessary. In cases of more severe dyslexic difficulty, pupils have access to support from teachers who are experienced in the teaching of dyslexic pupils.

In the Republic of Ireland the report of the task force on dyslexia, produced by the Department of Education and Science (Government of Ireland, 2002), gathered together 399 written submissions from individuals, educational institutions and organizations; 896 oral submissions were accumulated from individuals by telephone. This clearly represented a large-scale government-directed attempt to gather specific information and guidance on the way ahead for practice and provision in dyslexia.

One of the features of the report is the tracking of the assessment process from initial identification of a learning difference from the ages of 3 to 5 years through a series of phases to phase 4 – age 12 onwards. This provides a clear, structured and informative set of guidelines for teachers. One of the interesting points to emerge from this and other policy documents is the precision with which what teachers should look for in identifying dyslexia can be pinpointed. Given the controversy over identification criteria for dyslexia (British Psychological Society, 1999) this is a welcome outcome and certainly a significant step from the vague general statements noted in some much earlier reports.

The Irish Republic report, for example, highlights indicators of dyslexia across the age span using single-line bullet points, followed by tables providing key points and personnel in the assessment process. The tables indicate the procedure, the main people involved and the outcomes for each of the phases, and provide clear and hopefully workable guidance on the assessment process.

Scotland

One of the significant features of provision for dyslexia in Scotland for some time now has been the high level of training related to dyslexia offered and taken up by education authorities (Reid, 2001). Reid reports that, in one year alone (1997/8), 5,600 teachers in Scotland undertook early intervention training and 3,300 teachers undertook training specifically in special educational needs issues. This programme is still ongoing and there has been some recent evidence of further impetus particularly in the area of early identification and intervention across Scotland (Crombie, 2002; see also Chapter 12 of this volume).

Throughout the 1990s, teachers across Scotland took up masters courses in dyslexia at university level (Reid, 2001) and, in 2002, one particular course, run at Moray House, was developed into a distance-learning course in partnership with the Open University. In initial teacher education there has also been some impetus in providing training in dyslexia to all students. For example, from October 2003, Moray House School of Education offered a new elective module in dyslexia in the postgraduate course for secondary teachers (PGCE), similar to the type of module already being offered to BEd primary students.

Unlike England and Wales, Scotland does not have a national curriculum but instead has a set of curriculum guidelines (5-14 Guidelines SEED). These can provide for more flexible managing of resources and intervention. In 2002 the Education (Additional Support for Learning) (Scotland) Bill was submitted for consultation in draft form. Two key aspects of the Bill are the notion of 'additional support needs' and 'co-ordinated support plans'. In essence these involve partnership and collaboration, not only between the personnel in the school, but also involving those outwith the school, and particularly with parents. The Bill's key aim is to provide all pupils with a positive, inclusive educational experience and the necessary support to help them towards achieving their full potential. It aims to reform terminology and increase support to pupils. The Bill will therefore replace the term 'special educational needs' (SEN) with 'additional support needs' (ASN). Additional support needs will extend beyond traditional special educational needs to encompass children and young people who, for whatever reason, require support to access and benefit from school education. The Bill will also replace the record of needs (RON) document with a co-ordinated support plan (CSP). The CSP will focus on individuals' educational outcomes and the support required to achieve these. Unlike the RON, the CSP will be reviewed annually or if a pupil's circumstances change. It is important, in this crucial time of change in Scotland, that the needs of dyslexic children and adults are not forgotten. There are encouraging signs as already a number of dyslexia projects are well under way.

For example, as part of the special educational needs innovation grants programme, Dyslexia Scotwest secured funding for a dyslexia-friendly schools programme that will involve a development officer working with a local education authority to put together criteria that will have to be fulfilled by every school. Another ongoing project involves the development of materials for 'practical support to teachers and parents in the educational inclusion of learners with dyslexia across Scotland'. There are therefore good examples across Scotland of partnerships between policy and practice.

England and Wales

Some of the significant factors in England and Wales relating to dyslexia policy and practice have centred on initiatives such as the dyslexia-friendly schools campaign developed by MacKay (see Chapter 13 of this volume). Additionally, government-directed initiatives and statutory developments such as the Code of Practice (Department for Education and Skills, 2001), the National Literacy Strategy (Department for Education and Employment, 1998) and the National Numeracy Strategy (see Chapter 17 of this volume), the literacy hour requirements and the development and planning of individual education plans (IEPs) and school development plans, all have an effect on how the needs of pupils with dyslexia are met.

The Code of Practice (Department for Education and Skills, 2001) with the emphasis on 'school action' and 'school action plus' underlines the importance of initiatives such as the dyslexia-friendly schools campaign. As MacKay points out (Chapter 13 of this volume), the crucial aspects of a successful and effective dyslexia-friendly school include the degree of staff training and support from management. Initiatives, such as that commented on by Johnson (Chapter 14), on the partnership between Manchester Metropolitan University and the BDA (supported by a DfES SEN in-service fund grant) to develop a course for newly and recently qualified teachers to enable them to teach in 'dyslexia-friendly' classrooms are good examples of the way forward. Additionally, the report on the dyslexia-friendly initiative training (MacKay, 2002), which contains excellent suggestions from practising teachers, will be warmly welcomed. Other publications, such as those related to the National Literacy Strategy, supporting pupils with special educational needs in the literacy hour (Department for Education and Employment, 2000a), and supporting pupils working significantly below age-related expectations (Department for Education and Employment, 2000b) will hopefully make the necessary impact on the teaching of dyslexic pupils. These factors set against the backdrop of inclusion highlight the need to ensure that the diversity of students is not placed second to curriculum conformity. Such a potential conflict can have adverse consequences for dyslexic students. There are however many excellent examples of good practice using aspects of the National Literacy Strategy and the National Numeracy Strategy. Some of these include the work on the development of individual education plans (Tod, 2002) and staff development work with teachers on problem-based solutions that help to overcome the barriers to learning (Brough et al., 2002). There are, in fact, many initiatives – too many to mention here – that can contribute to the whole notion of dyslexia friendliness and can help to provide a more promising future for children with dyslexia.

English as an additional language

One of the areas that has gained significant momentum in recent years has been the acknowledgement of the need to promote appropriate and effective practices both in assessment and in intervention for students whose first language is not English, or those who have to use different languages at home and school. The BDA provided considerable impetus for this in 1999 when it hosted the first conference on multi-lingualism and dyslexia, held in Manchester. This was followed by a conference in Washington DC, held collaboratively by the International Dyslexia Association (IDA), the BDA and the EDA in 2002. At the 6th International BDA Conference in 2004 some of the speakers discussed prevention of dyslexia for children who have English as a second language (Siegal, 2004), early literacy skills of Ethiopian immigrants in Israel (Shany, 2004) and the dilemmas faced by teachers in international communities over the identification dilemma of multi-lingualism or dyslexia (Haigh, 2004).

This latter point regarding the dilemma in identification between dyslexia and multi-lingualism is crucial if identification of dyslexia among children who are using more than one language is to become a reality. The BPS report (BPS 1999: 60) on dyslexia, literacy and psychological assessment suggested that 'dyslexia may be masked by limited mastery in the language of tuition'. This implies that dyslexia may be undiagnosed because of the child's difficulty with the language of tuition. Any assumption that a child is failing to acquire literacy on account of using two languages at home and school is too simplistic. The same report suggested there was a need for culture-fair assessment and intervention. This is crucial and there have been attempts to address this (Smythe, 2002). Smythe suggests that identification should not stand alone, but that it should be linked to intervention and, in particular, the child's cognitive profile should be used to inform learning style and to develop an IEP. Smythe refers to his International Cognitive Profiling Test (ICPT) (Smythe, 2002) as a framework for identification. This test focuses on phonological segmentation and assembly skills, the auditory system, visual system, semantic lexicon, speed of processing, literacy attainment including listening and comprehension and non-verbal reasoning and maths.

Guron (2004) has also made significant headway in this area. She has focused on naming speed, word recognition and automaticity. Her view (Guron, 2000) is that, given adequate phonological skills, word decoding skills can be developed rapidly in L2 readers regardless of L1 origin. This point has been developed by Goulandris (2003) who makes cross-linguistic comparisons involving the nature of the language and the range of skills needed for reading in different languages. She argues that, in order to identify the presenting signs of dyslexia in a specific language, it is necessary to understand the relevant linguistic features of that language. Goulandris also suggests it is necessary to focus on the processes involved in the development of reading and spelling and the cognitive skills that underpin the acquisition of literacy development. This implies that the linguistic properties of each language can be influential in the case, or otherwise, of language acquisition in any particular language. This can have implications for those children who may have dyslexia. An example of that is the level of transparency of a language. This refers to how reliably a letter maps onto a speech sound. Goulandris discusses the continuum of how transparent a language is with reference to 'transparent', 'shallow' languages at one end of the spectrum and to 'opaque' and 'deep' languages at the other end. Wimmer (1993) suggests that transparent languages such as Italian, Spanish or Greek will provide fewer problems to young readers than inconsistent, opaque languages such as English, French and Polish.

The key areas in multi-lingualism and dyslexia therefore appear to centre around the availability of reliable, appropriate and culture-fair assessment. There has also been a recognition of the need to consider cultural aspects in teaching as well as individual learning styles and the factors associated with specific languages and, in particular, characteristics of languages such as transparency that can influence the outcome of tuition in that language for dyslexic children. It is also worth noting some of the factors identified by Cummins (1986), who suggests that the entire area of multi-lingualism is a whole-school responsibility and that the outcomes for children who are using more than one language rest on how adaptive the school is in terms of how the cultural aspects of minority pupils are embedded into the curriculum, the level of community participation in the school, the degree of interaction in the pedagogy and whether or not assessment incorporates aspects of the social and learning context of all pupils. This reinforces the dangers of focusing too narrowly on one particular aspect and highlights the need to adopt a holistic perspective involving the parents, the community, the school, the curriculum and the pupil in both assessment and intervention.

Other initiatives

There have been many interesting and effective initiatives that have been conducted in schools in relation to dyslexia over the last few years. Some of these are reported in this volume (see particularly Chapters 8, 12, 13 and 14).

Many of these have capitalized on the impetus initially provided by the highly successful dyslexia-friendly schools campaign, which saw constructive partnership between the voluntary sector and government departments with the campaign reaching every school in England and Wales. One such project that involved a high degree of collaboration between government departments, voluntary sector and commercial agencies is the one briefly described below – the SPELLIT project.

Study Programme to Evaluate Literacy Learning through Individualized Tuition (SPELLIT)

The results of the evaluation of this initiative were published in October 2002. The project was jointly funded by the DfES, WH Smith, the Community Fund and the Dyslexia Institute's Bursary Fund with the research conducted by the Dyslexia Institute and the University of York.

The project evaluated the effects of structured programmes of intervention for 7-year-olds with specific difficulties in learning to read, write and spell. The researchers found that pupils with literacy difficulties responded to early targeted intervention, with some pupils benefiting most from individual multi-sensory teaching and others benefiting more from a home support programme delivered by their parents. SPELLIT produced advice and guidance on assessment and on delivery of these learning programmes.

Awareness and training courses were provided for 30 schools that were involved in SPELLIT and, in many cases, materials and training have been given so that schools can apply some of the same teaching approaches that were used in the teaching and home support programmes. A number of the local education authorities (LEAs) involved in SPELLIT – notably Darlington, Hull, Sheffield, Lewisham and Portsmouth – have initiated or strengthened a partnership with the Dyslexia Institute to deliver services, provide advice and training or work on further research projects. Through collaboration with three LEAs in Glasgow, the Dyslexia Institute in Scotland has become involved in a project to develop home support materials and the experience of SPELLIT will be utilized in this project. SPELLIT has demonstrated how significant advances in educational theory and practice can be achieved through collaboration between voluntary sector, state sector and private sector organizations.

Evaluations of interventions

There has been considerable interest in innovative, as well as traditional, interventions for dyslexia. The Dyslexia, Dyspraxia and Attention Deficit Treatment (DDAT) programme, the evaluation of which featured in the *Dyslexia* periodical in February 2003, has caused considerable interest and a great deal of controversy (see *Dyslexia,* August 2003). The merits or otherwise of this programme – or any other – will not be discussed in this chapter but it is pleasing to note that those involved in innovation and perhaps controversial interventions are open to academic scrutiny and evaluation. It is interesting to note the comments of Silver (2001) regarding criteria for incorporating innovative approaches in dyslexia into some form of mainstream acceptance. He suggests that

> the process from initial concept of acceptance of a particular treatment approach is slow and can take years. Research must support a particular approach and the results should be published in a peer-reviewed journal. Often replication studies are undertaken. Then there is the process of publicising best practices and incorporating these approaches into standards of care. When research data are not available and the approach is based on an individual's belief and writings, information on such treatment approaches are usually found in a popular book, the newspapers, lay magazines, or in discussions in television shows. Often parents hear of such approaches before professionals. (Silver, 2001: 1)

It is important, therefore, that this process of academic scrutiny and peer comment is adhered to for all innovations in treatments and intervention.

It is heartening to note therefore that the Department for Education and Skills (DfES) initiated a series of reviews on different kind of approaches for dyslexia and literacy, including approaches on complementary therapies and traditional reading and phonological training therapies.

Fawcett (2002), in the third of these reviews for the DfES, evaluated traditional phonologically based interventions. She suggested that there may be a critical time for intervention and it does not seem to matter whether children are taught individually, in small groups, or as a class. The most effective approach she suggests would be to identify children as 'at risk' in the early years of school and provide a short structured intervention. This early support would 'accelerate' the literacy skills of the majority of the children, leaving a few children whose difficulties are particularly intractable. This could then be followed by a longer targeted intervention, which addressed the specific needs of the individual child. This would prove more effective and also more cost-effective, providing tailored support for children with real difficulties. This in many ways encapsulates the thrust of a number of chapters in this book, particularly in the section on practice.

Conclusion

This chapter has sought to identify and highlight the importance of recent and current initiatives in the field of dyslexia. There has been a trend to incorporate the various research areas in dyslexia within a broader framework, bringing in a range of interdisciplinary perspectives and recognizing the overlapping characteristics of dyslexia with other conditions, such as those involving attention, balance and co-ordination. This means that there have been attempts to pull together the range of theories that have been promoted in order to understand the causes of dyslexia. This interdisciplinary collaboration is beneficial for both the research field and those involved in practice. There has been an increasing understanding of the different aspects of dyslexia and it is encouraging to note that these different theories are not incompatible, and in fact the interconnections between them can often be very striking. This emphasizes that each theoretical strand is worthy of consideration and each can have an impact on practice, as well as increasing the knowledge base on dyslexia.

In relation to policy and practice there are also signs of a coherent link between research, policy and practice. There is evidence of evaluation of practical applications of programmes that have stemmed from theoretical developments. There is also evidence of increasing government interest in dyslexia and a number of new policy documents have emerged over the last few years. These have been informed by research and provided practical guidance to practitioners. The future trend will very likely continue along the lines of interdisciplinary collaboration in the sciences and in education. This should help to disentangle and clarify what at times can be a confusing array of ideas and hypotheses, for professionals and parents. This, and the further recognition of the preventative role of early identification, can ensure that the future for children and young people with dyslexia is more promising than ever before.

References

British Psychological Society (1999) Dyslexia, Literacy and Psychological Assessment. Leicester: BPS.

Brough M, Came F, Cooke G (2002) Assessing SEN in the Classroom: A Handbook for Class Teachers and Assistants. Marlborough: Learning Works.

Chase C, Ashourzadeh A, Kelly C, Monfette S, Kinsey K (2003) Can the magnocellular pathway read? Evidence from studies of colour. Vision Research 43, 10: 1211–22.

Coffin JM, Boegle A (2000) Failure of dyslexics to achieve eyeblink conditioning following five days of training. Society for Neuroscience Abstracts 26: 19.

Crombie M (2002) Dealing with diversity in the primary classroom – a challenge for the class teacher. In Reid G and Wearmouth J (eds) Dyslexia and Literacy. Chichester: Wiley, pp. 229–40.

Cummins J (1986) Empowering minority students: a framework for intervention. Harvard Educational Review 56(1): 18–36.

Department for Education and Employment (DfEE) (1998) The National Literacy Strategy; Framework for Teaching. London: Department for Education and Employment.

Department for Education and Employment (2000a) National Literacy Strategy: Supporting Pupils with Special Educational Needs in the Literacy Hour. London: Department for Education and Employment.

Department for Education and Employment (2000b) National Literacy Strategy: Supporting Pupils Working Significantly Below Age-related Expectations. London: Department for Education and Employment.

Department for Education and Skills (DfES) (2001) Special Educational Needs Code of Practice. London: Department for Education and Skills.

Department of Education Northern Ireland (2002) Report of the Task-group on Dyslexia. Bangor: DENI.

Eckert MA, Leonard CM, Richards TL, Aylward EH, Thomson J, Berninger VW (2003) Anatomical correlates of dyslexia: frontal and cerebellar findings. Brain 126: 482-94.

Facoetti A, Lorusso ML, Paganoni P, Cattaneo C, Galli R, Umilta C, Mascetti GG (2003) Auditory and visual automatic attention deficits in developmental dyslexia. Cognitive Brain Research 16: 185-91.

Fawcett AJ (2002) Evaluating therapies excluding traditional reading and phonological based therapies. A review for the Department for Education and Skills, the British Dyslexia Association and the Dyslexia Institute. Second review, February, http://www.dfes.gov.uk/sen.

Fawcett AJ, Maclagan F, Nicolson RI (2001) Cerebellar tests differentiate between poor readers with and without IQ discrepancy. Journal of Learning Disabilities 34(2): 119-35.

Goulandris N (2003) Introduction: developmental dyslexia, language and orthographies. In Goulandris N (ed.) Dyslexia in Different Languages, Cross-linguistic Comparisons. London: Whurr, pp. 1-14.

Government of Ireland (2002) Report of the Task Force on Dyslexia. Dublin: Department of Education and Science.

Guron LM (2000) Multilingualism and literacy in Sweden – multiple sources of reading difficulty. In Peer L and Reid G (eds) Multilingualism, Literacy and Dyslexia – a Challenge for Educators. London: David Fulton. pp. 94-101.

Guron LM (2004) First and second language rapid naming speed and word recognition automaticity. Paper presented at sixth BDA international conference, March, Warwick.

Haigh L (2004) Multilingual or Dyslexic? Practice from theory: dilemmas faced by teachers in international communities. Paper presented at sixth BDA international conference, March, Warwick.

Lyytinen H, Ahonen T, Eklund K, Guttorm TK, Laakso ML, Leinonen S, Leppanan PHT, Lyytinen P, Poikkeus AM, Puolakanaho A, Richardson U, Viholainen H (2001) Developmental pathways of children with and without familial risk for dyslexia during the first years of life. Developmental Neuropsychology 20: 535-44.

MacKay N (2002) Report on the Dyslexia Friendly Initiative Training. Bangor: Welsh Dyslexia Project/Prosiect Dyslecsia Cymru.

Moe-Nilssen R, Helbostad JL, Talcott JB, Toennessen FE (2003) Balance and gait in dyslexic children. Experimental Brain Research 150: 237-44.

Moores E, Nicolson RI, Fawcett AJ (2003) Attention deficits in dyslexia: evidence for an automatisation deficit? European Journal of Cognitive Psychology 15: 321-8.

Moretti R, Bava A, Torre P, Antonello RM, Cazzato G (2002) Reading errors in patients with cerebellar vermis lesions. Journal of Neurology 249: 461-8.

Morton J, Frith U (1995) Causal modelling: a structural approach to developmental psychopathology. In Cicchetti D and Cohen DJ (eds) Manual of Developmental Psychopathology, vol. 2. New York: Wiley, pp. 274-98.

Nicolson RI (2001) Developmental dyslexia: into the future. In Fawcett A (ed.) Dyslexia, Theory and Good Practice. London: Whurr, pp. 1-35.

Nicolson RI, Fawcett AJ (2000) Long-term learning in dyslexic children. European Journal of Cognitive Psychology 12: 357-93.

Nicolson RI, Daum I, Schugens MM, Fawcett AJ, Schulz A (2002) Eyeblink conditioning indicates cerebellar abnormality in dyslexia. Experimental Brain Research 143: 42-50.

Nicolson RI, Fawcett AJ, Dean P (2001) Developmental dyslexia: the cerebellar deficit hypothesis. Trends in Neurosciences 24: 508-12.

Raberger T, Wimmer H (2003) On the automaticity/cerebellar deficit hypothesis of dyslexia: balancing and continuous rapid naming in dyslexic and ADHD children. Neuropsychologia 41: 1493–7.

Rae C, Harasty JA, Dzendrowsky TE, Talcott JB, Simpson JM, Blamire AM, Dixon RM, Lee MA, Thompson CH, Styles P, Richardson AJ, Stein JF (2002) Cerebellar morphology in developmental dyslexia. Neuropsychologia 40: 1285–92.

Ramus F (2003) Developmental dyslexia: specific phonological deficit or general sensorimotor dysfunction? Current Opinion in Neurobiology 13: 212–18.

Reid G (2001) Specialist teacher training in the UK. Issues, considerations and future directions. In Hunter-Carsch M (ed.) Dyslexia: A Psychosocial Perspective. London: Whurr, pp. 254–64.

Scott RB, Stoodley CJ, Anslow PC, Stein JF, Sugden EM, Mitchell CD (2001) Lateralized cognitive deficits in children following cerebellar lesions. Developmental Medicine and Child Neurology 43(10): 685–91.

Shany M (2004) Mapping the development of cognitive, linguistic and early literacy abilities among senior kindergarten children of Ethiopian immigrants in Israel. Paper presented at sixth BDA international conference, March, Warwick.

Siegal L (2004) Early identification and intervention to prevent dyslexia in children who have English as a second language. Paper presented at sixth BDA international conference, March, Warwick.

Silver L (2001) Controversial therapies. Perspectives 27(3): 1–4.

Skottun BC, Parke LA (1999) The possible relationship between visual deficits and dyslexia: examination of a critical assumption. Journal of Learning Disabilities 32: 2–5.

Smythe I (2002) Diagnosing specific learning difficulties in multilingual children. In Johnson M and Peer L (eds) The Dyslexia Handbook 2002. Reading: BDA, pp. 234–41.

Snowling MJ, Gallagher A, Frith U (2003) Family risk of dyslexia is continuous: individual differences in the precursors of reading skill. Child Development 74(2): 358–73.

Sperling AJ, Lu ZL, Manis FR, Seidenberg MS (2003) Selective magnocellular deficits in dyslexia: a 'phantom contour' study. Neuropsychologia 41: 1422–9.

Stein J (2001) The sensory basis of reading problems. Developmental Neuropsychology 20: 509–34.

Talcott JB, Witton C, Hebb GS, Stoodley CJ, Westwood EA, France SJ, Hansen PC, Stein JF (2003) On the relationship between dynamic visual and auditory processing and literacy skills; results from a large primary-school study. Dyslexia 8: 204–25.

Tod J (2002) Individual Education Plans and Dyslexia: Some Principles. In Reid G and Wearmouth J (eds) Dyslexia and Literacy. Chichester: Wiley, pp. 251–70.

Vicari S, Marotta L, Menghini D, Molinari M, Petrosini L (2003) Implicit learning deficit in children with developmental dyslexia. Neuropsychologia 41: 108–14.

Wimmer H (1993) Characteristics of developmental dyslexia in a regular writing system. Applied Psycholinguistics 14(1): 1–33.

Wolf M (ed.) (2001) Dyslexia, Fluency and the Brain. Timonium MD: York Press.

PART ONE
RESEARCH

Introduction to Part One

It is particularly important, when preparing a general book on dyslexia, to include representatives of all the major theories of dyslexia. We have largely been successful in this endeavour, including here the cerebellar deficit hypothesis (Fawcett and Nicolson), the automatization deficit hypothesis (Van der Leij) and the phonological deficit hypothesis (Rack), as well as a chapter from the major proponent of the magnocellular deficit hypothesis (Stein), although in this instance his contribution is on the genetics of dyslexia.

These are interesting times for dyslexia research in that the complexity of the condition of dyslexia has now been widely recognized. It has become clear that the problems that dyslexic children face are far wider than just reading difficulties, and current theories attempt to explain some of this complexity. It is also now clear that these issues can be studied at different levels.

The first chapter in Part One, on the cerebellum and dyslexia, provides an update on the status of the cerebellar deficit hypothesis. It is now several years since this hypothesis was first proposed, and in the intervening years a range of evidence on the importance of the cerebellum has emerged from neuroscience generally. Moreover, other researchers have begun to evaluate the hypothesis and to examine their panels of dyslexics for cerebellar signs. At the same time various criticisms of the hypothesis have emerged. In this chapter, Fawcett and Nicolson consider the implications of recent findings in neuroscience for dyslexia, and address some of these emerging issues.

The next chapter, by Aryan Van der Leij, emphasizes the need for fluency in literacy and phonological skills. However, unlike the previous writers, this author does not subscribe to the cerebellar deficit hypothesis. Van der Leij argues for the need to integrate theories from different origins, linking learning and automaticity with its phonological underpinnings, via speech discrimination and timing. Much of the material reported here is drawn from the Dutch Longitudinal Family Study, emphasizing the importance of early identification of the precursors of dyslexia and the provision of appropriate support to prevent the erosion of self-esteem so often associated with dyslexia.

The third chapter in Part One, by John Stein, outlines the growing evidence about the genetic background to dyslexia. Significant progress in the area has been made, linking dyslexia with several well-established sites and examining issues such as the interaction of genes and the environment, along with the importance of handedness and autoimmune disorders.

The chapter by Berninger covers the widest spectrum of research in the area of dyslexia, moving from behaviour to the brain, via tools for diagnosis and intervention. This chapter emphasizes the constraints placed on the developing reading and writing system by the interactions between different areas of the brain. Berninger calls for a paradigm shift in our understanding of dyslexia and co-morbid conditions, based on these interactions between the brain and the environment.

Rack's chapter also draws on the phonological deficit hypothesis and addresses the issues of how this theoretical work has informed the development of remediation techniques. In an evaluation of the large-scale SPELLIT project, Rack argues that policy should take account of individual differences in the way in which children respond to remediation. He concludes that the style and programme of learning should be matched to the individual learner, in order to reach the most satisfactory outcome.

The final chapter in Part One, by Linda Siegel and Ian Smythe, addresses an area that is recognized increasingly as important in dyslexia research — how we identify children who are dyslexic when they use English as an additional language and speak a different language at home. In a series of striking multi-lingual research projects, the authors demonstrate that many children who have English as an additional language learn as well as, or better than, mono-lingual children, and conclude that culture-fair tests are needed to identify these problems more consistently.

The research presented here is at the cutting edge in terms of keeping the reader abreast of recent developments in dyslexia. Moreover, it is reassuring to note the concern that is clearly evident for the welfare of children with difficulties in the range of theoretical approaches. In our view, each of these theories contributes to our understanding of the complexities of dyslexia.

CHAPTER 2
Dyslexia: the role of the cerebellum

ANGELA J. FAWCETT, RODERICK I. NICOLSON

What has the cerebellum done for us?

Pick up a coffee cup. You monitor the progress of your hand with your eyes – a process of visual feedback. Once your fingers are round the handle you receive tactile feedback and then, as you lift it, proprioceptive feedback regarding the weight, balance and location. This information is fed back to many different brain regions by multiple pathways, but for our purposes here, a constant target is the cerebellum. The cerebellum is the brain's major system for integrating sensory information, for predicting the expected consequences of actions in terms of muscular outcomes and for tuning and automatizing actions. Now pick up the coffee cup with your eyes closed (it may be useful to use an empty one). Your arm snakes out and your fingers close on the handle without any visual feedback. The movement is a pre-planned 'feedforward' operation – presumably the actions of the previous movement are repeated. Now put down the cup, move a few inches, look at the coffee cup, close your eyes, and pick it up. The movements must have all been recalculated – the brain has calculated the 'inverse kinematics' needed to undertake the task ('I need to pick up the coffee cup at co-ordinates X, Y, Z relative to me. In order to do this I must make the following sequence of muscular commands: C1 at time t1, C2 at time t2' and so forth). It's fair to say that no one really quite knows how this is done, but there is general agreement that the cerebellum is centrally involved in undertaking the necessary calculations.

While we are talking about arm movements, it is also important to note that we don't move in a series of jerky movements like a robot. Rather, while ending one movement we are adjusting the muscles so that the next movement occurs as smoothly as possible – the two movements 'co-articulate'. The cerebellum presumably does this. A similar (and much more noted) process occurs for speech. Phonemes between words and within words are of course produced by muscles flexing the articulators (larynx, pharynx, tongue, hard palate, lower jaw, lips and so forth). As with arm movements, for fluent speech we attempt to smooth the muscular articulation. If, say, the jaw is not needed for the current phoneme we try to position it in the right place for the next phoneme, thereby improving the fluency. This occurs for almost all phonemes in fluent speech, but we do it so automatically that we have no realization whatsoever that we are doing so.

Now sit in a swivel office chair, look a friend in the eye, and swivel to and fro by 30 degrees or so, still looking at your friend. Your friend will see your eyes swivelling in precisely the opposite direction to your chair, thereby maintaining perfect fixation. We do this automatically of course. It is known as the vestibular-ocular reflex, and is a necessity to prevent images sliding all over the retina as we move. It relies upon the integration of information from the vestibular system (which detects acceleration) with commands to the eye muscles. This is known to be a cerebellar function, and is indeed one of the most fundamental of all visual reflexes. Without it, fixating a point would be like trying to study the rings of Saturn through binoculars – the 'jitter' destroys the acuity.

Now take a piece of scrap paper, crumple it up, and throw it in the wastebasket. If we were able to take a brain scan while you were doing this, the cerebellum (and other regions) would be found to be active. Now here's the rub: *imagine* throwing the paper into the wastebin. Your cerebellum would again be found to be active, for precisely the time that the action would have taken. Somehow the cerebellum is running through the 'throwing program' but without sending the commands to the muscles. Now remember the digits 3 7 5 9 2 for 10 seconds (without overtly rehearsing them). It turns out that the cerebellum is active during this memorization period. Presumably it is active in internalized speech in the same way that it is active with internalized actions. It is also active in fluent adult reading (Fulbright et al., 1999).

Now for something you shouldn't try at home. If one wears glasses containing inverting prisms, the entire visual scene is inverted on the retina. It's more than a little disconcerting – like trying to cut one's hair in the mirror but much worse – all one's movements have the opposite effect to that intended. However, in a couple of days one adapts fully to the changed visual configuration and moves around pretty much as normal. Again, it's the cerebellum that is the key structure in this adaptation. The cerebellum makes sure that actions and sensory input mesh properly together.

So, the cerebellum is seamlessly involved in almost all actions, whether speech or motor, whether explicit or internalized. It is seamlessly involved in the way we learned to make these actions in the first place, and how we learned to internalize them in the second place. And it is seamlessly involved in making sure that the world remains fixed while we move around. It is an extremely important structure for action, for speech, for learning and for automaticity. The only thing is, it is not accessible to consciousness – the very point is that it allows us to download our skills to a subconscious level, thereby permitting them to proceed more efficiently and in parallel with conscious thought. It succeeds in making extremely difficult tasks seem easy. Unfortunately, this deceptive simplicity appears to have fooled many eminent researchers into completely overlooking its role in the reading process and in problems in the reading process.

It is important to stress that the cerebellum never works alone. It acts as a central member of a 'team' of brain regions aimed at acquiring and executing skills. In conjunction with the sensory regions of the cerebral cortex it takes in information from the senses (visual, auditory, tactile) and from proprioception; in conjunction with the motor areas of the cerebral cortex it computes likely trajectories, predicts the effects of muscular commands, and puts together complexes of movements designed to achieve the current goal. In conjunction with sub-cortical regions such as the basal ganglia it inhibits some actions and 'gates through' other actions. In conjunction with many other brain regions it helps internalize skills such as movements, actions and thoughts. Until recently there has been a surprising imbalance between studies of cerebral cortex and studies of cerebellum in many cognitive tasks such as reading. In this chapter we attempt to start remedying this imbalance.

The cerebellar deficit hypothesis

We have produced a range of technical reports on the cerebellar deficit hypothesis (including a detailed account in the previous conference book – Fawcett and Nicolson, 2001). Here we provide a relatively non-technical overview.

In our original research (Nicolson and Fawcett, 1990) we argued that, unlike language, reading is not a 'special' skill for humans. We are not adapted to read as a result of evolution because, after all, few people could read at all until the last 200 or 300 years. Consequently, an analysis of the learning processes should cast some light on why dyslexic children fail to learn to read. One of the critical aspects of learning a skill fluently is to make it automatic, so that one can do it without thinking about it. A clear adult example of the importance of automatization is in learning to drive. The beginner can either steer, or change gear, but not both at the same time, because of the need to consciously attend to each procedure. An expert driver changes gear and steers 'automatically', thus leaving more 'capacity' for watching the traffic, planning a manoeuvre, or holding a conversation. Of course, automatization is a key requirement for reading, and there is extensive evidence that dyslexic children, even when reading well, are less fluent, requiring more time and effort to read than would a non-dyslexic child of the same reading age. Automatization of the processes in reading is no different from the general processes of automatizing any other complex skill, and so we started by putting forward the bold hypothesis that dyslexic children would have difficulty in automatizing any skill (cognitive or motor). Rather to our surprise, this hypothesis was clearly supported by a set of experiments in which we asked dyslexic children to do two things at once. If a skill is automatic, then one ought to be able to do something else at the same time (assuming it does not directly interfere with the first skill) with little or no loss of performance. Our most startling finding was for balance – a highly automatic skill with no language component. We found that although a group of dyslexic adolescents were normally able to balance as well as 'controls' (non-dyslexic children matched for age and IQ), their balance deteriorated very significantly when they had to do something else at the same time, whereas the controls' balance was not affected at all. We tried a range of secondary tasks, including counting or pressing a button on hearing a tone (and also we tried blindfolding them to prevent the children consciously attending to visual cues when trying to balance) and found the same pattern. We concluded, therefore, that our hypothesis was indeed supported, and that dyslexic children were not automatic even at the fundamental skill of balance. For some reason, dyslexic children had difficulty automatizing skills, and had therefore to concentrate harder to achieve normal levels of performance. We have used the analogy of driving in a foreign country – one can do it, but it requires continual effort and is stressful and tiring over long periods. On our account, life for a dyslexic child is like always living in a foreign country.

It should be stressed that automatization is not a conscious process – by dint of practice under reasonably consistent conditions most humans just 'pick up' skills without having to think at all. Our account gave an intuitively satisfying account not only of the reading problems but also of the phonological difficulties (because phonological awareness is a skill that is picked up initially just by listening to one's own language). Furthermore, it explained why it is that everything needs to be made explicit in teaching a dyslexic child, whereas for non-dyslexic children one can often get away with just demonstrating the skill. Perhaps most satisfying, many dyslexic people and dyslexia practitioners came to us to say that our account seemed exactly right to them – they did have to concentrate on even the simplest skills. On the other hand, what was not clear was why dyslexic children have problems in skill automatization, and until this puzzle has been solved, it is difficult to see how we would be able to test for dyslexia before school.

Interestingly, dyslexia has an established genetic basis – a male child with dyslexic parent or sibling has a 50% chance of being dyslexic. There should therefore be some underlying abnormality of the brain reflecting this genetic inheritance. Researchers have investigated the language area of the cerebral cortex, together with the relative size of corresponding regions of the right and left cerebral hemispheres (most right-handed people have the temporal lobe of the left hemisphere specialized for language processing). However, promising early leads seemed to peter out on further investigation. There have also been recent investigations of the magnocellular pathways – sensory pathways from the eye and ear that carry information rapidly to the brain – but it is not clear why sensory input difficulties might cause problems, say, in spelling. It had long been known that the cerebellum (the 'hind brain' – a primitive but very complex brain structure at the back of the brain) is involved in acquisition and execution of motor skills such as walking and reaching. Interestingly, however, when brain imaging techniques such as PET scanning were introduced in the early 1990s, it became clear that the cerebellum was highly active in a range of skills – when imagining a tennis stroke, when speaking, or even when trying to keep a list of words in memory (see Schmahmann, 1997 and Ivry and Fiez, 2000, for reviews). These findings tallied with an emerging view that the cerebellum was a key brain structure for the acquisition and use of a range of cognitive skills, including 'language dexterity'. Putting together the 'cognitive neuroscience' results on the role of the cerebellum in skill automatization, balance and language dexterity with our own findings with dyslexic children, it became clear that the cerebellar abnormality was a prime candidate for the cause of the difficulties suffered by dyslexic children.

Over the past 10 years we have completed a series of stringent tests of our cerebellar deficit hypothesis. First we undertook clinical tests of cerebellar dysfunction – both dysmetria (difficulty in precisely measured movements) and dystonia (low muscle tone) – on our panel of dyslexic and control children. We established (Fawcett et al., 1996) that the dyslexic children showed marked deficits on almost all of these clinical tests, and we then replicated these findings on further populations of dyslexic and control children, establishing that around 80% of our sample of dyslexic children showed clear 'cerebellar' symptoms (Fawcett and Nicolson, 1999). These findings were completely unexpected from the literature and were not predicted from any other theory of dyslexia, and consequently they provided strong support for the hypothesis. Nonetheless, it could still be argued that it was not the cerebellum itself, but perhaps some input to, or output from, the cerebellum that was causing the problems. This is by no means an unlikely hypothesis because the cerebellum has two-way connections with almost all parts of the brain, including the language areas. Consequently, in collaboration with colleagues in other laboratories, we carried out two direct tests of the cerebellar deficit hypothesis. Particularly striking results were obtained from a PET (brain imaging) study (Nicolson et al., 1999) involving learning a sequence of finger presses, known to result in considerable activation in the cerebellum with non-dyslexic adults. We established that our dyslexic adults showed only 10% of the normal cerebellar activation both when executing a previously overlearned (automatic) sequence and when learning a new sequence. This suggests strongly that, unlike non-dyslexic adults, dyslexic adults do not activate the cerebellum in these learning and automatic tasks – presumably because it does not help them in the normal way. Finally, there is a collection of dyslexic and non-dyslexic brains in the Beth Israel/International Dyslexia Association Brain Bank (Boston, USA) and our PhD student, Andrew Finch, was given permission to undertake neuroanatomical investigation of the cerebellar regions of these specimens. He established (Finch et al., 2002) significant abnormality, characterized by greater cell size, in both the cerebellum and in the inferior olive (a nucleus in the brain stem that sends input to the cerebellum).

Consequently, at least for the dyslexic children in our panel, we have found both behavioural and neurological evidence of cerebellar abnormality, thereby providing strong support for our cerebellar deficit hypothesis. Of course there is a great deal of research still to do, and indeed the hypothesis suggests a range of fascinating further studies, but those are for the future. This converging multi-disciplinary evidence of cerebellar abnormality led us to develop an 'ontogenetic causal chain' analysis in which we propose that cerebellar abnormality from birth leads to slight speech output dysfluency, then receptive speech problems (difficulties in hearing the speech sounds) and thence deficiencies in phonological awareness (Nicolson and Fawcett, 1999; Nicolson et al., 2001). Taken together with the problems in skill automatization and co-ordination associated with the cerebellar impairment, this analysis provides not only a good account of the pattern of difficulties suffered by dyslexic children, but also how they arise developmentally. This causal chain analysis still awaits confirmation via studies of pre-school 'dyslexic' children, but if supported by further research it provides a very significant analysis. It demonstrates how abnormality in a brain structure (the cerebellum) can lead, via difficulties in cognitive processes such as automatization and phonology, to deficits in arguably the pinnacle of cognitive skill, namely reading.

Note that the three criterial difficulties in the World Federation of Neurology definition – writing, reading and spelling – are all accounted for in different ways. It may be useful to distinguish between direct and indirect cerebellar causation. Cerebellar deficit provides a natural, direct, explanation of the poor quality of handwriting frequently shown by dyslexic children (Martlew, 1992). Handwriting, of course, is a motor skill that requires precise timing and co-ordination of diverse muscle groups. Literacy difficulties arise from several routes. The central route is highlighted. If an infant has a cerebellar impairment, initial direct manifestations will include a mild motor difficulty – the infant may be slower to sit up and to walk – and crucially, the direct effect on articulation would suggest that the infant might be slower to start babbling (see, for example, Ejiri and Masataka, 2001, for evidence relating babbling to motor control), and, later, talking (see Bates and Dick, 2002), Even after speech and walking emerge, one might expect that the skills would be less fluent, less 'dextrous', in infants with cerebellar impairment. If articulation is less fluent than normal, then one indirect effect is that it takes up more conscious resources, leaving fewer resources to process the ensuing

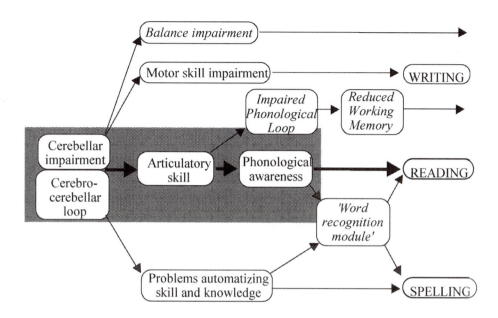

Figure 2.1 An ontogenetic causal chain.

sensory feedback. An additional indirect effect is that reduced articulation speed leads to reduced effective 'working memory' as reflected in the 'phonological loop', which in turn leads to difficulties in language acquisition (Gathercole and Baddeley, 1989). Furthermore, reduced quality of articulatory representation might lead directly to impaired sensitivity to onset, rime, and the phonemic structure of language (Snowling and Hulme, 1994) – in short, one would expect early deficits in phonological awareness. Cerebellar impairment would therefore be predicted to cause, by direct and by indirect means, the 'phonological core deficit' (Shankweiler et al., 1995; Stanovich, 1988) that has proved such a fruitful explanatory framework for many aspects of dyslexia. For spelling, the third criterial skill, problems arise from a number of indirect routes – over-effortful reading, poor phonological awareness, and difficulties in automatizing skills.

As noted above there is little high-quality evidence available for the pre-school period in dyslexia, primarily because dyslexia cannot be diagnosed formally until the child has failed to learn to read, and so an extensive prospective longitudinal study is required. Lyytinen et al. (2001) report just such a Finnish study. Interestingly, the team report no delay in early motor milestones, but that 'Children who were identified as late talkers at age 2 were still delayed at the age 3.5 in most features of language-related skills – but only if they belonged to the group at familial risk for dyslexia.'

In a further recent study (Nicolson et al., 2002) we used an eye-blink conditioning technique which had been shown to be sensitive to cerebellar lesions in humans (Daum et al., 1993), in order to probe further the involvement of the cerebellum. Individual analyses indicated that 85% of the dyslexic group showed either: no conditioning; abnormally poor conditioned response (CR) tuning and/or abnormally low orienting response (OR) habituation. The heterogeneity is interesting, in that there is evidence of abnormal habituation in patients with cerebellar lesions (Timmann et al., 1998; Maschke et al., 2000) and further that failure to acquire a classically conditioned limb withdrawal response was associated with lesions to the anterior and superior cerebellum, whereas patients with lesions confined to the posterior inferior cerebellum were relatively unaffected (Timmann et al., 2000). We concluded that the findings provide further converging evidence of cerebellar abnormality in dyslexia and, for the first time, demonstrate that there are fundamental abnormalities in the way that dyslexic people learn. Equally important, the eye-blink conditioning paradigm provides a method of investigating further both homogeneity and heterogeneity in the learning deficits underlying dyslexia and other developmental disorders.

The cerebellum and the discrepancy criterion

One of the most controversial issues in this controversial area is that of the discrepancy criterion for dyslexia – traditional definitions stress that there must be a discrepancy between the reading performance and that expected on the basis of the child's opportunity and intelligence. It is established that there are few, if any, qualitative differences in the reading of dyslexic children and poor readers with no discrepancy. Influential US researchers have argued forcefully that the discrepancy criterion is based on an outdated and indefensible construct (IQ), it does not distinguish between the reading of different groups of poor readers, and it has no obvious implications for differential teaching strategies – basically the teaching strategy used for dyslexic children is the same as that used for other poor readers. Consequently, they see no reason to maintain the IQ-based diagnostic criterion. In the view of most UK dyslexia researchers this would be a major step backwards in that a good individual educational plan requires understanding not only of the symptoms (poor reading) but also the underlying causes. Nicolson (1996) highlights the range of logical flaws in the anti-discrepancy analyses. One key issue is, of course, that the US researchers considered only reading. If they had cast their net wider in terms of symptoms, would they have found more interesting results? We addressed this issue in further research (Fawcett, Nicolson and Maclagan, 2001), comparing the performance of dyslexic poor readers (having an IQ of 90+ and therefore a discrepancy between reading and general function) with children with more generalized difficulties (IQ 85 and below). The expected (and equivalent) pattern of difficulties was found in both groups for phonology and speed, as one would expect from the US literature. However, we also assessed static and dynamic cerebellar performance. Both groups showed equivalent deficits on the dynamic tests (bead threading and other motor skills). However, the dyslexic group showed significantly greater deficits in static cerebellar tasks (postural stability and muscle tone), whereas performance of the non-dyslexic poor readers on these tasks was at normal levels. There is also evidence (see our Chapter 15) that children with balance difficulties may be particularly resistant to traditional reading interventions. This research was undertaken with only a limited sample of dyslexic and non-dyslexic poor readers. However, if replicated on larger samples it has a number of important implications. First, of course, it strongly supports the need to look beyond the symptoms of poor reading to the underlying causes of the poor reading. We really cannot stress this enough. Second, it confirms that it is vital to maintain the distinction between dyslexic and non-dyslexic poor readers. Third, it confirms the need to go beyond assessment of reading alone when diagnosing. Fourth, it provides a further line of evidence indicating the likely involvement of the cerebellum in dyslexia, and hints at the need to develop different intervention strategies for the two groups. Finally, it indicates one potent source of confusion in the literature. Many research groups include children with an IQ of 80 or above in their dyslexic group. This may not be a serious problem when one is assessing only reading-related skills, in that dyslexic and non-dyslexic poor readers show similar patterns of reading skill deficits. It is, unfortunately, disastrous when one turns to static cerebellar tasks such as balance. By including non-dyslexic poor readers, whose balance is normally very solid, one merely masks the true symptoms for dyslexia,[1] leading to spurious conclusions.

Changes since 2001: evidence from other research groups

Since the publication of our chapter in the previous BDA conference book in 2001 there has been considerable progress in understanding the role of the cerebellum in cognition and in reading, and some progress in the understanding the role of the cerebellum in dyslexia. We outline some of the major findings in each area.

---

1   This is not to say that no poor reader without discrepancy shows a cerebellar problem. It is likely that the incidence of cerebellar problems in the population of children with generalized learning difficulties is at least as high as the 5% or so in the general population. It is just that one must not include them in a population of children with specific learning difficulties if one wishes to investigate the cause of dyslexia. The real problem for understanding the causes of generalized learning difficulties is that the field has not enjoyed the quantity and quality of research dedicated to specific developmental disabilities.

The cognitive neuroscience of the cerebellum

As noted in our 2001 chapter, the evidence of substantial involvement of the cerebellum in a wide range of tasks related to speech and language had been building rapidly. Subsequent research has confirmed this picture. Evidence has accumulated both from neuroimaging studies and studies of cerebellar patients.

(a) Cerebellum and cognition

In 1995 controversy remained over the role of the cerebellum in cognition and language. By 2001, there was solid evidence. As Marien et al. (2001: 580) concluded:

> Growing insights in the neuroanatomy, of the cerebellum and its interconnections, evidence from functional neuroimaging and neurophysiological research, and advancements in clinical and experimental neuropsychology have established the view that the cerebellum participates in a much wider range of functions than conventionally accepted. This increase of insight has brought to the fore that the cerebellum modulates cognitive functioning of at least those parts of the brain to which it is reciprocally connected.

They argue that the cerebellum plays a 'modulator' role in various non-motor language processes such as lexical retrieval, syntax, and language dynamics and advance the concept of the 'lateralized linguistic cerebellum'.

Deficits identified in cerebellar patients include problems in articulation and phonation, and in particular apraxia of speech, which prevents the smooth and efficient translation of phonology into verbal-motor commands. In a study of word-finding deficits in a verbal fluency task, Leggio et al. (2000) demonstrated that impairments in phonological skills were greater than those in semantic skills, which they suggest reflects the need for novel and non-automatized searches. Further evidence from patients who have received cerebellar insult reveals symptoms ranging from deficits in attention and working memory (Malm et al., 1998) to problems in detecting moving patterns, and phonological discrimination. Most intriguingly of all in this context, Moretti and colleagues (2002) report increased reading errors in patients with damage to the cerebellar vermis, which they suggest may be attributable to the rich interconnections between the cerebellum and the language system.

Consequently, as we move into 2004, the role of the cerebellum in cognition has moved from controversy to orthodoxy. Researchers in cognitive neuroscience are trying to localize the precise anatomical basis of cerebellar activation in relation to different language tasks. For instance, a study by Gebhart and colleagues (2002) included an antonym generation task, a noun (category member) generation task, a verb selection task, and a lexical decision task. The authors argue that their findings on antonym generation suggest that it is not just the need for 'mental movement' in linking nouns to verbs which involves the cerebellum, but the internal generation of the words themselves in any two-word association task. Further, a study (Hanakawa et al., 2002) of non-motor mental operations, including numerical, verbal and spatial stimuli has shown activation of Brodmann's area and the cerebellum in all three tasks, although electrophysiological data shows no movement, either in articulation or eye movements. The numerical and verbal tasks showed right frontoparietal and right cerebellar activation, whereas the spatial task evoked activity bi-laterally.

(b) Cerebellum and sensory processing

Most excitingly, perhaps, from the viewpoint of the cerebellar deficit hypothesis, Bower and Parsons (2003) have derived a new hypothesis for the function of the cerebellum, based on their investigations of touch. They claim that the cerebellum is specifically involved in co-ordinating the sensory data acquired by the brain, rather than simply the motor skills. They provide evidence for this drawn from an elegant study comparing brain activation during a simple motor task (picking up and dropping small objects) and a sensory judgement task (identifying the same objects by touch). Surprisingly, the cerebellum was hardly activated during the motor task, but exceptional levels of activation were found in the sensory decision task. A similar pattern of intense activation was found during movement, or when the hands were still. The authors conclude:

> This observation added support to our idea that the cerebellum is more involved in sensory than pure motor function, and in particular that it is highly active during the acquisition of sensory data.

They argue that the cerebellum is a support structure for cognitive processing of all types, and that a radical re-interpretation of the role of the cerebellum is imminent. If further evidence supports these claims, this research provides further support for the cerebellar deficit hypothesis as a plausible causal theory for the range of deficits in dyslexia, encompassing both the phonological and the magnocellular deficit hypotheses, in addition to the wide range of deficits in dyslexia.

(c) Cerebellum and reading

Of course a key issue for causal theories of dyslexia is whether the structure in question is indeed involved in reading (or in learning to read). In a landmark study of the role of the cerebellum in reading, Fulbright et al. (1999: 1925) conclude that

> During phonologic assembly, cerebellar activation was observed in the middle and posterior aspects of the posterior superior fissure and adjacent simple lobule and semilunar lobule bilaterally and in posterior aspects of the simple lobule, superior

semilunar lobule, and inferior semilunar lobule bilaterally. Semantic processing, however, resulted in activation in the deep nuclear region on the right and in the inferior vermis, in addition to posterior areas active in phonologic assembly, including the simple, superior semilunar, and inferior semilunar lobules, CONCLU-SION: The cerebellum is engaged during reading and differentially activates in response to phonologic and semantic tasks. These results indicate that the cerebellum contributes to the cognitive processes integral to reading.

These findings have now been consistently supported. One meta-analysis (Turkeltaub et al., 2002) concluded that for reading single words aloud the brain regions reliably activated were bilateral motor and superior temporal cortices, pre-supplementary motor area, left fusiform gyrus, and the cerebellum. In a recent meta-analysis of 35 neuroimaging studies of the dual route to reading, Jobard et al. (in press) confirmed that the cerebellum is reliably activated, and intriguingly they go on to note that these findings are rarely discussed!

Dyslexia and the cerebellum

Several research groups have started to investigate the cerebellar deficit hypothesis of dyslexia. We distinguish between brain-level and cognitive-level studies. In terms of the former, there are suggestive (but not wholly conclusive) findings from a number of laboratories. Recent studies of brain structure have revealed clear differences between controls and dyslexic adults. Rae et al. (2002: 1285) conclude

> The relationship of cerebellar asymmetry to phonological decoding ability and handedness, together with our previous finding of altered metabolite ratios in the cerebellum of dyslexics, lead us to suggest that there are alterations in the neurological organisation of the cerebellum which relate to phonological decoding skills, in addition to motor skills and handedness.

Eckert et al. (2003: 482) conclude:

> The dyslexics exhibited significantly smaller right anterior lobes of the cerebellum, pars triangularis bilaterally, and brain volume. Measures of the right cerebellar anterior lobe and the left and right pars triangularis correctly classified 72% of the dyslexic subjects (94% of whom had a rapid automatic naming deficit) and 88% of the controls. The cerebellar anterior lobe and pars triangularis made significant contributions to the classification of subjects after controlling for brain volume. ... The cerebellum is one of the most consistent locations for structural differences between dyslexic and control participants in imaging studies. This study may be the first to show that anomalies in a cerebellar-frontal circuit are associated with rapid automatic naming and the double-deficit subtype of dyslexia.

It is fair to say that, in common with all studies of brain structure in dyslexia, studies have yet to converge on a clear consensus as to the precise nature of the differences, but it is evident that the cerebellum is one of the major structures affected.

In terms of cognitive-level performance, several research groups have investigated balance. Results have consistently indicated incidence of balance problems in at least 50% of the dyslexic subjects tested. A large-scale Norwegian study (Moe-Nilssen et al., 2003) established clear evidence of balance and gait deficits in dyslexic children:

> Tests of standing balance with eyes closed did not discriminate between groups. All unperturbed standing tests with eyes open showed significant group differences ($P < 0.05$) and classified correctly 70–77.5% of the subjects into their respective groups. Mean walking speed during very fast walking on both flat and uneven surface was = 0.2 m/s faster for controls than for the group with dyslexia. This test classified 77.5% and 85% of the subjects correctly on flat and uneven surface, respectively. (Moe-Nilssen et al., 2003: 347)

Studies by Ramus and his colleagues (Ramus, 2003; Ramus et al., 2003) have (as expected) identified clear difficulties in rapid automatized naming tasks in dyslexic students and children. Puzzlingly, they attribute the rapid naming deficit to phonological processing alone (rather than speed) despite the known need to dissociate the two (Wolf and Bowers, 1999). In terms of balance and motor skill, Ramus et al. (2003) found 4 out of their 16 dyslexic students had clear balance difficulties, but concluded that balance was not a significant factor. Ramus et al. (2003) found 59% of their dyslexic children had clear difficulties in balance and motor skill, but discount any association with the cerebellum because, unlike Nicolson et al. (1995), they found no differences in time estimation.[2] Consistent with previous research by Wimmer and his colleagues in Austria, Raberger and Wimmer (2003) confirm an association of balance difficulties with dyslexia, but argue that in fact it is only those dyslexic children who also have attention deficit who have the balance problems, and therefore that it is attention deficit rather than dyslexia that leads to balance difficulties.

Much of the evidence for the role of the cerebellum is emerging as a by-product of studies examining independent theoretical issues. Research from Paula Tallal's laboratory has investigated the brain basis of rapid auditory processing, which has been found to be impaired in children with dyslexia (Temple et al., 2000). In an imaging study, adults were presented with a series of low- and high-pitched tones, with instructions to press a button in response to the high-pitched tone. Comparisons were made between rapidly changing and slow changing stimuli for the two groups, revealing between-group differences for rapid stimuli in Brodmann's area and in the right posterior cerebellum. Controls showed greater activation of the cerebellum for rapid than slow stimuli, whereas the dyslexics showed a striking reversal, with highly significant increases in activation for the slow stimuli.

---

2   Their claim that time estimation is the critical indicator of cerebellar function is puzzling.

There have also been studies of the processes of attention and attention shifting in dyslexia. Facoetti et al. (2001) identify a problem in automatic attention shifting procedures (interestingly, this was substantially alleviated by a programme of 'visual hemisphere specific stimulation' in which the children were trained to orient effectively to briefly presented words in the visual periphery). Moores et al. (2003) concluded that an apparent difference in rapid switching of attention in dyslexia was best attributed to lack of automatization of basic skills in dyslexia. These studies represent an important new focus of dyslexia research, investigating fundamental processes of attentional allocation. We discuss the link with ADHD in the following section.

Finally, in a potential link between the brain, learning and dyslexia there have now been two studies of eye-blink conditioning and dyslexia. Eye-blink conditioning is thought to reflect the processes of classical conditioning – the fundamental form of 'automatic' learning by contiguity – and the cerebellum is considered to be the critical component of the brain circuitry involved. Nicolson et al. (2002) identified clear abnormalities in eye-blink conditioning, but with a relatively small sample (15 dyslexic subjects). Coffin et al. (in press) established clear-cut findings in a study that contrasted dyslexia, ADHD and foetal alcohol exposure (FAE). Both the dyslexic and FAE groups showed uniform failure to condition, whereas the ADHD (and controls) conditioned normally.

Overall, therefore, there is no doubt from recent research in cognitive neuroscience that the cerebellum plays a pivotal role in the acquisition and execution of speech-related cognitive skills. It may also play an important role in sensory processing. This research therefore completely vindicated and extended the theoretical basis for our cerebellar deficit hypothesis. In terms of specific evidence from studies of the cerebellum in dyslexia, in addition to research from our own laboratory there is now extensive evidence of cerebellar abnormality in dyslexia, and consistent evidence that around 60% of dyslexic children have difficulties in motor skills and balance. While one might consider that such high incidence levels would be construed as strong support for the hypothesis (given that no other theory of dyslexia predicts these problems), interpretation of these findings is still hotly disputed. We discuss the issue of interpretation in the following section, and conclude with a section on how best we can try to make progress in the field.

Criticisms of the cerebellar deficit hypothesis

The cerebellar deficit hypothesis was first made public nearly a decade ago, and it is not surprising that criticisms have been made.

Arguments from adult studies

A standard argument (see, for example, Zeffiro and Eden, 2001) is that the symptoms shown by dyslexic children might be expected to follow closely those of adults with acquired insult to the cerebellum. However, the fruitfulness of linking developmental and acquired disorders of reading has been seriously questioned (Snowling et al., 1996; Paterson et al., 1999). The value is particularly questionable when the cerebellum is the structure involved, in that the cerebellum may have a role in either or both skill acquisition and skill execution. As Ivry and Justus (2001) note,

> the cerebellum helps establish phonological representations. Once established these representations may be accessed without the cerebellum.

Other studies, many through necessity, use adult dyslexic participants. It is difficult to interpret failure to find standard cerebellar signs in adults. In almost all cases, skills improve to ceiling. The phonological tests needed to establish difficulty at 6 years (rhyme, phoneme deletion) are quite different from those needed at 16 years (Spoonerisms, non-word repetition, Pig Latin). Applying a 16-year-olds' test to 6-year-old children would lead to a null difference (floor effects for both dyslexic and control children) and applying a 6-year-olds' test to 16-year-old children would lead to a null difference (ceiling effects for both groups). Similarly, skills like balance improve with age, and sophisticated procedures may be needed to identify any remaining balance difficulties in adulthood.

Cerebellum too narrow

Zeffiro and Eden (2001) also make the point that, as the cerebellum receives input from a variety of brain regions (including sensory pathways), it may be that its inability to fully optimize the learning processes could reflect noisy input rather than faulty processing. Consequently, the real culprit may lie in the sensory pathways or perhaps in the perisylvian neocortex, with the cerebellum as 'innocent bystander'. There is no doubt that this is a complex issue. In addition to the well-known involvement of the cerebellum in visual processing (via the vestibulo-ocular reflex (VOR) among other mechanisms), there is now evidence of cerebellar involvement in other sensory systems including touch (Blakemore et al., 2001). It is difficult, but not impossible, to disentangle these possibilities. The most direct method of assessing the contribution of the sensory pathways is to undertake direct tests of magnocellular visual and auditory function. Such tests suggest a non-zero but still fairly low (approximately 20% to 33%) incidence (Ramus, 2001). Interactions with neocortex are more difficult to isolate, because the cerebellar/neocortical systems normally work seamlessly together. Nonetheless, the fact remains that the tests we have used are standard clinical tests for 'soft cerebellar signs'. The PET study (Nicolson et al., 1999), reported earlier, makes it clear that there is abnormal cerebellar function both in skill acquisition and in automatic skill execution, and in the latter case at least, this could not be attributed to some verbal labelling strategy by the controls.

Cerebellum just the 'head ganglion of the magnocellular system'

While recognizing the importance of the cerebellum, Stein (2001) argues for a different direction of causality between the cerebellum and dyslexia, in terms of the magnocellular deficit hypothesis. Stein argues that the focus on the cerebellum is particularly significant because this structure is the recipient of heavy projections from all the magnocellular systems throughout the brain. This includes not only the visual system, with the largest output quantitatively to the cerebellum, but also dynamic signals from muscle spindle fibres from the motor system. Furthermore antibodies selective for magnocells bind to the cerebellum very heavily. Distinctively for magnocellular theorists, Stein also argues that there are difficulties with eye movements, which he considers a causal mechanism for fluent reading. Thus Stein suggests that we can view the cerebellum itself as a quintessentially magnocellular structure, indeed as the 'head ganglion' of the magnocellular system. While the magnocellular and cerebellar deficit hypotheses share a variety of common features, and are entirely compatible, we would argue that the cerebellum is the more likely culprit in most cases. In terms of modelling clarity, we consider it valuable to maintain a distinction between sensory processing, cerebellar function and motor processing. Further research should indicate whether, as we believe, these may be dissociated, or as Stein believes, they are best viewed overall. Certainly, the latest hypothesis on the role of the cerebellum as a support structure for sensory co-ordination (Bower and Parsons, 2003) seems to support our view. Further research will be necessary to test the sensory cerebellar theory, and to disentangle these hypotheses empirically, although we have no doubt that evidence will be found in support of both hypotheses.

Cerebellum too broad

A further criticism goes somewhat like this:

> The cerebellum is a very large structure indeed, with half the brain's neurons. To say that the cause lies within the cerebellum is so vague as to be without value. It is a bit like saying that the problem lies somewhere within the brain.

We would have considerable sympathy with this argument were it not for the fact that the proponents tend to alternate between this critique and the 'too narrow' argument above. We make two points. It was never our intention to stop at the cerebellum. We have all along argued that the cerebellum is merely the first stage in analysis. Subsequent research should be targeted at issues such as: the parts of the cerebellum that are particularly vulnerable; whether there are in fact different sub-types of dyslexia reflecting the particular part(s) of the cerebellum affected; whether there are other systems involved (for example, whether there is a cerebellum plus sensory sub-type and a cerebellum minus sensory sub-type); the optimal support for children suffering from different sub-types, and so on. So, the cerebellum is merely one step on the research agenda. Second, if the theory is indeed so vacuous, why is it treated with such grave suspicion by 'mainstream' researchers?

Co-morbidity with attention deficit

A further important issue arises from the fact that there is a significant co-morbidity between dyslexia and attention deficit disorder (most likely those without hyperactivity). School- and clinic-based co-morbidity rates for attention deficit with dyslexia range from 11% to 40% (Hinshaw, 1992; Semrud-Clikeman et al., 1992; Shaywitz et al., 1994), with considerable variability deriving from differing inclusionary criteria. The DSM-IV definition of attention deficit (American Psychiatric Association, 1994) is considerably more inclusive than the DSM-III definition (American Psychiatric Association, 1987). Denckla (1985) claimed that motor disorders in dyslexic children were specific to those also suffering from attention deficit. Moreover, Wimmer et al. (1999) and Raberger and Wimmer (2003) have argued that balance abnormalities are specific to children with dyslexia and attention deficit. Unfortunately, the latter claim is hard to evaluate owing to difficulties in defining dyslexia in German-speaking children. Since the German language is sufficiently transparent that reading accuracy is extremely high for all children, slowness of reading was the key criterion used.

It may be valuable at this point to specify how participants in our studies were selected. The sample was not clinic based and it included any children whom we could find in the Sheffield area who satisfied the appropriate age category for a given study, who had a diagnosis of dyslexia (or were referred to us for diagnosis) and were willing to participate in a series of studies. Participants in studies were tested for reading age (latterly using the reading scale of the Wechsler Objective Reading Dimension, 1993) and for IQ (using the Wechsler Intelligence Scale for Children, 3rd Edition, 1992). A full-scale IQ of at least 90 together with a reading age at least 18 months behind chronological age was used as a criterion for inclusion in the dyslexic group. All of the dyslexic participants in the post-1992 experiments reported here were screened for ADD/ADHD (using the DSM-III), none satisfied the criterion, and there were no significant differences between dyslexic and control groups even on 'raw' ADD score on any of the studies reported here.

In short, the key point is that there are dyslexic children who show 'cerebellar' problems who are not classifiable as having ADD. It is quite likely that a higher proportion of dyslexic children with ADD will show 'cerebellar' problems than those without ADD, but that is an empirical issue. We await with interest results of suitably designed studies with English-speaking children with dyslexia and/or ADHD. Difficulties in this area reflect the lack of understanding of, and poor procedures for, diagnosis of ADD (Kupfer et al., 2000). A comparable issue arises with dyspraxia (see Jongmans et al., 2003, for a comparative analysis of dyslexia, dyspraxia and the effects of co-morbidity on balance).

Links to unproven intervention methods

One of the major concerns of the academic dyslexia community is that small-scale studies lead to espousal of at best unproven and at worst spurious methods of intervention, especially in cases where the developers of the interventions have financial interests in the outcomes. This concern applies not only to non-traditional reading methods that do not follow standard phonological lines but also to 'complementary' interventions that claim to improve a child's chances of benefiting from school-based reading support. We discuss this issue briefly in our Chapter 15 in this volume.

In our view, it is important to remain objective in analysis of these approaches. First, it is important not to make the category error of confusing cause, symptom and intervention. There are symptoms of abnormal cerebellar function in dyslexia. We have indeed attributed these symptoms – and the broader symptoms including phonological, reading and learning problems – to abnormalities of the cerebellum. This does not mean that attempts to improve cerebellar function will be successful in leading to improved learning (and hence improved reading if there is also reading support). Equally it does not mean that such attempts will not be successful. The cerebellar deficit hypothesis is silent on whether attempts to improve cerebellar function will generalize to reading. This is again an empirical matter. We look forward to the large-scale fully controlled studies that should indicate which sub-types of dyslexia are most likely to benefit from such interventions.

Second, it is important to maintain the perspective that learning to read is a skill. Learning a skill requires that skill to be practised. We have always advocated that, in order to teach a skill, one needs to make sure that the very best methods for teaching that skill are used. Nonetheless, if it is possible to improve the quality of the learning this will very much magnify the benefits of this high-quality teaching. As with so many false antitheses, there is no intrinsic clash between complementary and traditional approaches to reading support. The two approaches have different goals: improving the reading versus improving the learning. In our view it is necessary to maintain an open mind and undertake the research needed to identify the best ways of combining the two approaches.

Contributions of the cerebellar deficit hypothesis

In our view, where the above criticisms do have some force is against an extreme version of the cerebellar deficit hypothesis; namely: 'dyslexic children have abnormalities in the cerebellum, throughout the cerebellum and only in the cerebellum. These abnormalities are specific to dyslexia and dyslexia alone. Furthermore, these abnormalities are the only ones relevant to the acquisition of reading.' We do not make any of these claims. Nor do we believe them. Advocacy of the strong version of the cerebellar deficit is challenging enough.

As with any hypothesis in science, the CDH should be subjected to evaluation, refinement and maybe disconfirmation. That is the way of scientific progress. Even if the hypothesis proves significantly in error, one of the major criteria for a new approach is whether it is fruitful – whether it generates research questions that are likely to cause progression of theoretical understanding. We consider that this is definitely the case.

Links with mainstream cognitive neuroscience

For many years now mainstream researchers have looked down on dyslexia research as something of an anachronism – a seething backwater in which rather outdated theories are fought over by doctrinaire protagonists. There has been no expectation that dyslexia research might cast light on anything other than education. Our CDH framework links directly with 'mainstream' theories in cognitive psychology (learning and automatization) and in cognitive neuroscience (speech-based cognition and the cerebellum). This provides a natural channel for progress and cross-fertilization in both directions.

Levels and ontogeny

The explicit representation both of a 'biological' level of analysis (cerebellum) and a 'cognitive' level of analysis (automaticity and learning) provides an important link to genetics in one direction and education and treatment in the other. Furthermore, the 'ontogenetic' approach, which asks how the reading problems develop as a function of brain characteristics and experience (see also Lyytinen et al., 2001), facilitates the development of diagnostic techniques that can be undertaken before a dyslexic child starts (and fails) to learn to read (cf. Nicolson and Fawcett, 1996) and also provides potentially fruitful theoretical justifications for pre-school support methods. Most important, it makes it very clear that a developmental framework is the only legitimate framework for understanding a developmental disorder.

Learning

Arguably the most distinctive aspect of the cerebellar deficit hypothesis framework is that we have placed learning at the heart of the disorder. No other 'causal' framework (neither the phonological deficit hypothesis nor the magnocellular deficit hypothesis) has anything directly to say about learning. In our view, the only way to link from theory to diagnosis to support is via the issue of learning. This theme is developed further in Chapter 15 in this volume.

Inclusiveness

Because the framework is so much broader than alternative frameworks, there is scope for researchers of all spheres of expertise to attempt to work together. Those interested in speech and its disorders have a direct link to the precursors of dyslexia. Those interested in magnocellular function have a series of natural issues relating to the origins of the magnocellular problems. Those interested in motor skill and its development are empowered by the framework. Those interested in diagnostic methods are given a whole range of new issues and new methods to investigate – in particular the challenge of finding brain-based diagnostic methods rather than symptom-based methods. Those interested in developmental disorders other than dyslexia will find a range of fascinating parallels when they consider the overlaps. Those interested in education will find the clear emphasis on learning to be a refreshing change. In short, there is something in the framework for everyone.

The way forward

We emphasize that, despite the above desirable features, the cerebellar deficit hypothesis should be seen as incompletely proven at this stage, in that the dyslexia-related data provided are mostly from small-scale studies in our own laboratory. The approach raises many further theoretical questions. Are there sub-types of dyslexia corresponding to different loci of abnormality in the cerebellum? To what extent do cerebellar and magnocellular deficits co-occur? How do these specific issues relate to underlying genetic endowment? Are there other developmental disorders that might also correspond to cerebellar impairment? Is it possible to move toward diagnostic principles for developmental disability inspired by brain-based investigation rather than behaviour-based classification; above all, how can knowledge of underlying causality inform support and remediation? These are all potentially fruitful research issues, and we consider that their investigation will continue to illuminate the complex interplay between the brain, the environment and behaviour, in both normal and abnormal development.

Above all, we hope that the ecosystem (Nicolson, 2002) of policy makers, researchers practitioners and people with dyslexia – whatever their perspective – will combine to enhance, modify and transform the theoretical views expressed here (and by other approaches) so as to encompass the full range of potential causative factors, leading to a unified framework that integrates theory, diagnosis and support for children with dyslexia.

References

American Psychiatric Association (1987) Diagnostic and Statistical Manual of Mental Disorders (3rd edn). Washington DC.

American Psychiatric Association (1994) Diagnostic and Statistical Manual of Mental Disorders (4th edn). Washington DC.

Bates E, Dick F (2002) Language, gesture, and the developing brain. Developmental Psychobiology 40(3): 293–310.

Blakemore SJ, Frith CD, Wolpert DM (2001) The cerebellum is involved in predicting the sensory consequences of action. Neuroreport 12(9): 1879–84.

Bower JM, Parsons LM (2003) Rethinking the lesser brain. Scientific American 289: 50–7.

Coffin JM, Baroody S, Schneider K, O'Neill J (in press) Impaired Cerebellar Learning In

Children With Prenatal Alcohol Exposure: A Comparative Study of Eyeblink Conditioning in Children with ADHD and Dyslexia Cortex, in press.

Daum I, Schugens MM, Ackermann H, Lutzenberger W, Dichgans J, Birbaumer N (1993) Classical conditioning after cerebellar lesions in humans. Behavioral Neuroscience 107: 748-56.

Denckla MB (1985) Motor coordination in children with dyslexia: theoretical and clinical implications. In Duffy FH, Geschwind N (eds) Dyslexia: A Neuroscientific Approach to Clinical Evaluation. Boston MA: Little Brown.

Eckert MA, Leonard CM, Richards T, Aylward E, Thomson J, Berninger V (2003) Anatomical correlates of dyslexia: frontal and cerebellar findings. Brain 126(2): 482-94.

Ejiri K, Masataka N (2001) Co-occurrence of preverbal vocal behavior and motor action in early infancy. Developmental Science 4(1): 40-8.

Facoetti A, Turatto M, Lorusso ML, Mascetti GG (2001) Orienting of visual attention in dyslexia: evidence for asymmetric hemispheric control of attention. Experimental Brain Research 138: 46-53.

Fawcett AJ, Nicolson RI (1999) Performance of dyslexic children on cognitive and cerebellar tests. Journal of Motor Behavior 31: 68-79.

Fawcett AJ, Nicolson RI (2001) Dyslexia: the role of the cerebellum. In AJ Fawcett (ed.) Dyslexia: Theory and Good Practice. London: Whurr, pp. 89-105.

Fawcett AJ, Nicolson RI, Dean P (1996) Impaired performance of children with dyslexia on a range of cerebellar tasks. Annals of Dyslexia 46: 259-83.

Fawcett AJ, Nicolson RI, Maclagan F (2001) Cerebellar tests may differentiate between poor readers with and without IQ discrepancy. Journal of Learning Disabilities 24(2): 119-35.

Finch AJ, Nicolson RI, Fawcett AJ (2002) Evidence for a neuroanatomical difference within the olivo-cerebellar pathway of adults with dyslexia. Cortex 38: 529-39.

Fulbright RK, Jenner AR, Mencl WE, Pugh KR, Shaywitz BA, Shaywitz SE, Frost SJ, Skudlarski P, Constable RT, Lacadie CM, Marchione KE, Gore JC (1999) The cerebellum's role in reading: a functional MR imaging study. American Journal of Neuroradiology 20: 1925-30.

Gathercole SE, Baddeley AD (1989) Evaluation of the role of phonological STM in the development of vocabulary in children: a longitudinal study. Journal of Memory and Language 28: 200-13.

Gebhart AL, Petersen SE, Thach WT (2002) Role of the posterolateral cerebellum in language. In Highstein SM and Thach WT (eds) The Cerebellum: Recent Developments in Cerebellar Research (Special Issue of the Annals of the New York Academy of Sciences) 978: 318-33.

Hanakawa T, Honda M, Sawamoto N, Okada T, Yonekura Y, Fukuyama H, Shibasaki H (2002) The role of Rostral Brodmann Area 6 in Mental Operation tasks: an integrative neuroimaging approach. Cerebral Cortex 12: 1157-70.

Hinshaw SP (1992) Externalizing behavior problems and academic underachievement in childhood and adolescence - causal relationships and underlying mechanisms. Psychological Bulletin 111(1): 127-55

Ivry RB, Fiez JA (2000) Cerebellar contributions to cognition and imagery. In MS Gazzaniga (ed.) New Cognitive Neurosciences. Boston: MIT Press, pp. 999-1011.

Ivry RB, Justus TC (2001) A neural instantiation of the motor theory of speech perception - Comment. Trends in Neurosciences 24(9): 513-15.

Jobard G, Crivello F, Tzourio-Mazoyer N (2003) Evaluation of the dual route theory of reading: a metanalysis of 35 neuroimaging studies. Neuroimage, 20(2): 693-712.

Jongmans MJ, Smits-Engelman B, Bouwien CM, Shoemaker MM (2003) Consequences of co-morbidity of developmental co-ordination disorders and learning disabilities for severity and pattern of perceptual-motor dysfunction. Journal of Learning Disabilities 36(6): 528-37.

Kupfer DJ, Baltimore RS, Berry DA, 41 colleagues (2000) National Institutes of Health consensus development conference statement: diagnosis and treatment of attention-deficit/hyperactivity disorder (ADHD). Journal of the American Academy of Child and Adolescent Psychiatry 39(2): 182-93.

Leggio MG, Silverie MC, Petrosini L, Molinari M (2000) Phonological grouping is specifically affected in cerebellar patients. A verbal fluency study. Journal of Neurology, Neurosurgery and Psychiatry 69: 102-6.

Lyytinen H, Ahonen T, Eklund K, Guttorm TK, Laakso ML, Leinonen S, Leppanan PHT, Lyytinen P, Poikkeus AM, Puolakanaho A, Richardson U, Viholainen H (2001) Developmental pathways of children with and without familial risk for dyslexia during the first years of life. Developmental Neuropsychology 20(2): 535-54.

Malm J, Kristensen B, Karlsson T, Carlberg B, Fagerlund M, Olsson T (1998) Cognitive impairment in young adults with infratentorial infarcts. Neurology 51: 433-40.

Marien P, Engelborghs S, Fabbro F, De Deyn PP (2001) The lateralised linguistic cerebellum: a review and a new hypothesis. Brain and Language 79: 580-600.

Martlew M (1992) Handwriting and spelling - dyslexic children's abilities compared with children of the same chronological age and younger children of the same spelling level. British Journal of Educational Psychology 62: 375-90.

Maschke M, Drepper J, Kindsvater K, Kolb FP, Diener HC, Timmann D (2000) Involvement of the human medial cerebellum in long-term habituation of the acoustic startle response. Experimental Brain Research 133: 359-67.

Moe-Nilssen R, Helbostad JL, Talcott JB, Toennessen FE (2003) Balance and gait in children with dyslexia. Experimental Brain Research 150(2): 237-44.

Moores E, Nicolson RI, Fawcett AJ (2003) Attention deficits in dyslexia: evidence for an automatisation deficit. European Journal of Cognitive Psychology 15: 321-48.

Moretti R, Bava A, Torre P, Antonello RM, Cazzato G (2002) Reading errors in patients with cerebellar vermis lesions. Journal of Neurology 249: 461-8.

Nicolson RI (1996) Developmental dyslexia: past, present and future. Dyslexia: An International Journal of Research and Practice 2: 190-207.

Nicolson RI (2002) The dyslexia ecosystem. Dyslexia: An International Journal of Research and Practice 8: 55-66.

Nicolson RI, Fawcett AJ (1990) Automaticity: a new framework for dyslexia research? Cognition 35(2): 159-82.

Nicolson RI, Fawcett AJ (1996) The Dyslexia Early Screening Test. London: The Psychological Corporation.

Nicolson RI, Fawcett AJ (1999) Developmental dyslexia: the role of the cerebellum. Dyslexia: An International Journal of Research and Practice 5: 155-77.

Nicolson RI, Daum I, Schugens MM, Fawcett AJ, Schulz A (2002) Abnormal eye blink conditioning for dyslexic children. Experimental Brain Research 143: 42-50.

Nicolson RI, Fawcett AJ, Berry EL, Jenkins IH, Dean P, Brooks DJ (1999) Association of abnormal cerebellar activation with motor learning difficulties in dyslexic adults. Lancet 353: 1662-7.

Nicolson RI, Fawcett AJ, Dean P (1995) Time-estimation deficits in developmental dyslexia - evidence for cerebellar involvement. Proceedings of the Royal Society of London Series B - Biological Sciences 259: 43-7.

Nicolson RI, Fawcett AJ, Dean P (2001) Developmental dyslexia: the cerebellar deficit hypothesis. Trends in Neurosciences 24(9): 508-11.

Paterson SJ, Brown JH, Gsodl MK, Johnson MH, Karmiloff-Smith A (1999) Cognitive modularity and genetic disorders. Science 286(5448): 2355-8.

Raberger T, Wimmer H (2003) On the automaticity/cerebellar deficit hypothesis of dyslexia: balancing and continuous rapid naming in dyslexic and ADHD children. Neuropsychologia 41: 1493-7.

Rae C, Harasty JA, Dzendrowsky TE, Talcott JB, Simpson JM, Blamire AM, Dixon RM, Lee MA, Thompson CH, Styles P, Richardson AJ, Stein JF (2002) Cerebellar Morphology in Developmental Dyslexia. Neuropsychologia 40: 1285–92.

Ramus F (2001) Dyslexia – talk of two theories. Nature 412: 393–5.

Ramus F (2003) Developmental dyslexia: specific phonological deficit or general sensori-motor dysfunction? Current Opinion in Neurobiology 13: 212–18.

Ramus F, Pidgeon E, Frith U (2003) The relationship between motor control and phonology in dyslexic children. Journal of Child Psychology and Psychiatry and Allied Disciplines 54: 712–22.

Schmahmann JD (ed.) (1997) The Cerebellum and Cognition. New York: Academic Press.

Semrud-Clikeman M, Biderman J, Sprich-Buckminster S, Lehman BK, Faraone SV, Norman D (1992) Comorbidity between ADDH and learning disability. A review and report in a clinically referred sample. Journal of the American Association of Child and Adolescent Psychiatry 31: 439–48.

Shankweiler D, Crain S, Katz L, Fowler AE, Liberman AM, Brady SA, Thornton R, Lundquist E, Dreyer L, Fletcher JM, Stuebing KK, Shaywitz SE, Shaywitz BA (1995) Cognitive profiles of reading-disabled children – comparison of language-skills in phonology, morphology, and syntax. Psychological Science 6: 149–56.

Shaywitz BA, Fletcher JM, Shaywitz SE (1994) Interrelationships between reading disability and attention deficit-hyperactivity disorder. In Capute AJ, Accardo PJ and Shapiro BK (eds) The Learning Disabilities Spectrum: ADD, ADHD and LD. Baltimore MD: York Press.

Snowling M, Hulme C (1994) The development of phonological skills. Philosophical Transactions of the Royal Society of London Series B – Biological Sciences 346: 21–7.

Snowling MJ, Bryant PE, Hulme C (1996) Theoretical and methodological pitfalls in making comparisons between developmental and acquired dyslexia: some comments on A Castles, M Coltheart (1993). Reading and Writing 8: 443–51.

Stanovich KE (1988) Explaining the Differences between the dyslexic and the garden-variety poor reader: the phonological-core variable-difference model. Journal of Learning Disabilities 21(10): 590–604.

Stein J (2001) The sensory basis of reading problems. Developmental Neuropsychology 20: 509–34.

Temple E, Poldrack RA, Protopapas A, Nagarajan S, Salz T, Tallal P, Merzenich MM (2000) Disruption of the neural response to rapidly transient acoustic stimuli in dyslexia: evidence from fMRI. Proceedings of the National Academy of Sciences 97: 13907–12.

Timmann D, Baier PC, Diener HC, Kolb FP (2000) Classically conditioned withdrawal reflex in cerebellar patients 1. Impaired conditioned responses. Experimental Brain Research 130: 453–70.

Timmann D, Musso C, Kolb FP, Rijntjes M, Juptner M, Muller SP, Diener HC, Weiller C (1998) Postural responses to changing task conditions in patients with cerebellar lesions. Journal of Neurology, Neurosurgery and Psychiatry 65: 771–3.

Turkeltaub PE, Eden GF, Jones KM, Zeffiro TA (2002) Meta-analysis of the functional neuroanatomy of single-word reading: method and validation. Neuroimage 16: 765–80.

Wimmer H, Mayringer H, Raberger T (1999) Reading and dual-task balancing: evidence against the automatization deficit explanation of developmental dyslexia. Journal of Learning Disabilities 32: 473–8.

Wolf M, Bowers PG (1999) The double deficit hypothesis for the developmental dyslexias. Journal of Educational Psychology 91: 415–38.

Zeffiro T, Eden G (2001) The cerebellum and dyslexia: perpetrator or innocent bystander? Comment. Trends in Neurosciences 24(9): 512–13.

CHAPTER 3

Developing flexible mapping in an inflexible system?

ARYAN VAN DER LEIJ

Introduction

To understand the opportunities for preventing or treating developmental dyslexia it is essential to integrate theories that have different origins. The result should be of a 'dynamic' nature because both development and learning are involved. Dyslexia can be considered to be a *developmental* deficit with a genetic origin. The organism lacks the equipment to become a proficient reader. However, in contrast to other developmental deficits, dyslexia only becomes manifest at a relatively late age, when the ill-equipped organism is confronted with the need to learn how to read and spell. This need is not triggered by incidental learning at home but by *intentional learning* in an institutionalized context. The timing and conditions for reaching the desired developmental milestones are quite fixed. While there may be considerable tolerance for the different ages at which children learn how to walk, talk, ride bicycles or swim, they all have to learn reading, spelling and writing when they enter the first grade. The conditions of that grade are determined by culture, history and economy (most importantly age, school system, instruction method, writing system, orthography, teacher quality, and class size) but not by individual needs. In most cases this mismatch between developmental equipment and environmental demands is solved in time by the interaction between individual responsiveness to instruction and the adaptation of the instruction and guidance that the teacher can provide within 'normal' limits. However, poor readers and, in particular, dyslexics lack the coping mechanisms to deal with this mismatch, at least in time, whereas teachers struggle to expand the limitations of their time and expertise under 'regular' conditions.

The present chapter tries to describe this mismatch in terms of a task-specific model. It also considers the question of cross-linguistic universality and differences. An attempt will be made to integrate theories, in particular theories that relate to

- the development of reading, including individual differences;
- universality and script-dependency of the prerequisites and under-lying processes of reading that may be defective; and
- the treatment of reading disabilities.

The dyslexic system can be described as relatively inflexible – it is incapable of adapting its functioning to the varying demands of the task of learning to read and spell. According to Sternberg (1990: 210):

> Flexibility in strategy or information utilization means that an individual knows when to change strategy or transfer information and when not to do so.

With increasing reading and spelling skill, the level of automatization increases, necessarily reducing the level of consciousness involved. As a consequence, the use of strategy, with its connotation of 'top-down' and concept-driven activities, will be reduced to the minimum and flexibility will be defined by an accurate and rapid transfer of information.

Furthermore, from a 'dynamic' point of view it makes no sense to speak of all-or-nothing inflexibility at any point in time or in the course of development. It is evident that there are adult dyslexics who have not mastered the skills of reading and spelling in any automatized way, despite considerable effort. They made some progress at the start, most notably by learning letters and learning how to recognize some short words, but they missed the trend towards true automatization so characteristic of normal skill development. Their achievements do not follow the path of successful coping with increasing task demands such as unfamiliarity, word length, and phonological or orthographic complexities of words (Van der Leij and Van Daal, 1999a). Because they never caught up in any systematic way, their system can be called inflexible, at least with regard to learning how to read and spell and, importantly, in comparison to normally developing systems.

However, even the most severely affected dyslexic system is not completely inflexible. Dyslexics who seem to be unaffected by treatment have, nevertheless, still learned some of the sub-skills and some compensatory strategies to cope with their problems. Put positively, in terms of the dynamic system model they can be considered as intelligent organisms actively and adaptively dealing with the demands of a continuously changing external world (Thelen and Smith, 1994). They do what they can do, but the result of this dealing process is beneath the standards of mastery at the relevant age and under the present circumstances.

In contrast, cases of 'recovered', 'compensated' or even 'prevented' dyslexia are also well known. As a result, dyslexia on the individual level is not an absolute and stable syndrome but should be put on a continuum running from very severe via mild to light dyslexia and, in addition, in a longitudinal perspective that allows for changing positions on the continuum over time. This approach fits the dynamic systems model with its emphasis on intra- and inter-individual differences in development.

The development of reading and writing: a cross-linguistic view

To understand dyslexia, it is necessary to understand the act of reading and spelling and, in particular, the developmental process that leads to mastery of the act and the obstacles that have to be conquered during that process. Put in a longitudinal perspective, two stages may be differentiated (Seymour, 1999; Byrne et al., 2000): initial reading and acquisition of higher level orthographic coding.

During the initial stage of decoding and recognition of simple words, the novice in reading has to cope with a number of complexities such as unfamiliarity of phonemes and letters, lack of experience with manipulation of phonemes (for example, blending them into words and phonemic segmentation), confusable phonemes (/f/, /v/), confusable letters (b/d), inconsistent phoneme–grapheme correspondences (for example /c/ in cat and city), and inconsistencies in the spelling of simple words (such as set, sat, sad). In the next stage, the reader is faced with a number of higher level complexities related to larger orthographic units. First of all, even when all letters are known, most words are not (unfamiliarity of words). Inevitably, the same is true for sub-lexical units although some knowledge will have been gathered about codas and rimes of simple consonant–vowel–consonant (CVC) words in the initial stage. Increasing word length adds to the problems to be solved. Moreover, the number of graphemic and orthographic irregularities increases considerably. Some sounds are represented by two letters (for example, digraphs such as ng, ch, th, oa) or by different letters or letter combinations (such as eye, aye, ai, I, i, ie, y). Some letters affect other sounds in words while they remain silent (for example e in 'kite'). In the alphabetic system, the language has more sounds than can be represented by only 26 letters. Apparently, the development of the 26-letter system has been guided by the wish to make it simple and parsimonious. The problem of additional sounds has been solved by doubling or addition of letters, or addition of diacritics such as ø, ë or ç. The limited possibilities for designing letters and the history behind orthographic development meant that every language has inconsistencies with regard to the correspondence between sounds and the written form. Sounds that are not suited for extended left-to-right decoding have to be identified at a sub-lexical level.

Orthographies differ with respect to decodability. Two main complicating factors have been recognized (for example, by Seymour et al., 2003). One is a purely linguistic factor, the complexity of the syllabic structure, which affects decoding – in particular the presence of closed CVC syllables and complex consonant clusters in both onset and coda positions. Germanic languages (German, Danish, Norwegian, Swedish, Dutch and English) contain many of these complexities, in contrast to languages such as Italian, Spanish and Finnish with their many open consonant–verb (CV) syllables and few initial and final consonant–consonant (CC) clusters. The other is orthographic depth, which relates to orthographic complexities such as multi-letter graphemes, morphological effects, multi-letter inconsistencies and context-dependent rules. Again, English and Danish qualify as the most complex languages to be read and spelled, together with French and, to a lesser extent, Portuguese, Swedish and Dutch, while Finnish is on the very shallow side of this dimension, followed by Greek, Italian, Spanish, German and Norwegian (and semitic languages such as Hebrew). With regard to orthography, syllabic complexity is represented by multiple graphemes connected to multiple consonants, which complicate left-to-right decoding and sub-syllabic segmentation, probably because of an extra load on phoneme processing. Orthographic complexity appears in a variety of multi-letter-phoneme (for example, digraphs) and multi-letter-syllable (spelling patterns) rules that are unsuitable for left-to-right decoding and have to be learned by sight or by algorithms.

A model

A model of optional mapping is useful for describing the dynamics of reading and spelling. Mapping is a key concept in reading theory. Students have to learn how to map the sound of the heard word, the sight of the written word and the articulatory sequence of the spoken word on to each other (Ehri, 1992). Moreover, codes have to be learned concerning segments of word sounds and word spellings, specific sequences and letters and their relation to speech sounds (Paulesu et al., 1996). It is clear from many sources that the codes at the segmented (sub-lexical) level are essential in normal reading development (for example, Share, 1995; Goswami, 1999).

In general, the model presented here is in accordance with current reading theory, in particular the connectionist model of componential mapping (for example, Harm and Seidenberg, 1999). However, it is more explicit because it tries to define relevant sub-lexical components and to include syllabic and orthographic complexities that are inherent to the alphabetic system and vary across languages. The aim of the model is to describe differences between poor and good readers in terms that serve as a basis to categorize and possibly develop adequate interventions.

Figure 3.1 describes the options a reader has when he reads a word. Dependent on former experience, he will either recognize the written word directly as a whole word or try one or several of the sub-lexical options to 'construct' the whole word. After identification, the whole word is connected to meaning (with the exception of non-words) and, silently or aloud, used as output. Once one of the sub-lexical options has produced a successful identification, the connection adds to the representation of the whole word in memory (reverse broken line on top) and enhances the chance of direct word recognition next time. In addition, sub-lexical units are also represented in memory, probably connected to the representation of the word. Identification of unfamiliar words containing the sub-lexical

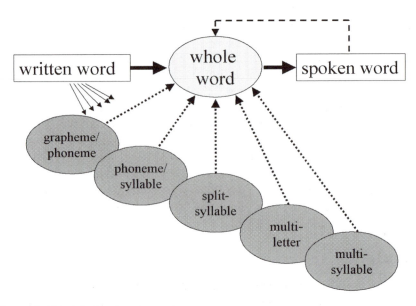

Figure 3.1 Model of optional mapping.

units may be facilitated by this knowledge. During the learning process the choice between options can be guided by conscious strategic control. However, optional mapping is increasingly automatized in normal development and it is therefore characterized by decreasing involvement of attentional resources. Strategic control is only a temporary tool that, in later stages, is only used for the identification of complex unfamiliar words. A strong indication that this developmental process has reached a high level of automatization is that unfamiliarity or word length no longer have any impact on accuracy and have very little impact on speed of identification. This stage will be reached earlier in a more shallow than in a deep orthography.[1]

1. Whole-word recognition

Whole-word recognition is both the most common of all the options of an experienced reader and, during the learning process, the aim of experience with the other options. It can also be described as (multi)-syllable mapping

---

1   In Dutch, the discrepancy in latency between high-frequency and non-words among 12-year-old normal readers varies only between 10 ms and 30 ms (one syllable) and 50 ms to 60 ms (two syllables) (Van der Leij et al., 2003). Using a slightly different approach (and, of course, other items) but comparable participants, Seymour (1986) reports larger discrepancies for English (119 ms to 212 ms).

because words can consist of one or more syllables. It is different from syllable mapping as described below in that the word is recognized as a whole, in most instances connected to the meaning.[2]

The identification process indicates automaticity which is,

> . . . a characteristic of specific words, not readers. Words move from the functional lexicon to the autonomous lexicon as a result of practice reading text.
>
> (Perfetti, 1992; Rayner et al., 2001: 40).

When he is not able to recognize a word, the reader will have to use one of the following options for identification.

2. Grapheme/phoneme translation

In the alphabetic system the most simple option is to translate graphemes into phonemes, one-by-one and from left to right. The first complexity is that it may be two-by-one as well. Digraphs – double letters – are connected to one phoneme and should be recognized accordingly. Typical for English is the 'th' sound, while the sound represented by 'ng' exists in many languages. In addition, some digraphs are complex because they are connected to different phonemes (for example ea in 'head', 'eat', 'great'). This kind of graphemic complexity is a well-known but little-investigated phenomenon that is part of the orthographic depth (and therefore of option 5). Conversions of graphemes (including simple digraphs) into phonemes are followed by blending of the sounds into the whole word. Although such a 'sounding-out' strategy is propagated to be used by initial readers and poor readers, because it affords control by the teacher, the use is mainly restricted to regular words – words with a high consistency between letters and sounds. Moreover, it is easier to apply when syllabic structure is simple (CV units with an open vowel at the end). Consequently, there are more opportunities to use this option in a language with a simple syllabic structure and a shallow orthography than in a language with syllabic complexity and a deep orthography. One of the main differences between reading development across languages is how soon the readers are confronted with the need to use more complex mapping options than grapheme/phoneme conversions. In turn, a wider range of cognitive skills will have to be engaged, making the learning process more difficult. This explains why learning how to read and spell results in lower word and non-word reading performance after the first year of instruction and practice in a deep orthography (English, followed by Danish, Portuguese and French) than in a more simple and/or

---

2 Meaning is not the main cause of the effect. Repeated practice with non-words tends also to lead to high levels of accuracy and speed of identification (Van den Bosch et al., 1995).

shallow one (Finnish, followed by Greek, Italian, Spanish, German) (Seymour et al., 2003). For example, at the end of grade one, in most European languages – with the exception of Danish – the children read words and non-words with an accuracy level of 70% or above, whereas the children in the UK still identify only about 30% correctly.

3. Phoneme/syllable mapping

Mapping grapheme clusters to syllables may be considered to be the most obvious of all options because languages are syllabic in nature. In most shallow orthographies, grapheme/phoneme conversions will be followed by syllable mapping of whole, simple words that are syllables (CVC). One could argue that this process overlaps with whole-word mapping as described in the model. However, there are two reasons to include it as a separate mapping option. First, the process of syllable mapping may still involve some effort, indicating that 'automatic' recognition of the word is not reached yet. Second, syllable mapping also relates to syllabic structures within words. All structures consisting of a vowel and (at least) one consonant (rimes, codas) are pronounceable syllables. Syllable mapping in the form of using onset-rime segmentation – the option of phoneme/syllable mapping – may be used to cope with some of the complexities at the grapheme/phoneme level. It is much used in English and French with their many inconsistencies but much less in transparent orthographies such as Greek and Spanish. As a consequence, phonological segmentation ability, in particular for end-rimes, is a strong predictor of reading development in English (Goswami and Bryant, 1990). In more shallow orthographies, it makes less difference where segmentations are made: C/VC or CV/C (Van Daal et al., 1994).

4. Split-syllable mapping

Split-syllable mapping concerns segmentation within the syllable. In contrast to segmentation of words into syllables, because this process is very different from natural speech, 'fragmentation' may be a better descriptor. As syllables consist of one or more consonants attached to one vowel, the key to sub-syllabic conversions is the split between the consonant(s) and the vowel (and vice versa). Apart from the fact that this is harder to accomplish than syllable segmentation, it may be assumed that syllabic complexities tend to complicate the splitting process. In particular, the processing of double or multiple consonants has been indicated as an important source of individual differences (Ramus, in preparation).

It is important to understand the difference between grapheme/phoneme conversions and split-syllable mapping. The first is strictly bottom-up and left-to-right, an extension of simple decoding, whereas the second is part of the repertoire of higher level orthographic coding used by readers who already have at least some experience and try to read unknown words by using sub-syllabic parts of known words. For example, this is the case when a consonant cluster from a known word is transferred to identify a word containing the same cluster (for example 'str' from the known word 'street' and in 'strong').

5. Multi-letter units

Multi-letter units violate the rules of grapheme cluster conversion into syllables. Because the pronunciation itself is perfectly syllabic (as it should be in any language), it is the orthographic rule that causes the problem. The degree of inconsistency at the multi-letter level defines the orthographic depth of the written form of a language. As noticed above, orthographies vary in depth. It is very easy to name orthographic complexities in English. The example of the pronunciation of 'ea' (as in 'head', 'eat', 'great') has already been mentioned. To take one other example, sometimes a letter is not pronounced but affects the pronunciation of a preceding letter (think of the many words ending with -ete, -ite, -ade, -ate, -ote, and so forth, in contrast to -et, -it, -ad, -at, -ot, and so on). In a more shallow orthography such as Dutch it is more difficult to find an example, but there is at least one very frequent one: the rules behind two syllable words. When the first syllable is stressed and a single vowel letter is followed by a single consonant, it is pronounced as a long ('open') vowel. For example, the single o in 'boten' is pronounced as a long vowel (as in English 'boat'). However, when the same single vowel letter is followed by a double consonant, it is pronounced as a short ('closed') vowel: the single o in 'rotsen' is pronounced as in English 'rock'. To determine the difference between the 'open' and 'closed' syllables, the reader has to identify letters of both syllables and apply multi-letter mapping.

6. Multi-syllable mapping

Words of two or more syllables can be identified by syllable (whole-word) mapping, using the first option repeatedly, or by mapping that includes more than one option. Multi-syllabic words consisting of two or more high-frequency syllables with stable pronunciation will demand only syllable mapping once the single syllables are known: 'redneck'. In many words, morphemes are helpful such as -en, -er, -ing, un-, pro-, -ity, -ation. However, multiple syllable mapping may not be enough to identify an unknown word, in particular when stress is different from what may be expected. An example is when a reader, knowing the syllable (high-frequency morpheme) un-, and the words 'family' and 'liar', needs to identify the word 'unfamiliar'. Direct transfer would generate the word /un/'/fa//mi/'/li//ar/ with the stress on the second and fourth syllable instead of on the first and third syllable: '/un//fa/'/mi//li//ar/. Additional sub-syllabic fragmentation is needed to produce the correct pronunciation. Another example is when very low-frequency patterns appear for the first time (Saskatchewan). In these cases, syllable mapping will have to be complemented by other mapping options.

Dyslexic development and optional mapping

It is widely accepted that dyslexics have trouble with all the options but opinions differ with regard to the question of whether they have more trouble with some of the options than with others. One approach is to interpret all differences between normal and dyslexic reading as quantitative differences. In particular, dyslexics are much slower and, as a consequence, word length affects their performance more, but syllabic or orthographic complexities do not contribute. Their reading profile across the mapping options is not different from the normal pattern and eventually they do not make more mistakes, other than what can be expected at their reading level. According to this interpretation, dyslexics are mainly slower readers (Landerl et al., 1997). The alternative approach is to stress qualitative differences in the reading profile. In particular, much attention has been paid to what has been called the non-word reading deficit (Rack et al., 1992). The hypothesis states that, as a consequence of their phonological deficit (Snowling, 2000), the performance of dyslexics deteriorates more than normally is the case when they are faced with unfamiliar words that have to be mapped onto the sound structure before identification can take place. Defective non-word reading (options 2 to 6) is considered to be a key characteristic of dyslexics. In contrast, reading familiar words (option 1) can be quite accurate, leaving the possibility open that direct word recognition is intact whereas phonological decoding is not.

In my opinion, it is more a matter of both quantitative and qualitative differences with the normal reading profile than of either of the two. It should be stressed that accuracy at the letter and word level does not imply that the system is partly unaffected. Even when overlearned words are recognized, speed is relatively slow (English: Seymour, 1986; German: Wimmer, 1993; German and English: Landerl et al., 1997; Dutch: Van der Leij and Van Daal, 1999b). It has been observed that, in normal reading development, only a few (and with increasing experience increasingly less) repeated identifications are sufficient to install direct word recognition but that poor readers require many more repetitions (Ehri and Wilce, 1983; Reitsma, 1983). Thus, both the effort and the outcome indicate that, although the dyslexic system at any point in time seems to cope better with familiar words than with unfamiliar ones, it does not reach normal levels of automatization in terms of rate of processing. The speed deficit, supporting the quantititative approach, is a persistent and cross-linguistic ('universal') characteristic of dyslexia. With regard to speed, there is no non-word-reading deficit per se, but there is a word-reading deficit, independent of familiarity. It is important to note that the speed deficit does not appear to be very specific in nature because it is also evident in a variety of reading-related auditory and visual processes (Breznitz, 2002) and in rapid naming of letters and digits (Korhonen, 1995; Wolf and Bowers, 1999; De Jong and Van der Leij, 2003).

However, there is some evidence that there may be qualitative differences too. To support this hypothesis, it should be proven that dyslexics find it harder to cope with some of the complexities than might be expected at their level of reading. Using the paradigm of increasing task demands we were able to show that the combination between unfamiliarity (non-word reading) and the need to process quickly (flashed presentations) had a much stronger negative effect on dyslexic performance than on normal performance, even when simple CVC words were used that were suitable for options 2 and 3 (Yap and Van der Leij, 1993). Apparently dyslexics have a specific deficit in the first phase of the reading act – fast perceptual processing to identify single graphemes and simple grapheme clusters. Furthermore, they find it harder to cope with unfamiliarity – requiring a switch to the right option – than normal readers, indicated by larger accuracy and speed effects along the word–non-word discrepancy line (see, for example, Seymour, 1986). Next, and with respect to mapping options more importantly, there is preliminary evidence that some of the orthographic and syllabic complexities have a relatively large effect on dyslexic performance. For example, it has been suggested that poor readers across languages struggle to cope with graphemic complexities, in particular digraphs (Elbro, personal communication). It has been observed that double (or multiple) consonants also seem to be a universal problem for dyslexics across languages that contain these syllabic complexities (for example, in English: Bruck, 1992; French: Rey et al., 2002). Furthermore, multi-letter mapping of CVCVC non-words ('open syllables') generates persistent and more errors in dyslexics, even in the relatively shallow orthography of Dutch. In contrast, single or double ('closed') syllable mapping of CVC or CVCCVC non-words shows more progress over time (Van der Leij and Van Daal, in preparation).

Universality and script dependency

To understand the origins of dyslexia in order to develop instruments and methods for identification and treatment, insight is needed into the processes and systems necessary for the underlying learning processes described in the mapping model. An important question is whether the cognitive prerequisites of learning how to read and spell (and, consequently, of dyslexia) are *universal* – that is, independent of environmental factors such as language, writing system, orthography and school and home factors. Although it has been assumed for a long time that this is the case, the cross-linguistic evidence to support the assumption has only been produced recently. A key observation is, that the sequence of phonological development is the same for children who grow up in different linguistic environments (Goswami, 1999). Furthermore, at the cognitive level, phonemic awareness, letter knowledge and productive language (in particular rapid naming) have been recognized as the strongest pre-school predictors of reading across languages (Elbro and Scarborough, in press a). In addition, neuropsychological studies have provided considerable evidence that the main defective mechanism leading to dyslexia is phonological in nature, in particular a basic defect in segmenting and manipulating the phoneme constituents of speech (Habib, 2000). As a consequence of universality, it may be assumed that learning how to read and spell is determined by central processes and, therefore, independent of orthography or writing system and comparable across languages. This idea is expressed by the 'central processing hypothesis' (Geva and Siegel, 2000). The impact of this hypothesis is threefold. First, reading and spelling develop in the same way across languages and orthographies. The only difference relates to the phonological, in particular syllabic, complexity of the languages. Second, differences in reading achievement (and poor and dyslexic reading) are cross-linguistically comparable, which leads to considerable if not complete overlap in characteristics of poor readers and the way to detect and treat them. Third, these differences transfer from first-language (L1) to second-language (L2) learning in reading and spelling because the engaged cognitive processes are essentially the same.

However, the conclusion of universality does not seem to be completely correct. Goswami (1999), reviewing cross-linguistic studies, states that, although the universality of the sequence of phonological development and the universality of phonemic awareness as a predictor of reading development are both supported by conclusive studies, rime awareness is a strong predictor of reading and spelling development in English, but not in more transparent orthographies of comparable syllabic complexity like German and Norwegian. Obviously, rimes represent an important level of orthographic structure in a deep orthography but not in shallower ones. Seymour et al. (2003) have demonstrated in a cross-linguistic study that syllabic complexity affects initial reading (in particular decoding unfamiliar words), a result that supports the central processing hypothesis. However, they also found evidence in favour of an influence of the orthography on reading familiar and unfamiliar words, a finding that supports the alternative to the central processing hypothesis, the 'script-dependent' or 'orthographic-depth' hypothesis (Katz and Frost, 1992).

As a consequence, the 'central' and 'script-dependent' processing hypotheses seem to be complementary. In all orthographies, including English, there are unambiguous grapheme–phoneme relationships that involve central (universal) processing and are the input for left-to-right decoding (Geva and Siegel, 2000). Script dependency varies with ambiguity and seems to be accompanied by cross-linguistic differences in the need to engage additional cognitive processes. However, what these cognitive processes are remains to be seen.

Recently, research that investigates the third of the implications of the 'central processing hypothesis' (transfer of L1 (dis)ability to L2) has produced somewhat surprising support for the 'script-dependent' idea. In contrast to the idea that learning a 'deep' second language after a 'shallow' first language should give dyslexic students at least comparable and probably more difficulties, some very poor readers in a 'shallow' L1 are considerably better in a 'deep' L2 (English). Evidence to support what is called a 'dyslexic preference for English reading' has been presented for Swedish (Miller-Guron and Lundberg, 2000) and for Dutch as L1 (Morfidi and Van der Leij, in preparation). Apparently these sub-groups are able to achieve meta-linguistic control over phonological structures that are important in learning to read in English that were of little use in learning to read in their own native language. Because both studies also describe a subgroup of poor L1 readers who lack the talent and show comparable poor reading in L1 and L2, it seems plausible to assume that reading achievement is not only related to the script to be learned but also to individual differences in script learning. In particular, a logographic process may be involved in the recognition and storage of familiar words (Ehri, 1992; Seymour, 1999).

It may be assumed that phonological deficits reflect a universal cause of developmental dyslexia that is to some extent language dependent (in particular syllabic complexity) but not script dependent. In addition, cross-linguistic differences may be found when script-bound skills are needed. These differences are related to some of the optional mappings, in particular option 3 (use of rime) and 5 (complex digraph and multi-letter identification). This leads to the hypothesis that the existence of an 'orthographic' sub-type that differs from the 'universal' phonological deficit sub-type is more likely when the orthography contains more complexities – in other words, more likely in English, French or Danish than, for example, in Italian, Finnish or German. The intriguing findings of the L1-L2 studies mentioned above support this hypothesis: while the dyslexics in the two studies could not be divided in sub-types in their first language, this could be done in L2 English.

Returning to the model of optional mapping, it may be assumed that general speed deficits slow down all the options including whole-word recognition (option 1), also indicated by a word length effect. In addition, specific phonological, in particular phonemic, deficits have a direct impact on the options that involve the left-to-right processing of simple syllables: options 2 and 3 – grapheme/phoneme conversion, phoneme/syllable mapping (for example, C-VC and CV-C segmentation) – and option 6 of multi-syllable mapping as far as it repeats options 2 and 3 (for example, double C-VC segmentation in CVCCVC). Option 4 – complex split-syllable mapping (for example, split between CC and V) – gives extra problems because phoneme processing is harder when more consonants are involved in the syllable (syllabic complexity). Option 5 of multi-letter mapping is a distinct problem because neither of the simpler options is useful: complex digraphs (for example, pronunciation of 'ea') have to be learned within the context of words and spelling patterns have to be learned as a whole. This analysis leads to the hypothesis that, in a cross-linguistic context, dyslexic reading will be comparable with respect to options 1, 2, 3 and 6 (simple syllables), in particular in reading speed. Differences (probably also including poorer accuracy) will be correlated with the amount of syllabic complexity (most notably multiple CCs) and of orthographic inconsistency (multi-letter spelling patterns and complex digraphs or polygraphs) and, thus, to options 4 and 5. Dyslexics who read languages with little complexities in split-syllable mapping and only a few multi-letter peculiarities such as Finnish, Italian and Hebrew should mainly be (very) slow readers. In contrast, languages such as English (and, possibly, French and Danish) with many multiple consonants and multi-letter inconsistencies should not only cause slow speed but also inaccuracy. Languages such as German and Dutch, with an intermediate level of syllabic and orthographic complexity, should be somewhere in between.

Treatment

After defining the dyslexic system as relatively inflexible in the use of optional mapping, indicated by slow speed of processing and proneness to errors we may consider how to 'flexibilize' that system. In general, two models are recognized to be used in special reading programmes. One is 'bottom-up' direct instruction with guided practice and intensive practice as integrated elements; the other is 'top-down' strategy training.

Direct instruction

Although there is some debate with regard to young children, direct instruction is recognized as a more effective approach than indirect and child-initiated instruction with little control of what is implemented and what is done (National Reading Panel, 2000; Rayner et al., 2001). With regard to treatment of dyslexia, elaboration of the direct instruction model has been advocated with regard to quantity and timing. Treatment has to capitalize on quantity: in comparison to the normal situation the amount of instruction, guidance and practice should be increased. Frequency of sessions should be high, many repetitions should be included, and intensive interactions with the tutor (or tutor system such as a computer) should be provided for, as well as many instances of immediate feedback. The dyslexic system needs many more highly qualified opportunities to learn the necessary connections between graphemes and orthographic units and sounds/sound structures than the non-dyslexic system. Consequently, the poor reader receives (much) 'more of the same' of what the normal reader is getting (or should be getting): phonemes, graphemes, words, sub-lexical units, and so forth. With regard to timing, it is recommended to start as early as possible to be able to train the brain when it is relatively plastic and is not overloaded yet by ill-defined representations.

Most programmes are based on the assumption of universality of the core deficit of dyslexia – a phonological deficit leading to problems with grapheme/phoneme conversions and sub-lexical processing. Moreover, most are clearly 'bottom up' in nature: directed at drill-and-practice of word-attack skills and aimed at automatization. Much attention is paid to stimulate phoneme awareness (sound segmentation and sound blending) as pre-requisites for word identification. Shortly after or in combination with phoneme learning, letter sounds are trained in a specified order. Individual sounds and small units are practised to stimulate the acquisition of the left-to-right decoding strategy. The principle of 'small differences' is used in the written material (cat – mat – fat) to practise phoneme/syllable segmentation. After the initial stage of phonemic awareness and decoding strategy, the emphasis on strategic control and monitoring of the student decreases when he enters the stage of acquisition of higher level orthographic coding, apart from general directives (such as 'read as accurately as you can', or 'take your time to identify the word before sounding it out'). Most drill-and-practice programmes are based on some sort of idea of how sub-lexical knowledge is acquired by the self-teaching mechanism (for example, by onset-rime segmentation) but the mechanism itself is not explained to the student. The identification processes – the mapping options – are triggered by manipulation of material conditions (for example, words, non-words, syllabic letter units, and split-syllabic letter units). In many programmes, words with overlapping letter units are given in lists or by way of a 'word-building' programme and the reader is asked to read them repeatedly (see, for example, McCandliss et al., 2003; Struiksma, 2003). The sub-lexical units are learned based on increased frequency, imitating the implicity of the normal self-teaching mechanism. Apparently, students do not have to 'know' how or even what they are learning (a common feature of drill practices). As a consequence, they will have little awareness of the different options in mapping and will not be able to monitor their own coping strategies at that specific level, with the exception of the most basic one: left-to-right phonological decoding ('sounding out and blend'). Above that level, 'flexibilization' is triggered, not taught.

Reviews indicate that the majority of effective programmes, across countries and languages, are based on the principles of 'bottom-up' direct instruction (Swanson et al., 1999). Effectiveness varies with age (an earlier start is more effective – see, for example, Torgesen, 2001), and focus (grapheme/phoneme-based reading programmes produce better results with regard to initial reading than purely phonological training – see, for example, Bus and Van Ijzendoorn, 1999). However, long-term effects of such programmes are stronger with regard to decoding skills (options 2 and 3) than with regard to real-word identification (option 1, but probably also related to split-syllable and multi-letter mapping). Moreover, a substantial sub-group of poor readers does not profit from the programmes or only learns what is taught without transfer to other words.[3] In addition, slow processing seems to be hard to beat (Torgesen, 2001). The older the dyslexic system is and the more it belongs to the 'resistors' to earlier treatments, the more it cannot only depend on quantity to learn something new (and replace the fuzzy representations that have been learned). More salient measures have to be introduced to alert and flexibilize the dyslexic system. There have been three kinds of attempts to solve this problem by adding a qualitative dimension to 'bottom-up' drill-and-practice:

- phonological: audio-support and manipulation of speech sounds;
- orthographic: manipulation of visual input; and
- involvement of additional modalities.

To give some examples, in the phonological domain auditory support (priming and feedback) has been tried with some success, in particular to aid whole-word (syllable) and phoneme/syllable mapping (Olson and Wise, 1992; Van Daal et al., 1994; Wise et al., 1997). This principle has become part of many treatment methods. Manipulation of speech sounds has been advocated as the solution of dyslexia (Merzenich et al., 1996; Tallal et al., 1996). Although it makes sense to increase the length of 'stop' consonants such as /b/, /d/, /p/ and /t/ to accommodate the speed to the slower rate of sound discrimination of the dyslexic system, the original studies have met serious criticism (see Habib, 2000, for a review). There is, however, some evidence that speech modification training improves phonological performance, in particular split-syllable segmentation (Habib et al., 2002).

With regard to the visual input, providing visual cues to letters (making letters or letter clusters more prominent: for example, by colours, extra symbols, fading pictures with embedded letters, altered letters) as a mnemonic aid has been used frequently but the specific contribution to the learning process is not clear yet. Manipulation of the visual input using flashed presentations of words and/or sub-lexical units (suggested by Frederiksen et al., 1985) has remained on the agenda because the results have been promising. Using flashed non-word presentations, Van den

---

3   Apart from their characteristic resistance to treatment and their obvious defective self-teaching mechanism, little is known yet about correlated cognitive or neurobiological variables. When IQ is controlled for, there does not seem to be anything special in the cognitive profile, at least not at the level of discrete IQ factors (see for example Kappers (1997) who was not able to differentiate between the extreme sub-groups of students who benefited very well from his treatment and students who did not benefit at all).

Bosch et al. (1995) reported length-independent word and non-word reading gains in speed without costs in precision, while reading-aloud training with time pressure only produced progress in accuracy. Das-Smaal et al. (1996) were able to show that perceptual unit training (detect CV, VC, VCC, CVC, VCV and CCC letter units in flashed words) has a positive effect on perceptual coding skills and multi-letter recognition in words, indicating a relation to options 3 to 6. When combined with phonological segmentation training of the units, perceptual unit training had positive effects on word and non-word reading (Yap and Van der Leij, 1994). This result supports the suggestion that componential spelling-to-sound mappings are the core of unfamiliar word generalization (Harm et al., 2003). Flashed word representation has also been applied successfully in a programme based on hemisphere-specific stimulation (flashed presentation in left or right visual half field – Van Strien et al., 1995; Kappers, 1997). In contrast to many other programmes, practice with flashed (non-)word presentation has a direct effect on reading speed. It should be noted that training studies to enhance rate of processing are scarce in comparison to accuracy-oriented training. Apart from flashed presentations, one of the few exceptions to this rule is reading rate acceleration by forcing the student to read a disappearing text (it is 'eaten up') at a relatively high pace (Breznitz, 1997). Because slow reading speed is the universal characteristic of dyslexics across languages, this issue should get more attention in future research.

The involvement of other modalities has a long history since Fernald published her VAKT method in 1943. In addition to the visual (V) and auditory (A) modality, movement (kinaesthetic: K) and touch (tactile modality: T) are involved. Although, to my knowledge, the principle of adding K and T has been the subject of very few studies, in many programmes some of it is present, mostly in a multi-modal fashion to support grapheme/phoneme connectivity and phoneme identification and discrimination (for example, 'see and feel' the place of articulation of the spoken phoneme). For example, it is part of an effective preventive method for pre-school children who are (genetically) at-risk (Borstrøm and Elbro, 1997).[4]

Strategy training

The second main approach of treatment is very different from the first because it is essentially 'top-down' in nature. In a sense, an unfamiliar word is

---

4   The idea of multi-modality is in harmony with the dynamic systems model: 'When stim-
    uli from a single modality are very strong, there is little functional advantage to be
    gained from amplification. In situations, however, where important stimuli are hard to
    detect, the multimodal enhancement is more critical' (Thelen and Smith, 1994: 190).

regarded as a puzzle that may be solved by consciously using certain rules, much in line with many special spelling programmes. These rules ('algorithms') may be based on a psycholinguistic analysis of the phonological and morphological structure of the words and transformed into a set of production rules. To give an example derived from a study by Tijms et al. (2002): 'If the last speech sound <S> of the syllable is a member of class <C>, then perform operation <O>.' In addition, orthographic inconsistencies (option 5) are presented as 'heuristic knowledge'. A computer and a redesigned keyboard (containing the sounds, classes and operations) are used to present the programme. Apart from consonants, short/long vowels and digraphs, morphemes are represented on the keyboard. Starting with grapheme/phoneme mapping in monosyllabic words, the length of the sub-lexical unit and of the words increases gradually in the reading and spelling practices. In the end, all the mapping options are explicitly and intensively covered by conscious operations of the student.

In general, this example is in agreement with other programmes developed to stimulate word-attacking strategies. It is important to note that these programmes have been born out of necessity. The conclusion has been drawn that many 'bottom-up' programmes successfully improve the phonologically based word attack and decoding skills (sounding out simple new words and non-words, options 1–3), but that the gains in terms of generalization to other aspects of reading acquisition (higher level orthographic coding – options 4, 5 and 6 – and text reading) have been disappointing (Moats and Foorman, 1997; Torgesen, 2001).

The only alternative seems to be to adopt a 'top-down' approach with conscious control by students of the word-attack strategies that they apply to identify words. It is important to note that dyslexic reading can be influenced by strategic control and, thus, is flexible in that sense (Hendriks and Kolk, 1997).

The alternatives do not exclude each other. After many years of thorough investigations, Lovett and her collegues (reviewed by Lovett, Lacerenza and Borden, 2000 – for an example, see Lovett et al., 1994) conclude that a combination of 'bottom-up' direct instruction and 'top-down' strategy training produces the best results when the goal is to acquire effective, flexible word-identification strategies. The 'bottom-up' part consists of instruction and practice of phonological analysis and blending, letter-sound association skills in the context of word recognition, and left-to-right phonological decoding strategy ('sounding out', which is the simplest one of five strategies and option 2 of the model in Figure 3.1). The 'top-down' part is a dialogue-based meta-cognitive training of four additional word identification strategies that offer different approaches to the decoding of unfamiliar words and exposure to different levels of sub-lexical segmentation. All strategies are explicitly taught (including self-monitoring and application to text-reading activities). In terms of optional mapping, identification by analogy ('riming') helps phoneme/syllable segmentation between onsets and rimes (option 3).[5]

Option 5, multi-letter mapping, is triggered by attempting different vowel pronunciations ('vowel alert') (for example in the case of 'eat', 'bread', 'great', or 'kit/kite'). Multi-syllable mapping (option 6) is executed by identification and segmentation of prefixes and suffixes ('peeling off': pro/nuncia/tion) and by identification of small, familiar parts in compound words (rain/coat) ('I spy').

Interestingly, in the integrated programme (Phonological and Strategy Training – PHAST – see Lovett et al., 2000), students attempt different vowel pronunciations later in time than segmentation of prefixes and suffixes. This is in harmony with the observation that – even in a transparent orthography like Dutch – multi-letter mapping (option 5) of orthographic inconsistencies ('open syllables') is harder to achieve (by all students but especially by dyslexics) than multi-syllable mapping (option 6). It is important to note that split-syllable mapping (option 4) is not trained as a separate strategy but presumably in the direct instruction part. Derived from the programme developed by Engelmann and colleagues (for example, Engelmann and Bruner, 1988), awareness of sub-syllabic units within spoken words is stimulated in segmentation training. In addition, visual cues are used, such as highlighting salient features of connected letters. However, the strategy of seeking known parts is probably also appropriate.

Table 3.1 gives an overview of the most frequent treatment principles.

Discussion

With regard to the stage of initial reading, when the child learns grapheme–phoneme conversions, simple whole word mapping and simple phoneme/syllable mapping (options 1 to 3 in the model in Figure 3.1), most 'bottom-up' methods try to help the young child to conquer the first complexities by training in phonemic awareness, grapheme/phoneme connections and isolated presentation or manipulation of confusable phonemes, letters and letter/sound inconsistencies. A growing amount of evidence suggests that direct instruction of phonemic awareness and letter knowledge in the pre-reading phase ('prevention') and in the first grade is beneficial to at-risk groups, including young children with language impairments, children from dyslexic families, children from socio-economically disadvantaged families, or children with poorly developed phonemic awareness (Elbro and Scarborough, in press b). The key observation is that, to learn the alphabetic principle and initial reading, at-risk children are dependent on direct and intensive instruction. As is

---

5   In transparent orthographies, segmentation would not only concern C-VC but also CV-C.

Table 3.1 Treatment principles

	Mapping option	Orthographic structure	Mapping on to	Direct instruction repeated practice presenting:	Strategy training teaching to use:
1	Whole word	Whole word	whole word	O: - whole words	- whole word knowledge - vocabulary - context
2	Grapheme/ phoneme	Single graphemes, for example, b Simple digraphs, for example, th, ng	single phonemes, for example, /C//V/ /V//C/ /C//V//C/	O: - letters - prominent letters - flashed letters - reading rate acceleration (letters) P: - phonemes - manipulated phonemes - audio-support (phoneme)	- labels of single phonemes (long, short, consonant, vowel) - connections of graphemes/ digraphs to single phonemes - sounding out left-to-right - blending sounds into words
3	Phoneme/ syllable	Grapheme clusters (including V)	phoneme/ syllables (segment C from simple syllable), for example, /C//VC/ /CV//C/	O: - (non-)words (CV, VC, CVC) - prominent clusters (syllables) - flashed non-words or clusters (syllables) - reading rate acceleration P: - manipulated phonemes in syllables - audio-support (phoneme/syllable)	- application of analogy rules (e.g. rimes)

4	Split-syllable	Grapheme clusters (excluding V)	phoneme(s)/ phoneme(s) (split CC from V in complex syllable), for example, /CV//CC/ /CC//VC/	O: - complex one-syllable (non-)words (CCV, VCC, CCVC, CCVCC, . . .) - prominent clusters (CC, . . .) - flashed (non-)words or CC-clusters - reading rate acceleration P: - manipulated CC in syllables - audio-support (CC, . . .)	- seeking of known parts
5	Multi-letter	Complex digraphs, for example, ea Grapheme clusters (spelling patterns), for example, CVCV CVCVC	syllables, for example, /CVC/ /CV//CVC/	O: - one- or multi-syllable (non-)words with inconsistent spelling patterns - prominent clusters (complex digraphs, spelling patterns) - flashed (non-)words or spelling patterns - reading rate acceleration P: - manipulated syllables mapped to spelling patterns - audio-support (syllables)	- attempting variable pronunciations or stress - application of spelling rules - use 'keywords' to recognize complex digraphs or spelling patterns (analogy rules)
6	Multi-syllable	Grapheme clusters (syllables)	syllables, for example, /CVC//CVC/	- multi-syllable (non-)words - see options 3–5	- peeling off prefixes/suffixes - seeking known parts - application of other strategies

Note: O = orthographic presentation, P = phonological presentation.

suggested by Byrne et al. (2000), apart from the effect of instruction in terms of mastery of (sub-)skills, their *responsiveness to instruction* serves as a strong predictor of later reading development. Although there may be very different ways to operationalize this concept, it fits well in the dynamic view proposed in this chapter.

With regard to the simpler mapping options, instruction can focus on clearly distinguishable prerequisite sub-skills such as sound blending, phonemic segmentation and grapheme–phoneme conversions and the identification of meaningful entities such as simple words. Obviously, the process is slow and, therefore, easily influenced by instruction and feedback in a straightforward way. However, the relation between instruction and the processes to be instructed becomes less clear in the stage of the acquisition of higher level orthographic coding, when mapping involves the more complex options of split-syllabic, multi-letter and multi-syllabic units and is characterized by an increase in processing speed. By repeated reading and, in particular, repeated sounding out the word as a whole, knowledge of words and sub-lexical units is gathered and used to identify words with equal parts. Put simply, ability in mapping results from experience with mapping. Thus, frequently read units – spelling patterns – will facilitate recognition of words containing the units. Adams (1990: 128) describes the result: 'For the skilled reader, the perception of words and syllables is effortlessly and automatically driven by the associative connections among letters in their memories.' However, when this level of mastery is not reached by drill-and-practice, the poor reader has to be forced to attend to the spellings of words or to use some kind of strategy to identify the words. Inevitably, these solutions will increase his attention level and, in many cases, slow the process down. Unfortunately, it is still unclear whether this approach eventually leads to a higher reading rate after increased performance in accuracy.

It is important to note that returning to phonology-oriented programmes is not an option. Wise et al. (2000) conclude that improving phonological skills does not in itself lead, by some 'self-teaching' mechanism, to independent and accurate reading. Possibly, this is caused by a switch in the primary unit that is processed. Once written words are recognized and stored in memory, they increasingly influence sub-lexical processing and generalization. In particular when syllabic and orthographic complexities frustrate the application of simple left-to-right decoding options (options 4 and 5: split-syllable or multi-letter), word-specific knowledge may become more important for sub-lexical operations than graphemes or grapheme clusters connected to simple syllables. The normal system seems to adopt the switching back-and-forth from small (graphemes) to large units (words) and back to sub-lexical units in a self-evident way. Possibly, the inflexibility of the dyslexic system is characterized most by the struggle with this switch. When it cannot be done by 'self-teaching' it has to be guided in an explicit way ('teaching by other'). Treatment involves either drawing the attention to the relevant sub-lexical unit within the word by manipulation of input or audio-support, or teaching the right strategies to cope with sub-lexical options. The important question is whether these kinds of treatment in the phase of higher level orthographic coding eventually lead to the same result as the more implicit ('normal') way of drill-and-practice. It all depends on whether the mechanism is temporarily penetrable by prominent or salient input or rule-based guidance at some level of consciousness, in order to escape from the wrong identification routines. After learning an effortful and self-regulated way to solve the identification problem, the system has consequently to learn to do without the manipulated input or the rules and take the pathway to automatization with its characteristic of decrease of attentional effort. It should be noted that this is a fairly good description of the way spelling is learned, but the question remains whether it applies to reading acquisition. A strong proof of such dynamics of the dyslexic system in reading would be generalization and transfer of decoding proficiency to fluent word reading. Unfortunately, in spite of gains on the (sub-)skills directly trained as a result of strategy instruction, generalization to reading acquisition has been reported to be poor (Moats and Foorman, 1997; Olson et al., 1997). In particular, it can be assumed that the lack of speed of the dyslexic system is hard to beat. Although in many of the better controlled studies progress has been reported with regard to accuracy, rate stays comparatively slow. Torgesen (2001: 198), reflecting on his data, concludes:

> Even if word reading accuracy is dramatically increased through the more efficient use of analytic word reading processes, reliance on analytic processes will not produce the kind of fluent reading that results when most of the words in a passage can be recognized 'by sight'.

Concluding comments

Returning to the question of how to develop flexible mapping in an inflexible system, the answer seems to be by providing one or, if necessary, more of three conditions:

- intensive direct instruction (as early as possible);
- practice with manipulation of input or support that draw the attention to relevant phonological and orthographic features; and
- teaching of strategies to control the mapping options.

In contrast with normal readers, these conditions may not result in a fast data-driven 'bottom-up' process. Reading of 'hard-core' dyslexics will probably remain slow and not fully automatized, because basic processing speed consumes too much attention or effort (the 'automatization deficit' hypothesis – Van der Leij and Van Daal, 1999a, b), or because 'top-down' and concept-driven strategies slow it down (Spear and Sternberg, 1987). Presumably, many dyslexics will show signs of both characteristics. Consequently it may be assumed that, when the flexibilization of the system is not 'normalized', the aim should be gains in accuracy, reading level and, as a result, in reading comprehension, but not in reading speed (other than acquired by higher accuracy). The hypothesis that repeated exposure to words will produce fluency after effortful mastery of a certain level of accuracy (suggested by Torgesen, 2001), is challenging but not supported by the evidence reviewed by Kuhn and Stahl (2003: 18) who state: '. . . fluency-oriented instruction seems to have salutary effects in a number of areas but not in the area that it was intended for, rapid recognition of isolated words.' However, as was suggested before, it may be worthwhile to put manipulations such as speech modification, flashed presentations and reading rate acceleration higher on the research agenda, while early intervention also seems to be promising (for example, Borstrøm and Elbro, 1997; Nicolson et al., 1999; Torgesen et al., 1999; Byrne et al., 2000; see also Elbro and Scarborough, in press b).

Two specific issues require special attention in future investigations. Because the syllable is the natural segment of speech, and deficits in sub-syllabic segmentation are a main characteristic of dyslexia, it makes sense that anything that complicates identification of the syllable as an orthographic unit will contribute to defective reading.

First, split-syllabic fragmentation of syllables with multiple consonants into CC/V or V/CC (option 4) seems to be particularly defective in comparison to single consonants and phoneme/syllable segmentation. While it is not clear yet what role the double consonants play, the phenomenon itself may be attributed to the phonemic impairments that are typical for dyslexics. The fact that normal readers hardly have problems with double consonants in one-syllable words supports this conclusion. Moreover, segmenting consonants from the vowel seems to be a universal problem of dyslexics across the languages that contain many multiple consonants (in particular double Cs) (see, for example, studies using English: Bruck, 1992; French: Rey et al., 2002; Dutch: Van der Leij and Van Daal, 1999b, in preparation). In an intriguing study, Struiksma (2003) was able to demonstrate that responsiveness to training that demanded fragmenting the vowel from the double consonant, sharply differentiates the hard-core dyslexics from otherwise poor readers. The effect of repeated practice with CCVC- and CVCC-word families was measured. When after 20 sessions the change was made from CC clusters with the same vowel (slaaf – slaag – slaat) to CC clusters with varying vowel (slaaf - sloeg - sloot), a substantial sub-group showed decline of their achievement curve, which had previously been progressing. Moreover, they never recovered from the 'shock' and did not reach their old level in the next 20 sessions. The other sub-group began to progress again after a short delay. These results indicate the importance of split-syllable mapping as a subject of further study.

Second, multi-letter mapping (option 5) of complex digraphs and spelling patterns should receive further investigation. In contrast to the split-syllable mapping, executed by central processes, multi-letter mapping is more script dependent. As a consequence, there should be a correlation between inconsistencies in this respect and reading problems. Dyslexics who learn English, French or Danish as their first language should be more victimized than dyslexics who learn shallow orthographies such as Finnish, Spanish or Hebrew. However, there are complications to deal with in a cross-linguistic study. It is a very normal problem to struggle with orthographic complexities. Between dyslexics and normal readers it is more a matter of degree than of all or none. In addition, if it is true that there may be dyslexics with a talent for gathering orthographic knowledge (as was shown in an earlier section by Swedish and Dutch dyslexics learning English as L2), some may compensate for their problems in decoding. To be able to make cross-linguistic comparisons, sub-types along the dimension orthographic processing/phonological decoding should be included, even in languages with a more shallow orthography. If successful, sub-type studies of this kind may provide a basis for development of aptitude-treatment interaction programmes with regard to multi-letter mapping.

References

Adams MJ (1990) Beginning to read. Thinking and learning about print. Cambridge MA: MIT Press.

Borstrøm I, Elbro C (1997) Prevention of dyslexia in kindergarten: effects of phonemic awareness training with children of dyslexic parents. In Hulme C and Snowling M (eds) Dyslexia: Biology, Cognition and Intervention. London: Whurr, pp. 235–53.

Breznitz Z (1997) Increasing the reading of dyslexics by reading acceleration and auditory masking. Journal of Educational Psychology 89(1): 236–46.

Breznitz Z (2002) Asynchrony of visual-orthographic and auditory-phonological word recognition processes: an underlying factor in dyslexia. Reading and Writing: An Interdisciplinary Journal 15: 15–42.

Bruck M (1992) Persistence of dyslexics' phonological awareness deficits. Developmental Psychology 28: 874–86.

Bus A, Van Ijzendoorn M (1999) Phonological awareness and early reading: a meta-analysis of experimental training studies. Journal of Educational Psychology 91(3): 403–14.

Byrne B, Fielding-Barnsley R, Ashley L (2000) Effects of preschool phoneme identity training after six years: outcome level distinguished from rate of response. Journal of Educational Psychology 92(4): 659–67.

Das-Smaal EA, Klapwijk MJG, Van der Leij A (1996) Training of perceptual unit processing in children with a reading disability. Cognition and Instruction 14(2): 221–50.

De Jong PF, Van der Leij A (2003) Developmental changes in the manifestation of a phonological deficit in dyslexic children learning to read a regular orthography. Journal of Educational Psychology 95(1): 22–40.

Ehri LC (1992) Reconceptualizing the development of sight word reading and its relationship to reading. In Gough P and Treiman R (eds) Reading Acquisition. Hillsdale NJ: Lawrence Erlbaum, pp. 107–43.

Ehri LC, Wilce LS (1983) Development of word identification speed in skilled and less skilled beginning readers. Journal of Educational Psychology 75: 3–18.

Elbro C, Scarborough H (in press a) Early identification. In Bryant P and Nunes T (eds) International Handbook of Children's Reading. Dordrecht: Kluwer.

Elbro C, Scarborough H (in press b) Early intervention. In P Bryant and T Nunes (eds) International Handbook of Children's Reading. Dordrecht: Kluwer.

Engelmann S, Bruner E (1988) Reading Mastery I/II Fast Cycle: Teacher's Guide. Chicago: Science Research Associates.

Fernald GM (1943) Remedial Techniques in Basic School Subjects. New York: McGraw-Hill.

Frederiksen JR, Warren BM, Rosebery AS (1985) A componential approach to training reading skills: Part 1. Perceptual units training. Cognition and Instruction 2(2): 91–130.

Geva E, Siegel L (2000) Orthographic and cognitive factors in the concurrent development of basic reading skills in two languages. Reading and Writing: An Interdisciplinary Journal 12: 1–30.

Goswami U (1999) Towards a theoretical framework for understanding reading development and dyslexia in different orthographies. In Lundberg I, Tønnesen FE and Austad I (eds) Dyslexia: Advances in Theory and Practice. Dordrecht: Kluwer Academic Publishers, pp. 101–16.

Goswami U, Bryant P (1990) Phonological Skills and Learning to Read. Hove: Erlbaum.

Habib M (2000) The neurological basis of developmental dyslexia. An overview and working hypothesis. Brain 123: 2373–99.

Habib M, Rey V, Daffaure V, Camps R, Espesser R, Joly-Pottuz B, Démonet J-F (2002) Phonological training in children with dyslexia using temporally modified speech: a three-step pilot investigation. International Journal of Language Communication Disorders 37(3): 289–308.

Harm M, Seidenberg M (1999) Phonology, reading acquisition, and dyslexia: insights from connectionist models. Psychological Review 106(3): 491–528.

Harm M, McCandliss B, Seidenberg M (2003) Modeling the success and failures of interventions for disabled readers. Scientific Studies of Reading 7(2): 155–82.

Hendriks AW, Kolk HJ (1997) Strategic control in developmental dyslexia. Cognitive Neuropsychology 14(3): 321–66.

Kappers EJ (1997) Outpatient treatment of dyslexia through stimulation of the cerebral hemispheres. Journal of Learning Disabilities 30(1): 100–25.

Katz L, Frost R (1992) The reading process is different for different orthographies: the orthographic depth hypothesis. In Frost R and Katz L (eds) Orthography, Phonology, Morphology and Meaning. Amsterdam: Elsevier, pp. 67–84.

Korhonen T (1995) The persistence of rapid naming problems in children with learning difficulties. Journal of Learning Disabilities 28: 232–9.

Kuhn M, Stahl S (2003) Fluency: a review of developmental and remedial practices. Journal of Educational Psychology 95(1): 3–21.

Landerl K, Wimmer H, Frith U (1997) The impact of orthographic consistency on dyslexia: a German–English comparison. Cognition 63: 315–34.

Lovett MW, Borden SL, DeLuca T, Lacerenza L, Benson NJ, Brackstone D (1994) Treating the core deficits of developmental dyslexia. Evidence of transfer of learning after phonologically- and strategy-based reading training programs. Developmental Psychology 30(6): 805–22.

Lovett MW, Lacerenza L, Borden SL (2000) Putting struggling readers on the PHAST track: a program to integrate phonological and strategy-based remedial reading instruction and maximize outcomes. Journal of Learning Disabilities 33(5): 458–76.

McCandliss B, Beck I, Sandak R, Perfetti C (2003) Focusing attention on decoding for children with poor reading skills: a study of the word building intervention. Scientific Studies of Reading 7(1): 75–104.

Merzenich MM, Jenkins WM, Johnston P, Schreiner C, Miller SL, Tallal P (1996) Temporal processing deficits of language-learning impaired children ameliorated by training. Science 271(5245): 77–81.

Miller-Guron L, Lundberg I (2000) Dyslexia and second language reading: a second bite at the apple? Reading and Writing: An Interdisciplinary Journal 12: 41–61.

Moats L, Foorman B (1997) Introduction to the special issue of SSR: components of effective reading instruction. Scientific Studies of Reading 1(3): 187–9.

Morfidi E, Van der Leij A (in preparation) The use of orthographic information in L1 and L2 reading: a comparison of Dutch normal and poor readers.

National Reading Panel (2000) Teaching Children to Read: An Evidence-based Assessment of the Scientific Research Literature on Reading and its Implications for Reading Instruction. Washington DC: National Institute of Child Health and Human Development.

Nicolson RI, Fawcett AJ, Moss H, Nicolson M, Reason R (1999) Early reading intervention can be effective and cost-effective. British Journal of Educational Psychology 69: 47–62.

Olson R, Wise B (1992) Reading on the computer with orthographic and speech feedback. Reading and Writing: An Interdisciplinary Journal 4(2): 107–44.

Olson R, Wise B, Johnson M, Ring J (1997) The etiology and remediation of phonologically based word recognition and spelling disabilities: are phonological deficits the 'hole' story? In Blachman B (ed.) Foundations of Reading Acquisition and Dyslexia: Implications for Early Intervention. Mahwah NJ: Erlbaum, pp. 305–26.

Paulesu E, Frith U, Snowling M, Gallagher A, Morton J, Frackowiak S, Frith C (1996) Is developmental dyslexia a disconnection syndrome? Evidence from PET scanning. Brain 119: 143–57.

Perfetti CA (1992) The representation problem in reading acquisition. In Gough PB, Ehri LC and Treiman R (eds) Reading Acquisition. Hillsdale NJ: Lawrence Erlbaum, pp. 145–74.

Rack JP, Snowling MJ, Olson RK (1992) The nonword reading deficit in developmental dyslexia: a review. Reading Research Quarterly 27(1): 28–53.

Ramus F (in preparation) Outstanding Questions about Phonological Processing in Dyslexia. London: Institute of Cognitive Neuroscience, University College.

Rayner K, Foorman B, Perfetti C, Pesetsky D, Seidenberg M (2001) How psychological science informs the teaching of reading. Psychological Science in the Public Interest 2(2): 31–74.

Reitsma P (1983) Word-specific knowledge in beginning reading. Journal of Research in Reading 6: 41–56.

Rey V, De Martino S, Espesser R, Habib M (2002) Temporal processing and phonological impairment in dyslexia: effect of phoneme lengthening on order judgment of two consonants. Brain and Language 80: 576–91.

Seymour P, Aro M, Erskine J (2003) Foundation of literacy acquisition in European orthographies. British Journal of Psychology 94: 143–74.

Seymour PHK (1986) Cognitive Analysis of Dyslexia. London: Routledge & Kegan Paul.

Seymour PHK (1999) Cognitive architecture of early reading. In Lundberg I, Tønnesen E and Austad I (eds) Dyslexia: Advances in Theory and Practice. Dordrecht: Kluwer Academic Publishers, pp. 59–73.

Share D (1995) Phonological recoding and self-teaching: sine qua non of reading acquisition. Cognition 55: 151–218.

Snowling MJ (2000) Dyslexia. Oxford: Blackwell.

Spear LC, Sternberg RJ (1987) An information-processing framework for understanding reading disability. In SJ Ceci (ed.) Handbook of Cognitive, Social and Neuropsychological Aspects of Learning Disabilities. Hillsdale NJ: Lawrence Erlbaum Associates, pp. 3-31.

Sternberg R J (1990) Thinking styles: keys to understanding student performance. Phi Delta Kappan 71(5): 366-71.

Struiksma AJC (2003) Lezen gaat Voor [Reading First]. Amsterdam: University of Amsterdam (doctoral dissertation).

Swanson HL, Hosky M, Lee C (1999) Interventions for Students with Learning Disabilities. New York: Guilford.

Tallal P, Miller S, Bedi G, Byma G, Wang X, Nagarajan S, Schreiner C, Jenkins W, Merzenich M (1996) Language comprehension in language- learning impaired children improved with acoustically modified speech. Science 271: 81-4.

Thelen E, Smith LB (1994) A Dynamic Systems Approach to the Development of Cognition and Action. Cambridge MA: MIT Press.

Tijms J, Hoeks J, Paulussen-Hoogeboom M, Smolenaars P (2002) Long-term effects of a psycholinguistic treatment for dyslexia. Journal of Research in Reading 25(3): 259-79.

Torgesen J (2001) The theory and practice of intervention: comparing outcomes from prevention and remediation studies. In A Fawcett (ed.) Dyslexia Theory and Good Practice. London: Whurr, pp. 185-202.

Torgesen J, Wagner R, Rashotte C, Rose E, Lindamood P, Conway T (1999) Preventing reading failure in young children with phonological processing disabilities. Group and individual responses to instruction. Journal of Educational Psychology 91: 579-93.

Van Daal VHP, Reitsma P, Van der Leij A (1994) Processing units in word reading by disabled readers. Journal of Experimental Child Psychology 57: 180-201.

Van den Bosch K, Van Bon WHJ, Schreuder R (1995) Poor readers' decoding skills: Effects of training with limited exposure duration. Reading Research Quarterly 30: 110-25.

Van der Leij A, De Jong PF, Van Daal VHP (2003) De ontwikkeling van dyslexie [The development of dyslexia]. Pedagogische Studien 80(4): 309-27.

Van der Leij A, Van Daal V (1999a) Automaticity automatization and dyslexia. In Lundberg I, Tonnesen FE and Austad I (eds) Dyslexia: Advances, Theory and Practice. Dordrecht: Kluwer Academic Publishers, pp. 75-90.

Van der Leij A, Van Daal V (1999b) Automatization aspects of dyslexia: speed limitation in word identification sensitivity to increasing task demands and orthographic compensation. Journal of Learning Disabilities 32(5): 417-28.

Van der Leij A, Van Daal VHP (in preparation) The Development of Developmental Dyslexia.

Van Strien J, Stolk B, Zuiker S (1995) Hemisphere-specific treatment of dyslexia across subtypes: better reading with anxiety-laden words? Journal of Learning Disabilities 28(1): 30-4.

Wimmer H (1993) Characteristics of developmental dyslexia in a regular writing system. Applied Psycholinguistics 14: 1-33.

Wise B, Olson RK, Ring J (1997) Teaching phonological awareness with and without the computer. In Hulme C and Snowling M (eds) Dyslexia. Biology, Cognition and Intervention. London: Whurr, pp. 254-74.

Wise B, Ring J, Olson RK (2000) Individual differences in gains from computer-assisted remedial reading with more emphasis on phonological analysis or accurate reading in context. Journal of Experimental Child Psychology 77: 197-235.

Yap R, Van der Leij A (1993) Word processing in dyslexics. An automatic decoding deficit? Reading and Writing: An Interdisciplinary Journal 5: 261-79.

Yap R, Van der Leij A (1994) Automaticity deficits in word reading. In Fawcett A and Nicolson R (eds) Dyslexia and Children. The Acquisition and Development of Skills. Hemel Hempstead: Harvester Wheatsheaf, pp. 77–107.

CHAPTER 4

Dyslexia genetics

JOHN STEIN

In his book *Hereditary Genius* (1869), Galton proposed that a system of arranged marriages between men of distinction and women of wealth should eventually produce a superior race. He coined the term 'eugenics' in 1883 to describe these arrangements and continued to expound their benefits until his death in 1911. Although Henry Maudsley, after whom the Bedlam Hospital was renamed, was initially interested in these ideas, later his psychiatric experience caused him to oppose them strongly. As the foremost psychiatrist of his day he had observed that most of the great creative and successful families in Victorian England sheltered relatives who had 'mental' problems. He judged it dangerously simplistic to believe that mental disease was entirely hereditary and he feared quite rightly that eliminating the genes that influence mental health might also eliminate creativity and imagination. He had worked out intuitively that the genes that help to cause conditions like dyslexia, depression and schizophrenia would not be as common as they were unless they also contributed to the talents that made these families successful.

Galton's theories remained very popular in the US. The American Eugenics Society was founded in 1926 to support the proposition that the wealth and social position of the upper classes was justified by their superior genetic endowment, ignoring the important contribution that their advantageous economic and social circumstances made to their success. Eugenicists in the US also supported restrictions on immigration from nations with 'inferior' stock, such as Italy, Greece, and the countries of Eastern Europe, and strongly argued for the sterilization of insane, retarded and epileptic citizens in the US. As a result of their misinformation to Congress, sterilization laws were passed in more than half of the US states and isolated instances of forced sterilization continued into the 1970s. Eugenic theories only came under serious attack in the 1930s after the German Nazis began to exploit them to support their extermination of Jews, blacks, and homosexuals.

I begin this chapter on this note of caution to urge readers to ponder whether we should be studying the genetic basis of dyslexia at all. We certainly should not be trying to root out 'dyslexia genes' because we would thereby eliminate our chances of benefiting from future highly talented dyslexics, the likes of Einstein or Churchill. If pure curiosity to unravel the genetic basis of dyslexia were to have that effect then it should be vigorously opposed.

However, understanding how genes influence reading ability should have far more positive effects. Perhaps the most important gain that has already accrued from the uncontested demonstration that dyslexia has a strong genetic component is that this proves absolutely that dyslexia is a real neurological condition, and not a convenient word to be used by anxious mothers to hide their children's laziness or stupidity. Demonstrating that it has a genetic basis makes it impossible to maintain that it is 'purely psychological' as it has a clear biological reality. Knowing that a child's dyslexia is a respectable neurological diagnosis, and not another word for laziness or stupidity, can transform his self-image. From losing all self-esteem because he could not keep up with his peers' reading skills, acquiring the diagnosis of dyslexia gives him self-respect and hope and the confidence to exploit the talents that have been submerged by his shame.

Writing was only invented 4,000 years ago, so literacy itself is not likely to be under direct genetic control. Instead, reading and writing depend on more fundamental sensory and motor processing functions that originally evolved for other purposes. Hence another strong reason for studying the genetics of dyslexia is to elucidate the mechanisms by which inherited control of the development of the nervous system contributes to reading skills. Then we will have a better chance of understanding not only more about these basic neural processes but also the way in which they mediate reading. The great advantage of studying cognitive reading skills from this point of view is that they are much easier to measure precisely than many other higher functions, such as emotion, motivation or delusional thinking.

Basic biology

Most of the trillion (10^{12}) cells that make up our bodies have a nucleus that contains 23 pairs of chromosomes (one pair of XX or XY sex chromosomes and 22 'autosomes'). These are made up of long strands of the double helix, DNA, wound around proteins called histones. DNA consists of a long ladder of pairs (base pairs) out of a possible four kinds of nucleotides, so that each cell has a total of about 3 billion DNA base pairs. Only about 5% of these form the 30,000 different genes that are now known to exist; thus there are c. 10,000 base pairs per gene. The rest is known as junk DNA and the function of most of it is not really understood. Triplets of the base pairs code for specific amino acids and their order in proteins. When a gene is switched on this code is transcribed from the nucleus by messenger RNA which directs the linkage of the amino acids in the right order by ribosomes outside the nucleus, to form the proteins upon which life depends.

Thus genes control the synthesis of proteins. In the case of dyslexia currently it seems most likely that the proteins concerned are involved in brain development. Galaburda and his colleagues studied a number of brains of known dyslexics *post mortem*, and found that they had mild neuropathological abnormalities (Galaburda and Kemper, 1979). These probably occur towards the end of the second trimester of foetal development, at around 24 weeks' gestation when the cerebral cortex is developing and folding most rapidly. The most common of these abnormalities are cortical ectopias that are found mainly in the temporo-parietal and frontal association areas in both hemispheres, but particularly on the left, language, side. These brain 'warts' are about 1 mm in size and they form because disobedient developing neurones migrate past the outer limiting membrane to form an abnormal outgrowth on the surface of the cortex. The cause of this breaching of the outer limiting membrane is unknown. But the outgrowths are associated with both anatomic and biochemical disruption of all the normally neat six layers of cortex beneath them, for several millimetres on either side, and also in equivalent, 'homotopic', areas in the opposite hemisphere to which they are connected by fibres travelling in the corpus callosum. Every one of us has a few of these ectopias but the dyslexic brains had noticeably more, particularly in the left hemisphere language areas.

The phenotype

It is not easy to recognize these mild neurodevelopmental abnormalities. The first essential for successful genetic studies is to be able to identify subjects with the putative genetic trait (known as 'probands') reliably. The way the genes express themselves in terms of the subjects' symptoms and signs is known as the 'phenotype'. If your sample is contaminated with people who haven't really got the condition at all (do not display the phenotype), clearly it is going to be far more difficult to find the responsible genes. In fact this is a serious difficulty in the case of dyslexia, because there is no agreement about how to define the phenotype reliably. In fact our hope is the other way about; we believe that understanding more about its genetic basis will make it possible to define the dyslexia phenotype more rigorously.

The most widely accepted criterion for diagnosing developmental dyslexia is if a subject's single word reading is significantly lower than would be expected from his age and general intelligence measured in a way that does not depend on his reading ability – in other words, non-verbal IQ. Even this has been contested, however. There is a school of thought that says that the general intelligence of the subjects is irrelevant because children with low IQ have the same kind of phonological problems as dyslexics with higher IQ. However, even though children with an IQ of 70 to 80 can be taught to read successfully, nevertheless significant reading problems are much more common in those with low IQ.

It has also been suggested that dyslexia should only be diagnosed if the subject demonstrates deficient ability to translate letters into sounds – significantly decreased phonological ability. However, there are several aspects to phonology and no agreement about which is the most important. Phonological awareness is the knowledge that words can be broken down into separate sounds. At the syllabic level this can be assessed by testing rhyming ability; or at the single phoneme level it can be measured by phoneme deletion tests; for example, 'say cat without the c' – 'at'. Phonological decoding can be assessed by testing accuracy and speed of reading 'non-words' such as 'tegwop', because such nonsense words can only be read by translating each letter into its corresponding sound. Short-term phonological memory can be tested by asking subjects to repeat non-words read to them; for example, repeat flepisterslop. In our studies we use non-word reading and non-word repetition to cover most aspects of phonological processing.

It is widely agreed, however, that not all those with reading problems have significantly impaired phonological ability. Furthermore, some argue that a commoner cause of impaired phonological ability is specific language impairment, developmental dysphasia, rather than developmental dyslexia. So we can hardly elevate tests of phonological processing to the status of diagnosing dyslexia.

In fact there are strong arguments for supposing that tests of visual orthographic skill may be more important. It has been shown that understanding that the sounds of words can be broken down to the level of separate phonemes depends on a child learning that the word can be represented as a sequence of separate letters (Morais and Bertelson, 1979). In other words, acquiring detailed phonemic skill bootstraps on learning the letter level orthography of a word. A good test of orthographic skill is Olson's pseudohomophone spelling test: 'which is the correct spelling, rain or rane?'. Sounding out the word will not provide the correct answer; the subject has to know the correct visual orthographic form of the word. Likewise reading and spelling irregular words calls on memory of the orthography of the word. These orthographic tests actually correlate better with overall reading ability than any of the phonological tests and are more heritable – they are likely to be more strongly genetically regulated.

Two other kinds of deficit have been strongly associated with reading problems. Dyslexic children are remarkably slow at simply naming letters or digits or even pictures, in a test known as rapid automatic naming (RAN). These tests seem to tap into the speed with which they can perform many of the operations that underlie reading, so that dyslexics' RAN performance also correlates strongly with their phonological and orthographic scores. The other test that is often used is digit span. The tester reads out an increasingly long random sequence of digits and the subject has to repeat them. This is a test of short-term memory and, again, it correlates strongly with phonological and orthographic scores.

So we have a plethora of different possible phenotype tests to use with no agreement about which is the most important. One strategy is to use all of them and then to correlate each with the genotype separately. But since they all intercorrelate a better strategy is to use principal component analysis to summarize them all in a smaller number of summary variables or to use multivariate analysis (Marlow et al., 2003).

Arguments about the best phenotype definition will continue until we have a clearer understanding of the biological basis of dyslexia. Such understanding should also provide us with explanations of why reading problems are so often associated with other neurodevelopmental anomalies. 50% of dyslexics have symptoms of specific language impairment, developmental in-co-ordination (dyspraxia) and attention deficit hyperactivity disorder. Likewise, 50% of subjects with these conditions also have dyslexic symptoms. Hence 'pure' examples of any of these conditions without symptoms of the others are rare. These conditions also share many other common features: they all involve problems with the accurate direction of visual, auditory or motor attention, hence of the correct sequencing of letters, sounds or movements; they are all commoner in males; they are all associated with weakly established lateral dominance, which manifests as mixed handedness, eyedness and footedness, and probably a reduced degree of asymmetry in critical language areas such as the planum temporale, which is a language association area situated at the back of the temporal cortex.

Furthermore, autoimmune problems such as allergies, eczema and hay fever all seem to be commoner than normal in subjects with these disorders, as well as in other family members. This suggests that there might be some connection between immunological processes and the development of the nervous system. Recent genetic discoveries have supported this idea more and more as we shall see. Finally, many of these conditions have been associated with signs of deficiency of omega three essential fatty acids (fish oils) and we have shown that fish oil supplements can improve many of their symptoms. Hence one set of candidate genes that we are studying consists of those that influence essential fatty acid metabolism.

The highly disparate set of features that characterize neurodevelopmental disorders is reminiscent of the odd juxtaposition of symptoms and signs that is found in many rare hereditary neurological syndromes, such as ataxia telangectasia. Their apparent arbitrariness stems from the mutations having their major effect on genes concerned with very basic aspects of the development of the foetus, not directly with reading or any other higher function, so that they can affect many different systems. Likewise, this is likely to be true of the genetic basis of dyslexia as we shall see.

Familiality versus heredity

There is no agreement on how to define the dyslexic phenotype, and our 46 different chromosomes consist of 3 billion DNA base pairs of nucleotides. It is really amazing, therefore, that in the last few years we have actually discovered more about the genetics of reading disability than of any other higher cognitive function. This is partly because dyslexia is so common and so important but also because reading ability and its component skills can now be measured so precisely and correlated with modern DNA assays.

The first important step that was made in the 1980s and 1990s was to prove that vulnerability to reading problems is indeed inherited. In 1896 Pringle Morgan guessed that word blindness, as he called dyslexia, was congenital (either inherited or acquired in the womb). Since then the family histories of dyslexics have shown indisputably that dyslexia has a strong genetic basis. In fact, however, a strong family history does not at all prove that a trait is inherited. Pedigrees do not prove that genes are involved because members of the same family share such a similar environment and upbringing; and this could explain why two members both have reading problems.

However, comparing the reading of identical (monozygotic – MZ) with that of non-identical (dizygotic – DZ) twins does enable us to distinguish hereditary from shared environmental influences. Both MZ and DZ twins share the same family environment, but only identical (MZ) twins have exactly the same genes, whereas DZ twins share only 50% of their genes. So if one identical twin has reading problems, his identical twin will inherit any genes that caused them. However if he has a non-identical twin the latter is less likely to have the problem because he is 50% less likely to inherit them; but he will have the same amount of shared environment and upbringing. With enough twins, therefore, we can calculate how much reading disability is due to inherited genes and how much to shared environment.

Two large twin studies in southern England (Stevenson et al., 1987) and Colorado (DeFries et al., 1987) have thus shown that approximately 50% of reading disability is due to inherited genetic influences, and 50% due to upbringing and environment. However, these and other studies have also made it clear that there is unlikely to be just a single gene that underlies reading problems. The best guess is that there will be 5 to 10 genes that all have to act in consort to cause the problems.

Gene exploration

How do we go about trying to find these genes in dyslexics? There are three broad kinds of approach: *candidate gene*, *linkage* and *association studies*. Of course these methods can be combined. The simplest approach is to decide on theoretical grounds which gene is a likely candidate, look it up in the human genome, and find and sequence it in your sample of dyslexics to see if it is mutated in them. However, the cognitive skills required for reading are so far removed from the proteins, the synthesis of which each gene controls, that we have no real idea how to relate the two. Hence at present there are seldom sufficiently strong grounds for committing the considerable funds, time and energy required to any particular one of the 30,000 genes as a candidate to study.

In association and linkage studies we make use of single nucleotide polymorphisms (SNPs) to identify particular chromosomal sites. Each of us has around 1 million sites amongst our 3 billion DNA base pairs where one nucleotide is different in some people from others. Few of these are situated in the protein coding regions of the gene, so they are functionally unimportant. But we know their location on each chromosome precisely, so they can be used as markers of that particular site on the chromosome.

Eggs and sperm contain only 23 chromosomes so that when they fuse during fertilization the somatic cells that form the foetus contain the normal complement of 46. During meiosis, when the reduction division occurs, portions of paternal chromosomes exchange with maternal by means of 'crossovers'. These have the effect that, over hundreds of generations, the further away from a marker a gene is, the more likely it is to have separated from it during crossover. The corollary of this is that if a marker SNP is found significantly more often in dyslexics than in good readers it is likely that it lies close to a gene that affects reading. 'Close' in this context is relative; it can still be 30 million base pairs away.

Armed with a map of where these marker SNPs are located on each chromosome, modern high throughput molecular genetic techniques now allow us to 'type' large numbers of subjects for linkage or association studies. We obtain the volunteers' DNA either from white cells from a blood sample or from cells scraped from the inside of the cheek. Using the polymerase chain reaction (PCR) the small amount of DNA obtained from the white blood cells or cheek scrapings can be amplified as much as needed.

For linkage studies we recruit as many whole families as possible with at least one dyslexic child; in our genetic project we have so far typed 300 families. We take DNA samples from mother, father, dyslexic child (proband) and other sibs. In the children, we measure cognitive and reading skills to ascertain whether they really are dyslexic and for later quantitative correlations, but this is not necessary in their parents. Our studies use the British Ability Scales (BAS) matrices, similarities, digit span, reading and spelling tests, the Castles and Coltheart non-word (phonological) and irregular word (orthographic) tests together with other physiological tests that we are interested in, namely hand skill, visual motion sensitivity and auditory frequency discrimination sensitivity (Fisher et al., 1999, 2002).

Genotyping enables us to determine whether a particular SNP in the child was derived from mother or father. Then, using powerful computerized statistical programs, we calculate whether a particular marker is shared within families by 'affected' individuals more often than by chance. To scan all 23 chromosome pairs (the whole genome) we use about 400 markers spread evenly over the chromosomes. This amounts to a marker every 7.5 million base pairs.

We can define 'affected' children as dyslexic or not according to whether their reading is significantly behind that expected from their IQ (derived in our case from the matrices and similarities subtests of the BAS). However, a more powerful technique is to take advantage of the fact that reading and the other skills we measure are continuous quantitative variables. So we can use their variation in the probands and their sibs to correlate with their inheritance of the markers; this is called quantitative trait linkage (QTL).

Association studies depend on already having strong evidence of where on a chromosome a gene affecting the trait in question is likely to be found, so not many have been conducted in dyslexia yet. The assumption is made that unrelated individuals with dyslexia will all have the same mutation. Large numbers of dyslexics and control good readers matched for age, sex and IQ are collected. Their cognitive and reading skills are measured and they are typed using much more closely spaced SNP markers in the region that has already been shown to be linked, each separated by only approximately 15,000 base pairs. If we find strong linkage at this stage then we should be able to home in on the actual gene involved by candidate gene mutation analysis.

Linkage results – chromosome 6

Figure 4.1 shows the sites on chromosomes 1, 2, 3, 6, 15 and 18 where more than one study has shown linkage with reading problems. The strongest linkage evidence so far connects reading problems with a site on the short arm of chromosome 6. This site has now been confirmed in at least seven different studies (Grigorenko, 2003). It was at first argued that the strongest loading was for phonological skill and therefore that the C6 site was selective for phonology. But it turned out that real word reading, spelling and orthographic skill also link to the same site, and this was confirmed by principal component and multivariate analysis. These results imply that the gene or genes concerned affect the development of nerve cells that influence all the auditory, visual, memory and motor processes required for reading.

As mentioned earlier there is great overlap between attention deficit hyperactivity disorder (ADHD) and dyslexia; 50% of dyslexics have attention deficit symptoms and 50% of ADHD have reading problems. It is therefore very significant that it has now been shown that ADHD links to the same site on C6 (Willcutt et al., 2002). This strongly suggests that the effects controlled by the chromosome 6 site extend to other neurodevelopmental disorders as well as dyslexia.

This C6 location is of particular interest for another reason: it is very close to the family of genes that controls important aspects of the immune response. This system of genes is called the major histocompatibility

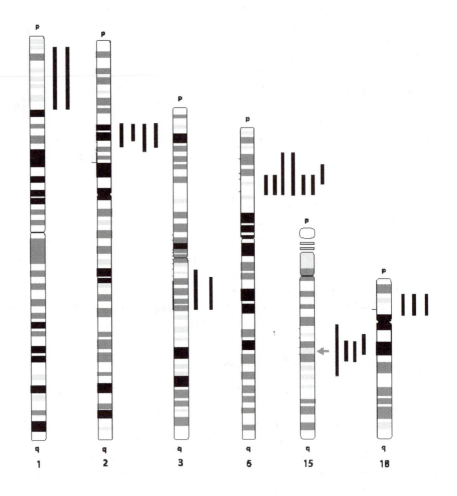

Figure 4.1 Linkage results – chromosome 6.

complex (MHC) because it is the system that controls the expression of the
surface signature molecules by which the immune system recognizes an
individual's own, as opposed to foreign, cells. Successful transplantation of
organs from another person depends on these histocompatibility antigens
from the donor not being too dissimilar from the recipient's.

In fact this possible linkage with C6 genes affecting immune function was
first suggested because it was known that dyslexics and their families suffer a
greater than normal incidence of problems with their immune systems, such
as allergies, asthma, eczema, hay fever and other autoimmune diseases
(Hugdahl et al., 1990). It has therefore been speculated that dyslexic
neurodevelopmental abnormalities might possibly be the result of autoimmune attack during early intrauterine development.

All mothers generate antibodies to their foetuses because, sharing only half her genes, they are treated as foreign bodies by her immune system. But the foetus's placenta inactivates most of these antibodies before they can harm the foetus. Nevertheless occasionally antibodies can cross the placenta and affect the foetal brain. We have therefore injected serum containing antibodies from a mother who had had two dyslexic children into the uterus of pregnant mice. After birth we found that the co-ordination of the pups was impaired. We could attribute this to malfunction of the mice's cerebellum because we showed that cerebellar metabolism was depressed. Furthermore, we found that the mother's antibodies were bound to the mice's cerebellar Purkinje cells (Vincent et al., 2002). This demonstration of possible involvement of the cerebellum is of great interest because the cerebellum is the centre of the brain's magnocellular timing systems and many dyslexics exhibit in-co-ordination, impaired motor learning and other signs of mild cerebellar abnormality (Nicolson et al., 1999).

Chromosome 18

The strongest linkage that we obtained from our scan of the whole genome revealed another important linkage site on chromosome 18 (Fisher et al., 2002). We are hopeful that we might identify the actual gene involved relatively quickly because this region happens to contain only five to 10 genes. Again, the linkage is not confined to a single reading sub-skill. Even though single word reading achieved the highest statistical significance, phonological and orthographic measures also linked to this same site, and multivariate analysis showed that there was no way of choosing between them.

The K family – specific language impairment

'Man has an instinctive tendency to speak, as we see in the babble of our young children,' wrote Charles Darwin in 1871, 'while no child has an instinctive tendency to bake, brew, or write.' Darwin's insight that there was probably a genetic basis to language was given strong support by my colleagues under Tony Monaco at the Wellcome Trust Centre for Human Genetics at Oxford University. They found a gene that is mutated in a hereditary disorder of speech and language. They studied a large single family, the K family, who had been first identified by Faraneh Vargha-Khadem at the Institute of Child Health, London. Many members of this family are unable to control their vocal or facial muscles properly (orofacial dyspraxia), which causes profound speech impairments – severe lisps and robotic sounding speech that is very difficult to understand, and these are accompanied by grammatical and phonological impairments. Tony Monaco and his team were able to link these problems to a small region of chromosome 7. They were then fortunate to find an unrelated individual with similar speech problems who had a break in the middle of this part of chromosome 7 in a known gene called FOXP2 (Lai et al., 2001). They then showed that this gene is mutated in the K family by a single guanine nucleotide being replaced by adenine.

FOXP2 belongs to a family of genes that encode proteins that control the transcription of other genes (transcription factors) into the proteins they specify. These genes are therefore particularly important during the early development of the brain. F stands for the 'forkhead domain' that binds to the DNA whose transcription is to be controlled. The K family has one deficient version of this gene but the other is normal. Hence it seems that at some point in neural development having only half the normal amount of the factor alters the development of the brain slightly, leading to these language problems. Why only speech, language and orofacial movements are affected is not clear however.

What is even more interesting is that the mutation seen in the K family is at one of the only two nucleotide positions in the FOXP2 gene that distinguishes this gene in humans from that in our closest relative, the chimpanzee, who cannot speak at all. Remembering that 99% of our DNA is identical to that in chimpanzees, this implies that one of the important distinctions lies at this very early stage of development of the brain. These exciting discoveries also show that the new molecular genetics are going to provide powerful new insights even into our evolutionary past.

Unfortunately, however, the FOXP2 mutation has turned out to be a rare cause of specific language impairment, and despite the overlap between this and dyslexia it is probably connected with dyslexia even more rarely. There is some recent evidence for linkage of reading problems to chromosome 7, but mutations here will rarely account for dyslexia. This does not diminish the importance of the K family and FOXP2. Elucidating their mutation has advanced our understanding of neurodevelopment immeasurably.

DYXC1

In September 2003, a Finnish group found the first candidate gene for dyslexia not on chromosome 6, as we all expected, but on chromosome 15 (Taipale et al., 2003). They found a family with several generations of dyslexics. As for the K family, part of the long arm (q) of one chromosome (in this case chromosome 2) had exchanged with chromosome 15q. Whereas the breakpoint on chromosome 2 was far away from the short arm (p) site that has been linked to reading problems, that indicated by the arrow shown in Figure 4.1 on chromosome 15 was squarely centred on the region that has also been linked to dyslexia. It turned out that the break split a gene that is now christened DYXC1 and this break causes the family's dyslexic problems. DYXC1 codes for a 420 amino acid protein that is expressed within the nucleus of many large nerve cells in the brain. Like FOXP2, it only differs from our chimpanzee relatives at two sites. Although, unfortunately, we do not yet know precisely what its function is, it seems likely that it is associated in some way with general learning performance as many of the Finnish family members have general learning in addition to their reading problems. As for FOXP2 again, however, it seems that unfortunately DYXC1 will account for relatively few cases of dyslexia because, even in the relatively homogeneous population of Finland, less than 10% of dyslexics unrelated to the original family showed mutations in this gene.

Handedness

Many dyslexics appear to have weaker establishment of cerebral dominance and handedness than good readers. Furthermore, recent research suggests that there may be a genetically mediated association between language or reading deficits and impaired motor co-ordination. So we measured right-versus left-hand skill (relative hand skill) in our dyslexic and control subjects by timing how long they take to move 10 pegs from one set of holes to another with each hand. We confirmed that hand motor skill is significantly inherited; the heritability in our sample of 195 siblings was 41%. Hand motor skill was also significantly, though weakly, correlated with real word, non-word and irregular word reading.

We found very strong linkage of relative hand skill to a site on chromosome 2 close to those shown in Figure 4.1 which have been implicated in reading problems (Francks et al., 2002). This relationship may be inherited more strongly from the father, suggesting a degree of paternal imprinting. Furthermore, in a sample of 241 pairs of schizophrenic siblings we have found similar linkage of schizophrenic symptomatology to this same site and similar paternal imprinting. No convincing linkage of dyslexia to the sex chromosomes has ever been reported, so this paternal imprinting may begin to explain why dyslexia appears to be more common in boys. But even this is disputed. There is some evidence that the sex difference may have been exaggerated by under-referral of girls because they tend to be less troublesome and make less fuss.

Conclusions

Application of modern molecular genetic techniques to the problem of the inheritance of developmental dyslexia has been remarkably successful. When we started our project we were specifically refused funding to study dyslexia because it was thought to be too unreliable a phenotype. Other labs told us that they had faced the same scepticism. But we continued on a shoestring, and our faith has been rewarded. Six well-replicated linkage sites have been found and the gene involved in one of these on chromosome 15 has probably been identified, although we do not yet know what it does. Other sites have offered us tantalising glimpses of how we may begin to understand the neurodevelopmental, immunological and nutritional mechanisms underlying failure to acquire reading skills. One thing is clear. These molecular genetic techniques are proving so powerful that the next few years are going to bring many more discoveries.

References

DeFries JC, Fulker DW, Labuda MC (1987) Evidence for a genetic aetiology of reading disability in twins. Nature 329: 537-9.

Fisher SE, Marlow AJ, Lamb J, Maestrini E, Williams DF, Richardson AJ, Weeks DE, Stein JF, Monaco AP (1999) A quantitative-trait locus on chromosome 6p influences different aspects of developmental dyslexia. American Journal of Human Genetics 64(1): 146-56.

Fisher SE, Francks C, Marlow AJ, MacPhie IL, Newbury DF, Cardon LR, Ishikawa-Brush Y, Richardson AJ, Talcott JB, Gayan J, Olson RK, Pennington BF, Smith SD, DeFries JC, Stein JF, Monaco AP (2002) Independent genome-wide scans identify a chromosome 18 quantitative-trait locus influencing dyslexia. Nature Genetics 30(1): 86-91.

Francks C, Fisher SE, MacPhie L, Richardson AJ, Marlow AJ, Stein JF, Monaco AP (2002) A genomewide linkage screen for relative hand skill in sibling pairs. American Journal of Human Genetics 70: 800-5.

Galaburda AM, Kemper TL (1979) Cytoarchitectonic abnormalities in dyslexia. Ann Neurol 6: 94-100.

Galton F (1869) Hereditary Genius. London: Macmillan

Grigorenko EL (2003) The first candidate gene for dyslexia. PNAS 100: 11190-2.

Hugdahl K, Synnevag B, Satz P (1990) Immune and autoimmune diseases in dyslexic children. Neuropsychologia 28(7): 673-9.

Lai CSL, Fisher SE, Hurst JA, Vargha-Khadem F, Monaco AP (2001) A forkhead-domain gene is mutated in a severe speech and language disorder. Nature 413: 519-23.

Marlow AJ, Fisher SE, Francks C, McPhie IL, Richardson AJ, Talcott JB, Stein JF, Monaco AP, Cardon LR (2003) Use of multivariate linkage analysis for dissection of complex cognitive trait. American Journal of Human Genetics 72(3): 561-70.

Morais JL, Bertelson P (1979) Does awareness of speech as a sequence of phones arise spontaneously? Cognition 7: 323.

Nicolson RI, Fawcett AJ, Berry EL, Jenkins IH, Dean P, Brooks DJ (1999) Motor learning difficulties and abnormal cerebellar activation in dyslexic adults. Lancet 353: 43-7.

Stevenson J, Graham P, Greman G, McLoughlin V (1987) A twin study of genetic influences on reading and spelling. J Child Psych 28: 229-47.

Taipale M, Kamine N, Nopola-Hemmi J, Haltia T, Myllyluoma B, Lyytinen J, Muller K, Kaaranen M, Lindsberg OJ, Hannoula-Joupi K, Kere J (2003) A candidate gene for developmental dyslexia encodes a nuclear tetratricopeptide repeat domain protein dynamically regulated in brain. Proceedings of the National Academy of Sciences 100: 11553-8.

Vincent A, Deacon R, Dalton P, Salmond C, Blamire AM, Pendlebury S, Johansen-Berg H, Rajogopalan B, Styles P, Stein JF (2002) Maternal antibody mediated dyslexia? Evidence for a pathogenic serum factor in a mother of 2 dyslexic children shown by transfer to pregnant mice shown by behavioural and MRS studies. Journal of Neuroimmunology 130(1-2): 243-7.

Willcutt EG, Pennington BF, Smith SD, Cardon LR, Gayan J, Knopik VS, Olson RK, DeFries JC (2002) Quantitative trait locus for reading disability on chromosome 6p is pleiotropic for attention-deficit/hyperactivity disorder. American Journal of Medical Genetics 114(3): 260–8.

CHAPTER 5

Brain-based assessment and instructional intervention[1]

VIRGINIA W. BERNINGER

According to Minsky (1986), understanding the complexity of the human brain and its role in learning will require many small theories. Premature elimination of small theories by treating them as competing alternatives to rule among rather than as potential explanations of different phenomena in complex systems may stifle scientific progress. Churchland (1986) cautioned that theory-driven scientific research on the human brain will probably result in psychologists rethinking (and even possibly discarding) psychological constructs of mental processing that were created to explain phenomena at the behavioural level of analysis before knowledge generated by cognitive neuroscience was available. One such construct that is likely to be discarded as the result of increasing knowledge of the role of the brain in human learning is the overly simple notion of *linear causality*, which served physics well but is proving inadequate for advancing knowledge in molecular biology. The current paradigm in molecular biology is grounded in complex systems that have multiple constraints, all of which must be considered in offering scientific explanations (Gallagher and Appenzeller, 1999).

Likewise, reading research, whether aimed at normal reading or reading disorders such as dyslexia, would benefit from replacing the search for the single theory and the single linear causal mechanism with approaches that allow for constraints in complex systems. The complexity arises from the interacting components within and across functional brain systems, which can be understood at the micro-level and macro-level of different neural substrates, and the interactions with external environments that can also be modelled at many different levels of analysis (Berninger and Richards, 2002). Functional brain systems are not only independent variables that constrain

1   Based on a presentation to the International Dyslexia Association in San Diego, November 13, 2003 and the Sixth British Dyslexia Association International Meeting, March 28, 2004, in Warwick, England. Grants HD R01 25858 (since 1989) and P50 33812 (since 1995) from the National Institute of Child Health and Human Development (NICHD) supported preparation of this chapter.

reading development but are also dependent variables that may be changed in some predictable ways by variables in the external environment, such as instruction, that exert effects on the brain (Richards et al., 2000). In this way, complex systems can develop *multi-level, bidirectional causal influences.*

In this chapter I describe one line of developmental neuropsychological research launched in the mid-1980s – before the cognitive neuroscientific revolution made possible by the introduction toward the end of the twentieth century of *in vivo* brain imaging. The goal of this programmatic research was to add to basic scientific understanding of how reading and writing are acquired and to improve assessment and treatment of reading and writing disorders by applying this basic knowledge to clinical and teaching practice. The research began with a few small theories of the role of the brain in learning to read and write. These theories were tested with behavioural data in assessment studies and modified when data indicated revision was needed. These theories continue to guide our research but now are confirmed, disconfirmed, or revised on the basis of *in vivo* brain imaging, genetic, and treatment studies.

This chapter is divided into six parts. First, I review the findings from our studies guided by developmental neuropsychological theories of reading and writing prior to the availability of *in vivo* brain imaging studies; I point out when the findings are consistent with those of subsequent brain imaging studies. I also explain how our small theories have been modified based on our research findings and those of others. Second, I discuss the translation of these findings into psychometric assessment instruments that can be used to identify students needing instructional treatment and to monitor progress of students over the course of instructional intervention. Third, I summarize findings to date from our family genetics study of dyslexia, which also have implications for diagnosis and treatment of reading and writing disorders. Fourth, I describe the lesson plans that have resulted from the instructional studies and can be used by teachers, psychologists, and speech and language therapists to prevent and remediate reading and writing problems. Fifth, I explain the rationale and findings of our brain imaging studies, which have often combined brain imaging and instructional treatment to show that biologically based reading and writing disorders are treatable. Finally, I outline further research directions that are needed to expand our scientific knowledge of nature–nurture interactions in understanding normal reading and writing, and reading and writing disorders.

1. Understanding reading and writing from a developmental neuropsychological perspective

Several small theories guided this initial longitudinal research on how children, who were studied repeatedly near the end of kindergarten and four times during first grade, learn to read and spell written words.

Multiple mappings in beginning reading and spelling

One small theory was *redundancy* – this held that words are coded in multiple formats in memory: auditory or phonological word forms and visual or orthographic word forms. The seminal positron emission tomography (PET) studies by Posner and colleagues (for example, Posner et al., 1988) confirmed the existence of multiple codes by showing that visible word forms activated different brain regions than did audible word forms.

Another small theory was *normal variation* (individual differences that are not attributable to learning disabilities and that fall within the normal range for a child's age and grade) in each of these coding processes – for phonological and orthographic word forms. The longitudinal study of kindergarten and first-grade children documented normal variation (interindividual and intraindividual differences) in development of orthographic and phonological coding abilities (Berninger, 1986).

Yet another small theory was *multiple mapping* – this held that children can make multiple maps or connections between the orthographic and phonological word forms they code into memory: between alphabet letters and phonemes, between all letters in a word and a lexical-level phonological name code, and between written and oral syllables. When this research programme began, many researchers assumed that pronouncing unfamiliar written words was a phonological process and that pronouncing familiar well-learned words or spelling words was an orthographic process. Many reading researchers and practitioners still believe this – as if the phonological and orthographic processes function alone in reading and writing. The alternative view guiding this research was that orthographic and phonological processes are separate coding processes in the brain but that during the process of learning to read children create maps to relate these codes – by noting connections between units of phonology and units of orthography of corresponding size.

A brain imaging study confirmed that more than one kind of orthographic-phonological mapping occurs when written words are read. Direct recording from the brain during neurosurgery indicated that the posterior fusiform gyrus activated during *sub-lexical-level* orthographic–phonological mapping, whereas the anterior fusiform gyrus activated during *lexical-level* orthographic–phonological mapping (Nobre et al., 1994).

Based on the work of others (for example, Treiman, 1985; Wise et al., 1990) and our subsequent instructional interventions studies (for example, Berninger, Vaughan, Abbott, Brooks, Abbott, Reed, Rogan and Graham, 1998), we revised the original multiple connections model to substitute sub-syllabic onset-rime mapping for syllabic mapping (Berninger and Richards, 2002). Because syllable structure is less salient and varies with speed of articulation in English, it is a less reliable mapping cue for beginning readers of English who primarily encounter one- and two-syllable words. Accumulating evidence from many studies (reviewed by Berninger and

Richards, 2002) indicates that the most important orthographic–phonological mappings in beginning word reading and spelling are *alphabetic principle* (graphemes of one- or two- letters and corresponding phonemes), *onsets at the beginning of syllables* (handled by alphabetic principle), *rimes at the end of syllables* (multi-letter units that are typically larger units than the graphemes in alphabetic principle but have predictable pronunciations and correspond to analogies or word families), and *lexical units* (all letters in the orthographic word form and its corresponding phonological name code, co-articulated segmental phones and suprasegmental intonational contour).

A related small theory hypothesized that some children may follow *alternative developmental pathways* in creating these maps between orthographic and phonological word forms. The normal developmental patterns for acquiring orthographic codes and for acquiring phonological codes were studied first, and then the focus switched to the alternative developmental paths in children whose orthographic or phonological word form development is delayed.

Normal development for processing the orthographic word form showed a progression from whole-word coding to coding a letter in the word form to coding a letter group in the word form (Berninger, 1987). Initially most children (following a brief, computer-controlled exposure of a written word) could code the word into short-term memory and then hold it in working memory while making a decision as to whether the written word presented next (containing all the same letters as the first word on half the trials and differing by only one letter on half the trials) matched the first word exactly. Later, they could judge whether a single letter (which followed the briefly presented written word) had (half the trials) or had not (half the trials) appeared in the prior word. Finally, they were able to judge whether a group of letters (mostly two letters) (which followed the briefly presented written word) had (half the trials) or had not (half the trials) appeared in that prior word in exactly the same letter order. This developmental pattern for the orthographic word form has been replicated (Berninger, Yates and Lester, 1991). *Normal development for processing the phonological word form* replicated the same progression found by Liberman et al. (1974) – from syllable segmentation to phoneme segmentation.

If both orthographic and phonological word forms follow the typical developmental progressions, children should be able to construct maps between letters or letter groups and phonemes at about the same time in their literacy development. *Both* letter and letter-group coding are skills needed to learn to map phonemes onto graphemes in alphabetic principle underlying written American English (Venezky, 1970, 1995, 1999). However, some children were delayed in the development of coding skills for one of the word forms. For example, some children could code the letter or letter group in the orthographic word form but not the phoneme in the spoken word form, or conversely, could code the phoneme in the spoken word but not the letter or letter group in the orthographic word form. In either case, the child struggled with learning to decode written words into spoken words – but for different reasons. In some cases the bottleneck in orthographic-phonological mapping was orthographic and sometimes it was phonological.

Children constructed other kinds of orthographic–phonological maps too. Another study provided converging evidence that beginning readers can process orthographic units corresponding to whole-word units early in literacy acquisition. Before they could decode the words orally, beginning readers could make reliable judgements about whether letter strings could be real words (Berninger, 1988). Presumably, children had abstracted from printed words to which they were exposed some knowledge in implicit memory about the permissible letter sequences in English words (orthotactics). This early orthotactic knowledge may support fast mapping of whole written words onto whole-name codes in forming a small set of familiar words that can be named. Some children also learned to map written and spoken syllables. In fact, the number of different kinds of mappings that children could do – because the corresponding orthographic and phono-logical skills were comparably developed – predicted reading achievement in the longitudinal study (Berninger, Chen and Abbott, 1988), a cross-sectional study (Berninger and Abbott, 1994), and a subsequent instructional study (Berninger and Traweek, 1991).

Of all the kinds of orthographic–phonological mapping studied, the combination of receptive coding of letter groups in written words and phoneme coding in spoken words was the best (unique) predictor of individual differences in word reading achievement (Berninger, 1986). This finding meshes with more recent findings that (a) two-letter spelling units (graphemes that correspond to phonemes) are more frequent than one-letter spelling units in high frequency grapheme–phoneme correspondences in high frequency words in primary grade reading programmes, and thus capture much of the predictability of alphabetic principle in American English (Berninger, 1998a, 1998b); and (b) ability to code letter groups in the orthographic word form differentiated the beginning readers who grew significantly in both real word and pseudoword reading and those who grew only in real word reading (Berninger, Abbott, Vermeulen, Ogier, Brooksher, Zook and Lemos, 2002). Growing in only real word reading is of concern because failure to grow in pseudoword reading is associated with later reading problems.

Reading researchers have argued about whether phonics rules that correspond to alphabetic principle or analogies that correspond to the rime unit of the syllable (for example, Goswami, 1988; Seidenberg and McClelland, 1989) should be the goal of instruction, but our evidence pointed to the conclusion that children could learn both and benefited from being taught both (Hart et al., 1997). That is, multiple computational or mapping paths had added value over single ones: the more developed the multiple orthographic and phonological codes underlying reading and spelling development were, the higher the probability that children would construct the multiple maps of orthographic-phonological correspondence and the higher their reading and spelling achievement was (Berninger and Abbott, 1994).

Our studies of the interrelationships of learning to read words silently, decode them orally, and spell them in writing also have implications for multiple mapping theory. Developmentally, as is consistent with the emergent literacy perspective, written word learning was acquired in waves in which partial learning preceded mastery learning but different kinds of word-level tasks peaked before others. Silent lexical judgements preceded oral decoding, which preceded written spelling (Berninger, 1988). In general, lexical-level mapping may contribute to lexical judgments, sub-lexical mapping to decoding, and both lexical and sub-lexical mapping to written spelling, but subsequent instructional studies found considerable individual differences in how children constructed orthographic-phonological maps in response to the same reading or spelling instruction (Berninger and Abbott, 1992; Abbott et al., 1997; Hart, Berninger and Abbott, 1997). Integrated reading-writing instruction resulted in the construction of more orthographic-phonological mappings than did decoding instruction alone (Traweek and Berninger, 1997).

Multiple mappings in developing word reading and spelling

As our assessment and instructional research moved up the developmental continuum of literacy learning, we learned that orthographic-phonological mapping can model beginning reading well but is insufficient to explain how older students learn to read longer, more complex words, particularly words of Latinate or Greek origin. In our current work, *Triple Word Form Awareness and Mapping Theory* underlies our assessment, instructional intervention, genetics, and brain imaging research (Berninger, in press; Berninger, Abbott, Billingsley and Nagy, 2001; Berninger, Nagy, Carlisle, Thomson, Hoffer, Abbott, Abbott, Richards and Aylward, 2003; Berninger and Richards, 2002; Nagy et al., 2003). Recent brain imaging research (see Berninger, in press, for review) provides evidence for unique neural signatures (patterns of brain activation) for the phonological, morphological and orthographic word forms.

According to Triple Word Form Theory, the phonological, morphological and orthographic word forms contribute to learning to read and spell written words. The instructional goal is to help students become aware of the parts of each of the three word forms so that multiple maps of phonological, morphological and orthographic interrelationships can be computed and the word parts can be co-ordinated in real time during word reading and spelling. Early in literacy development, *inflectional suffixes* contribute to these mappings – for example, the three phonological representations (/t/, /d/, or /_d/) for the past tense marker spelled 'ed' and the three phonological and two orthographic representations for plural forms spelled 's' or 'es' (/s/, /z/, or /_z/). Nevertheless, the central goal in beginning word reading is to learn multiple orthographic–phonological mappings. Then, beginning about fourth grade (age 9) and continuing through high school, *derivational suffixes* that mark grammatical parts of speech and link lexical representations to syntactic structures play an increasing role in the mapping of phonological, morphological and orthographic word forms and their parts that contribute to word reading and spelling and other literacy outcomes (Nagy et al., in preparation).

Levels of language and functional language systems

Although language is often assumed to be a single mental construct, both linguistic science and neuroscience indicate that it is not: language can be analysed and is represented in the brain at different levels or units (see Berninger and Richards, 2002, for review of the evidence for this claim). Thus, a small theory guiding our cross-sectional studies was that *intraindividual differences in different levels of language* influence both reading achievement (Berninger, 1994; Berninger, Abbott and Alsdorf, 1997) and writing achievement (Berninger, Mizokawa, Bragg, Cartwright and Yates, 1994; Whitaker, Berninger, Johnston and Swanson, 1994) and have implications for assessment and instruction. For example, children's word reading and sentence understanding skills may not be comparably developed and children should be taught to pay attention to and co-ordinate both word-level decoding skills and sentence-level syntactic skills in developing sentence comprehension ability. Likewise, children's word-choice, sentence-construction and text-organization skills may not be comparably developed and children should be taught planning, drafting and reviewing/revising skills at the word, sentence and text levels.

Not only does language have different levels of representation but it is also organized into different systems, depending on which end organ connecting it to the external environment is involved. Liberman (1999) had the fundamental insight that because language has no end organs of its own it teams up with sensory or motor processes to create systems for language by ear (listening), language by mouth (speaking), language by eye (reading) and language by hand (writing). Our current theory-driven longitudinal and instructional research programme on the connections between and among these different language systems (see, for example, Berninger, 2000a; Berninger, Abbott, Abbott, Graham and Richards, 2001) is guided by this small theory of *multiple language systems.*

Functional systems in reading and writing

The various components of these multiple language systems exhibit properties that are captured by two other small theories: *functional systems* and *flexible orchestration*. Functional systems are constructed from other existing systems to perform new goal-directed functions, and the newly created functional systems co-ordinate many different processes to accomplish their goals. Functional reading and writing systems draw on common as well as unique brain structures, on other language systems (for listening and speaking), and on non-language systems (for example, sensory, motor, attention, memory and executive); they are flexibly reorganized according to the task at hand and the language-users' stage of language development (Berninger and Richards, 2002). Our studies of the normal development of the complex functional reading system and the complex functional writing system have drawn on the systems theory and research of Hughling Jackson, A. R. Luria, Marvin Minsky, Michael Posner and J. Fuster (see Berninger, in press).

In our recent research on dyslexia, we focus on the working memory system and how it is orchestrated differently for reading and writing goals. Regardless of the goal at hand, it has three components, each of which draws on some kind of phonological process: word form storage (in phonological, morphological, and orthographic codes), a phonological loop that mediates new word learning, and a supervisory attention system in the executive network for co-ordinating phonology with other language codes (Berninger, in press; Berninger, Dunn and Alper, in preparation). In the context of this model of working memory, the phonological core deficit of dyslexia and the working memory deficit theory of dyslexia are reconciled (Berninger, in press). However, this reconceptualization of reading within a working-memory architecture is changing our views of the constructs of phonology, attention, memory, and executive functions, much as Churchland predicted. It is no longer possible to view each of these constructs as a separate, unrelated process in the functional systems of the brain. Executive control in working memory depends on both the phonological loop and the supervisory attentional system, and words are temporarily stored in multiple formats – phonological, morphological and orthographic codes. Although the phonological word form code is clearly of major importance in learning to read (mapping aural/oral language onto the written word), accumulating evidence shows that orthographic and morphological word forms also play an important role in written language acquisition (Nagy et al., 2003).

2. Translating cross-sectional assessment research findings into psychometric instruments

In a series of cross-sectional studies, large test batteries of widely used psychometric tests and experimenter-devised measures of neuropsychological processes (referred to as process measures) and specific reading and writing skills were given to 600 first through sixth graders (50 girls and 50 boys at each grade level) that were representative of the US population in ethnicity and mother's level of education. Measures of neuropsychological processes (process measures) that were correlated at p < 0.001 with specific reading and writing skills were then (a) entered into multiple regression to identify which contributed additional unique variance to the specific reading or writing skills, or (b) used as indicators of factors in structural equation modelling to identify whether paths in structural models were significant, indicating that they contributed unique variance to the reading and writing outcome factors. In one case, a computerized experiment was used to validate the process measures (primary grade reading comprehension). In this section, the main findings are summarized about which process measures are unique predictors of reading and writing achievement and thus are valid measures to use in assessment of reading and writing problems.

These measures were then translated into a standardized, normed psychometric test by the Psychological Corporation. The neuropsychological processing model underlying the resulting Process Assessment of the Learner (PAL) Test Battery of Reading and Writing (Berninger, 2001) is then presented in Table 5.1 and discussed. In both the primary (grades 1 to 3) and intermediate (grades 4 to 6) samples, a prorated WISC-R Verbal IQ was used, based on the Information, Similarities, Vocabulary, and Comprehension sub-tests, which is comparable to the Verbal Comprehension Factor on the Wechsler Intelligence Scale for Children, Fourth Edition (WISC 4, Psychological Corporation, 2003). The PAL Test Battery was designed for use with the WISC 4 and the Wechsler Individual Achievement Test, Second Edition (WIAT II) (Psychological Corporation, 2001). Levels of language theory informed the development of the WIAT II Reading Comprehension and Written Expression sub-tests.

Assessment research findings

Primary-grade word reading

Measures of multiple orthographic codes – whole word, letter in a word, and letter group in a word – and of multiple phonological codes – whole phonetic codes, syllables, and phonemes – were entered into the multiple regressions (Berninger and Abbott, 1994; also see Berninger, Yates and Lester, 1991). For reading real words, each orthographic and phonological code contributed uniquely. For pseudoword reading, each code except letter in a word contributed uniquely, but the interaction between letter group and syllable contributed uniquely too. These results (letter groups contribute uniquely and the significant interaction) indicated that orthographic units larger than the single letter play a role in phonological decoding. For written spelling, all the orthographic and phonological codes contributed uniquely except the whole word orthographic code, but again the interaction between letter group and syllable contributed uniquely. Taken together, these results supported the view that beginning readers and spellers are learning to map orthographic and phonological codes of different unit size. On the PAL Test Battery, Receptive Coding A, B and C assess coding of whole orthographic word forms, a letter in the word form, and a letter group in the word form, respectively. The PAL Test also has syllable, phoneme, and rime tasks to assess phonological coding for primary-grade children. These orthographic and phonological measures can be given with the WIAT II Word Reading and Pseudoword Reading sub-tests to pinpoint why primary-grade children struggle with reading.

Primary-grade reading comprehension

Beginning readers need to learn to co-ordinate word decoding and computation of sentence meaning in order to comprehend the text they read. Meaningful sentences or sentences containing only real words in which one did not make sense in sentence context were computer-administered to second or third graders in one of two formats – one word at a time highlighting single word units, or one sentence at a time highlighting sentence units (Berninger, 1994; Berninger, Abbott and Alsdorf, 1997). This task requires careful attention to word reading and unfolding sentence context in order to judge whether a sentence is meaningful or not. Intraindividual differences in processing word and sentence units were found (Berninger, 1994). Both word unit processing and sentences unit processing were significantly correlated with a standardized measure of reading comprehension (Berninger, Abbott and Alsdorf, 1997). This task was adapted for the PAL Test Battery by presenting a trio of sentences all containing only real words but only one of which is a meaningful sentence that the student is asked to underline. This PAL Sentence Sense sub-test, a measure of silent reading fluency, can be given with WIAT II Reading Comprehension for a fuller picture of the comprehension problems readers may have.

Primary-grade handwriting

Three measures contributed uniquely to handwriting – receptive coding of letter groups, fine motor planning and execution of sequential finger movements, and automaticity of legible letter production (Berninger, Yates, Cartwright, Rutberg, Remy and Abbott, 1992). These processes can be assessed with PAL Receptive Coding C, Finger Sense – Succession, and Alphabet Writing sub-tests, respectively. Structural equation modelling (Abbott and Berninger, 1993) showed that the path from the orthographic coding factor had a direct, significant path to the handwriting factor, but the fine motor factor did not – it contributed to handwriting only indirectly through the orthographic coding factor. Handwriting is not a pure motor skill – it is also language by hand. Representing the orthographic letter form precisely in memory and retrieving letter forms automatically and efficiently from memory are critical processes in learning to write.

Primary-grade spelling

Three measures contributed uniquely to spelling – phoneme deletion, pseudoword reading (mapping letters and phonemes) and automaticity of legible letter production (Berninger et al., 1992). These processes can be assessed with PAL Phonemes, Pseudoword Reading and Alphabet Writing, respectively, to pinpoint reasons for low achievement on WIAT II Spelling or other measures of spelling.

Primary-grade composition

The same measures that contributed uniquely to handwriting also contributed uniquely to compositional fluency (number of words written in 5 minutes), consistent with other findings in our research group that handwriting constrains compositional fluency and quality during the elementary grades (Berninger et al., 1992). However, when compositional quality (based on ratings of content and text organization) was also considered, Verbal IQ also contributed uniquely (Berninger et al., 1992). Thus, to explain low achievement on WIAT II Written Expression, in the first three grades, valid tests that might be used include PAL Alphabet Writing, Receptive Coding C, and Succession and WISC 4 Verbal Comprehension Factor.

Intermediate-grade word reading

Multiple orthographic codes – mapping orthographic word form and semantic codes, long-term memory representations for orthographic word form (when phonology is equated), and integration of receptive and expressive orthographic word forms; *multiple phonological codes* – receptive phoneme localization across word pairs, articulation of target phoneme, and syllable/rime/phoneme deletion; and *Verbal IQ* were entered into the multiple regressions for word reading, decoding and spelling (Berninger, Cartwright, Yates, Swanson and Abbott, 1994). For real word reading, all orthographic and phonological coding measures and Verbal IQ contributed uniquely. For pseudoword reading, all orthographic and phonological codes except mapping orthographic and semantic codes and Verbal IQ contributed uniquely. For spelling, all orthographic and phonological codes and Verbal IQ contributed uniquely. Taken together, these results support the claim that both orthographic and phonological codes contribute uniquely to reading and spelling written words in normally developing upper elementary students in grades 4 through 6. Both should be assessed to explain poor achievement in word reading, decoding and spelling on WIAT II or other standardized measures.

Intermediate-grade reading comprehension

Phonological (phoneme localization), orthographic (long-term representation of the orthographic word form), working memory (at the word and transword levels), and Verbal IQ contributed uniquely to reading comprehension (Berninger, Cartwright et al., 1994). Also, see Swanson and Berninger (1995). PAL Phonemes, Word Choice, and Working Memory (available 2005) and WISC 4 Verbal Comprehension Factor are valid measures to use in assessing upper elementary children with reading comprehension problems. PAL Sentence Sense, a measure of silent reading fluency, can be used along with WIAT II Reading Comprehension to assess reading comprehension problems in older students that often surface as the curriculum requirements increase in reading comprehension. See Berninger, Abbott and Alsdorf (1997) for evidence that the experimental measure, on which Sentence Sense is based, was correlated with reading comprehension achievement in intermediate-grade students.

Intermediate-grade handwriting

Automaticity of legible letter production and expressive orthographic coding (of whole words, a letter in a word, and a letter group in a word) contributed uniquely to handwriting (Berninger, Cartwright et al., 1994). PAL Alphabet Writing and Expressive Coding A (whole orthographic word form), Coding B (letter in the word form), and Coding C (letter group in the word form) assess these skills. In contrast to the receptive coding sub-tests that require a yes/no judgement, the expressive sub-tests require a written response (whole word, letter or letter group). As was the case with the primary grade sample, in the intermediate grade sample, the orthographic coding factor had a significant, direct path to the handwriting factor, but the motor coding factor did not – it accounted for handwriting only indirectly via its relationship to coding of the orthographic word form and its constituent letters.

Intermediate-grade spelling

Three *orthographic coding measures* – orthographic–semantic mapping, long-term orthographic word form representation and expressive coding of the whole orthographic word form, a letter in the word form, and a letter group in the word form, a *phonological coding task requiring phonemic analysis*, and *Verbal IQ* contributed uniquely to spelling (Berninger, Cartwright et al., 1994). Thus, PAL Word Choice, Expressive Coding, and Phonemes, and WISC 4 Verbal Comprehension Factor are valid measures to assess upper elementary students who score poorly on WIAT II Spelling or another measure of spelling.

Intermediate-grade composition

Automaticity of legible letter production, planning and execution of sequential finger movements, and working memory contributed uniquely to compositional fluency (number of words written in five minutes), but when ratings of compositional quality were also considered, Verbal IQ also contributed uniquely along with automaticity of legible letter production and working memory (Berninger, Cartwright et al., 1994). Also, see Swanson and Berninger (1996). Thus, to assess upper elementary students who score poorly on the WIAT II Written Expression sub-test or other measure of written composition, valid diagnostic measures include PAL Alphabet Writing, Finger Succession, and working memory (available 2005) and WISC 4 Verbal Comprehension Factor.

Neuropsychological Process Model

Table 5.1 summarizes the model of neuropsychological processes related to reading and writing acquisition and the PAL sub-tests designed to measure each of the processes in the model. The PAL Test Battery is the only psychometric measure providing comprehensive assessment of the orthographic word form and its constituent parts. Elementary grade children need to become aware of this word form and its parts in order to learn to read and spell words. The various measures assess both short-term/working memory representation of the orthographic word form and long-term representation of these word forms. They also assess receptive and expressive orthographic processes involved in reading and spelling words. All handwriting (expressive orthographic tasks) is timed and assess different aspects of automatic letter production that is rapid and effortless. Copy Task B does not have memory requirements and assesses formation of each alphabet letter – in a different order than alphabetic order and in word context. The Alphabet Writing Task does have long-term memory requirements and the letters have to be produced in alphabetic order. Performance on Copy Task A and Alphabet Writing can be compared to determine if the bottleneck in handwriting is in letter formation (no memory requirement) or in memory search and retrieval, respectively. Copy Task B assesses more sustained automatic letter production in word context.

Fine motor processes are assessed that involve only execution (Finger Sense Repetition) and planning and execution (Finger Sense Succession). Because the number of finger taps is held constant across these measures, the relative time for executing finger taps that do and do not require grapho-motor planning for sequential movements can be compared. Finger Succession has greater ecological validity for writing tasks than does Finger Repetition (Berninger and Rutberg, 1992), which provides a control in case problems in execution are also operating.

Table 5.1 Neuropsychological process constructs and measures in the Process Assessment of the Learner (PAL) Test Battery for Reading and Writing

Receptive Orthographic Processes:

Short-term memory storage of orthographic word form. A briefly presented word (1 s) must be held in temporary storage until a receptive judgement or expressive task is completed.

RECEPTIVE CODING and EXPRESSIVE CODING

Processing orthographic word forms in working memory. While the briefly presented orthographic word form is held in temporary storage, processing in working memory renders a decision or prepares a written response.

RECEPTIVE CODING and EXPRESSIVE CODING

Long-term word representations of the orthographic word form. From a set of three written words or pseudowords, all of which have equivalent phonological word forms, the correctly spelled real word is chosen.

WORD CHOICE

Expressive Orthographic Processes:

Reproducing letters and written words without memory requirements. Letters are produced without memory requirements by copying from written text.

COPY A and COPY B

Rapid, automatic retrieval and production of letter forms from long-term memory.

ALPHABET WRITING

Executive co-ordination of receptive and expressive orthographic word forms. Following judgement in working memory about a briefly stored word in short-term memory, an orthographic word form or a letter or letter group in it is written.

EXPRESSIVE CODING

Phonological Processes:

Rhyming.

Detecting the non-rhyme in a set of three words RHYMING TASK A

Generating rhymes RHYMING TASK B

Syllables.

Deletion real words SYLLABLES (K-3)

Deletion pseudowords SYLLABLES (4–6)

Phonemes.

Detection real words PHONEMES TASK A

Deletion real words PHONEMES TASKS B, C

Deletion pseudowords PHONEMES TASK D

Rimes.

Deletion real words RIMES TASK A

Deletion pseudowords RIMES TASK B

Table 5.1 Cont.

Orthographic–Phonological Mapping:
>   Translating letters into phonemes and synthesizing phonemes into a pseudo-name.

PSEUDOWORD READING

Rapid Automatic Naming (RAN):
>   Rapid Naming of Single Letters and Rapid Naming of Letter Groups
>   RAN Letters
>   Rapid Naming of High Frequency, Partially Decodable Words
>   RAN Words

Rapid Automatic Switching (RAS):
>   Rapid Naming of Switching Categories — Words and Double Digit Numbers

RAN WORDS AND NUMBERS

Finger Sense:
>   *Execution of repetitive finger movements.* Imitative, repetitive touches of index
>   finger and thumb.

REPETITION

>   *Planning and execution of sequential finger movements.* Imitative, sequential
>   touches of thumb and each of the other fingers in sequential order.

FINGER SUCCESSION

>   *Sensory-motor integration.* Pointing to the finger touched by the examiner
>   behind a screen.

FINGER LOCALIZATION

>   *Sensory-symbol-motor integration.* Naming the finger touched by the examiner
>   behind a screen. Naming a number written on fingertip by examiner.

FINGER RECOGNITION and FINGERTIP WRITING

Executive Functions for Language Processes and Systems:
>   *Co-ordinating word-level and sentence-level processing.* Deciding which
>   sentence is meaningful (makes sense) in a set of three sentences.

SENTENCE SENSE

>   *Co-ordinating listening and writing.* Taking notes while listening to a 'pseudo'
>   lecture about fictional information.

NOTE TAKING A

>   *Co-ordinating reading and writing.* Composing based on lecture notes.

NOTE TAKING B

In contrast to other psychometric measures of phonological skills, the PAL measures are organized by unit of analysis and a developmental order of acquisition. For syllable, phoneme, and rime units, the deletion task is first performed on real words, which are easier because both phonological and orthographic codes in long-term memory may be used to do the task, and then on pseudowords, which are harder because only phonological codes in short-term memory can be used to do the task. At present the PAL Test has measures of the phonological and orthographic word forms and their constituent parts. Measures of morphological word form and its parts are under development and when available will permit assessment from the perspective of triple word form awareness and mapping theory.

In contrast to other psychometric measures of rapid automatic naming (RAN), the PAL measures assess naming of both single letters and letter groups (see Berninger, Yates and Lester, 1991). Also, to assess fast mapping of lexical-level orthographic codes and phonological name codes (see Berninger et al., 1991; Berninger, Abbott and Alsdorf, 1997), PAL RAN Words assesses speed of naming high frequency words that are only partially decodable. For rapid alternating switching (RAS), an index of executive regulation of switching attention or the supervisory attentional system, PAL RAS alternates between high frequency, partially decodable words and double-digit numerals.

Many of the PAL sub-tests assess executive functions for co-ordinating different processes in a language system or different language systems. For example, pseudoword reading assesses mapping of orthographic and phonological codes onto word level productions on the oral-motor channel. Finger Sense assesses processes underlying production on the grapho-motor channel, when symbol (linguistic) coding is (Finger Recognition and Finger Tip Writing) and is not (Repetition and Successions) involved. Sentence Sense, which is timed, assesses ability to co-ordinate single words and sentence level units in silent reading fluency. Note Taking A assesses ability to co-ordinate language by ear (listening) with language by hand (writing). Note Taking B assesses ability to co-ordinate language by eye (reading) with language by hand (writing).

3. Implications of findings of a family genetics study for assessment of dyslexia

Phenotypes

Structural equation modelling was used to evaluate the flexible orchestration of four predictor factors – orthographic coding, phonological coding, rapid automatic naming and Verbal IQ – for six academic outcomes – reading accuracy, reading rate, reading composition, handwriting, spelling and composition in 102 child dyslexics (Berninger, Abbott, Thomson and Raskind, 2001). For reading accuracy, spelling and written computation, the paths from the orthographic factor and the phonological factor were significant for three academic outcomes – reading accuracy, spelling and written composition, thus demonstrating once again the importance of children learning to map the relationships between the orthographic and phonological representations that each make common as well as unique contributions to these aspects of literacy acquisition. For reading rate, the orthographic and rapid automatic naming factors had significant paths. For reading comprehension, the phonological factors and Verbal IQ had significant paths. For handwriting, only the orthographic factor had a significant direct path. Thus, of the six academic outcomes, five had a significant direct path from the orthographic factor. Even though none of the orthographic tasks used as indicators of the orthographic coding factor required reading, individual differences in the level to which the orthographic word form was developed significantly influenced the ability of children with dyslexia to read and write.

Genotypes

Initial aggregation analyses in our family genetics study targeted the most probable genetic constraints in dyslexia to be in these single phenotypes – coding of phonological word forms in short-term memory, accuracy and rate of phonological decoding, and written spelling (Raskind et al., 2000). Phenotypic measures for these potential genotypes include (a) Nonword Repetition on the Comprehensive Test of Phonological Processing (CTOPP) (Wagner et al., 1999) or WISC 4 Digit Span for coding phonological word forms in short-term memory; (b) WIAT II or PAL Pseudoword Reading or Woodcock–Johnson, Third Edition (WJ III) (Woodcock et al., 2001) Word Attack for accuracy of phonological decoding; (c) Test of Word Reading Efficiency (TOWRE) Phonemic Reading (Torgesen et al., 1999) for rate of phonological decoding; and (d) Wide Range Achievement Test, Third Edition (WRAT 3) (Wilkinson, 1993) or WIAT II Spelling or PAL Word Choice.

Subsequent aggregation analyses and more recent phenotype analyses (in preparation) also point to supervisory attentional difficulties in the executive management system of dyslexics who do not meet diagnostic criteria for attention deficit hyperactivity disorder (Hsu et al., 2002). The Inhibition sub-test on the Delis–Kaplan test (Delis et al., 2003) appears to be a valid way to assess this difficulty in attending to the relevant linguistic code and ignoring the irrelevant linguistic codes (Berninger and O'Donnell, in press). The Verbal Fluency sub-test on the Delis–Kaplan test is another measure that captures their observed difficulty in executive control for managing the memory search and retrieval processes for verbal codes (Berninger et al., submitted). Both the RAN (Wolf et al., 1986) deficit and the RAS (Wolf, 1986) deficit occur frequently in affected family members in our sample. The RAS may provide yet another index of the supervisory attention deficit in the executive system for language in dyslexia. However, because of the time scores that are skewed in distribution on RAN and RAS, it is proving challenging to model these measures genetically.

Initial segregation analyses demonstrated that coding phonological word forms for word-like stimuli (pseudowords) and digits probably share a common genetic pathway but also have a unique genetic pathway (Wijsman et al., 2000). Subsequent segregation analyses (Chapman et al., 2003) confirmed earlier aggregation analyses (Hsu et al., 2002) that the accuracy and the rate of phonological decoding have separate genetic pathways, and the rate of phonological decoding may exert the greater genetic constraint. Despite these genetic constraints, effective instructional intervention leads to compensated dyslexics, as has been long known. Current clinical assessment results based on many small theories (Berninger and O'Donnell, in press) support a model in which individual dyslexic children and adults may have constraints in any aspect of the behavioural expression of the working memory architecture for reading-related and writing-related goals: in *temporary storage of word forms* (phonological, orthographic and/or morphological; in the *phonological loop for new word learning* and/or in the *supervisory attention system*. Recent brain imaging studies are increasing understanding of the probable brain circuitry underlying each of the components of the working memory architecture.

4. Translating research findings into lesson plans

Since the mid-1990s we have conducted three kinds of instructional intervention studies, organized around a three-tier model for prevention (Tier 1), optimization (Tier 2), and compensation (Tier 3). Both Tier 1 (Early Intervention and Prevention) and Tier 2 (Increasing the Number of Students Who Pass High Stakes Standards) have involved controlled experiments in which children are randomly assigned to treatments, which have been delivered in school settings. The Tier 3 studies, which have been conducted at the university clinical research laboratory, for the purpose of remediating persisting dyslexia and/or dysgraphia, have sometimes been controlled experiments and have sometimes been design experiments to create a desired achievement outcome.

Recently we translated each of 15 instructional studies into lesson plans (five at each of the three tiers). Table 1 in the PAL Research-Supported Reading and Writing Lessons (Berninger and Abbott, 2003) contains the citations for the published studies. Many of these use the previously published instructional materials: (a) phonological and orthographic awareness lessons (Berninger, 1998a), (b) the PAL Talking Letters Program for teaching alphabetic principle based on Berninger, Abbott, Brooksher et al. (2000), Berninger, Vaughan et al., (1998), and Venezky (1970, 1995, 1999), (c) syllable awareness activities (PAL Speaking Syllables) based on Berninger, Vaughan et al. (2000), or (d) PAL Handwriting (Automaticity) Lessons based on Berninger, Vaughan et al. (1997)

Part IV of the PAL Lessons explains the instructional design principles underlying these research-generated lesson plans so that practitioners can develop their own lessons based on them. These principles include the following:

- Teach to all levels of language close in time within the same lesson so that the various levels of language can become interconnected within the functional reading and writing system. Thus, all lessons have instructional activities at the sub-word, word and text levels. For example, all lessons start with alphabet principle training and linguistic awareness training to foster awareness of word form parts (phonological and/or orthographic in beginning readers and writers and phonological, morphological and orthographic in older readers); then they have word work in which they learn how to transfer that prior sub-word training to reading or spelling words; and finally they learn self-regulated strategies for applying the sub-word and word knowledge to reading or composing text.
- Teach low-level skills (such as letter production, spelling, word recognition) to automaticity to free up time- and space-limited working memory for the high-level skills of composing and comprehending (see Berninger, 1999; Berninger and Richards, 2002).
- To avoid tuning out through habituation or excessive novelty seeking create a balance between familiar, predictable routines that do not drain attentional resources and novel, intellectually engaging activities that stimulate but do not overwhelm attentional resources.
- Draw on all the brain's learning mechanisms: social imitation, associative learning, repeated practice to automatize, focal attention through shared reference (pointing, naming, manipulating), strategies and rules for transfer to new contexts, and reflection (making the taught concept an object of conscious thought).
- Use instructional time efficiently by preparing highly pre-planned lessons with varied activities and sufficient progress monitoring so that both the student and the teacher know how much learning is taking place.
- Review the progress monitoring measures so that instruction can be adapted if necessary.
- Include both play with language (humour with riddles and puns, word games and so forth) and work with language (effortful mind expanding activities).

All sessions begin with readers' or writers' warm-up with the Talking Letters Student Card (with or without the teacher using the overheads for group instruction) (Berninger, 1998b). The instructional activities are designed to develop orthographic awareness for letters that are named, phonological awareness for phonemes embedded in names of pictured words that are pronounced in word context and in isolation, and automatic correspondences between the letters and phonemes that are named and pronounced, respectively, by the teacher and the child, in a fast paced, rhythmic turn-taking activity (like the parent–child interactions in which aural/oral language is acquired).

Next, instruction focuses on word work with the goal of transferring linguistic awareness and automatic knowledge of alphabetic principle acquired in the initial phase of the lesson to words that are carefully selected, based on past research, to foster generalization of word decoding or spelling across word contexts. Not only does the teacher model and the student imitate these strategies for transfer but also a progress monitoring system is included that has lists of taught words and transfer words and growth graphs for accuracy (frequency or percent correct), time and rate. These word lists are provided both in whole-word format and in a form in which they are parsed by spelling units to facilitate phoneme mapping and blending.

Finally, a transition occurs to reading text for meaning or composing for authentic communication goals. During this phase children are taught self-regulation strategies for applying the knowledge learned during warm-up and word work to their independent reading or writing.

Given the likely genetic constraints found so far, many of the lessons are aimed at treating these constraints. To treat the *deficit in phonological word forms* (make them less fuzzy), PAL Lesson Sets 2, 5, 11 and 15 and the phonological treatment in Berninger, Nagy et al. (2003) begin with the phonological word form and do not show children the orthographic word form until they develop a more precise phonological word form representation through counting syllables and counting phonemes (with small coloured discs to represent each phoneme). Because of the *deficit in speed of phonological decoding*, some of our interventions emphasize rate of learning letter–sound correspondences (Berninger, Abbott, Billingsley and Nagy, 2001; Berninger, Nagy et al., 2003; and PAL Lesson Sets 9, 10 and 11) and use curriculum-based progress monitoring to assess rate and accuracy of (a) knowledge of correspondences between phonemes and letters and (b) application of these correspondences to decoding Jabberwocky words; teachers plot children's time, accuracy, and rate of correct responding on the growth graphs. Because of the *executive problems* dyslexics face in self-regulating language learning, teachers provide explicit, adult-regulated instruction for each component reading and writing skill.

Words used in the reading and spelling lessons begin with high-frequency monosyllabic Anglo Saxon words (PAL Lesson Sets 1 and 4) and proceed to high-frequency one- and two-syllable Anglo Saxon words (Lesson Sets 2 and 5) to foster awareness of types of syllables in English (which are more reliable decoding cues than are syllable boundaries in English). Vowels on the vowel side of the Talking Letters card are organized by these syllable types. Reading (PAL Lesson Set 6) and writing (PAL Lesson Set 7) lessons then proceed to high-frequency structure words (prepositions, pronouns, conjunctions and articles) that are partially but not fully decodable in many cases, and high-frequency content words, which are easier to learn than structure words because they are typically fully decodable. Students with dyslexia have great difficulty learning structure words. The lists of structure and content words (taught from word card decks) have instructional cues on the back for the teacher to use in teaching the orthographic, phonological and morphological units in the words. This explicit linguistic instruction is more effective in teaching structure words than the common practice of telling students to memorize structure words because they are irregular (they are not totally irregular when many linguistic cues are considered) (see Berninger, Vermeulen, Abbott, McCutchen, Cotton, Cude, Dorn and Sharon, 2003). Also, a list of high-utility prefixes and suffixes in the personal dictionary is used to introduce morphological awareness in decoding longer more complex words, many of which are of Latinate origin, in the Tier 3 Lessons. All these instructional materials are in a supplementary manual. Both the lessons and the supplementary instructional materials can be copied for instructional purposes – so a school or clinic only needs one set of the instructional and reproducible manuals.

5. Combining *in vivo* brain imaging and treatment studies to understand constraints and their plasticity in dyslexia

Phenotypic constraints

Participants in our brain imaging studies are in the age range of 9 to 12 and grades 4 to 6. They meet the inclusion criteria for our family genetics study (Berninger, Abbott, Thomson and Raskind, 2001): their accuracy and rate of single-word and text oral reading and spelling is below the population mean and discrepant from their Verbal Comprehension Factor. They have deficits in orthographic, phonological and rapid automatic naming (the more of these deficits, the more severe their dyslexia: Berninger et al., 2001), but are at the population mean, on average, in morphological and syntactic awareness, planning skills related to expressive language, and oral-motor planning. This profile contrasts with another sub-type also referred to our clinic and other research projects. People with language learning disability are impaired in those morphological, syntactic, language planning and formulation, and/or oral-motor skills, as well as having phonological, orthographic and rapid naming problems. Speech and language pathologists who work with the learning disabled also report difficulty with word retrieval processes, which may interfere with planning for oral expression. The language-learning disabled tend to have more severe problems in using language to learn than do the dyslexics and more pervasive problems in learning across the curriculum than in just reading and spelling specifically (see Berninger and O'Donnell, in press). In all our brain imaging studies the dyslexics are matched on age and Verbal IQ to good readers who serve as the controls and are imaged at the same times as the dyslexics are.

Neuroanatomical constraints

Our structural magnetic resonance images (MRI) are analysed by a research team at the University of Florida at Gainesville – Eckert (an imaging researcher) and Leonard (a neuroanatomist and an imaging researcher). Eckert et al. (2003) used jackknife classification procedures in which they were blind to group but were able to classify accurately most of the dyslexics and matched controls on the basis of a few structures – bilateral par triangularis in inferior frontal gyrus (Broca's area) and the right cerebellum. Other researchers have found structural differences between dyslexics and controls in insula. In functional imaging we found that individual dyslexics did not activate in insula. The right cerebellar-insula-left inferior frontal network may be a circuit for the phonological loop that mediates verbal learning of new words in working memory (see Berninger, in press, for a review of the evidence). That may be why dyslexics have such great difficulty in learning to read new words.

Functional magnetic resonance spectroscopic (fMRS) imaging studies

On an auditorially presented phonological rhyming judgement task, dyslexics and controls differed in lactate activation in the left frontal regions (including but not localized to Broca's area). Lactate is a chemical involved in neural metabolism during energy utilization and may be a marker of neural efficiency. Dyslexics were significantly more activated than controls before treatment – suggesting that their phonological processing was inefficient neurologically (Richards et al., 1999). Because the phonological task did not require reading (it was aurally presented and involved a rhyming task that even pre-reading pre-schoolers can do successfully), the results are consistent with a causal mechanism involving a phonological core deficit. However, following a comprehensive treatment (Berninger, 2000b), the dyslexics did not differ from the controls in lactate activation during the phonological rhyming judgement task (Richards et al., 2000) – suggesting that as a result of instructional treatment they became more efficient in phonological processing. Richards et al. (2002) replicated the results before and after treatment in lactate activation in left anterior regions during the auditorially presented phonological rhyming task. However, because this time the dyslexics were randomly assigned to a phonological or morphological awareness treatment (Berninger, Nagy et al., 2003), we could analyse treatment-specific effects.

At the behavioural level, a significant interaction occurred in a psychometric measure of rate of phonological decoding – those in the morphological awareness treatment improved significantly more in efficiency of phonological decoding on the TOWRE than those in the phonological awareness treatment. This result is consistent with triple word form awareness and mapping theory, which hypothesizes that efficient word decoding requires awareness of the phonological, orthographic and morphological word forms and their parts and interrelationships. The dyslexics had received considerable prior instruction in phonics (orthographic–phonological mapping) but not in morphological awareness – so teaching awareness of morphological word form and its constituent parts helped their word-decoding module operate more efficiently.

Likewise, at the brain level, the fMRS images after treatment showed that those in morphological treatment were significantly more likely to decrease in lactate activation, whereas those in the phonological treatment stayed the same or increased in lactate activation, suggesting that their word processing was still inefficient because they were not aware of morphological word form parts.

Functional magnetic resonance imaging (fMRI) studies

In our first fMRI study (Corina et al., 2001), the same phonological rhyme judgement task was used and differences between dyslexics and controls were found in blood flow in the planum temporale, inferior temporal gyrus, insula, pre-central gyrus, middle frontal gyrus and orbital frontal gyrus. Differences between dyslexics and controls in the left–right aymmetry of the planum temporale structures have been reported in many studies, beginning with autopsy studies of the brain's microscopic neuroanatomical structures; so it was interesting to find this functional activation difference. Individual brains in the control group activated in inferior temporal gyrus and insula but individual brains in the dyslexic group did not activate in either of these structures. The inferior temporal gyrus may be involved in mapping phonology and semantics. Insula may be associated with automatization of articulation processes. The pre-central gyrus is probably involved in articulation and articulatory awareness. The middle frontal gyrus may be part of the working memory system. The frontal orbital cortex may be part of the executive management system. (For further discussion of these findings and original sources for the functions associated with particular structures, see Berninger, in press; Berninger and Richards, 2002; and Corina et al., 2001). However, Corina et al. also found differences between dyslexics and controls on a lexical judgement task, which required attention to semantics and disregard of phonology, and proposed that dyslexics also have difficulty with executive co-ordination of different linguistic codes (the code co-ordination deficit).

In the second fMRI study (Aylward et al., 2003) another phonological task was used – phoneme mapping. For the target (on task), which alternated with the control (off task), children were shown a pair of pseudowords each of which had one or two letters in pink and were asked to decide if the pink letters in each word could stand for the same sound (phoneme). For the control task, children decided whether both letter strings in a pair matched exactly. Prior to treatment, the brain activation that was unique to the phoneme judgements (and not the orthographic judgements when these were directly compared) was significantly different for the dyslexics and matched control good readers. However, after treatment, the dyslexics changed significantly in the inferior frontal gyrus and parietal regions during this phoneme mapping task and their activation in these two regions was no longer significantly different from the controls. This result suggested that, despite the genetic, neuroanatomical, and pre-treatment blood flow differences – all of which are constraints interfering with reading acquisition, it is possible, with explicit, systematic, intensive treatment to 'normalize' the dyslexic brain processing sufficiently so that it can respond to instruction. Although we do not know how permanent the effects of this short-term intervention are, this result certainly shows that if appropriate instruction for dyslexia was made available on a daily basis throughout a school year, affected students may be able to compensate. In this study dyslexics seemed to use the same neural circuits as good readers but needed very intense instruction to activate those circuits. (See Aylward et al., 2003, for further discussion of these issues.)

In that second fMRI study, a morpheme mapping (on task) was also given in which children were asked to decide if one word (for example, 'corner' or 'builder') came from a second word (for example, 'corn' or 'build'); in one case the word did because the common spelling pattern ('er') functioned as a morpheme, but in the second case it did not (the common spelling pattern was not a morpheme). The control (off task) for morpheme mapping was a synonym task (general semantic features) so that the comparison of the on- and off-task yields brain activation effects that are specific to morphological word form. The controls showed different brain signatures (patterns of blood flow) for the phoneme mapping task and the morpheme mapping task, consistent with the claim that the language system draws on many different processes that have distinct spatial representation in the brain. Again, the dyslexics differed in blood flow activation before but not after treatment – on morpheme mapping the pre-treatment differences that normalized occurred in right fusiform gyrus and parietal regions. (See Aylward et al., 2003, for more details.)

6. Future research directions

Many potential genetic, neurological and instructional constraints may affect how easily dyslexics learn to read. Given the complexity involved, it is important not to rule out prematurely any factors that may ultimately explain the aetiology or lead to effective treatment. Multiple constraints may be operating and it is important to understand how each of the constrained processes contributes and is co-ordinated in real time (see Wolf, 2001; Fawcett and Nicolson, 2001; Ivry and Keele, 1989) in functional systems.

Sub-cortical structures such as the cerebellum, which contains 50% of the neurons of the brain and neurons that are distinctively different from the cerebral cortex, may play an important role in the temporal co-ordination of these processes during learning and subsequent automatization (Nicolson and Fawcett, 2001). However, it is unlikely that any one structure alone controls timing – it is more likely that circuits of connected structures contribute to the timing mechanisms. At least for motor skills that may play an important role in the temporal co-ordination of these processes during learning and subsequent automatization is the cerebellum. At least for motor skills (and reading involves the co-ordination of language with the oral-motor system), different circuits appear to activate during learning a motor skill than during performance of a practised, automatic motor skill (Van Mier et al., 1998). Van Mier et al. found that learning motor skills changed activation patterns in supplementary motor areas and the left cerebellum, and Mazziotta et al. (1991) found that basal ganglia activate only after overlearning that leads to a skill being on automatic pilot. When adults learned a motor sequence of key presses with auditory feedback for correct presses, the cerebellum activated during both the learning phase and after practice (Nicolson et al., 1999). As already discussed, the right cerebellum seems to be involved in circuits in working memory that mediate new word learning. Neuroanatomical anomalies in the right cerebellum uniquely predicted individual differences in orthographic word form coding (Eckert et al., 2003). However, there is also evidence that different circuits in the cerebellum may activate during learning and after skills are well honed and automatic (for review, see Berninger and Richards, 2002; Berninger, in press).

During learning, component processes must be orchestrated in time so that they begin to function as a system for goal-directed activity. Once the system is functional (typically as the result of learning and practice), it may shift to an automatic brain pathway, where the retrieval and execution processes are orchestrated in time for automatic production. If this analysis is correct, then the most effective treatment for dyslexia is not to practise the function associated with an isolated brain structure (such as the cerebellum) but rather to create learning environments in which all the necessary circuits of the functional reading and writing systems are activated and co-ordinated in time. One way to do this is to teach to all levels of language close in time within the same lesson with the goal of automatizing low-level decoding and word recognition, handwriting, and spelling to free up the limited, time-constrained as well as capacity-constrained, working memory resources for the high-level (non-automatic, controlled) processes of reading comprehension and written expression (see Berninger and Richards, 2002). In general, the field of cognitive neuroscience is moving away from a model that focuses on single neural structures in isolation as causal mechanisms to an emphasis on the interconnectivity of neural structures within systems for performing specific functions. Not all neural networks distributed through the brain are on the same time scale, so it is unlikely that simple sequential models of linear neural transmission or univariate causality will be sufficient to explain the brain at work (Berninger, in press). These interconnected neural circuits may be modifiable, to some degree, depending on how attentional resources are allocated and what happens in the instructional environment. Much remains to be learned about the nature–nurture interactions as brain systems and instructional systems are manipulated in systematic ways. The resulting knowledge will likely shed light on the complex multi-level, bidirectional causal mechanisms that underlie human learning.

References

Abbott R, Berninger V (1993) Structural equation modelling of relationships among developmental skills and writing skills in primary and intermediate grade writers. Journal of Educational Psychology 85(3): 478-508.

Abbott S, Reed L, Abbott R, Berninger V (1997) Year-long balanced reading/writing tutorial: A design experiment used for dynamic assessment. Learning Disabilities Quarterly 20: 249-63.

Aylward E, Richards T, Berninger V, Nagy W, Field K, Grimme A, Richards A, Thomson J, Cramer S (2003) Instructional treatment associated with changes in brain activation in children with dyslexia. Neurology 61: 212-19.

Berninger V (1986) Normal variation in reading acquisition. Perceptual and Motor Skills 62: 691-716.

Berninger V (1987) Global component and serial processing of printed words in beginning readers. Journal of Experimental Child Psychology 43: 387-418.

Berninger V (1988) Acquisition of linguistic procedures for printed words: neuropsychological implications for learning. International Journal of Neuroscience 42: 267-81.

Berninger V (1994) Intraindividual differences in levels of language in comprehension of written sentences. Learning and Individual Differences 6: 433-57.

Berninger V (1998a) Process Assessment of the Learner (PAL) Guides for Intervention. San Antonio TX: The Psychological Corporation.

Berninger V (1998b) Process Assessment of the Learner (PAL) Intervention Kit with Manuals for Talking Letters and Handwriting Automaticity Lesson. San Antonio TX: The Psychological Corporation.

Berninger V (1999) Coordinating transcription and text generation in working memory during composing: Automatized and constructive processes. Learning Disability Quarterly 22: 99-112.

Berninger V (2000a) Development of language by hand and its connections to language by ear, mouth and eye. Topics in Language Disorders 20: 65-84.

Berninger V (2000b) Dyslexia an invisible treatable disorder: the story of Einstein's Ninja Turtles. Learning Disability Quarterly 23: 175-95.

Berninger V (2001) Reading and Writing PAL; Math PAL in progress. Process Assessment of the Learner. San Antonio TX: The Psychological Corporation.

Berninger V (in press) The reading brain in children and youth: A systems approach. To appear in Wong B (ed.) Learning about Learning Disabilities, 3rd edn. San Diego CA: Academic Press.

Berninger V, Abbott R (1992) Unit of analysis and constructive processes of the learner: key concepts for educational neuropsychology. Educational Psychologist 27: 223-42.

Berninger V, Abbott R (1994) Multiple orthographic and phonological codes in literacy acquisition: an evolving research program. In Berninger V (ed.) The Varieties of Orthographic Knowledge I: Theoretical and Developmental Issues. The Netherlands: Kluwer Academic Publishers, pp. 277-317.

Berninger V, Abbott S (2003) PAL. Research-supported Reading and Writing Lessons. San Antonio TX: The Psychological Corporation.

Berninger V, Abbott R, Abbott S, Graham S, Richards T (2001) Writing and reading: connections between language by hand and language by eye. Journal of Learning Disabilities 35: 39-56.

Berninger V, Abbott R, Alsdorf B (1997) Lexical- and sentence-level processes in comprehension of written sentences. Reading and Writing: An Interdisciplinary Journal 9: 135-62.

Berninger V, Abbott R, Billingsley F, Nagy W (2001) Processes underlying timing and fluency: efficiency, automaticity, coordination and morphological awareness. In Wolf M (ed.) Dyslexia Fluency and the Brain. Baltimore: York Press, pp. 383-414.

Berninger V, Abbott R, Brooksher R, Lemos Z, Ogier S, Zook D, Mostafapour E (2000) A connectionist approach to making the predictability of English orthography explicit to at-risk beginning readers: evidence for alternative effective strategies. Developmental Neuropsychology 17: 241-71.

Berninger V, Abbott R, Thomson J, Raskind W (2001) Language phenotype for reading and writing disability: a family approach. Scientific Studies in Reading 5: 59-105.

Berninger V, Abbott R, Thomson J, Wagner R, Swanson HL, Raskind W (submitted) Modeling phenotypes in developmental dyslexia in children and adults. Evidence for the phonological care and working memory deficits.

Berninger V, Abbott R, Vermeulen K, Ogier S, Brooksher R, Zook D, Lemos Z (2002) Comparison of faster and slower responders: implications for the nature and duration of early reading intervention. Learning Disability Quarterly 25: 59-76.

Berninger V, Cartwright A, Yates C, Swanson HL, Abbott R (1994) Developmental skills related to writing and reading acquisition in the intermediate grades: shared and unique variance. Reading and Writing: An Interdisciplinary Journal 6: 161-96.

Berninger V, Chen A, Abbott R (1988) A test of the multiple connections model of reading acquisition. International Journal of Neuroscience 42: 283-95.

Berninger V, Dunn A, Alper T (in press) Integrated multi-level models of branching, instructional and differential diagnosis. In Prifitera A, Saklofske D, Weiss L and Rolfhus E (eds) WISC-IV. Clinical Use and Interpretation. San Diego CA: Academic Press.

Berninger V, Mizokawa D, Bragg R, Cartwright A, Yates C (1994) Intraindividual differences in levels of written language. Reading and Writing Quarterly 10: 259-75.

Berninger V, Nagy W, Carlisle J, Thomson J, Hoffer D, Abbott S, Abbott R, Richards T, Aylward E (2003) Effective treatment for dyslexics in grades 4 to 6. In Foorman B (ed.) Preventing and Remediating Reading Difficulties: Bringing Science to Scale. Timonium MD: York Press, pp. 382-417.

Berninger V, Richards T (2002) Brain literacy for educators and psychologists. New York: Academic Press.

Berninger V, Rutberg J (1992) Relationship of finger function to beginning writing: application to diagnosis of writing disabilities. Developmental Medicine, Child Neurology 34: 155-72.

Berninger V, O'Donnell L (in press) Research supported differential diagnosis of specific learning disabilities. In Prifitera A, Saklofske D, Weiss L and Rolfhus E (eds) WISC IV. Clinical Use and Interpretation. San Diego CA: Academic Press.

Berninger V, Traweek D (1991) Effects of two-phase reading intervention on three orthographic-phonological code connections. Learning and Individual Differences 3: 323-38.

Berninger V, Vaughan K, Abbott R, Abbott S, Brooks A, Rogan L, Reed E, Graham S (1997) Treatment of handwriting fluency problems in beginning writing: transfer from handwriting to composition. Journal of Educational Psychology 89: 652-66.

Berninger V, Vaughan K, Abbott R, Brooks A, Abbott S, Reed E, Rogan L, Graham S (1998) Early intervention for spelling problems: teaching spelling units of varying size within a multiple connections framework. Journal of Educational Psychology 90: 587-605.

Berninger V, Vaughan K, Abbott R, Brooks A, Begay K, Curtin G, Byrd K, Graham S (2000) Language-based spelling instruction: teaching children to make multiple connections between spoken and written words. Learning Disability Quarterly 23: 117-35.

Berninger V, Vermeulen K, Abbott R, McCutchen D, Cotton S, Cude J, Dorn S, Sharon T (2003) Comparison of three approaches to supplementary reading instruction for low achieving second grade readers. Language Speech and Hearing Services in Schools 34: 101-15.

Berninger V, Yates C, Cartwright A, Rutberg J, Remy E, Abbott R (1992) Lower-level developmental skills in beginning writing. Reading and Writing: An Interdisciplinary Journal 4: 257-80.

Berninger V, Yates C, Lester K (1991) Multiple orthographic codes in acquisition of reading and writing skills. Reading and Writing: An Interdisciplinary Journal 3: 115-49.

Chapman N, Raskind W, Thomson J, Berninger V, Wijsman E (2003) Segregation analysis of phenotypic components of learning disabilities II. Phonological decoding. Neuropsychiatric Genetics 121B: 60-70.

Churchland P (1986) Neurophilosophy. Toward a Unified Science of the Mind/Brain. Cambridge MA: MIT Press.

Corina D, Richards T, Serafini S, Richards A, Steury K, Abbott R, Echelard D, Maravilla K, Berninger V (2001) fMRI auditory language differences between dyslexic and able reading children. Neuroreport 12: 1195-201.

Delis D, Kaplan E, Kramer J (2003) Delis–Kaplan Executive Function System. San Antonio TX: The Psychological Corporation.

Eckert M, Leonard C, Richards T, Aylward E, Thomson J, Berninger V (2003) Anatomical correlates of dyslexia: Frontal and cerebellar findings. Brain 126(2): 482-94.

Fawcett A, Nicolson R (2001) Speed and temporal processing in dyslexia. In Wolf M (ed.) Dyslexia Fluency and the Brain. Extraordinary Brain Series. Baltimore: York Press, pp. 23-40.

Gallagher R, Appenzeller T (1999) Beyond reductionism. Introduction to special issue on complex systems. Science 284: 79.

Goswami U (1988) Orthographic analogies and reading development. Quarterly Journal of Experimental Psychology 40A: 239-68.

Hart T, Berninger V, Abbott R (1997) Comparison of teaching single or multiple orthographic-phonological connections for word recognition and spelling: implications for instructional consultation. School Psychology Review 26: 279-97.

Hsu L, Berninger V, Thomson J, Wijsman E, Raskind W (2002) Familial aggregation of dyslexia phenotypes: paired correlated measures. American Journal of Medical Genetics/Neuropsychiatric Section 114: 471-8.

Liberman A (1999) The reading researcher and the reading teacher need the right theory of speech. Scientific Studies of Reading 3: 95-111.

Liberman I, Shankweiler D, Fisher F, Carter B (1974) Explicit syllable and phoneme segmentation in the young child. Journal of Experimental Child Psychology 18: 201-11.

Mazziotta J, Grafton S, Woods R (1991) The human motor system studied with PET measurements of cerebral blood flow: topography and motor learning. In Lassen N, Ingvar D, Raichle M, and Friberg L (eds) Brain Work and Mental Activity. Alfred Benzon Symposium 31: 280-90.

Minsky M (1986) The Society of Mind. New York: Simon & Schuster.

Nagy W, Berninger V, Abbott R, Vaughan K, Vermeulin K (2003) Relationship of morphology and other language skills to literacy skills in at-risk second graders and at-risk fourth grade writers. Journal of Educational Psychology 95: 730-42.

Nicolson RI, Fawcett AJ (2001) Dyslexia, learning and the cerebellum. In Wolf M (ed.) Dyslexia, Fluency and the Brain. Timonium, MD: York Press, pp. 159-87.

Nicolson RI, Fawcett AJ, Berry E, Jenkins I, Dean P, Brooks D (1999) Association of abnormal cerebellar activation with motor learning difficulties in dyslexic adults. The Lancet 353: 1662-7.

Nobre A, Allison T, McCarthy G (1994) Word recognition in the human inferior temporal lobe. Nature 372: 260-3.

Posner M, Petersen S, Fox P, Raichle M (1988) Localization of cognitive operations in the human brain. Science 240: 1627-31.

Psychological Corporation (2001) Wechsler Individual Achievement Test, 2nd edn. WIAT II. San Antonio TX: The Psychological Corporation.

Psychological Corporation (2003) Wechsler Individual Intelligence Test for Children, 4th edn. WISC IV. San Antonio TX: The Psychological Corporation.

Raskind W, Hsu L, Thomson J, Berninger V, Wijsman E (2000) Family aggregation of dyslexic phenotypes. Behavior Genetics 30: 385-96.

Richards T, Berninger V, Aylward E, Richards A, Thomson J, Nagy W, Carlisle J, Dager S, Abbott R (2002) Reproducibility of proton MR spectroscopic imaging: comparison of dyslexic and normal reading children and effects of treatment on brain lactate levels during language tasks. American Journal of Neuroradiology 23: 1678-85.

Richards T, Corina D, Serafini S, Steury K, Dager S, Marro K, Abbott R, Maravilla K, Berninger V (2000) Effects of phonologically-driven treatment for dyslexia on lactate levels as measured by proton MRSI. American Journal of Radiology 21: 916-22.

Richards T, Dager S, Corina D, Serafini S, Heidel A, Steury K, Strauss W, Hayes C, Abbott R, Kraft S, Shaw D, Posse S, Berninger V (1999) Dyslexic children have abnormal chemical brain activation during reading-related language tasks. American Journal of Neuroradiology 20: 1393-8.

Seidenberg M, McClelland J (1989) A distributed developmental model of word recognition and naming. Psychological Review 96: 523-68.

Swanson HL, Berninger V (1995) The role of working memory in learning disabled readers' comprehension. Intelligence 21: 83-108.

Swanson HL, Berninger V (1996) Individual differences in children's working memory and writing skills. Journal of Experimental Child Psychology 63: 358-85.

Torgesen J, Wagner R, Rashotte C (1999) Test of Word Reading Efficiency (TOWRE). Austin TX: PRO-ED.

Traweek D, Berninger V (1997) Comparison of beginning literacy programs: alternative paths to the same learning outcome. Learning Disability Quarterly 20: 160-8.

Treiman R (1985) Onsets and rimes as units of spoken syllables: evidence from children. Journal of Experimental Child Psychology 39: 161-81.

Van Mier H, Temple L, Perlmutter J, Raichle M, Petersen S (1998) Changes in brain activity during motor learning measured with PET: effects of hand performance and practice. Journal of Neurophysiology 80: 2177-99.

Venezky R (1970) The Structure of English Orthography. The Hague: Mouton.

Venezky R (1995) From orthography to psychology to reading. In Berninger VW (ed.) The Varieties of Orthographic Knowledge II: Relationships to Phonology Reading and Writing. Dordrecht: Kluwer, pp. 23-46.

Venezky R (1999) The American Way of Spelling. New York: Guilford.

Wagner R, Torgesen J, Rashotte C (1999) Comprehensive Test of Phonological Processing (CTOPP). Austin TX: PRO-ED.

Whitaker D, Berninger V, Johnston J, Swanson L (1994) Intraindividual differences in levels of language in intermediate grade writers: implications for the translating process. Learning and Individual Differences 6: 107-30.

Wijsman E, Peterson D, Leutennegger A, Thomson J, Goddard K, Hsu L, Berninger V, Raskind W (2000) Segregation analysis of phenotypic components of learning disabilities I. Nonword memory and digit span. American Journal of Human Genetics 67: 631–46.

Wilkinson G (1993) Wide Range Achievement Test – Third Edition. Wilmington DE: Wide Range.

Wise B, Olson R, Treiman R (1990) Subsyllabic units in computerized reading instruction: onset-rime versus post-vowel segmentation. Journal of Experimental Child Psychology 49: 1–19.

Wolf M (1986) Rapid alternating stimulus (RAS) naming: a longitudinal study in average and impaired readers. Brain and Language 27: 360–79.

Wolf M (ed.) (2001) Dyslexia, Fluency and the Brain. Baltimore: York Press.

Wolf M, Bally H, Morris R (1986) Automaticity retrieval processes and reading: a longitudinal study in average and impaired reading. Child Development 57: 988–1000.

Wolf M, Bowers P (1999) The double-deficit hypothesis for the developmental dyslexias. Journal of Educational Psychology 91: 415–38.

Wolf M, Bowers P, Biddle K (2000) Naming-speed processes timing and reading: a conceptual review. Journal of Learning Disabilities 33: 387–407.

Woodcock R, McGrew K, Mather N (2001) Woodcock–Johnson III. Itasca IL: Riverside.

CHAPTER 6

The theory and practice of specialist literacy teaching[1]

JOHN RACK

In this chapter I shall review some of the research studies that have evaluated specialist literacy teaching programmes and also present results from some Dyslexia Institute projects that have used these methods in applied settings. I shall argue that there is strong evidence that children with dyslexia can improve their literacy skills when given teaching that is appropriate to their profile of strengths and weaknesses. Research evidence points to the need for a balance of decoding and text-based strategies and suggests that the greatest gains come when multi-sensory links are made explicit. I argue that there are important individual differences that can mask differences in group studies and that the optimum benefits will only be achieved if these are taken into account.

Practitioners know that there are children who do not respond to the normal classroom and home-based teaching of early literacy skills, but do seem to make progress when they are taught in a different way by specialist teachers. The methods used by specialist teachers have been informed by theory, but it is probably fair to say that the ongoing development of 'what works' has been primarily an applied exercise. Teaching pioneers from Samuel Orton, through Gillingham and Stillman, Hickey, Hornsby, Bramley, Walker have developed and refined the core multi-sensory methods in the light of their direct teaching experience. This is the way that many techniques in teaching – and in other disciplines – have evolved, and no criticism is intended. Most people in the field of dyslexia and reading difficulties will know, and have great respect for, highly experienced teachers who seem to find ways of getting the most challenging pupils to learn. They do this not necessarily because they know a lot of theory but because they have a wealth of experience to draw on. One feature of this kind of expertise is that it can be hard to describe, and hard to pass on to others; teachers can often more easily show what they know rather than explain it, hence the typical 'apprentice' model of training used in education. However, this can create a problem if the effectiveness of the

---

1 The SPELLIT project described in this chapter was supported by grants from the Community Fund, WH Smith and the Department for Education and Skills.

methods is challenged. For example, someone may come along and say that there is a better way of doing things, or that this kind of 'expert' teaching can be done by others with less training and experience. To some extent, these challenges can be responded to by pointing out that experience shows that other people doing things in other ways often does not work. But an argument based on experience is never as satisfactory as one based on 'evidence'. This is why there is a need for theory and research alongside practical experience. Let us begin therefore by looking at what the current research evidence is telling us about effective intervention.

Hatcher et al. (1994) conducted a study with 7-year-old children in Cumbria who were experiencing difficulties learning to read. The children were randomly assigned to 'no training', 'reading alone', 'phonological skills training alone' and 'reading with phonology' groups. The reading programme was based on the Reading Recovery programme of Clay (1985), which includes extensive practice in reading from books, with progression to the next level of difficulty only when a consistent level of accuracy (94%) has been achieved. The 'phonology-alone' group followed a programme of activities including rhyme detection, identification of sounds within words, segmenting, substituting and deleting sounds from words. The reading plus phonology (R+P) group had roughly half the amount of time on each of the R and P programmes plus specific linkage activities that included letter–sound associations, sound categorization supported by plastic letters and phonologically based writing tasks.

The mean reading ages on the British Abilities Scales test of Word Reading are shown in Table 6.1, along with the ratio gain in months of reading age per month of elapsed time. A similar pattern was obtained for measures of prose reading accuracy and comprehension and measures of spelling.

Table 6.1 Mean reading ages on the British Abilities Scales test of Word Reading

BAS reading age	Pre-test	Post-test	Ratio gain (months/month)
Reading and phonology	5.85	6.73	1.42
Reading alone	5.90	6.60	1.07
Phonology alone	5.90	6.55	1.05
Control	5.96	6.60	1.03

It can be seen that the greatest gains in reading were made by the reading and phonology group who received the programme in which phonological activities and reading experience were linked explicitly. The effect size for gains in reading for the reading and phonology group compared to the control group was 0.53 (Hatcher, 2003). What this means is that, for every unit of improvement made by the control group (in this case months of reading age), the reading and phonology group was making 'half as much progress again'. Based on their initial findings Hatcher and colleagues went on to develop the reading intervention programme using 'sound linkage' methods and this programme has been used extensively in Cumbrian schools. Hatcher (2003) reported further data on the effectiveness of the reading intervention approach for a group of 10-year-old children with dyslexia. Those children made 2.89 months of progress in reading for every month on the programme and 2.07 months per month in spelling, providing further data on the effectiveness of the approach.

Wise et al. (2000) tested two models of intervention, which involved groups of four students working on their own computer with one input from one teacher. Two hundred children from Colorado took part; they were aged between 7 and 12 and in the lowest 10% on a measure of word reading. There were two intervention groups, both of which were given computer reading experience in which they read graded stories on the screen with the opportunity to request speech-feedback on unknown words. One intervention group was termed the 'phonological analysis' (PA) group and the children in this group were given additional activities and computer exercises learning about phonemes through their association with articulatory motor movements (Lindamood and Lindamood, 1975). The second intervention group, termed 'accurate reading in context' (ARC), had a greater emphasis on accurate reading of stories, on and off the computer, and were given explicit training in comprehension strategies.

The students received training in half-hour sessions over a period of 4 months amounting to a total of around 29 hours; they were post-tested at the end of the intervention and a year later.

Table 6.2 shows that both the ARC and PA programmes were making progress at a rate that allowed them to begin to catch up with their peers. The gains of seven to nine points in reading were achieved with around 29 hours' teaching and this therefore shows rates of growth per hour compare favourably to other studies, as discussed later. There was no untreated control group in this study so the effect sizes reflect the gains expressed in standard deviation units. There were few differences between the two intervention conditions. The PA group showed an advantage on the post-

Table 6.2 Comparison of phonological analysis and accurate reading in context

	Pre-test standard score	Gain in standard score units	Effect size
Word reading (WRAT)			
ARC	74.6	7.0	0.31
PA	74.0	9.0	0.26
Spelling (WRAT)			
ARC	75.9	3.1	0.04
PA	76.4	3.6	−0.15

training tests on measures of phoneme awareness and phonological decoding (non-word reading), which is perhaps not surprising as their programme had included more work on these skills. Thus, as with the Hatcher et al. study, the group who received most training in phonological awareness made the greatest gains on measures of that skill. However, the benefit of improved phonological skills did not translate to advantages on other measures of word identification and comprehension or on measures of spelling. There was one exception to this for the younger children in the study who did show advantages in word reading, but only on untimed tests. The ARC group, on the whole, showed advantages on timed reading tests. Thus the more phonologically explicit training programme was effective in producing benefits in terms of phonological skills, but not in terms of more general reading skills (and at some expense in terms of speed).

Torgesen et al. (2001) conducted a study using 60 pupils from Florida, aged between 8 and 12, selected to be in the lower 2% of the population on national norms. The pupils received very intensive intervention amounting to an average of almost 68 hours of instruction over a 2-month period. Two intervention groups were compared; both were taught letter–sound decoding rules, but the emphasis of each programme was different. The auditory discrimination in depth (ADD) group was also based on the Lindamood programme and was similar to the PA group from the Colorado study. The embedded phonics (EP) group had a greater emphasis on letter–sound decoding rules, but in the context of text reading. This programme was similar in many ways to the accurate reading in context of Wise et al. and to the reading intervention group of Hatcher et al. in which rules are applied and reinforced in context.

Table 6.3 shows the standard scores on a measure of word identification for the two intervention groups immediately before and after the programmes and at two follow-up points. The percentage of children scoring below the low end of the average range, defined here as a standard score of

Table 6.3 Standard scores in Torgesen et al. (2001)

	Pre-test	Post-test	One-year follow up	Two-year follow up
Word attack				
ADD	68.5 (100)	96.4 (16)	90.7	91.8 (31)
EP	70.1 (100)	90.3 (54)	87.0	89.9 (46)
Word identification				
ADD	68.9 (100)	82.4 (72)	82.7	87.0 (61)
EP	66.4 (100)	80.5 (83)	78.2	83.9 (67)
Passage comprehension				
ADD	83.0 (65)	91.0 (40)	92.8	94.7 (15)
EP	82.2 (75)	92.0 (46)	91.5	96.9 (21)

90, is shown in brackets for the three times of measurement. It can be seen that the participants in the Torgesen et al. study made substantial progress over the 2 months of the intervention and, more importantly, these gains were maintained at the one-year and two-year follow ups.

As can be seen in Table 6.3, post-test and follow-up scores on measures of single word identification and passage comprehension were remarkably similar for the two groups. The ADD group was found to make greater gains on measures of phonological decoding during the intervention, however this advantage for the ADD group was not maintained at the follow-up tests. Moreover, this short-term advantage in terms of phonological decoding did not translate to more general benefits in terms of other reading skills.

Discussion

Torgesen et al. suggest that a useful measurement of progress is the standard score gain divided by the number of hours of intervention. For word identification the gain per hour was 0.20 for the ADD group and 0.21 for the EP group. Putting this another way, 10 hours of intervention would produce a gain of 2 points; 50 hours would produce a gain of 10 points and so on. The figure of about 0.2 compares very closely with the results of other studies. For example, the gain ratios for word recognition were 0.22 to 0.33 from the Wise et al. (2000) study, discussed above, and a similar figure of 0.22 was found in an earlier study by Wise et al. (1999). The gain ratios for phonological decoding in the Torgesen et al. study were 0.41 for the ADD programme and 0.30 for EP, again comparing well with 0.31 from Wise et al. (1999). Gains for passage comprehension were the least impressive in the Torgesen study at 0.12 of the ADD group and 0.15 for the EP group and the same was true for the Wise et al. study where a gain of 0.14 was obtained. Whilst this might be thought of as rather disappointing, the participants in these studies were typically starting out with better comprehension levels. At the end of the intervention, as the above table shows, comprehension remained the least of the children's difficulties.

The evidence from Hatcher et al.'s work is that improving poor readers' phonological skills does not, on its own, bring about substantial improvement in reading skills. Rather, development of phonological skills linked to reading experience and practice is required. The inclusion of phonological skills training is important, since reading experience and practice, on its own, does not produce significant gains. Hatcher et al.'s work, building on Bradley and Bryant's (1985) seminal study, suggests that children with poor phonology need the linkage between spoken sounds and written letters to be made explicit. Moreover, it suggests that the teaching of word-level and sub-word-level decoding strategies must be explicitly linked to reading of connected text. In the reading plus phonology group the teachers would highlight and consolidate taught rules during structured reading practice. This is an important practical point: it is not simply a matter of teaching phonic rules and then practising them in isolation; rather the practice provides opportunities to reinforce the rules and to demonstrate their use explicitly in context.

The work of Wise et al. and of Torgesen and colleagues is consistent in showing that the same kinds of results can be obtained using two rather different methods. Both research groups used a programme that emphasized decoding rules with a highly structured progression and an emphasis on awareness of sound patterns via articulatory gestures. These were phonological analysis in the Colorado studies and auditory discrimination in depth in the Florida study. Both groups also used an approach that emphasized the application of word decoding skills in context – accurate reading in context in Colorado and embedded phonics in Florida. It should be stressed that the programmes were delivered by experienced specialist teachers and that the differences were more in the 'mix' of the activities rather than one programme having all one type of activity and the contrasting programme having completely different activities.

The most striking aspect of the Florida study is the rapid gains in standard scores that can be made with very intensive intervention. As has been pointed out, these gains 'per hour' are not necessarily better than has been achieved by some other studies over a longer period but the effect for the individual is dramatic. Importantly, these rapid gains seem also to be sustainable. The argument is similar to that for early intervention – progress can be made at a later time but it is clearly much better to effect the 'catch-up' at an early time and so avoid a constant feeling of being behind despite making progress.

Intervention in practice

The Dyslexia Institute, for over 30 years, has been delivering individualized multi-sensory literacy teaching to children and adults, many of whom could not, or did not, learn to read, write and spell with traditional methods. Rack and Walker (1994) presented an analysis of the progress of 145 pupils who had attended the Dyslexia Institute in Sheffield. Prior to entering the Dyslexia Institute programme, pupils had made an average of just over 6 months' progress in reading per calendar year and just under 6 months' progress in spelling per calendar year. After about 2 years in teaching, the rate of progress of the Sheffield pupils had doubled so that, on average, progress in reading was just over one year in a calendar year and spelling about one year per calendar year. Thus, pupils were, on average, 'catching up' in reading and making age-appropriate progress in spelling. A number of specialist residential schools have a track record of publishing their progress results (for a review, see Thomson 1990). In some cases, progress of more than 2 years in reading and 18 months in spelling per calendar year has been obtained.

Pupils attending the Dyslexia Institute are given standardized tests twice a year to assess their progress. Table 6.4 shows the scores on the Wide Range Achievement Tests of reading and spelling given one year apart for a sample of pupils attending three of the teaching centres at the relevant time. The sample consisted of all those who had a full assessment that enabled a Dyslexia Index (Turner 1997) to be calculated and who had received two progress tests. The 113 pupils were divided according to severity, assessed using the Dyslexia Index. Thirty-nine pupils were rated as most severe (categories E and F) and 74 were rated as less severe (categories C and D). Characteristics of the groups, and progress made on the Wide Range Achievement Test in Reading and Spelling are shown in the table below. Note that the WRAT tests are given at the same time each year which, for some, could be fairly soon after their initial assessment and, for others, could be after a longer time during which teaching has been provided.

Table 6.4 Wide Range Achievement Test scores of reading and spelling

	Total sample N = 113		Most severe N = 39		Less severe N = 74	
	Mean	SD	Mean	SD	Mean	SD
Age	9.7	1.77	10.26	1.72	9.40	1.73
IQ (WISC-III)	111	13.2	118.1	12.62	107.7	12.98
Reading (WORD)	84.7	11.11	80.90	10.51	86.35	11.03
Spelling (WORD)	82.50	9.07	78.59	8.52	4.57	8.72
WRAT Scores						
Reading 1	87.15	13.62	85.54	13.97	88.61	13.43
Reading 2	94.00	12.98	94.82	14.13	93.57	12.42
Spelling 1	82.15	10.12	79.56	9.16	83.47	10.39
Spelling 2	86.55	10.26	83.41	9.93	88.20	10.11

The gains made for the total sample were around seven points for reading and four points for spelling, indicating that the pupils were catching up to their peers, which in both cases was statistically significant. The gains made by the more severe group were significantly larger than the gains made by the less severe group in reading ($F(1,118) = 6.71$, $p < 0.05$) but not in spelling.

It is worth emphasizing that even someone whose standard score remains the same from year to year is making progress, but that individual's ability relative to their peer-group is not changing. Thus standard scores can enable progress to be evaluated in relation to the progress that would be expected simply with the passage of time. However, this is not completely satisfactory because what would be expected for someone with average skills is not the same as for someone with weak skills. We therefore need to know what is the typical progress made by pupils who are identified as having difficulties but who do not receive any intervention. Data of this kind can best be collected as part of a research study and that is what we attempted with SPELLIT – the Dyslexia Institute's Study Programme to Evaluate Literacy Learning through Individualized Tuition (Rack and Hatcher, 2002).

In the SPELLIT research, we assessed a national sample of about 350 7-year-old pupils and selected the 240 with the weakest literacy skills to take part in the study. On average, the pupils were reading and spelling in the lower 10% on standardized tests – at around the 6-year age equivalent level compared to their chronological age of 7 years and 6 months. The sample covered a wide range on measures of general intellectual ability with the mean for the whole sample almost exactly 100, the expected population average.

The pupils from the first phase of recruitment were allocated at random to one of three groups: teaching for 2 hours per week at Dyslexia Institute centres; a programme of home support delivered by parents with guidance and training from Dyslexia Institute teachers; and a 'waiting list' control group that received no additional support from the project. The waiting list control group provided the important information about what would happen to children who are having difficulties if no extra support is given. This is the group that is so often missing in applied research as there is strong pressure to provide support once difficulties have been formally recognized. In common with other intervention studies, the waiting list control group received support after the first intervention phase.

The teaching took place over a 9-month period with a maximum of 48 hours' input provided and a similar amount of input on the home support programme. During this time the average reading age for those in the teaching group went from 5 years and 9 months to 6 years and 8 months. This was reflected in a gain of around two standard score points, on average, showing that there is some 'catching up' to age-group norms. The waiting group did make progress – from 5 years and 10 months, on average, to 6 years and 4 months. This reflects progress at a slower rate than would be expected and thus they were falling further behind their age peers. Their standard scores were, on average, about two points lower than at the start of the programme. The home support (only) group progressed at a rate somewhere in between. Their reading increased, on average, from 5 years and 10 months to 6 years and 7 months and their standard score increased by about one point, on average.

The gains made by pupils in the teaching and home support groups may sound small but they show that children were, on average, keeping pace with their peers at a time when their peers were moving ahead quite fast. This is underlined by the scores for the waiting group which, although making gains, was falling further behind its peers.

Differential response to the teaching and home support programmes

For comparison with previous studies, which have tended to select participants with poor phonological skills and poor reading, we divided our sample into sub-groups. The resulting sub-groups were small and the findings must therefore be regarded as tentative, but they point to a finding that we think is interesting and, potentially, important. Figure 6.1 shows the progress made by the pupils with

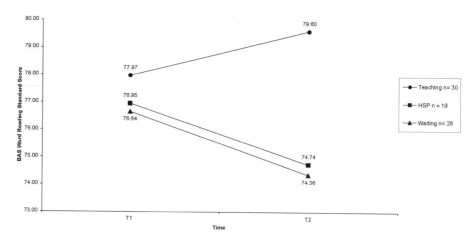

Figure 6.1 Progress made by pupils with more severe difficulties.

more severe difficulties reading, standard scores below 85 and lower scores (< 7) on the Test of Auditory Analysis Skills (Rosner, 1993).

As was the case with the Dyslexia Institute sample described above, the benefits of teaching were greater for pupils with the more severe difficulties. Comparing the teaching and waiting groups, there is a significant statistical interaction ($F1,56 = 4.209$, $p < 0.05$) with an effect size of 0.65. Children with the more severe difficulties seemed not to do particularly well with the home support programme (HSP). Firstly, we found that they were overrepresented in the group that withdrew from the programme. The dropout rate was much higher for the HSP group in general but, perhaps unsurprisingly, those with the most severe difficulties found it harder to persist. Secondly, as can be seen in Figure 6.1, those with severe difficulties who did persist with the programme, made less progress.

A comparison of the teaching and the HSP programmes for the sub-group who have more severe difficulties gives an effect size of 0.56 for reading and 0.33 for spelling. This is an important contrast as it allows us to reject the possibility that the gains made were due to a non-specific effect of receiving extra attention (a placebo or 'Hawthorne' effect).

When we looked at the pupils who had less severe difficulties, we found the opposite pattern – at least for reading. As can be seen in Figure 6.2, pupils with relatively good reading and phonological skills seem to do better with the home support programme. (The gains made by those in the HSP group are significant, but the interaction is not significant ($F = 2.09$).) Comparing pupils with these characteristics in the HSP and the waiting groups, there is a difference of four standard score points, which gives an effect size of 0.42.

The different pattern of results for the two sub-groups is, we believe, an important finding. It is not the case that one programme is always best; one programme is better for pupils with one set of characteristics and another

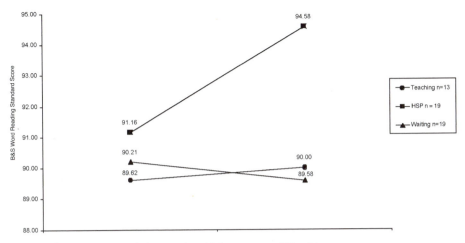

Figure 6.2 Progress made by pupils with less severe difficulties.

programme is better for children with a different set of characteristics. The findings suggest that those children with the more severe difficulties with reading and phonological awareness are those who need the fine-grained structured language teaching used in the Dyslexia Institute and other programmes. However, those children who had less severe reading and phonological difficulties seemed to benefit more from some aspects of the HSP. Our tentative interpretation is that the HSP was providing more opportunities to practise decoding skills and other strategies in context and thus promoting greater reading experience (giving more 'exposure to print'). These results suggest that we need to broaden our ideas about what makes particular kinds of interventions effective, to ask instead what kinds of interventions are effective for which children and at what stages of literacy learning.

The findings of the Dyslexia Institute's 'SPELLIT' suggest one reason why other studies, such as the Colorado and Florida studies, have not found differences between the two intervention programmes that were compared. If the sample contains some children who benefit more from one programme than the other, that effect would not show up if there are also within the sample a second group of children who show the opposite pattern. In the SPELLIT study, the sample was deliberately heterogeneous – the children were poor at reading but their other abilities such as phonological skills and general conceptual abilities were free to vary. Whilst these findings need to be investigated further with a larger sample, the clear suggestion is that differences in programme outcomes are more likely to be found for sub-groups.

General discussion

In this chapter, we have examined four important intervention studies from Cumbria, Colorado, Florida and York. Several consistent findings have emerged. First and foremost, these studies show that children who have failed to make satisfactory progress with 'standard' methods can make good progress with the kind of multi-sensory teaching methods that originated with Orton and have been developed and refined by organizations such as the Dyslexia Institute over the past 30 years. The effect size statistic is typically around 0.5 which means that for every unit of progress made by the control group, the intervention group makes the same progress and half as much again. Second, the findings are consistent in suggesting that developing phonological skills is necessary but not sufficient to bring about literacy gains. Hatcher et al.'s data, for example, require us to reject a strong version of the phonological deficit theory, which predicts that those whose phonological skills improve the most will improve the most in reading. In that study, the 'phonology only' group improved most on the phonological tests but the reading and phonology group improved most in reading. Thus, it seems that there is a certain threshold of phonological awareness that needs to be reached in order to support the use of reading skills in context. However, once this threshold is reached, direct teaching of strategies and provision of structured opportunities for practice is also needed. It is an open question as to whether other factors to do with underlying cognitive abilities, self-esteem, motivation or something else altogether may play a role in shaping progress. It seems reasonable to suppose that other factors will be relevant but further research is needed to establish what these are.

Thirdly, the Colorado and Florida studies discussed here show that similar gains can be achieved with different kinds of programmes when delivered by skilled teachers. It should be stressed that the programmes being compared both involved systematic teaching of phonic rules with the differences primarily in the emphasis or balance of the components of the programme. Most researchers would find it difficult to include an intervention programme that they believed would be unlikely to yield *some* benefits. It should also be noted that skilled teachers will often find a way of adapting activities according to the individual needs of the child; or, in other words, a good teacher will be doing different things with different children, even though that activity might be listed as the same thing on a research protocol! With this in mind, the findings from the SPELLIT study that suggest individual differences in response to two different programmes are rather encouraging. The SPELLIT results also introduce a note of caution when interpreting differences (or lack of differences) between programme outcomes as differential effects may be masked by individual differences.

In conclusion, I suggest that there is a pleasing convergence between the research findings and the practical experiences of skilled, specialist teachers. At the core of the teaching methods that originated with Orton is the idea of making multi-sensory connections between print, sound, movement and meaning to support the learning of reading and spelling skills. The weight of evidence from the studies reviewed here, and from others, is that learning programmes need to include a range of activities, working at different levels of text, and that the benefits are greatest when the linkage is made explicit. The evidence of studies that have used different models of providing support is encouraging as it suggests that there are important roles for computer activities and for home support activities alongside individual and class-based methods.

References

Bradley LL, Bryant PE (1985) Rhyme and reason in reading and spelling. Ann Arbor: University of Michigan Press.

Clay M (1985) The Early Detection of Reading Difficulties. Auckland: Heinemann.

Hatcher P (2003) A conventional and successful approach to helping dyslexic children acquire literacy. Dyslexia 9: 140–5.

Hatcher P, Hulme C, Ellis AW (1994) Ameliorating early reading failure by integrating the teaching of reading and phonological skills: the phonological linkage hypothesis. Child Development 65: 41–57.

Lindamood P, Lindamood C (1975) Auditory Discrimination in Depth. Columbus OH: Science Research Associates Division, Macmillan/McGraw-Hill.

Rack JP, Hatcher J (2002) A Three-year National Research Project to Investigate Literacy Difficulties in Primary School Children, to Develop Methods of Assessment and to Evaluate Different Methods of Teaching including Specialist Teaching and Home Support Programmes. Staines: The Dyslexia Institute

Rack JP, Walker J (1994) Does Dyslexia Institute teaching work? Dyslexia Review 2: 12–17.

Rosner J (1993) Helping Children Overcome Learning Difficulties, 3rd edn. New York: Walker.

Thomson ME (1990) Developmental Dyslexia, 3rd edn. London: Whurr.

Torgesen JK, Alexander AW, Wagner RK, Voeller K, Conway T, Rose E (2001) Intensive remedial instruction for children with severe reading disabilities: immediate and long-term outcomes from two instructional approaches. Journal of Learning Disabilities 34: 33–58.

Turner M (1997) The Psychological Assessment of Dyslexia. London: Whurr.

Wise BW, Ring J, Olson RK (1999) Training phonological awareness with and without attention to articulation. Journal of Experimental Child Psychology 72: 271–304.

Wise BW, Ring J, Olson RK (2000) Individual differences in gains from computer-assisted remedial reading with more emphasis on phonological analysis or accurate reading in context. Journal of Experimental Child Psychology 77: 197–235.

CHAPTER 7

Dyslexia and English as an additional language (EAL): towards a greater understanding

LINDA SIEGEL, IAN SMYTHE

Case studies

Sandra (Pavan)

Sandra, 7 years old, speaks Urdu at home and goes to school in a partially Urdu-speaking environment – that is, English in the classroom and Urdu in the playground. Her pronunciation and vocabulary appear to be similar to those of her classmates. However, her reading and spelling skills are developing more slowly than other children of the same age. Are her difficulties the result of her bilingual background or is she dyslexic?

Henry

Henry, 13 years old, was brought up in Hong Kong, but moved to Canada at the age of 10. He studied some English during his schooling in Hong Kong, using norms for monolingual children. His word reading and spelling skills are appropriate for his age. However, he has trouble sounding out new words, his vocabulary skills are not well developed and his score on a reading comprehension test is at the tenth percentile. Does Henry have dyslexia or are his problems with reading comprehension and phonological decoding a result of his Chinese language background?

Gareth

Gareth, 10 years old, lives in Wales. In Wales, a child may be educated through the medium of either English or Welsh. Furthermore, the language of the home may not be the language of instruction in the school that the child attends. Gareth's parents decided to send him to a Welsh-medium school. Consequently, some children will start at a Welsh-medium school not knowing any of the Welsh language. The implications of this are that some children cannot speak to their parents in the language in which they are learning. Although this may appear to be the same as for Gujarati speakers who cannot discuss homework with their children in English, the difference is that there are few resources available to a child who experiences difficulty in this situation. A similar situation exists in Canada, where there are two official languages, English and French. Many parents elect to send their children to French immersion in which the children, although English speaking at home, are educated in French. Gareth's parents, who speak English at home, wanted their son to be educated in a Welsh-medium school.

Gareth had difficulties reading the material for his courses, especially when a course required a great deal of reading. When it came to attending college, Gareth was unable to apply for the disabled students' allowance, which would have provided the technology to support him, because there were no tests for dyslexia available in Welsh to assess whether or not he was dyslexic.

Michael

Michael's parents are of Afro-Caribbean background and, despite their frequent discussions with the school, they were told that their son's difficulties were due to his accent and language and not dyslexia. Only when he left school, without qualifications, and obtained a formal assessment through the disability officer of his local job centre, was it realized that his difficulties were consistent with those of monolingual dyslexics. The education system had failed him by making assumptions that were incorrect and failing to cater for his needs.

Implications

These true cases illustrate a number of issues and all of these cases raise questions.

In Sandra's case the following questions, among others, emerge:

- Were Sandra's vocabulary and pronunciation similar to those of her native English-speaking classmates? How can these be assessed?
- Were Sandra's reading and spelling skills significantly lower than those of children of her grade level?
- If there are only norms for native English-speaking children, how can we find the answers to these questions?
- How can we develop norms for EAL children? Does their first language matter – that is, if the child's first language is Chinese and another's is Spanish, will that influence the development of their literacy skills in English?

The questions are similar for Henry's case but there are additional ones. In Henry's case, the following questions, among others, emerge:

- How do we measure reading comprehension? What impact does cultural and linguistic background have on the measurement?
- The passages in reading comprehension tests may involve background knowledge, vocabulary and understanding of culturally specific information. How can we be sure that Henry's low score is actually a comprehension problem and not the result of a lack of vocabulary or culturally specific knowledge?

Gareth's case raises the following questions, among others:

- If countries have an official policy of bilingualism and if students are being educated in a language that is not the language of their home ('immersion'), are resources available if they experience reading and spelling difficulties?
- What type of resources are available for assessment and intervention in these 'immersion' programmes?

Michael's case raises the following additional questions:

- How can our assessments accurately take account of dialect differences?
- How can the system deal with cases like Michael?
- What type of programmes do we need to prevent, or at least reduce, the severity of literacy problems for students like Sandra, Henry, Gareth and Michael?

In this chapter we will explore some of the answers to these questions.

Dyslexia versus English as an additional language (EAL) difficulties

All of these students have similar problems; they are having difficulty in reading and/or spelling and are being educated in a language other than English, their first language. When children attend a school in a situation where their first language is not the language of instruction, and they start to experience difficulties with the acquisition of reading, spelling and/or writing skills, the question of possible dyslexia is raised. Specifically, the issue is whether or not the student has dyslexia or whether the problem is a lack of proficiency in English. One of the critical issues in the education of multi-cultural students is an attempt to understand what happens when language-minority children and youths experience academic difficulties in school. Specifically, the issue is whether or not the student has dyslexia or whether the problem is a lack of proficiency in English.

Defining dyslexia

An examination of these issues needs to start with a definition of dyslexia. We propose the following:

> Dyslexia is a difficulty in the acquisition of literacy skills that is neurological in origin. It is evident when accurate and fluent word reading, spelling and writing develop very incompletely or with great difficulty. This does not negate the existence of co-morbid difficulties, including receptive and expressive oral language deficits, developmental coordination difficulties and dyscalculia. The manifestation of dyslexia in any individual will depend not only upon individual cognitive differences, but also the language used.

Using the term 'literacy skills' allows not only reading and spelling to be included but also comprehension. The second part of the definition may be recognized as being an adaptation of the BPS definition, which in turn is based on the Netherlands Health Ministry definition. 'Accurate and fluent' is now also at the core of US definitions (for example, the definition given by the International Dyslexia Association and the National Institute of Child and Human Health Development). The third part of the definition reminds us that these individuals often have other conditions. For example, speech difficulties are often found in the dyslexic individual. Developmental co-ordination difficulties (otherwise known as dyspraxia) such as poor handwriting skills and difficulties with tying shoe laces are often quoted as indicators of dyslexia, but are not dyslexia in themselves.

Assessing dyslexia

To assess the possibility of dyslexia, an assessment battery should include some essential measures. In order to assess reading ability, assessment should include a measure of word recognition skills. Reading single words is an important skill to measure; this skill is critical for gaining meaning from print. Tests of reading single real words typically require the individual to read a set of words aloud.

Phonological processing is another critical skill that is the basis of a reading disability (see, for example, Bruck, 1990; Felton et al., 1990; Shafrir and Siegel, 1994). This is a key skill necessary for decoding words in an alphabetic language and can be assessed by the reading of pseudowords – pronounceable combinations of letters that produce a 'word' with no meaning. A reasonable question to ask is why the reading of pseudowords is important. When do we ever read words that are not real? It is important to remember that when we encounter a word that we have never seen before it is like a pseudoword. We must sound it out. Guessing from context is very inaccurate (Share and Stanovich, 1995). Decoding this new word is possible only if we know the letter–sound correspondences of the language in question. When an individual reads a particular word correctly, there is no indication of whether she or he has merely memorized this word; this is not the case in the reading of pseudowords. Therefore, the assessment of reading pseudowords is essential to identify phonological awareness difficulties. Reading of pseudowords can be assessed by the Word Attack sub-test in the Woodcock–Johnson Reading Mastery Test – Revised (Woodcock, 1987).

It is necessary that the assessment battery includes a reading comprehension test. Reading comprehension tests typically require the student to read a passage and answer multiple-choice questions about the passage. These tests are usually timed. This means that the student may know the answers but not have enough time to finish enough of the questions to achieve a good score. Low scores may be a result of slow reading, not actually a failure to comprehend the material.

Reading comprehension tests may also assume that the readers possess a certain knowledge about the culture. Unlike the assessment of reading single words or pseudowords, the assessment of reading comprehension is more complex. Text processing is usually measured by reading sentences and paragraphs. In both cases, there are clues to the meaning of words from the surrounding context. In this case, it is difficult to assess whether an individual read the word, or made a good guess based on the context. Sentences or paragraphs can be read silently or aloud. If we were to assess silent reading there would be no way of assessing what the individual is actually reading.

Spelling is another required skill in an academic setting. Therefore, a test of dictation words should be included in the assessment battery.

There should also be an assessment of writing skills. There are various reasons why this type of assessment is quite difficult. The time needed to allow someone to write may be extensive because one must allow time for planning as well as the actual writing. Moreover, many individuals have learned to use a computer and prefer to write using a computer. Therefore, a proper assessment of writing might use a computer but this is not feasible in most assessment contexts. It may be acceptable to ask the individual to bring in a sample of his or her writing but some type of brief assessment in the context of the assessment is useful. The scoring of these written products is subjective and there does not appear to be agreement on what constitutes a widely accepted scoring system. However, Berninger (1994) has proposed a system that appears to have potential as a system to evaluate writing. She suggests six dimensions to evaluate writing: (a) handwriting quality (legibility); (b) handwriting fluency (number of words copied within time limits); (c) spelling single words from dictation (on standardized lists of increasing difficulty); (d) spelling in composition (percentage of correctly spelled words); (e) composition fluency (number of words produced within time limits); and (f) composition quality (content and organization of paragraph construction).

For all of these assessments, it is important to determine if the errors that a child makes are reflective of his or her first language. In tests measuring reading, spelling and oral language proficiency, it may be that the errors that a child makes are reflective of his or her first language. Alternatively, they may be the same type that native speakers make. Assessments of working memory, syntactic awareness, visual and auditory processing may also be useful.

The role of the first language

The first language of the child can make a difference in the ease or difficulty with which English can be acquired. We compared groups of children with six different first languages – Chinese, Farsi, Slavic languages, Japanese, Romance languages and Tagalog – in their learning of literacy skills to native English speakers in the school classroom. The results indicated that children who spoke languages in which there were few if any inflections (Chinese, Japanese) had poorer scores in English syntax tasks, and children who spoke a Slavic language (these languages are heavily inflected) performed better than native speakers. Children who had experience with Chinese and Japanese performed very well in word-reading tasks, in some cases better than native English speakers, but worse on phonological tasks. These results show the importance of considering the first language in the assessment of ESL children.

The role of IQ

Although, traditionally, a discrepancy between IQ scores in achievement has been used to define dyslexia, more recent conceptualizations do not include the use of IQ but concentrate on significantly low academic achievement. In addition, IQ tests require expressive language, understanding of vocabulary, culture-specific knowledge, and verbal memory. It is obvious that administering an IQ test to language-minority children and youths is problematic because they are at a disadvantage in terms of language and culture.

An 'intelligence test' is still sometimes used to allocate resources, which does not make sense, particularly when there is so much cultural bias inherent in all of the tests. It is worth remembering that they are not valid for identification of the dyslexic individual, as well as totally inappropriate for a multi-lingual population.

Despite this, some education authorities or school districts will still fail to give adequate provision without a measure of intelligence. This is surprising since even the British Psychological Society accepts that IQ is irrelevant (Siegel, 1989; BPS, 1999). Any attempt to impose a measure of intelligence should be resisted. Furthermore, it may be pointed out that many of the IQ tests have significant cultural bias and favour only those who are schooled in the taking of such tests. Therefore they are intrinsically biased against the dyslexic multi-lingual individual.

Diagnosing dyslexia

Dyslexia should be assessed with standardized achievement tests of reading, spelling and, if possible, writing. If an individual has a low score on any of these achievement tests, in the absence of co-occurring conditions such as mental retardation, severe neurological problems (such as autism) and/or severe social or emotional difficulties, then the individual may have dyslexia. The diagnosis is complicated when individuals are being educated in a language that is not their first language.

The critical question is whether their poor performance is due to a general language-related disability that would manifest itself in whatever language they were learning, or whether it is specific to the second language learning situation.

Research strategies

A number of research strategies have been used to answer these questions.

One possible strategy is to compare the performance of language-minority students who are having difficulty with first-language students who are also experiencing reading difficulties. If the magnitude and pattern of difficulties is the same in these two groups, then it is possible that it is dyslexia, not inadequate second-language skills, that is the main determining factor of the learning disability in the EAL. If the pattern is different, then it may be the second-language problem that is the major cause of the difficulty.

Another research strategy is to compare more successful and less successful learners within the EAL group and determine the patterns of differences and similarities. The study of these individual difference factors may help us understand the difficulties experienced by language-minority children and youths. The questions can be raised as to whether those whose performance is below average have a 'real learning disability' but after some exposure to the second language it seems reasonable to conclude that a student having a great deal of difficulty has a genuine disability. We do not know how much exposure is enough; hopefully, future research will answer that question.

Yet another strategy is to compare the performance of the student in his or her first and second languages. If there are indications of difficulty in the first language this would suggest that problems found with acquisition of reading and spelling skills in a second language may be related to a more general language deficit.

Literacy and EAL

A number of studies have used these research strategies to produce some answers to these questions, usually tentatively. We will review studies that address the question of individual differences in literacy development in children receiving schooling in a language other than their first language.

Phonological awareness

A number of studies have examined individual differences in groups of children with English as a second language. Typically, these studies compare children who have reading or spelling difficulties with children who seem to be making normal progress.

For example, Wade-Woolley and Siegel (1997) found that grade 2 English second language (ESL) poor readers had significantly lower scores than ESL average readers on a sound mimicry test that required them to imitate pseudowords and a *phoneme* deletion test that required them to say a word without the first phoneme – for example, pink without the /p/. The ESL poor readers showed similar difficulties to language-majority children with reading problems. These studies indicate that the children sharing reading or spelling difficulties in a second language appear to have phonological deficits in a manner similar to native English speakers with dyslexia and different from children with EAL who are not having difficulties.

Similarly, Everatt et al. (2000) studied bilingual Sylheti (Bengali) English children who spoke Sylheti at home and were educated in English in England. They divided the 7–8-year-old children into those who had low scores on a spelling dictation test and those whose scores on the same test were in the average range. The children with the low spelling scores had deficits in phonological skills including the detection of rhymes and the repetition of non-words compared to their peers matched on a non-verbal ability task who did not have disabilities. There were no differences on phonological tasks involving the repetition of words, the discrimination of sounds, or recognizing which words started with the same sound.

These studies indicate that the children who have reading or spelling difficulties in a second language appear to have phonological deficits in a manner similar to native English speakers with dyslexia and different from children with EAL who are not having difficulties.

Decoding skills

As noted earlier, the reading of pseudowords is a critical test of phonological skills. A number of studies have found differences in pseudoword reading skills between ESL readers who were experiencing word reading and spelling problems and those who were not. In general, these individual differences in the ESL group show a pattern very similar to that found with monolinguals.

We have already seen that Wade-Woolley and Siegel (1997) found that grade 2 ESL poor readers had significantly lower scores than ESL average readers on pseudoword reading tasks. Other studies have reached similar conclusions.

The Everatt et al. (2000) study of bilingual Sylheti English children, mentioned above, found that children with low spelling scores had deficits in pseudoword reading compared to the children whose spelling scores were in the average range.

Da Fontoura and Siegel (1995) studied Portuguese–English bilingual children in grades 4 to 6 who were being educated in English in Canada. The children who were poor readers on an English reading test had significantly lower scores on pseudoword reading tests than the bilingual good readers. Their pattern of performance matched monolingual reading disabled English first-language children. However, they had significantly *higher* scores on a pseudoword reading test than the native speaking English first-language reading disabled children, perhaps the result of a positive transfer from the more regular and predictable orthography of Portuguese.

Abu Rabia and Siegel (2002) studied bilingual Arabic–English children, aged 9 to 14, in Toronto. The children all spoke Arabic at home but were being educated in English. The children were divided into normally achieving readers and children with a reading disability, based on their scores on an English reading test. On word reading, visual and orthographic tasks (described earlier), the scores of the bilingual reading disabled group were similar to a group of English first-language children with a reading disability. However, on a pseudoword reading task and on the phonological task described earlier, the bilingual children with a reading disability had *higher* scores than the English first-language group with a reading disability.

D'Anguilli et al. (2002) studied bilingual Italian–English-speaking 9 to 13-year-old children in Toronto, Canada. Within the bilingual group, the less skilled readers had significantly lower scores than the skilled readers on word and pseudoword reading tests. However, the less skilled readers had significantly *higher* scores than less skilled monolingual English first-language students on word and pseudoword reading tasks, perhaps reflecting a positive transfer from the regular, predictable grapheme–phoneme correspondences in Italian to the less regular orthography of English.

In a study involving 10th grade Israeli students learning English as a foreign language, Abu Rabia (1997) measured a wide range of component skills in the two languages, English and Hebrew. He found that corresponding skills were highly correlated across languages, and that real-word and pseudo-word reading abilities were closely related both within and across languages.

Abu Rabia (1997) divided grade 10 native-speaking Hebrew students learning English as a *second* language into two groups based on their performance on Hebrew reading tests. These groups were skilled and less-skilled Hebrew readers. The skilled readers had significantly higher scores on

English word and pseudoword reading tests. In addition, the students were given a phonological task in which they had to recognize which of two pseudowords (joak-joap) was pronounced like a real English word, a visual task in which they had to recognize the correct spelling of a word in contrast to a pseudohomophone (brain-brane), and an orthographic awareness task in which they had to recognize which of two letter strings could be an English word (filv-filk). The skilled readers had significantly higher scores than the less skilled readers on the phonological and visual task but not on the orthographic task. Performance of the latter task depends on considerable experience with English print.

Spelling

Wade-Woolley and Siegel (1997) studied the spelling of grade 2 ESL poor and average readers. The ESL poor readers had significantly lower scores than the ESL good readers on pseudoword and real-word spelling tasks. If the ESL speakers were poor readers, their spelling patterns resembled those of poor readers who had English as a first language. Therefore, the difficulties of the ESL students appear to be related to underlying cognitive deficits or learning disabilities and were not a result of their language-minority status.

The Da Fontoura and Siegel (1995) study mentioned above found that children who were poor readers on an English reading test had significantly lower scores on an English spelling dictation test than the bilingual good readers. However, they had significantly *higher* scores on an English spelling test than the native speaking English L1 reading disabled children, which again could result from a positive transfer from regular, predictable Portuguese orthography.

The Abu Rabia and Siegel (2002) study mentioned above found that the bilingual group with a reading disability had higher scores on an English spelling test than the first-language English group with a reading disability.

The D'Anguilli et al. (2002) study mentioned above found that, within the bilingual group, the less skilled readers had significantly lower scores than the skilled readers on an English spelling dictation test. The less skilled readers had significantly higher scores than less skilled monolingual English first-language students, again perhaps reflecting a positive transfer from the regular, predictable grapheme-phoneme correspondences in Italian to less regular English orthography.

The spelling difficulties experienced by some ESL students appear to be a manifestation of an underlying cognitive deficit, not necessarily a result of lack of exposure to the second language. On the basis of some studies, it appears that exposure to a more regular predictable language than English such as Arabic, Italian or Portuguese may actually result in a positive transfer for EAL students, especially if they have spelling difficulties.

Fluency

The Everatt et al. (2000) study described above found that the children with spelling difficulties had lower scores on a rapid naming task that required the child to name pictures as rapidly as possible. It should be noted that the language-minority children without spelling problems had significantly *better* scores on this task than the native speakers.

Wade-Woolley et al. (1997) found that ESL grade 2 students who were poor readers made significantly more errors on a rapid naming task than ESL students who were average readers.

Summary

There appears to be a considerable range of individual differences in language-minority children and youths after the same period of exposure to English. In all these studies, there appears to be a range of abilities within the language-minority group, the performance of certain students being clearly below average and similar to a first-language dyslexic group. At this point in time there is not sufficient empirical evidence to determine whether these individual differences are a result of instruction or of differences in levels of language proficiency. The instruction explanation, which cannot be ruled out, seems unlikely as the children within these studies were typically from the same schools and classrooms where there were not large differences in instruction.

These findings suggest that individual differences may be more important than native language in determining the acquisition of literacy skills. Clearly, language-minority children and youths constitute a heterogeneous group and attention must be paid to individual differences within this group. Although definition issues are complicated and there are no easy solutions, it is clear that many language-minority children and youths are performing at levels similar to their native-speaking peers and that there is a group of individuals who appear to have difficulties in their second language that resemble learning disabilities, particularly in the area of literacy skills.

Longitudinal study

We have used a longitudinal study to attempt to provide an answer to the questions raised earlier. Since 1998 we have been conducting a longitudinal study that addresses some of the issues raised in this chapter. We have studied groups of kindergarten children from school entry at age 5 (called kindergarten in North America and reception year in the UK) until the ages of 9 to 10 in grade 4. All the children in a school district in the Vancouver area are included in the study. There are approximately 1,000 children in the sample and approximately 20% of them have English as a second or additional language. There are, in total, 38 languages spoken by the children.

The most common languages are Cantonese and Farsi, but Tagalog, Serbian, Mandarin, Spanish, Punjabi and Romanian are some of the other languages.

The children were given tests of phonological and language processing at the beginning and at the end of kindergarten (Chiappe, Siegel and Gottardo, 2002). Children with ESL performed worse than the children whose native language was English on most measures of phonological and linguistic processing. Knowledge of the alphabet and phonological awareness skills were important predictors of early reading skills in both groups.

As knowledge of the alphabet and phonological awareness skills were significant predictors of reading skill in both the children with ESL and the native English speakers it is quite possible that these measures could be used as predictors of subsequent literacy difficulties in the EAL group (Chiappe, Siegel and Wade-Woolley, 2002). This finding suggests that individual differences are present from the beginning of school and that if children are having difficulty, even if they are EAL, they would benefit from early intervention before they have a chance to fail.

Within the sample both the ESL and the native speakers were divided into two groups: children who performed significantly below average or were identified as being at risk in kindergarten. On tasks measuring letter identification, spelling, rhyme detection, pseudoword repetition, syllable and phoneme identification and phoneme deletion, and speed of naming pictures, the performance of the 'ESL at-risk group' and 'at-risk native English group' was lower. Both the 'at-risk native speakers' and the ESL groups performed significantly worse than the children who were not at-risk from both groups. In other words, the ESL 'at-risk' group showed a pattern that was very similar to the children with reading problems who were native speakers. The ESL group whose reading scores were in the normal range showed performance on all these tasks that was very similar to the native speakers who were not at risk.

This pattern of findings indicates that individual differences within the ESL group emerge early and that not all ESL children have reading difficulties. In fact, most do not. However, the group that is showing reading difficulties is clearly at risk for reading problems later and may be showing early manifestations of dyslexia.

A very similar pattern was found in grade one. The performance of the ESL children who had low reading scores was similar to the performance of the native-speaking children who had low scores on a reading test, word reading, pseudoword reading, spelling pseudowords, rapid naming of picture and on measures of phonological processing, including pseudoword repetition, phoneme deletion and substitution, and spelling of real words. Similarly, the performance of native speakers and ESL on a sentence repetition task was very similar when children had low scores in a reading test group. The scores of the children with reading difficulties were significantly lower on a sentence repetition task than children with reading scores in the average range. The pattern of results was very similar for the native speakers and the children who had English as a second language. Similar results have been found in grade two, grade three and in grade four. These findings indicate that the children who have reading difficulties and who have ESL were very likely to have dyslexia. Their performance resembles native-speaking dyslexics and their problems were not entirely the result of English being their second language.

In general, the children in this study did quite well. The school district to which the children belonged is one that has made a commitment to a balanced reading-acquisition programme that includes phonological awareness instruction. Early identification of at-risk children was an important part of this programme. Following the kindergarten assessment, each school received feedback on the performance of the children who participated in the study. Those children who were classified as being at risk for reading failure were identified within the feedback. The phonological awareness training took the form of classroom-based and small-group activities for all children in kindergarten. Although 37% of the ESL children, and 25% of the native English-speaking ones, were at risk in kindergarten, approximately 3% were having significant reading difficulties in grade 4. The small groups consisted of both ESL and L1 speakers matched on phonological awareness ability. The classroom teachers as well as the school resource teachers provided the intervention 3 to 4 times a week for 20 minutes. The kindergarten phonological awareness training for all children was presented in the context of a variety of literacy activities, which included a combination of activities with an explicit emphasis on the sound–symbol relationship as well as independent activities such as co-operative story writing and journal writing using invented spelling. Given the commitment of the district to early identification and intervention for children at risk for reading failure, the phonological awareness intervention continued into grade 1 for some children in the study and took the form of small-group and individually targeted interventions. It should be noted that most of this instruction took place in the classroom, so help in developing language skills was available to all. Early identification and intervention are clearly the most efficient and successful routes to reduce the incidence of dyslexia.

Conclusion

Geva and Wade-Woolley (in press) made a series of observations that provide a good checklist when thinking about assessing the possibility of dyslexia. These included:

- Do assess as many of the areas known to be related to dyslexia as possible.
- Do assess in English and the home language where possible.
- Do monitor progress and learning over time.

- Do look beyond oral language proficiency.
- Do provide direct instruction in reading skills.
- Do provide language enrichment opportunities.
- Do consider the transfer of specific skills from the first language.

- Do not wait or delay assessment until oral language proficiency has reached an 'appropriate' level.
- Do not assume that word recognition and word attack skills are unimportant.
- Do not assume persistent language and reading difficulties will 'catch up' if ignored.
- Do not seek to establish a discrepancy in order to justify a label of reading disability.
- Do not assume that persistent difficulties across-the-board merely reflect 'negative' transfer from the first language.
- Do not use test norms based on the child's first language.

Children whose first language is not English and who are being educated in English may be dyslexic. It is important to attempt to understand their difficulties, if and when they have them. It should not be assumed that reading difficulties, when they occur, are due entirely to EAL status. Children experiencing reading, spelling and writing difficulties should receive help whatever their language status. For a discussion of specific techniques to help the multi-lingual child experiencing difficulties see Smythe and Siegel (2003).

References

Abu Rabia S (1997) Verbal and working-memory skills of bilingual Hebrew–English-speaking children. International Journal of Psycholinguistics 13: 25–40.

Abu Rabia S, Siegel LS (2002) Reading, syntactic, orthographic and working memory skills of bilingual Arabic-English speaking children. Journal of Psycholinguistic Research 31: 661–78.

Berninger VW (1994) Future directions for research on writing disabilities: integrating endogenous and exogenous variables. In Lyon GR (ed.) Frames of Reference for the Assessment of Learning Disabilities: New Views on Measurement Issues. Baltimore: Paul H. Brookes, pp. 419–40.

British Psychological Society (1999) Working Party of the Division of Educational and Child Psychology of the British Psychological Society. Dyslexia, Literacy and Psychological Assessment. Leicester: British Psychological Society.

Bruck M (1990) Word recognition skills of adults with childhood diagnoses of dyslexia. Developmental Psychology 26: 439–54.

Chiappe P, Siegel LS, Gottardo A (2002) Reading-related skills of kindergartners from diverse linguistic backgrounds. Applied Psycholinguistics 23: 95–116.

Da Fontoura HA, Siegel LS (1995) Reading, syntactic, and working memory skills of bilingual Portuguese-English Canadian children. Reading and Writing: An Interdisciplinary Journal 7: 139–53.

D'Anguilli A, Siegel LS, Serra E (2002) The development of reading in English and Italian in bilingual children. Applied Psycholinguistics 22: 479–507.

Everatt J, Adams E, Smythe I, Ocampo D (2000) Dyslexia screening measures and bilingualism. Dyslexia 6: 42–56.

Felton RH, Naylor CE, Wood FB (1990) Neuropsychological profile of adult dyslexics. Brain and Language 39: 485–97.

Geva E, Wade-Woolley L (in press) Component processes in becoming English-Hebrew biliterate. In Durgonoglu A, Verhoeven L (eds) Acquisition of Literacy in a Multilingual Context: a Cross Linguistic Perspective. Cambridge: Cambridge University Press.

Shafrir U, Siegel LS (1994) Subtypes of learning disabilities in adolescents and adults. Journal of Learning Disabilities 27: 123–34.

Share D, KE Stanovich (1995) Cognitive processes in early reading development: accommodating individual differences into a model of acquisition. Issues in Education: Contributions from Educational Psychology 1995: 1: 1–57.

Siegel LS (1989) IQ is irrelevant to the definition of learning disabilities. Journal of Learning Disabilities 22: 469–78, 486.

Smythe I, Siegel LS (2003) Helping the multilingual dyslexic child. Unpublished manuscript.

Wade-Woolley L, Siegel LS (1997) The spelling performance of ESL and native speakers of English as a function of reading skill. Reading and Writing: An Interdisciplinary Journal 9: 387–406.

Woodcock RW (1987) Woodcock Reading Mastery Tests-Revised. Circle Pines MN: American Guidance Service.

POLICY

Introduction to Part Two

One of the consequences of the many breakthroughs in the field of dyslexia is the emergence of formal – and in some cases legislative – policy on dyslexia. Policy is crucial, as it should provide protection and reassurance to those involved in the area of dyslexia. Protection and reassurance have been lacking for many years and parents and teachers have felt exposed and vulnerable, not knowing how best to deal with the challenges they faced in the identification, intervention and emotional development of dyslexic children.

Recent years have witnessed many advances in this area, with examples of government-supported working-party investigations into dyslexia and the formulation of policy and subsequent guidance and training programmes for teachers. Part Two seeks to provide a flavour of these developments from both Europe and the US, and from the perspectives of children, parents and adults.

Early identification and intervention are key factors in the accessing of appropriate teaching for dyslexic children and this is dealt with in the chapter by Crombie, Knight and Reid. In making a strong case for policy and practice in early identification they also warn against the negative aspects that can be associated with premature labelling. They maintain that the objective of early identification is not to label but to intervene, to monitor and to ensure that the child's progress does not unexpectedly lag behind that of his/her peers. This implies that policy and intervention should not be based on the presence of a label but on the identification of need. In this chapter the authors describe a range of approaches for early identification and intervention from both sides of the Atlantic, as well as highlighting the role of parents and the value of collaboration for policy and practice.

Collaboration is the theme of the chapter by Lindsay Peer, which looks at the development of policy at a national level in the UK. Dr Peer discusses the implications of the revised Code of Practice in the UK, including the parent partnership service (PPS), which is part of the Code of Practice.

Peer reports that it was a condition of the Code that local education authorities set up a parent partnership service on a statutory basis. The Code recognized that 'all parents of children with special educational needs should be treated as partners.'

The essence of any policy is to ensure that the curriculum is accessible to all. Peer argues that, in the UK, the Literacy and Numeracy Strategies that were introduced in 1998 and 1999 offered the first real opportunity to ensure that materials resulting from policy were introduced to aid the dyslexic learner. Peer also comments on the dyslexia-friendly schools campaign, which is discussed in detail in the subsequent part of this book, and argues that the campaign witnessed attitudinal changes amongst those involved in educational policy in local education authorities. As Peer argues, this helped to shape the successful package of a triangular model of working relationships involving schools, parents and children.

Policy and its effect on practice in the US are discussed in the chapter by Reid Lyon, Shaywitz, Chhabra and Sweet. In this chapter the authors discuss the political role in educational decision making, as well as the role of science in shaping national reading policy. They address issues relating to funding, monitoring and accountability in relation to the 'No Child Left Behind'/'Reading First' legislation. They argue that the implementation of Reading First will be stronger and more focused than preceding programmes. They suggest that, unlike previous programmes, Reading First will provide an opportunity for students and teachers in classrooms in every state to participate, and all states will have the resources to use proven methods of reading instruction to improve student achievement.

They conclude by claiming that 'there remains an unforgiveable gap between what we know about reading development and effective reading instruction and the instruction provided in many of our schools. This must stop. There are no more excuses.'

Policy and provision for adults with dyslexia has for many years been a neglected area. In a chapter providing a US perspective, Young and Browning discuss the research bias in studies involving adults with dyslexia. They argue that many studies have a selection bias towards those with dyslexia identified at school. They suggest, however, that this sample only represents around one-third of those with dyslexia and, furthermore, that this identified sample is representative of those who have been very successful or those who have had accommodations. So although there are now policy and services to help those adults with dyslexia, Young and Browning argue that many adults were not identified at school and remain unidentified throughout their lives. This means that this group will not qualify for services and support such as vocational rehabilitation and social security disability insurance (SSI). The authors advocate very strongly that the approach to successfully identify and support adults with dyslexia should be based on a disability-focused approach.

McLaughlin takes a different perspective – that of empowerment. He argues that empowerment comes from self-understanding and understanding by others, particularly employers. He argues that, to take advantage of the Disability Discrimination Act, individuals do not have to establish that they are dyslexic but that their difficulties constitute a disability that has significant adverse day-to-day effects.

McLaughlin describes the key points of the Act and discusses some of the contentious issues relating to the notion of reasonable adjustment. Adults with dyslexia often find themselves surrounded by confusing procedures and red tape before they can access the support to which they are entitled. McLaughlin, in this chapter, seeks to clarify this and provides helpful information relating to dyslexia and employment. It is through such clarification that policy can have an impact on practice and on the daily lives of all involved in dyslexia.

Part Two therefore raises many issues relating to policy but also seeks to provide some guidance and clarification for teachers, parents and individuals with dyslexia.

CHAPTER 8

United Kingdom policy for inclusion

LINDSAY PEER

There have been significant changes in policy and practice in the UK since 1993 that have been of considerable benefit to dyslexic learners. These changes have occurred as a result of research and effective practice, together with substantial lobbying that was designed to raise awareness at a political level. The Education Act 1993 was followed by the Code of Practice (CoP) (1994) (Department for Education, 1994), which has since been revised as the Code of Practice (2001) (Department for Education and Skills, 2001). It can be argued that these statutory documents have been beneficial to the whole field of dyslexia - to teachers, parents and children.

Code of Practice (2001)

This document is a substantial focal point of a range of documentation relating to equal opportunities. One of the most important paragraphs is the following:

> A statement should specify clearly the provision necessary to meet the needs of the child. It should detail appropriate provision to meet identified need [para 8:36/7].
>
> Provision should normally be quantified (e.g. in terms of hours of provision, staffing arrangements) although there will be cases where some flexibility should be retained in order to meet the changing needs of the child concerned.

The CoP was published with a 'toolkit', which is a collection of guidance booklets together with a circular on inclusive schooling.

It is significant that, for the first time, dyslexia is found in a section entitled 'Cognition and learning' (in paragraph 7:58). The CoP recognizes that 'each child is unique' (paragraph 7:52). Educators are required to identify the specific needs of an individual child and make provision, rather than trying to fit the child into the framework of the school.

Schools are able to use the code flexibly but are required to 'have regard' to it. There is little objection if schools offer something equivalent to what is suggested and it is feasible. However, there is far less choice regarding issues of assessment and statementing as these sections relate to matters of law.

The 2001 CoP has new sections relating to pupil and carer/parent involvement. This reflects current thinking that 'good' schools ensure that pupils are involved in all plans made for them. These new sections have equal weight to those relating to parent partnership; these are all requirements for provision to be made by local education authorities (LEAs).

Parent partnership service (PPS)

Chapter 2 of the CoP recognizes the importance of parent partnership services. The Code required LEAs to set them up on a statutory basis. The Code recognized that:

all parents of children with special educational needs should be treated as partners. They should be supported so as to be able and empowered to:

● Recognise and fulfil their responsibilities as parents and play an active and valued role in their children's education;
● Have knowledge of their children's entitlement within the SEN framework;
● Make their views known about how their child is educated; and
● Have access to information, advice and support during assessment and any related decision-making process about special educational needs.

(CoP para 2.2)

An effective parent partnership scheme ensures that parents are in a position to make informed choices.

Core activities of the PPS include:

● working with parents;
● offering information and publicity;
● training;
● offering advice and support;
● networking and collaborating and helping to inform and influence local special educational needs policy and practice.

The PPS also includes access to an independent parental supporter (IPS) for those parents who request such a person.

The IPS works in a voluntary capacity and has an interest in issues relating to special educational needs. He or she may offer parents advice in how to work effectively with the school, the LEA or cope at a tribunal. They may offer support at meetings or reviews at school and even contribute to assessment. They often help in explaining the implications of decisions and by offering options for a child's provision.

The Code assumes that schools make provision for the teaching of all children with difficulties in mainstream classrooms through their inclusion framework. It encourages teachers to value and work with difference. Co-ordinators and heads of department are expected to be able to make recommendations to advise on teaching and learning for common special needs such as mild specific learning difficulties, thus freeing up the special needs co-ordinators to work on specific issues and more serious areas of concern. This is reflected in advertising for new teaching posts in many schools.

The Code also outlines strands of 'differentiation' – thereby matching provision to need. Teachers are expected to consider:

- assessment, planning and review;
- grouping for teaching purposes;
- additional human resources;
- curriculum and teaching methods.

National Curriculum Inclusion Statement

Many of the points mentioned above are reflected in the National Curriculum Inclusion Statement.

Section B of the statement is entitled: *responding to pupils' diverse learning needs*. This implies that teachers are required to:

- create effective learning environments;
- secure motivation and concentration;
- provide equality of opportunity through teaching approaches; and
- set targets for learning.

Section C is titled 'Overcoming potential barriers to learning and assessment for individuals and groups of pupils'.

Teachers must make provision, where necessary, to support individuals or groups of pupils to enable them to participate effectively in the curriculum and assessment activities. During the end of key stage assessments, teachers should bear in mind that special arrangements are available to support individual pupils.

As a result, teams of inspectors from Ofsted will look at the whole of a school's planning system when inspecting for successful inclusion in relation to special educational needs and disability.

Special Educational Needs and Disability Act 2001

The Disability Discrimination Act, passed in 1995, was amended in 2001 and schools became subject to its requirements. This was a landmark in legislation as it directly promotes the inclusion of children with special educational needs and disabilities in mainstream schools.

The Act states that a person with a disability is: 'One who has a physical or mental impairment, which has a substantial and long-term adverse effect on his/her ability to carry out normal day-to-day activities.' (Note that the 'impairment' has a long-term effect if it has lasted or is expected to last for at least 12 months or for the rest of the individual's life. 'Substantial' means neither minor nor trivial.)

It suggests that a 'mental impairment' should include learning difficulties and that 'normal day to day activities' incorporate memory or ability to concentrate, learn or understand. It would therefore appear that those experiencing persistent difficulties related to dyslexia would be included in the definition of disability.

It is now unlawful for a responsible body to discriminate against learners with a disability. Discrimination can take place in two ways:

- treating learners 'less favourably' than others for reasons relating to their disabilities;
- failing to make 'reasonable adjustment' to ensure they are not placed at a 'substantial disadvantage' for a reason relating to their disabilities.

These issues must be considered in relation to all other school documentation – for example staff development, behaviour and exclusion policies and extracurricular activities.

Each and every person holding a role within a school has a responsibility to both know and comply with checklists compiled for governors by the Disability Rights Commission.

Local education authorities are required to prepare an accessibility strategy (and further strategies if and when required). All strategies must be in writing. They should be kept under review and should be implemented.

National Literacy Strategy

The National Literacy Strategy was introduced into all schools in England in 1998 with the intention of raising educational standards for all primary-age pupils. The author was invited to sit on the steering groups once it was up and running. This was the first real opportunity to ensure that materials were introduced to aid the dyslexic learner.

Initially the Strategy was geared solely to children who had no difficulties with the learning process. At later stages, three waves were introduced that were designed to address the needs of a range of readers. Under the Literacy Strategy all pupils receive a daily dedicated literacy hour, which maximizes opportunities for oral work, guided reading and writing, structured teaching of phonics, spelling and grammar. The literacy hour shifts the balance of teaching from individualized work towards more whole-class and group teaching, which means that pupils spend more time learning and working together. In the literacy hour, pupils spend about three-quarters of their time being taught as members of a whole class or a smaller ability group and a quarter of their time is spent on independent reading or writing work. As this takes place every day, children with more complex needs are able to work in small groups using a range of programmes more dedicated to their needs. One of the programmes recommended for children at Key Stages 1 and 2 with difficulties in reading is the multi-sensory system for the teaching of reading (MSTR) (Johnson et al., 1999).

National Numeracy Strategy

The National Numeracy Strategy was introduced to all schools in England in 1999. The Strategy is well structured and assisted many aspects of learning for the dyslexic child. The BDA was responsible for the production of the booklet on dyslexia and dyscalculia aimed to support teachers working with dyslexic children.

Most schools teach a daily mathematics lesson, which uses a three-part structure, starting with oral work and mental calculation involving whole-class teaching. The main part of the lesson can be used for teaching new topics or consolidating previous work, making clear what will be learned and how long it will take. Finally, the plenary plays an important role, allowing teachers to draw together what has been learned.

The Key Stage 3 National Strategy

This focuses on raising the standards for all pupils in their first three years of secondary education. There are five strands in the Strategy: English, mathematics, science, the foundation subjects and information and communications technology (ICT), plus the cross-curricular elements of literacy and numeracy. English and mathematics, together with cross-curricular elements of literacy and numeracy, were introduced into all schools in 2001–2, and science, foundation subjects and ICT were introduced in 2002–3.

The Strategy is based on four main principles:

- *expectations* – establishing high expectations for all pupils and setting challenging targets for them to achieve;
- *progression* – strengthening the transition from KS2 and ensuring good progression in teaching and learning across KS3;

- *engagement* – promoting approaches to teaching and learning to engage and motivate pupils and demand their active participation;
- *transformation* – strengthening teaching and learning through a programme of professional development and practical support.

The Strategy has provided extra support in the form of catch-up and booster materials and the introduction of summer schools to develop the learning and achievement of pupils operating at level 3. Many dyslexic learners function at this level.

Implications of political change

The BDA has been campaigning tirelessly to ensure that change is incorporated into all facets of the education system. It is clear that this is now happening. No longer am I asked to 'prove' that dyslexia exists. Now it is a matter of ensuring that awareness is raised and that parents and educators know what to do when faced with each and every dyslexic individual. We know from experience that early identification, effective assessment and appropriate provision lead to success in learning. It is vital to ensure that dyslexic children are never left to feel as though they are failures and to develop the low self-esteem that is unfortunately so common. As a result of this thinking, the dyslexia-friendly schools campaign was born in 2000, supported by the DfES. Since then 45,000 dyslexia information packs have been distributed across the UK encouraging schools and LEAs to provide an environment in which dyslexic children will flourish (see, for example, British Dyslexia Association, 2000). I outline the philosophy below.

The 'dyslexia-friendly' schools campaign

Relevant research findings have influenced policy and practice over the past few years, leading to significant changes within the education system.

It is clear from research and practice that what is educationally sound for dyslexic learners is of value to all, particularly when learning in a mainstream inclusive classroom. Learners without difficulties may not need such detailed strategies but those who are dyslexic cannot cope without them. Dyslexic people who are successful feel confident and contribute to society. Emotional, academic and financial barriers to inclusion are therefore removed. As a result of this understanding, many learners are now succeeding in ways that were previously impossible for them.

The principle of working towards the facilitation of all people to reach their educational potential – regardless of challenge or disability – is fundamental to the principle of 'dyslexia friendliness'. As up to 20% of children at any one time experience a form of special educational need (SEN) there is a moral obligation to place the needs of this substantial group on all agendas to ensure that their voices are heard and needs are met. Moreover, now that there is a growing body of evidence highlighting good practice internationally, as a nation we should be able to facilitate successful change in the UK at all levels and stages of educational practice. We recognize that leaders in schools are the key people who have the power to influence this agenda and, by so doing, determine the philosophy, policy and practices of their institutions.

It is fully recognized that only when a headteacher leads the way for such changes in attitude do teachers feel empowered, parents confident and children successful. We are working towards changes in working practices to ensure the inclusion of all learners. Should this fail then exclusion will result.

Dyslexic people have a great deal to offer every society, with creativity, skills and talents that so often lie dormant. We often see frustration and anxiety in traditional educational environments. A dyslexia-friendly environment with its appropriate support will open doors for those who have experienced failure. This will ensure success and confidence for all concerned – teachers, parents and dyslexic people themselves.

Attitudinal changes

- Local education authorities should provide clear, written guidelines for teachers.
- The needs of dyslexic learners should be an integral part of the whole school's policy, enabling children with dyslexia to develop strengths at the same time as addressing their weaknesses.
- Headteachers need to ensure that being 'dyslexia friendly' underpins the philosophy of the school.
- All current and new staff need to 'buy into' the dyslexia-friendly philosophy of the school.
- Schools should adopt an open and formative approach encouraging communication between all relevant parties, including the school staff, external agencies where appropriate, parents and dyslexic learners themselves.
- There must be high expectations of all learners. This is only deliverable by acceptance of appropriate philosophy and effective support.
- Policies must be in place to encourage the self-esteem of children who find learning through traditional methodologies frustrating.
- Ensure that the needs of those learners who enter the education system with more than one language are met as effectively as those who speak one language only.

Whole school

- Specialist teachers working in an advisory capacity should make regular visits to schools to evaluate, support and advise on how to improve provision.
- Establish a whole-school approach to ensure policies are translated into action. This should be done by:
  - comprehensive and appropriate training for different levels of staff;
  - a common approach;
  - target setting;
  - putting monitoring and evaluation systems in place.
- All staff are made responsible, within their roles, for the progress of each individual learner.
- Teachers must have available to them a range of alternative methodologies to ensure success for all learners.
- Study skills must be taught across the whole school.
- Staff should encourage the active participation of parents to support both the individual child and the school.
- Whole-school marking, assessment and homework policies should be introduced.
- Schools should develop a culture of teaching, which reflects a range of learning styles.
- Introduce a thinking skills programme.

Discrete provision

- Individual target setting should aim at the level learners have already reached, rather than at where they should be according to age.
- Intellectual potential should be recognized and supported whilst appropriate individual teaching of areas of weakness takes place.
- Group education plans should be introduced where appropriate with individual education plans for specific needs.
- Multi-sensory teaching methodologies should be used to enhance learning capabilities.
- Programmes should be introduced to enhance development of those areas underlying the dyslexic weaknesses, for example, speed of processing, memory, language, organization.
- All staff, regardless of subject specialism, should be responsible for and use methodologies that will benefit dyslexic learners across the curriculum.

Concluding comment

We will succeed in our goal by taking advice from those who have created such change successfully and by working with other leaders who feel that they have the drive and ability to facilitate the modifications necessary. We are aware that schools which see children as individuals and answer their needs appropriately ensure best practice for all. We know that good practice for *dyslexic* learners benefits all learners. We are striving towards the recognition and acceptance of diversity, which we see as an imperative on a national scale. Together we will help schools reach their targets of academic, emotional and social achievement and concurrently shape the successful package of a triangular model of working relationships – schools, parents and children with special educational needs themselves.

References

British Dyslexia Association (2000) Dyslexia Friendly Schools Resource Pack. Reading: BDA.

Department for Education (1994) Code of Practice on the Identification and Assessment of Special Educational Needs. London: Department for Education.

Department for Education and Skills (2001) Special Educational Needs Code of Practice. London: DfES.

Johnson M, Philips S, Peer L (1999) Multisensory System for the Teaching of Reading. Manchester: Manchester Metropolitan University.

CHAPTER 9

Evidence-based reading policy in the US

G. REID LYON, SALLY E. SHAYWITZ, VINITA CHHABRA,
ROBERT SWEET

Introduction

Since the early 1990s much of educational policy in the US has shifted away from its philosophical and ideological foundations and towards the application of converging scientific evidence to forge policy directions and initiatives. This has been particularly the case for early (kindergarten through grade 3) reading instructional policies and practices. The reasons for this are discussed below. The use of scientific evidence rather than subjective impressions to guide any aspect of educational policy represents a dramatic shift in educational thinking. In this chapter, we will review selected reading policy initiatives to underscore this shift. Our goal is to explain why and how some educational policy initiatives in the US now reflect a reliance on findings from rigorous scientific research rather than opinion, ideology, fads and political interests. For in-depth reviews of these new research to policy trends, the reader is referred to the work of Cecil Miskel and his group at the University of Michigan (McDaniel et al., 2001; Song et al., in press) and Sweet (in press).

Why reading?

Within American educational policy writ large, the area of reading has become the focal point for education legislation based on scientific research. There are two major reasons for this specific emphasis. First, reading proficiency is the most fundamental skill, critical to most, if not all, academic learning and success in school. No doubt mathematics, social studies, science and other content domains are essential for academic and intellectual development, but learning specific information relevant to these disciplines is extraordinarily difficult if you cannot read. Moreover, in the US, the ability to read proficiently is significantly related to one's quality of life – not only occupational and vocational opportunities, but public health outcomes as well (Lyon, 2002; Shaywitz, 2003).

161

Second, despite its critical importance, an unacceptable number of children in the US cannot read proficiently. For example, the National Center for Educational Statistics (NCES) within the US Department of Education (USDOE) recently published the 2003 Reading Report Card as part of the results of the National Assessment of Educational Progress (NAEP) (NCES, 2003). This current snapshot of the reading ability of fourth-, eighth- and twelfth-grade students reflects a persistent and abysmal trend. In the fourth grade alone, 37% of students read below the basic level nationally, which essentially renders them illiterate. To further underscore the pervasiveness of the problem, the data show that only 31% of students are reading proficiently or above. If these results are not disappointing enough, consider the outcomes when the national reading data are disaggregated by sub-group. Sixty per cent of African American children and 56% of Hispanic/Latino youngsters read below basic levels, with only 12% and 15% reading proficiently or above, respectively. In New York City alone, over 70% of minority students cannot read at a basic level. To be clear, it is not race or ethnicity that portends this significant underachievement in reading – it is poverty – and minority students happen to be overrepresented among disadvantaged families. These findings of the dismal status of reading are all the more unfortunate (and unnecessary) given the converging evidence that most children can learn to read when provided with well-trained teachers, effective instructional programmes, and strong educational leadership (Lyon et al., 2001; Torgesen, 2002).

Reading failure: the role of philosophically based instruction

A comprehensive discussion of the maladies that have plagued education, education research, and education policies in general, and reading research and instruction in particular, is beyond the scope of this chapter and readers are referred to Adams (1990), Coleman (1966), Hirsch (1996), Lagemann (2000), Lagemann and Shulman (1999), Ravitch (1983, 2001), Sowell (1993), and Stanovich (2000) for historical and recent reviews. However, the reviews cited above point to the consistent finding that curricula and instruction for reading have been based primarily on untested theories and assumptions, if not romantic beliefs about learning and teaching.

A notable example of this is the large-scale implementation, despite little to no evidence of its effectiveness, of the whole-language approach. Thus, this invalidated approach is used to guide teacher preparation and licensing, the development of classroom instructional materials, classroom reading instruction, and reading assessment practices. Rooted, in part, in constructivist views of learning and development, proponents of whole language claim that learning to read *should be as natural as learning to talk*

(Goodman, 1967; Smith, 1973, 1977). For example, Goodman (1986) pointed to the ease and naturalness of the development of listening and speaking abilities and argued that learning to read would be equally natural and easy if meaning and the purposes of reading were emphasized. Both Goodman and Smith reasoned that children can learn phonics rules on their own and primarily through reading itself, that decoding words will slow children down and disrupt comprehension, and that too much direct instruction will produce memorization and rote reading rather than conceptual learning and deep understanding (Moats, 2000). With respect to the instructional implications for this view, Smith (1973) concluded that, beyond providing materials and opportunities for reading, the teacher's most important job was one of providing sensitive feedback. Later, Smith again repeated his view that 'reading is a process in which the reader picks and chooses from the available information only enough to select and predict a language structure which is decodable [to meaning] . . . it is not a process of sequential word recognition' (Smith, 1973: 164).

A review of the reading literature indicates that whole language is a *philosophy* of instruction rather than an instructional method (Adams, 1991; Adams and Bruck, 1995a, 1995b), although it has also been described as an approach, a theory, a perspective, an attitude of mind, and a theoretical orientation. Clearly whole language represents many things to many people. Despite this, some consistent themes can be identified as critical to the whole-language concept (Moats, 2000):

- Learning to read is a natural process similar to learning to talk. Indeed, phonemic awareness, phonics, spelling and other written language skills can be learned naturally through exposure to reading and writing activities.
- Phonics and spelling should be taught only on an 'as needed' basis – that is, after students make errors on words they are reading or writing.
- Reading is the construction of meaning, where the emphasis is placed on reading comprehension.
- Too much phonics instruction is harmful to children. Phonics instruction out of context is viewed as harmful in that it may produce 'word callers' rather than children who read for meaning.
- The skilled whole-language teacher is a coach, a model and a guide. Teachers should develop instructional interactions where students discover concepts, rather than being directly taught about them, as discovery leads to higher order thinking.

Between 1975 and 1995, the educational community embraced many of these themes even without the availability of a concise definition of what whole-language instruction actually meant (Stahl and Miller, 1989) or credible scientific evidence supporting the validity of its instructional principles (Adams, 1991; Adams and Bruck, 1995a, 1995b; Foorman et al., 1998; Stanovich, 2000). This acceptance of whole language, even in the presence of significant reading failure rates associated with it, was reinforced by the belief that instructional programme effectiveness and objective measurement of reading outcomes was 'unauthentic' and irrelevant to reading instruction. Thus, the use of reading assessment to measure reading achievement outcomes and to guide instruction was typically rejected and replaced with alternative assessments that, instead, probed attitudes, motivation, self-esteem and enjoyment (Moats, 2000). The assumption was that a positive attitude and a love for reading would motivate children to learn to read and to read independently. The goal of reading instruction during this 20-year span became a love of reading, not the ability to read (Moats, 2000; Stanovich, 2000), seemingly without the realization that the ability to read is a necessary precursor to a love of reading.

That many tenets of the whole-language philosophy remained popular among educators despite an unacceptable rate of reading failure, particularly among children from disadvantaged backgrounds, begs the question of how a flawed philosophical approach to reading instruction remained so fashionable among teachers in the US for so long. As Adams and Bruck (1995a, 1995b) have pointed out, several factors accounted for its currency. First, whole language emphasized teacher empowerment. Second, it advocated a child-centred method of instruction in which the child is seen as an active and thoughtful learner who constructs knowledge with guidance from the teacher. Third, it stressed the importance of integrating reading and writing instruction. These factors proved appealing to many teachers who felt, among other things, unappreciated as professionals and constrained by published reading programmes, and whose perceptions of children reflected their beliefs in the capacity of children to learn on their own under proper conditions.

To be sure, some of these themes are compatible with effective instruction if incorporated in a knowledgeable manner. The problem is that children do not learn to read naturally (Adams and Bruck, 1995a; Lyon, 1998; Rayner et al., 2001; Shaywitz, 2003; Stanovich, 2000). Most children will have difficulty learning to read if they are not systematically provided with information about the letter–sound relationships from which the English writing system is built, about vocabulary and about domain-specific background knowledge. This conclusion is firmly supported by converging scientific evidence on how children learn to read, why some have difficulties, and what can be done to prevent failure and this information has been available over the past decade (Adams and Bruck, 1995a, 1995b; NICHD, 2000; Rayner, et al., 2001; Shaywitz, 2003). So why has the educational establishment resisted using objective scientific evidence rather than philosophical beliefs to guide reading policies and reading instruction? And how can this resistance be replaced by reliance on evidence-based instructional practices?

What took so long?

There are a number of factors that have impeded the systematic use of scientific research evidence to guide the development and implementation of reading policies in the US; three stand out. First, as Adams and Bruck (1995b) have pointed out, there was, and continues to be, a decided anti-scientific research spirit within the education profession in general, and within the whole-language movement in particular. Many proponents of whole language explicitly reject traditional scientific approaches to the study of reading development and instruction and promote post-modern concepts of what constitutes truth and reality. From a whole-language perspective, the value of any evidence, scientific or not, is in the eye of the beholder – truth is relative and framed via one's own experience and culture (Ellis and Fouts, 1997; McKenna et al., 1994). The majority of teacher preparation and professional development programmes embrace a whole-language philosophy; consequently, many prospective and veteran teachers have been taught to discount the role of scientific research in informing them about reading development and instruction.

Second, often confusing scientific jargon combined with a lack of robust training in the principles of scientific research evidence make it difficult for teachers and administrators to discriminate between research findings that are valid and findings that are invalid (Lyon and Chhabra, in press). In the past, much of the existing educational reading research was notoriously weak and educators were frequently assaulted by the next 'research-based' instructional magic bullet without having had the necessary preparation to distinguish between valid claims of effectiveness and instructional voodoo. When such 'magic bullets' failed, as they invariably do, many teachers lost trust in the ability of research to inform their teaching. This should not be a surprise. It is difficult, if not impossible, for teachers to apply educational research information that has historically been of poor scientific quality, which lacks the authority of valid evidence, which is not communicated in a clear manner, and which is woefully impractical (Kennedy, 1997).

Third, historically, it has also been rare for policy makers at either the federal or state levels to have a firm understanding of the role that scientific evidence can play in educational policy development and implementation. Even when there is recognition that scientific research is critical to other policy environments (for example, public health, agriculture, commerce), education has been typically viewed as more value driven and primary policy input is obtained from politicians and diverse special interest groups rather than educational scientists. Thus, educational policies have been forged almost entirely within a political, rather than a scientific, context.

While political input continues to play a major role in educational decision making – indeed education and educational policies are inherently political – the role of scientific evidence in shaping national reading policy has increased dramatically. Why the shift?

Science to policy to practice: critical factors

As Song et al. (in press: 2) point out, in order for new policy directions and actions to occur, '. . . a societal condition must capture policy makers' attention and be recognized as a problem that demands action'. Moreover, shifts or new directions in educational policies require proposed new solutions to problems; the public will to solve the problems(s); sufficient indication that the solutions can work; significant input from policy actors including specialists who are clear about their interests; and compromise (McDaniel et al., 2001).

Recognition

To be sure, reading failure in the US has become a recognized societal condition that demands action. As McDaniel et al. (2001: 111) point out: '. . . the importance of improving the reading abilities of American school children has likely evolved into a permanent national concern'. But this recognition did not occur rapidly. One can see glimmers of concern and recognition of the problem in 1989 when President George Herbert Walker Bush and the nation's governors proposed: '. . . by the year 2000, every adult American will be literate and will possess the knowledge and skills necessary to compete in a global economy and exercise the rights and responsibilities of citizenship' (Campbell, 1992: 40). With the 1992 and 1994 NAEP scores continuing to show persistent reading problems among fourth- and eighth-grade students *and* significant declines in the reading abilities of high school seniors, it became apparent to some policy makers that not only would this goal be difficult, if not impossible, to achieve but that the country was actually dealing with a 'reading crisis' (McDaniel et al., 2001). This concern was apparent in President Clinton's State of the Union Address in 1996 when he announced that 40% of fourth-grade students could not read at grade level and urged Americans to support his goal that every child learns to read.

Proposed early solutions and the role of scientific evidence

To achieve this goal, President Clinton proposed a programme titled *America Reads*, which relied upon volunteers to work with struggling readers to ensure reading proficiency by the fourth grade. The Administration proposed $2.6 billion for this programme.

However, as Sweet (in press) explains, the Congressional House Committee on Education and the Workforce, under the leadership of Chairman Bill Goodling, held several face-to-face briefings with reading scientists (including the first author) and formal hearings to determine the status of the scientific research relevant to the national reading deficit and whether the types of volunteer activities proposed within the *America Reads* programme had been proven to reduce reading failure. These inquiries represented the first time that Congress had relied substantially on the scientific reading community to summarize extant evidence relevant to reading development and instruction and to help determine the effectiveness of particular educational programmes. In these briefings and hearings, Chairman Goodling and his committee relied heavily on reading scientists from the National Institute of Child Health and Human Development (NICHD) within the National Institutes of Health (NIH) to summarize the current scientific understanding of reading and reading instruction. The NICHD Reading Research programme and the findings from its 44 research sites are described and summarized elsewhere (Fletcher and Lyon, 1998; Lyon, 1995a, 1995b, 1998; Lyon et al., 2003; Shaywitz, 2003). In short, reports from the NICHD as well as from other reading research (see for example, Adams, 1990; Snow et al., 1998, 2000) clearly indicated that the 'instructional' interactions typically observed in volunteer tutoring programmes were only minimally effective, particularly with disadvantaged children.

Thus, on the basis of the existing scientific evidence, the committee proposed a different solution to the reading crisis from that embodied in *America Reads*. Specifically, on 21 October 1998, the Reading Excellence Act (REA) was signed into law. A bipartisan coalition, including representatives from the US Department of Education, the White House and Congress, agreed to provide $260 million annually to states for the provision of scientifically based reading programmes for children, from kindergarten through the third grade, at risk for reading failure.

The REA had three major goals:

- to provide children with the readiness skills and instructional support they need in early childhood in order to learn to read once they enter school;
- to teach every child to read by the end of the third grade; and
- to improve the instructional practices of teachers and their instructional staff in elementary schools.

The REA was unique in three significant ways. First, this was the first time that reading specifically became the focus of federal legislation. Second, the REA provided a specific definition of 'reading' that was described as including the understanding of how speech sounds (phonemes) are connected to print, the ability to decode unfamiliar words, the ability to read fluently, and the development of sufficient background information and vocabulary to foster reading comprehension. Third, the REA required that funding be provided for only those reading programmes that were based upon scientific research. Within this context, peer review groups were convened by the US Department of Education to review state REA applications for funding. State applications had to ensure that all reading programmes and teacher professional development programmes purchased with REA funds had to be developed on the basis of 'scientifically based reading research (SBRR)'. The term SBRR was carefully defined to reflect the manner by which scientific research is conducted by the National Science Foundation, the National Institutes of Health, and the National Academy of Sciences. Scholars from across the nation had been asked to review the definition of SBRR, and after many months of discussion, modifications and review, it was agreed upon (Sweet, in press). The definition of SBRR, as presented in the REA, follows:

> The term 'scientifically based reading research' – (A) means the application of rigorous, systematic, and objective procedures to obtain valid knowledge relevant to reading development, reading instruction, and reading difficulties; and (B) shall include research that
>
> (i)   employs systematic, empirical methods that draw on observation or experiment;
> (ii)   involves rigorous data analyses that are adequate to test the stated hypotheses and justify the general conclusions drawn;
> (iii) relies on measurements or observational methods that provide valid data across evaluators and observers and across multiple measurements and observations; and
> (iv)   has been accepted by a peer-reviewed journal or approved by a panel of independent experts through a comparably rigorous, objective, and scientific review.
>
> (Reading and Literacy Grants to State Educational Agencies. Title II (C) Sec. 2252 (5) [20 U.S.C. 6661a])

It was critically important that this definition provided the scientific foundation that ultimately led to the inclusion of more than 110 references to 'scientifically-based research' in the No Child Left Behind Act of 2001 (P.L. 107-110 [20 U.S.C. 7801] Title IX - General Provisions, Part A, Sec. 9101 (37) DEFINITIONS; Whitehurst, 2001) (Sweet, in press).

As with any new federal policy initiative, a great deal was learned from the attempt to implement the REA in states and local school districts. First, the REA did not achieve the goals for which it was intended for one major reason. Initial federal peer review of state applications provided quality control over the criteria that states would employ to ensure that REA applications from eligible districts would implement only instructional and professional development programmes that were based on scientific research, but the states themselves did not implement these standards in a reliable and systematic manner. Later site visits to many states indicated that reading programmes in use before REA funding were still in use irrespective of their scientific underpinnings. Given that many of these non-scientific programmes were allowed to be implemented or remain in practice, it is not surprising that many children continued to fail in reading. In short, flawed federal and state implementation/monitoring systems allowed federal funds under REA to be provided for 'business as usual'. Moreover, the federal government underestimated the resistance to the implementation of scientifically based reading programmes within the local reading education communities and within the professional development community. Finally, the experience with the REA indicated significant gaps in state, local and school understanding of scientifically based reading programmes and limited capacity to provide professional development at the university, state and district levels.

The role of reading scientists in reading policy

The lessons learned from the difficulties with the implementation of the REA were critical in preparing future reading legislation. First, it was evident that both federal and state programme monitoring had to be increased to ensure use of SBRR in selecting and implementing appropriate professional development and reading instruction. Second, it was apparent that states must be explicitly accountable for the implementation and effectiveness of their federally supported reading programmes. Third, it was clear that significant efforts must be undertaken to educate the larger educational, reading and policy communities about scientific reading research and its relation to instruction through clearly written and scientifically rigorous summaries of reading research. The monitoring and accountability lessons will be addressed in the discussion of the No Child Left Behind/Reading First legislation. The role of scientists in educating the public about the use of scientific reading research in guiding policy initiatives and instructional practice was highlighted in the development of two major research reports on reading.

Preventing Reading Difficulties in Young Children

The report *Preventing Reading Difficulties in Young Children* (PRD) (Snow et al., 1998) signalled an attempt to underscore the critical role of converging evidence in understanding reading development and preventing reading failure and to also end the so-called 'reading wars' that had been raging for decades (Sweet, in press). The PRD committee was convened by the National Research Council of the National Academy of Sciences and supported by the NICHD and the US Department of Education.

A broad scientific consensus about beginning reading development and reading instruction was forged by highly respected reading researchers representing diverse perspectives relevant to reading. The conclusion reached by the PRD Committee is summarized in the following quotation:

> All members agreed that reading should be defined as a process of getting meaning from print, using knowledge about the written alphabet and about the sound structure of oral language for the purpose of achieving understanding. All thus also agreed that early reading instruction should include direct teaching of information

about sound-symbol relationships to children who do not know about them. And that it must also maintain a focus on the communicative purposes and personal value of reading. (Snow et al., 1998: 6)

The National Reading Panel (NRP)

To date, the objectivity and veracity of the consensus findings of the PRD Committee have not been challenged scientifically. However, in reviewing the findings, Senator Thad Cochran (R–MS) and Representative Anne Northup (R–KY) were concerned that while the PRD Committee had been able to determine *which* skills were critical for reading proficiency, they had not been able to focus scientifically on *how* those skills are most effectively taught. Thus, Cochran and Northup were instrumental in convening the NRP to provide the first evidence-based summary of the effectiveness of different reading instructional approaches and methods. Building on the conclusions of the PRD, the *Report of the National Reading Panel* (NRP) was published in April 2000. This panel was established as follows:

In 1997, Congress asked the 'Director of the National Institute of Child Health and Human Development (NICHD), in consultation with the Secretary of Education, to convene a national panel to assess the status of research-based knowledge, including the effectiveness of various approaches to teaching children to read.' This panel was charged with providing a report that 'should present the panel's conclusions, an indication of the readiness for application in the classroom of the results of this research, and, if appropriate, a strategy for rapidly disseminating this information to facilitate effective reading instruction in the schools.'
(National Institute of Child Health and Human Development, 2000: 1)

Dr Donald Langenberg, Chancellor of the University of Maryland, chaired the Panel.
In his testimony before Congress after the release of the report, he stated:

In what may be the Panel's most important action, it developed a set of rigorous methodological standards to screen the research literature relevant to each topic. These standards are essentially those normally used in medical and behavioral research to assess the efficacy of behavioral interventions, medications or medical procedures. (Langenberg, 2000)

The report of the NRP has had a profound impact on public policy in America. It was the most rigorous and comprehensive review of reading research literature relevant to teaching reading ever undertaken, and provided clear and unequivocal evidence that the majority of children could learn to read if teachers were given the training necessary to implement effective scientifically validated instruction. There were six NRP sub-groups that reviewed those studies that were considered by the panel to be methodologically sound: first a sub-group to establish rigorous methodology; and then content sub-groups including alphabetics (phonemic awareness and phonics), fluency, comprehension, teacher education, and technology (National Reading Panel, 2000: iii) and the results of this review are presented in the *Reports of the Subgroups* (National Institute of Child Health and Human Development, 2000). Copies of the full NRP report have been sent to virtually every school district in America, and the distribution continues through the National Institute for Literacy, the US Department of Education and the NICHD. The significance of this report cannot be overemphasized; it became the basis of the Reading First legislation initiated by President George W. Bush and included in the No Child Left Behind Act of 2001.

Both the PRD and the NRP reports made it clear that a comprehensive, scientifically based approach to reading instruction is necessary if all children are to learn to read efficiently and effectively. Based on the scientific evidence, the essential components of any reading programme must include *systematic* and *direct* instruction in phonemic awareness, phonics, reading fluency, vocabulary development, and comprehension strategies.

The No Child Left Behind Act (NCLB) and the Reading First legislation

As noted earlier, the REA did not meet stated objectives primarily because of weak implementation at the state level and limited federal and state monitoring of REA activities and outcomes. In addition, whereas the REA mandated the use of SBRR in identifying effective instructional programmes, an evidence-based reading instructional synthesis like the NRP report was not then available to provide a more comprehensive analysis of effective reading instruction.

During his transition into office, President George W. Bush and his Domestic Policy staff, as well as the Secretary of Education and his staff, were briefed in detail about the strengths and weaknesses of the REA and the new research information that had been provided by the NRP. Because President Bush's major domestic policy focus was to be education and reading, he was intent not only on learning from the implementation failure of the REA but also building on its scientific foundation through the use of the NRP. After reviewing all of the relevant information President Bush proposed the No Child Left Behind policy initiative. Similar to the REA, the NCLB mandated that federal funds could only be provided for educational programmes that had been determined to be effective through rigorous scientific research. To ensure high fidelity implementation of programmes, NCLB also mandated accountability for results. At the same time, as long as states implemented effective programmes and ensured the measurement of results, they, and local districts, were provided with flexibility to identify instructional professional development programmes. In short, a prescribed 'National Curriculum' was not proposed.

To ensure that the NCLB 'pillars' of scientifically based programmes, accountability, flexibility and local control, and increased choices for parents were applied specifically to reading, President Bush proposed the Reading First grant programme within the NCLB to ensure that all children would be proficient readers by the end of the third grade and the Early Reading First grant programme, which extended the NCLB and Reading First goals to pre-schoolers.

The idea behind the Reading First programme

The development and implementation of the Reading First initiative was built on:

- the recognition that many children in the US, particularly those from disadvantaged environments, continued to struggle in reading;
- the continuing convergence of scientific evidence on reading development, reading difficulties and effective reading instruction;
- the need to increase the identification and implementation of reading and professional development programmes based on scientific research;
- the need to redefine the federal role in education by requiring all states to set high standards of achievement and to create a system of accountability to measure results;
- the need to provide flexibility to states and local districts in meeting their specific needs; and
- the need to significantly improve the federal and state grant application process and the federal and state Reading First monitoring process at the local (grantee) level in order to provide technical assistance where necessary and to terminate programs where necessary.

In order to achieve these goals, the Reading First initiative significantly increased the federal investment in scientifically based reading instruction in the early grades. Approximately $1 billion per year for a 6-year period would be provided to eligible states and local school districts for the implementation of instructional programmes based on SBRR. This substantial funding increase was also predicated on data indicating that investment in high quality reading instruction at the K to 3 levels would help to reduce the number of children requiring later special education services for reading failure.

It was clear that any increase in funding for reading programmes would result in increased student achievement if, and only if, the US Department of Education developed and put in place programmatic policies and procedures to ensure successful implementation. Within this context, the probability of children benefiting from the Reading First (and Early Reading First) programmes is significantly increased by the following factors:

- *Strong statute.* The Reading First grant programme states clearly that all programme activities must be based on scientifically based reading research. It also requires the submission of detailed state plans and annual performance reports and explicitly allows for the *discontinuance* of states that are not making significant progress in reducing the number of students reading below grade level.
- *Significant National Activities funds.* Reading First is allotted up to $25 million each year for National Activities. This allows the Department of Education to provide unprecedented funds for technical assistance and monitoring activities to support the implementation of Reading First. A specific, focused multi-million dollar contract has been awarded that will provide on-site monitoring in *each* state, *each* year. Other well-funded pending contracts will specifically support the competitive sub-grant process across the nation and ongoing, technical assistance for sub-grantees.
- *Rigorous application process.* The rigorous Reading First application process has not only sent the clear message to states that weak, sub-standard plans will not be funded, but it has also required each state to create a detailed blueprint of its Reading First plan. States have not been allowed to provide vague overviews of any facet of their plans. As a result, monitors will be able to assess whether states are implementing their plans exactly as approved.
- *Solid relationships with state education agencies (SEAs).* The application process has provided an opportunity for relationship building between state programme co-ordinators and federal Reading First programme staff. Programme staff are in frequent, ongoing contact with states in both the application and implementation phases.
- *Performance reporting.* States must submit an annual performance report documenting their progress in reducing the number of students reading below grade level. In their applications, states have had to describe how reporting requirements will be met. States will not be able to claim they do not have the appropriate data. States have also had to describe how they will make funding decisions, including discontinuation, based on the progress of participating districts and schools.
- *External review.* One important requirement of the Reading First programme to enhance accountability is the implementation of an external independent review of the degree to which states and local school districts are increasing the number of students who read proficiently. The external review also evaluates whether all the essential components of reading assessment instruction are being implemented and taught consistently and with appropriate fidelity. The funding for this evaluation is sufficient to complete the review effectively. Results will be used to improve the implementation of Reading First and to ensure that all students are learning to read.

● *Improving on REA.* For all of these reasons, the implementation of
Reading First will be stronger and more focused than preceding
programmes such as the REA. Unlike previous programmes, Reading First
provides an opportunity for students and teachers in classrooms in every
state to participate, and all states will have the resources to use proven
methods of reading instruction to improve student achievement. A major
difference between Reading First and the REA is that all states and local
districts are held accountable for ensuring that federal funds are explicitly
tied to student reading achievement.

Why scientific research must guide reading policies and reading instruction

For the last three decades, a significant number of children in America's
public schools have not learned to read. The failure of children in the US
to read proficiently is an all too consistent finding and this trend is
remarkable in its persistence. But it does not have to be this way. The
reading research supported and conducted by the NICHD and other
federal agencies has led to the development of assessment strategies that
can identify children at risk for reading failure and monitor their progress
as we teach them. The scientific evidence has shown us that reading must
be taught – directly and systematically – and that the children most at risk
require the most systematic instruction with the best-prepared teachers.
Science has taught us that millions of children's lives have been
squandered through illiteracy – not because they did not have the ability
to learn to read but because teachers who understood what the scientific
research indicates did not teach them. Still today, teachers are being
prepared to teach reading on the basis of romantic and disproved
philosophies and concepts. Untested assumptions and belief systems
continue to guide the most important instruction a teacher can provide –
instruction to teach reading. In short, there remains an unforgiveable gap
between what we know about reading development and effective reading
instruction and the instruction provided in many of our schools. This must
stop. There are no more excuses.

References

Adams M J (1990) Beginning to Read: Thinking and Learning about Print. Cambridge: MIT
    Press.
Adams MJ (1991) Why not phonics and whole language? In Ellis W (ed.) All Language and
    the Creation of Literacy. Baltimore: Orton Dyslexia Society, pp. 40–53.
Adams MJ, Bruck M (1995a) Resolving the 'great debate'. American Educator 19(2): 10–20.
Adams MJ, Bruck M (1995b) Word recognition: the interface of educational policies and
    scientific research. Reading and Writing 5: 113–39.
Campbell C (1992) The National Educational Goals Report: Building a Nation of Learners.

Washington DC: National Educational Goals Panel.

Coleman JS (1966) Equality of Educational Opportunity. Washington DC: US Department of Health Education and Welfare Office of Education.

Ellis AK, Fouts JT (1997) Research on Educational Innovations, 2nd edn. Larchmont NY: Eye on Education.

Fletcher JM, Lyon GR (1998) Reading: a research-based approach. In W Evers (ed.) What's Gone Wrong in America's Classrooms? Stanford CA: Hoover Institution Press.

Foorman BR, Francis D, Fletcher JM, Schatschneider C, Mehta P (1998) The role of instruction in learning to read: preventing reading failure in at-risk children. Journal of Educational Psychology 90: 1–15.

Goodman KS (1967) Reading: a psycholinguistic guessing game. Journal of the Reading Specialist 6: 126–35.

Goodman KS (1986) What's Whole in Whole Language? Portsmouth NH: Heinemann.

Hirsch Jr ED (1996) The Schools We Need and Why We Don't Have Them. New York: Anchor Books.

Kennedy MM (1997) The connection between research and practice. Educational Researcher 26: 4–12.

Lagemann EC (2000) An Elusive Science: The Troubling History of Education Research. Chicago: The University of Chicago Press.

Lagemann EC, Shulman LS (eds) (1999) Issues in Education Research. San Francisco: Jossey-Bass.

Langenberg DN (2000) Testimony of Donald N Langenberg, Committee on Education and the Workforce, September 26.

Lyon GR (1995a) Toward a definition of dyslexia. Annals of Dyslexia 45: 3–27.

Lyon GR (1995b) Learning disabilities: past, present and future perspectives. The Future of Children 6: 24–46.

Lyon GR (1996) Learning disabilities. In Mash E, Barkley R (eds) Child Psychopathology. New York: Guilford Press, pp. 390–435.

Lyon GR (1997) Why kids can't read. Testimony of Lyon GR to Committee on Education and the Workforce, July 10th 1997.

Lyon GR (1998) Why reading is not a natural process. Educational Leadership (March): 14–18.

Lyon GR (2002) Reading development, reading difficulties and reading instruction: educational and public health issues. Journal of School Psychology 40: 3–6.

Lyon GR, Chhabra V (in press) The science of reading research and its importance to teaching reading. Educational Leadership.

Lyon GR, Fletcher J M, Shaywitz SE, Shaywitz BA, Torgesen JK, Wood FB, Schulte A, Olson R (2001) Rethinking learning disabilities. In Finn CE, Rotherham RAJ and Hokanson CR (eds) Rethinking Special Education for a New Century. Washington DC: Thomas B Fordham Foundation and Progressive Policy Institute, pp. 259–87.

Lyon GR, Shaywitz SE, Shaywitz BA (2003) A definition of dyslexia. Annals of Dyslexia 53: 1–14.

McDaniel JE, Sims CH, Miskel CG (2001) The national reading policy arena: policy actors and perceived influence. Educational Policy 15(1): 92–114.

McKenna MC, Stahl SA, Reinking D (1994) A critical commentary on research politics and whole language. Journal of Reading Behavior 26: 211–33.

Moats LC (2000) Whole Language Lives On: The Illusion of 'Balanced' Reading Instruction. Retrieved November 25 2003 from http://www.ldonline.org/ld_indepth/reading/whole_language_lives_on.html

National Center for Educational Statistics (2003) National Assessment of Educational Progress: The Nation's Report Card. Washington DC: US Department of Education.

National Institute of Child Health and Human Development (2000) Report of the National Reading Panel Teaching Children to Read: An Evidence-based Assessment of the Scientific Research Literature on Reading and its Implications for Reading Instruction: Reports of the Subgroups (NIH Publication No 00-4754). Washington DC: US Government Printing Office.

Ravitch D (1983) The Troubled Crusade: American Education 1945-1980. New York: Basic Books.

Ravitch D (2001) Left Back: A Century of Battles over School Reform. New York: Simon & Schuster.

Rayner K, Foorman BR, Perfetti CA, Pesetsky D, Seidenberg MS (2001) How psychological science informs the teaching of reading. Psychological Science in the Public Interest 2(2): 31-74.

Shaywitz SE (2003) Overcoming Dyslexia. New York: Knopf.

Smith F (1973) Understanding Reading. New York: Holt, Rinehart & Winston.

Smith F (1977) Making sense of reading and of reading instruction. Harvard Educational Review 47: 386-95.

Snow C, Burns S, Griffin P (eds) (1998) Preventing Reading Difficulties in Young Children. Washington DC: National Academy Press.

Snow CE (2000) On the limits of reframing: rereading the National Academy of Sciences Report on Reading. Journal of Literacy Research 32(1): 113-20.

Song M, Coggshell J, Miskel C (in press) Where does policy come from and why should we care? In McCardle P and Chhabra V (eds) The Voice of Evidence in Reading Research. Baltimore: Brookes.

Sowell T (1993) Inside American Education: The Decline, the Deception, the Dogmas. New York: The Free Press.

Stahl SA, Miller PD (1989) Whole language and language experience approaches for beginning reading: a quantitative research synthesis. Review of Educational Research 59(1): 87-116.

Stanovich KE (2000) Progress in Understanding Reading: Scientific Foundations and New Frontiers. New York: Guilford Press.

Sweet R (in press) The big picture: where are we nationally on the reading front? In McCardle P and Chhabra V (eds) The Voice of Evidence in Reading Research. Baltimore: Brookes.

Torgesen JK (2002) The prevention of reading difficulties. Journal of School Psychology 40(1): 7-26.

Whitehurst G (2001) Beginning Reading Development in Early Childhood. The White House Summit on Early Childhood Cognitive Development. Washington DC: US Department of Education.

CHAPTER 10

Dyslexia and the workplace – policy for an inclusive society

DAVID MCLAUGHLIN

Introduction

In 1994 Whurr Publishers introduced the first UK book to include the words 'adult' and 'dyslexic' in the same title: *Adult Dyslexia: Assessment, Counselling and Training* (McLoughlin et al., 1994). Since then a number of other books devoted to the issues facing dyslexic adults have been published,[1] those specifically addressing employment matters being Bartlett and Moody (2000), Reid and Kirk (2001) and McLoughlin et al. (2003).

There has also been more research into the problems facing adults, and the needs of adults, but studies have concentrated on students in further and higher education. Conducting research with adult dyslexics where they are not a captive audience is difficult, finding a representative sample being a particular problem. Volunteers are likely to be the 'most needy', others being reluctant to participate. The closest we have to a large-scale study is the results of the International Literacy Survey (Carey et al., 1997). This included people with 'self-reported' learning disabilities and a subsequent analysis of the data (Fawcett, 2003) identified significant numbers of individuals with severe persisting literacy problems. In the absence of a large body of quantitative data we have to rely on the small-scale studies that exist, as well as the individual experiences of dyslexic people and those working with them.

Eighty per cent of the population of the United Kingdom is over 16 years of age. This implies that the same percentage of dyslexic individuals is

---

1   It has been suggested that it is preferable to refer to 'people with dyslexia' rather than 'dyslexic people' or 'dyslexics'. Consistent with the theme of empowerment and the suggestion of Reiff, Gerber and Ginsberg (1993) that adults with learning difficulties should participate in the process of description and definition I continue to use phrases such as 'dyslexic people' or the word 'dyslexic'. I have met few who have described themselves as 'an adult with dyslexia'. Some have specifically disregarded phrases such as 'a person with dyslexia' because of its medical connotations.

beyond the age of compulsory schooling, but the needs of this group have been given far less attention than those of children still at school. Dyslexia has remained more of an educational issue than one that affects daily living, including employment. Although the past decade has seen a greater interest in dyslexic adults, this does not necessarily mean they have been recognized as a distinct population, with needs that are quite different from their younger counterparts. Provision has often been an 'add on', the same practices as employed with children being applied to adults.

Models and definitions of dyslexia

There is still a need for a fundamental shift in thinking on behalf of professionals, researchers, and all the organizations, including employers, concerned with providing for dyslexic people. If dyslexic people are to be *included*, the emphasis should be on empowerment or enablement rather than a model of disability that perceives the 'dyslexic as a victim'. Empowerment comes from:

- Self understanding – dyslexia is often referred to as a 'hidden disability'. Dyslexic people do, therefore, have to advocate for themselves, and can only do so if they have a good understanding of the nature of their difficulty, how it affects them and what they need to do about it to improve their performance.
- Understanding by others, particularly their employers – if dyslexic people have to deal with managers and colleagues whose understanding of the nature of the syndrome is limited then they will be excluded rather than included.

The persistence of dyslexia in the adult years raises important issues about definition, with consequent implications for practice. To take advantage of the provisions of the Disability Discrimination Act (1995), for example, individuals do not have to establish that they are dyslexic but that their difficulties constitute a disability that has significant adverse day-to-day effects. A narrow literacy-based view will not protect dyslexic people from discrimination, nor will it oblige employers to make adjustments that will 'level the playing field'.

Defining dyslexia has however remained an elusive business, most definitions focusing on literacy. The Division of Educational and Child Psychology (DECP) of the British Psychological Society (1999) produced a report that offered as a working definition 'Dyslexia is evident when accurate and fluent word reading and/or spelling develops very incompletely or with great difficulty' (p. 5). This is despite the fact that almost 10 years earlier Miles and Miles wrote that 'there is no contradiction in saying that a person is dyslexic while nevertheless being a competent reader; and indeed many dyslexic adults come into this category' (Miles and Miles, 1990: ix). Some authors now refer to 'literate dyslexic', recognizing that there are problems that extend beyond literacy. Dyslexia continues to undermine the performance of literate dyslexic adults. They are still dyslexic, regardless of whether they have learned to read, write and spell. Returning to literacy-based definitions sets back a decade the understanding of dyslexia as it affects adults. It is usually the way in which dyslexic people process information that is of interest to employers, not their literacy skills. Trainers are concerned with matters such as following procedures.

Reid (2003) suggests that definitions should recognize that dyslexia is contextual. We do, therefore, need to consider the syndrome as it is manifested in the adult years, specifically in the workplace. Dyslexic adults and their employers require sensible and comprehensive models that they can understand and:

- explain all the primary difficulties;
- allow for the anticipation of what might be difficult in the future;
- enable employees and employers to see the relevance of specific strategies and adjustments.

In considering definitions we also need to consider the language we use. As dyslexia has been and continues to be regarded as an educational issue, much of the language surrounding it belongs to the world of learning and teaching. Viewed from the adult perspective a good deal of the terminology is inappropriate. One should not, for example, suggest that the manager seeking to improve his report-writing skills is in need of 'remedial help'. Even 'dyslexia' is often incorrectly used interchangeably with 'specific learning difficulty' or 'reading difficulty', the focus being on literacy. It is a specific learning difficulty but only one of a number.

Even the generic term 'learning difficulty' is inappropriate for many adult dyslexics as they have learned very well, albeit differently, but continue to have a 'performance difficulty'. I am using the word 'dyslexia' here in its very broadest sense; that is, as 'a family of lifelong manifestations that show themselves in many other ways than poor reading' (Miles et al., 1998). Dyslexic people can find learning difficult but in the adult years their ability to 'perform' in social, family and work settings, as well as their ability to adapt to transitions in these settings, is of greater concern. The definition I advance is therefore:

Dyslexia is an inefficiency in the cognitive processes that underlie effective performance in conventional educational and workplace settings. It has a particular impact on written and verbal communication, as well as organization, planning and adaptation to change.

Dyslexia at work

Being dyslexic is not necessarily a barrier to occupational success; there are too many dyslexic people in all occupations to refute this. Some occupations are more dyslexia-friendly than others, tapping the dyslexic people's strengths rather than their weaknesses. There are undoubtedly dyslexic people who are in the wrong job – that is, they are in a situation where the demands on tasks they find difficult outweigh those on their competencies and strengths. Career guidance/counselling geared towards the needs of dyslexic people is arguably one of the most important but underresourced professional activities. There is also a lack of systematic transition planning, leading to people becoming a 'victim of their own success'. That is, they have not been given the opportunity to develop the skills they will need to cope with increased demands, working only to long-term rather than short-term goals.

Dyslexia is often misunderstood and so the difficulties facing individuals at work can be exacerbated because the challenges they face are not obvious, being concerned with organization, social skills and coping with transitions rather than literacy. Many dyslexic people, having survived the traumas of the school system and leaving with few qualifications, find learning 'on the job' more effective. As they deal with the problems they face, they may learn to avoid situations involving literacy skills and become very well organized in work. They certainly may have more confidence than they had in school, being evaluated on their performance rather than through tests and examinations. This will, however, only be maintained if they have opportunities to continue developing the literacy, learning and technological skills and if, like any employee, they feel valued.

The employers' role

Responsibilities

One of the major influences on the increasing interest in dyslexia during adulthood has been the introduction of the Disability Discrimination Act (1995). Section 1 of the Act defines 'disabled person' as a person with 'a physical or mental impairment' that has a substantial and long-term adverse effect on his ability to carry out normal day-to-day activity. Dyslexia is not listed as a disability but can be covered under the heading of 'memory or ability to concentrate, learn or understand'. There is, however, an illustrative example in the Code of Practice that refers to dyslexia as a specific case of a disability. The Act recommends that account should be taken of the person's ability to remember, organize his or her thoughts, plan a course of action and execute it or take in new knowledge. This includes considering whether the person learns to do things more slowly than is normal.

In some ways this is more satisfactory than the use of labels. However, concern has been expressed at the parameters recommended by the legislators. The examples given are that it would be reasonable to regard as a substantial effect:

- Persistent inability to remember the names of familiar people such as family or friends.
- Inability to adapt to minor change in work routine.

It would not be reasonable to regard as a substantial effect:

- Occasionally forgetting the name of a familiar person such as a work colleague.
- Inability to concentrate on a task requiring application over several hours.
- Inability to fill in a long, detailed technical document without assistance.
- Inability to read at speed under pressure.

Under the Act, employers, trade organizations such as unions, as well as professional organizations:

- may not discriminate against a disabled person in recruitment, promotion or dismissal;
- must make reasonable adjustments to the job or the workplace to help a disabled person do a job.

If employees feel that they have been discriminated against illegally, they can take their employer to an employment tribunal.

Dyslexic people should never assume that they are automatically entitled to protection under the Act, nor should employers think they are not. Dyslexic people have successfully and unsuccessfully lodged complaints with employment tribunals. At a tribunal three specific issues are considered. These are:

- Whether dyslexia is a disability for the purposes of the Act.
- Whether the person's dyslexia affects their ability to carry out normal day-to-day activities.
- Whether an employer has made reasonable adjustments for the dyslexic person.

Establishing that dyslexia is a disability should not be difficult. Paragraph 4.12 of the Code of Practice expressly contemplates it as such in a given example. Further, although not specifically mentioned in the World Health Organization International Classification of Diseases or the Diagnostic and

Statistical Manual (IV), the behavioural characteristics of dyslexia are listed under headings such as Specific Reading Disorder.

Demonstrating that there are adverse affects on the ability to carry out normal day-to-day activities can be more difficult. Dyslexia is not well understood as an information processing difficulty so employers, as well as lawyers, are likely to focus on literacy skills alone. If someone does have very basic reading, writing and spelling skills this inevitably has an effect on day-to-day functioning. Literate dyslexics are in a more difficult position, however.

Those supporting dyslexic people need to focus on the extent of the information processing. The Act does specifically refer to the person's ability to remember, organize his or her thoughts, plan a course of action and execute it, or take in new knowledge. Someone who has good academic qualifications and advanced literacy skills but needs to get to work much earlier than everyone else, and leave later in order to complete all the tasks that would be required in a normal day, is being affected on a day-to-day basis.

The matter of 'reasonable adjustment' is also contentious. Under Section 5.2 of the Disability Discrimination Act, if an employer fails to make reasonable adjustments under Section 6 of the Act, that failure in itself is an act of discrimination. There is a duty on employers not to discriminate against disabled people in recruitment, selection, promotion, retention and dismissal. As part of 'retention' employers are required to act on the recommendations made to support dyslexic people. This can include the provision of training, equipment and supervision.

The implications for practitioners working with dyslexic people are that:

- They need to adopt a definition that allows them to be very specific about the nature of dyslexia in its widest context if
  (a) it is to be interpreted as a disability, and
  (b) adverse day-to-day affects are to be established.
- They need to make very specific recommendations about appropriate skill development training, compensations and adjustments.

One of the ways in which employers are required to make adjustments is in the process of recruitment and selection. The Employers' Forum on Disability recommends flexibility, as often minor changes can make a significant difference, and a focus on 'what' is to be achieved in the job rather than 'how' it is to be achieved, allowing for a dyslexic person's different working style.

Usually the recruitment process begins with the completion of an application form. A simple format with a clear typeface, acceptance of emailed applications so that they can be typed and checked for spelling and perhaps the use of different coloured paper can all accommodate the needs of dyslexic people.

There have been particular concerns where psychometric tests measuring abilities and attainments are used. Dyslexia does affect performance in test situations, especially where there are time constraints, and dyslexic people might therefore be prevented from demonstrating their abilities. Some could, for example, be very good at verbal reasoning but this is not reflected in their performance when they complete 'pencil-and-paper' tests. It is common for dyslexics to gain lower scores on group administered tests of ability than those they achieve when tests are administered individually and verbally.

In making adjustments the key issue is to 'obtain an accurate assessment of those job-relevant abilities/aptitudes, while minimising the influence of job-irrelevant factors' (Meehan et al., 1998: 6). Adjustments for dyslexic people during the selection process could include:

- Applicants should be contacted to provide information about the assessment process and the different types of task involved. This would enable them to say if they are likely to have any difficulties and how these can be best overcome.
- Applicants should be encouraged to provide information about the ways in which they would normally deal with a 'pencil-and-paper' task.
- Test publishers should be contacted as they might have materials required in the format the candidate can use.
- Untimed tests could be used or candidates could be given extra time. Changing time allowances can create problems in interpretation, however, especially when speed is integral to the test. Determining how much extra time should be allowed is difficult. Too little might not lessen the disadvantage; too much might increase it, fatigue being a factor (Nester, 1993).
- How the person would use the skill being measured on the job and whether the adapted version of the test measures the same ability is a key consideration.
- A qualitative view should be taken in making a decision, integrating all the information about the candidate, including test scores, exercise results and ratings. The skills the candidate may have gained from just managing his or her disability should not be underestimated
- Employers who use methodology such as an interview could allow dyslexic people to refer to notes.

Valuing difference

Making reasonable adjustments so that dyslexic people can use their skills and abilities is a matter of establishing what has been termed 'goodness of fit' (Gerber et al., 1992). It can be improved through encouraging a positive attitude towards dyslexic people. The ideal situation is one in which there is a 'whole-organization approach'. That is where there is a good understanding of dyslexia and a network throughout the organization to support the dyslexic employee.

One of the problems facing dyslexic people is that dyslexia is a 'hidden disability'. Dyslexic people can be 'different' but supervisors and colleagues don't know why. A whole-organization approach should therefore begin with awareness training, directed towards increasing everyone's understanding. It should include information about the nature of dyslexia, how it affects people individually and in the workplace. The emphasis should be on solutions rather than problems, and stress that many of the adjustments made for dyslexic people can improve the working environment for everyone. There is, however, a need for balance; it is easy to exaggerate the difficulties, portraying dyslexia as an insurmountable problem, when it isn't. At the same time, by highlighting simple solutions the difficulties experienced by dyslexic people on a day to day basis can be underestimated.

Awareness training can be followed up by establishing support groups, identifying named staff who can be contacted for advice, setting up a mentoring system and arranging specialist input when necessary. In general, there should be co-ordination of and co-operation with staff responsible for human resources, equal opportunities and in-house differentiation in selection, training and appraisal.

In designing an awareness-training programme it is important to acknowledge that, in general, people are comfortable with their 'sameness'. Walker (1994: 212) has recommended that organizations should value differences as an approach to affirmative action and equality of opportunity. Rather than allow differences to create discomfort and conflict, she suggests that they should be seen as something which can 'fuel creative energy and insight . . . (as) points of tension that spark alternative viewpoints and ideas, and ignite the kindling process behind creativity and innovation.'

Walker's Valuing Differences Model is based on four principles:

● People work best when they feel valued.
● People feel most valued when they believe that their individual and group differences have been taken into account.
● The ability to learn from people regarded as different is the key to becoming fully empowered.
● When people feel valued and empowered, they are able to build relationships in which they work together interdependently.

She suggests that valuing difference is a way of helping people think through their assumptions and beliefs about all kinds of differences, facilitating both individual personal growth and an organization's productivity. Recognizing and valuing the 'differences' manifested by dyslexic people will facilitate their success and contribute to that of the organization. As Armstrong has written: 'Managing diversity is about ensuring that all people maximise their potential and their contribution to the organisation. It means valuing diversity, that is, valuing the differences between people and the different qualities they bring to their jobs which can lead to the development of a more rewarding and productive environment' (Armstrong, 1999: 804).

Employers do, however, need to take action through specific initiatives. Among the most successful of those that would be relevant to dyslexic people, described by Kandola and Fullerton (1994), are: buying specialized equipment, employing helpers, and training trainers in equal opportunities. Employers should consider the 'reasonable adjustments' that can be made to allow dyslexic people to show themselves at their best. They need to be aware of their legal responsibilities, specifically meeting the requirements of the Disability Discrimination Act (DDA). Employers should be able to answer the following questions (adapted from Wehman, 1996):

- Do you provide information to job applicants and employees about their rights under the DDA?
- Have you informed supervisory staff of their responsibilities under the DDA?
- Have you ensured your employment practices and procedures do not discriminate against applicants or employees who are dyslexic?
- Do you make adjustments for dyslexic applicants during the selection process and when employed by you?
- Can you identify the main skills involved in jobs, and do interview questions focus on whether an applicant has or can acquire these skills?

Employers do need to consider financial issues but often cost considerations are minimal. The two questions they really need to address are:

Can we alter the job?
- Restructure the job.
- Extend a training period.
- Provide alternative training.
- Modify work schedules.
- Reassign tasks.
- Provide a mentor or coach.

Can we alter the workplace?
- Change the workstation.
- Provide organizational aids.
- Allow flexible working hours.
- Provide appropriate technology.

The employee's role

Inclusion is also fostered through advocacy, especially self-advocacy.

> Advocacy is the representation of the views, feelings and interests of one person or group of people by another individual or organisation. Self-advocacy is the action of a person on their own behalf without the intervention of another. The shift in focus from advocacy to self-advocacy is a natural extension of the process of empowerment. (Garner and Sandow, 1995)

Advocacy for dyslexic people in the UK has been best represented by the work of organizations such as the British Dyslexia Association. Self-advocacy is reflected in the work of adult support groups.

Organizations advocating for the interests of dyslexic people have been quite effective in promoting a better understanding of the needs of adults, but without allowing for self-advocacy they can find that the very people they are trying to help become aggressive towards them. At the same time self-advocacy needs to be based in self-understanding and empathy, otherwise those seeking their rights and greater equity can alienate those who are trying to help them. It should be recognized that rather than there being 'experts in dyslexia' there are a variety of people who have an expertise. There are professionals, for example, who know how to diagnose, advise and train dyslexic people. Dyslexic individuals do, however, have their own views and an understanding based on their personal experience. The way forward is therefore to ensure that there is partnership between advocates, including professionals, and those engaging in self-advocacy.

Self-advocacy

Self-advocacy is particularly important to dyslexic individuals. It is a 'hidden disability' and this means that their difficulties are less obvious and less well understood. Many struggle with the issue of 'disclosure' – that is, the question of whether they should tell an employer or a prospective employer that they are dyslexic. If they wish to access resources and be protected under the terms of the Disability Discrimination Act, they need to do so, although tribunal panels have acknowledged that it is often difficult for people with disabilities to admit to the problems they experience.

To avoid discrimination and ensure that they are properly understood, dyslexic people need to be able to explain what dyslexia is, how it affects them, the way in which they work best, and what an employer can do to assist them. This applies during the process of selection and whilst in the job. Whilst it is never easy to know how much to say or when to say it, dyslexic people must:

1. Understand themselves.
- *Know their strengths.* We all have talents and abilities and dyslexic people need to know what theirs are and feel positive about them.
- *Know their weaknesses.* We all have these and need to work around them. It is important to be realistic and know one's limitations.
- *Know what adjustments enable them to do their best.* Employers and colleagues can only know what to do if they are aware exactly what is being asked for.
- *Know what situations to avoid.* There are those that will present insurmountable difficulties.

2. Be specific.
- *Dyslexic people should only tell what is necessary to those who need to know.* They should therefore be discreet and selective. There will be people who are not ready to hear what they have to say.
- *They should talk about what they can do.* If they have particular needs, they should tell people what they need rather than what their problem is.
- *Dyslexic people should try to give a complete picture*, and be able to describe the problem, the cause and the solution.

3. Provide information.
It can be helpful to others to provide information, both verbally and in written form. Authoritative handouts provided by appropriate organizations can add credibility. These can include articles and books or videos about dyslexia, and suitable adjustments.

Essentially, dyslexic people will get what they need by telling people what they need, not what their problem is.

Policy and practice in employment

Responsibility for supporting dyslexic people at work lies within the Disability Service of the Department for Work and Pensions. The Service offers a wide range of programmes designed to help people find and maintain employment, including the following:

- It offers a variety of services, including practical help directed towards enabling dyslexic people to find work for the first time or to return to work.
- Occupational psychologists work within the Disability Services Division and provide specialist assessment, counselling and training for people with disabilities, including dyslexics.
- Disability employment advisers are based in job centres and are engaged to help and advise individuals who are encountering barriers to employment because of their disabilities. They work with occupational psychologists.

The Employment Service conducts a number of programmes, the most recently developed being the New Deal, which was designed to help unemployed people generally but has specific provision for people with disabilities. The programme is delivered with the aid of personal advisers. Access to Work is designed to provide help for people with disabilities securing and maintaining employment with practical support such as the provision of special aid and equipment and adaptations to premises, support workers and other assistance in meeting personal needs. For a comprehensive review of provision in employment readers are referred to Reid and Kirk (2001).

References

Armstrong M (1999) A Handbook of Human Resources Management Practice. London: Kogan Page.

Bartlett D, Moody S (2000) Dyslexia in the Workplace. London: Whurr.

Carey S, Low S, Hansboro J (1997) Adult Literacy in Britain. London: OCNS.

Division of Educational and Child Psychology of the British Psychological Society (1999) Dyslexia, Literacy and Psychological Assessment. Leicester: BPS.

Fawcett A (2003) The International Adult Literacy Survey in Britain: impact on policy and practice. Dyslexia 9(2): 99–121.

Garner P, Sandow S (1995) Advocacy, Self-Advocacy and Special Needs. London: Fulton.

Gerber PJ, Ginsberg R, Reiff HB (1992) Identifying alterable patterns in employment success for highly successful adults with learning disabilities. Journal of Learning Disabilities 25(8): 475–87.

Kandola R, Fullerton J (1994) Managing the Mosaic: Diversity in Action. London: Institute of Personnel and Development.

McLoughlin D, Fitzgibbon G, Young V (1994) Adult Dyslexia: Assessment, Counselling and Training. London: Whurr.

McLoughlin D, Leather C, Stringer P (2003) The Adult Dyslexic: Interventions and Outcomes. London: Whurr.

Meehan M, Birkin R, Snodgrass R (1998) Employment assessment (EA): issues surrounding the use of psychological assessment material with disabled people. Selection Development Review 14(3): 3–9.

Miles TR, Miles E (1990) Dyslexia: a Hundred Years On. Milton Keynes: Open University Press.

Miles TR, Haslum MN, Wheeler TJ (1998) Gender Ratio in Dyslexia. Annals of Dyslexia 48: 27–57.

Nester MA (1993) Psychometric testing and reasonable accommodations for persons with disabilities. Rehabilitation Psychology 38(2): 75–85.

Reid G (2003) Dyslexia: A Practitioner's Handbook, 3rd edn. Chichester: Wiley.

Reid G, Kirk J (2001) Dyslexia in Adults: Education and Employment. Chichester: Wiley.

Reiff HB, Gerber PJ, Ginsberg R (1993) Definitions of learning disabilities from adults with learning disabilities: the insiders' perspectives. Learning Disability Quarterly 16: 114–25.

Walker BA (1994) Valuing differences: the concept and a model. In Mabey C and Iles P (eds) Managing Learning. London: Routledge, pp. 211–23.

Wehman P (1996) Life Beyond the Classroom. Baltimore: Brookes.

CHAPTER 11

Learning disability/dyslexia and employment: a US perspective

GLENN YOUNG, JANE BROWNING

Introduction

In this chapter the term 'learning disability/dyslexia' ('LD/dyslexia') will be used to cover both the US and the UK definitions of dyslexia. This chapter will examine the lack of appropriate research, and other issues, relating to employment and LD/dyslexia. The inherent bias in past and present research is one of the key factors that will be discussed here, and particularly its effect on employment outcomes of persons with learning disabilities and dyslexia. The authors suggest that problems in research bias are actually preventing persons with LD/dyslexia from attaining both academic and employment success.

Research into employment and adults with LD/dyslexia

As of mid-2003 there has been no comprehensive study of employment outcomes for persons with LD/dyslexia despite the issue being raised as early as 1991. Prior studies and research have been largely anecdotal, and/or rife with 'selection bias' and support and promote intervention models that were 'normed' on very limited populations (Reiff et al., 1997).

Many groups have not been included in the general research on adults with LD/dyslexia because their LD/dyslexia had not been identified, or they lost their status as persons with learning disabilities upon leaving school. Therefore most, if not all, of the studies on LD/dyslexia are tainted with 'selection bias' towards those with LD/dyslexia identified in schools, who are least moderately successful or alternatively those who have been very seriously affected to the point that they have little expectation of success. The pool of students identified with LD used for the studies may only represent a third of those with LD/dyslexia at best and the two extremes of those with LD/dyslexia (highly successful or very seriously affected). This figure is based on the NICHD findings that the actual rate of those with reading disabilities in childhood is about 15% to 17%.

One aspect that has been missing from previous research is an evaluation of the issues from the 'adults' perspective'. Most studies about adults with LD/dyslexia have focused on reading skills and how to address and remediate these. This approach assumes that:

- reading skill deficits are the only, or the major, impact on the lives of persons with LD/dyslexia (which has not been proven);
- reading interventions can really work for adults with LD/dyslexia, considering the complexity of adult lives (which also has not been proven); and
- interventions are the same for 20-year-olds as for 45-year-olds, perhaps with 20-year-old children of their own.

Most studies on adults with LD/dyslexia in the past and present are focused on child issues (failure to read) and child solutions (learning to read) and conducted on individuals in their late teens or early twenties, using inadequate sampling.

We need to be asking the research questions from an adult's perspective. What do adults with LD/dyslexia need in order to become functional as adults within the confines of the complexity of adults' lives (throughout the adult span) and the impact of their disability?

This question can only be answered by greatly expanding the pool or the populations included in the research, and by using methods of investigation that account for variables such as age, race, gender, language and past failure to identify the disability (Young et al., 1999).

We suggest here that the available research on the employment prospects of persons with LD/dyslexia falls into two main pools: the experiences of individuals who have been 'successful', or those with very severe LD/dyslexia, who are most affected and least likely to become successful in education and work.

Some research in the US on adults with LD/dyslexia has expanded to include studies on the prevalence of these disorders within 'unsuccessful' adult populations. This research has looked at single parents on state support, adults enrolled in literacy and basic-skills programmes, or in prison. By looking at these populations we see a very different result and pattern (and general outcomes) compared to those identified in schools, in those who graduated from high school and went on to college.

Many within this 'unsuccessful population' of adults were not identified with LD/dyslexia in schools and are likely to remain 'unidentified' throughout their lives. These 'unsuccessful populations' have not been included in the general research on adults with LD/dyslexia, in large part simply because their LD/dyslexia had not been identified, or they lost their status as persons with learning disabilities upon leaving school.

When we really look at the 'failure' rates of persons with LD/dyslexia in school and in post-academic settings, even among those who have been identified and have received services, we are faced with the conclusion that what has been happening in schools has mostly not worked in preparing most people with LD/dyslexia for adult life and the world of employment.

Identification and support

There is now substantial evidence based on NICHD studies to suggest that more than two-thirds of those with LD/dyslexia are not identified and have never received services for their disability. These 'unidentified' people are those who make up the bulk of the 'great middle' group of persons with LD/dyslexia. There are many reasons for this unidentified 'middle' in the US – the historic failure to identify most of the persons with LD/dyslexia – including issues of funding and parental concerns over labelling to name just two, and they are beyond the scope of this chapter. However, over the 25 years of federally funded special education in the US, the combined factors have resulted in the vast majority of those with LD/dyslexia struggling, without special education services, and not considered as persons with disabilities/dyslexia. These unidentified K-12 students of the recent past now make up the 'great middle' of adults with LD/dyslexia.

The NICHD research now indicates about 17% of children have reading disabilities, which supports the higher end of the range for LD. (See NICHD Keys to Success Summit on Learning Disabilities, Washington DC, May 1999.) Part of the problem in identifying the actual number of persons with LD/dyslexia includes significant conflicts in definitions and diagnostic procedures between the various entities for both adult populations and the K-12 populations, and even the variations between definitions from state to state in the US. It is also worth noting that people are usually counted as having LD/dyslexia only if they 'qualify' for something.

In the US, for children, this means qualification for 'special education programmes'. In the US, the schools over the past 25 years have identified about 5% of all students each year as having LD/dyslexia. This 5% figure is not really the number of children with LD in the US. This is only the 5% of all students in schools who have been evaluated and found to have LD/dyslexia to a degree that qualifies them for special education services. There are many others, children both in and out of schools, with LD/dyslexia, but some of those children have been identified through testing and found not 'severe enough' for special education (less than 2 years behind peers). Some others, for a number of reasons (often associated with assumptions about gender and also lack of school funds), are showing signs of LD/dyslexia but are not tested for LD/dyslexia. Some are tested, but not properly evaluated, (due to bias in the testing or the test administrator, or language issues, gender issues, and so forth). For example, there are few bilingual and bicultural evaluators qualified to test in languages other than English. Moreover, some people were found to have LD/dyslexia, but designated as having a different disability than LD, such as emotional or behavioural disability or listed in the special education category of 'multiple disabilities'.

This means that if 15% of the US population has LD/dyslexia, as speculated in the past, and now supported by the NICHD research, then as many as two-thirds of those with LD/dyslexia, in the present school cohort, are not receiving services that they need in public schools. The same can be said for every cohort of students that has gone through school since the inception of special education (and before).

The undercount of those with LD/dyslexia is not just in schools, but continues into adulthood. However, in the adult world, the undercount becomes even more dramatic as in adulthood those counted as having LD/dyslexia are those with official documentation, and are involved in systems that require 'proof of disability', such as colleges, or high-school equivalency testing. Less than 0.5% of people taking the high-school equivalency exams are accommodated as having LD/dyslexia (see American Council on Education, 1995 through 2000, in the further reading section at the end of this chapter).

In the past, most people with LD/dyslexia relied on schools for documentation of the disability. However, with the passing of IDEA (Individuals with Disabilities Education Act) 97 amendments there has been a marked decrease in testing of older students for LD (with schools relying on testing that may be 7 to 10 years old). Most students with LD, on leaving high school, will therefore not have 'proof' of their disability (testing within 3 years) for these other entities, unless 'new' testing is provided. Once out of the school systems, the schools have no legal requirement to provide new testing.

It has been estimated that less than 1% of the 15% of all adults with LD/dyslexia have the current documentation required by a college to prove that they have the disability. The traditional source of testing for adults (and re-establishing the disability status), other than family resources, has been a programme in the US called Vocational Rehabilitation (VR) Services. This source of testing has also all but been eliminated for adults with LD/dyslexia.

State Vocational Rehabilitation programmes were ordered by the federal government to provide services to persons with 'most severe' disabilities first, based on resources available. Since that time, of the 50 states, 39 are under this 'order of selection' requirement. Almost all states have responded by eliminating or sharply reducing most services for persons with LD/dyslexia (because they have no obvious physical disorders that are severe).

Another major resource in the US for children with severe disabilities, including LD/dyslexia, has been a financial support programme called Supplemental Security Income (SSI) and Social Security Disability Insurance (SSDI). With recent reforms, most adults with LD/dyslexia no longer qualify.

Moreover, not being able to qualify for VR or SSI/SSDI also limits the ability of adults with LD to gain access to work through targeted disabilities programmes.

Therefore, without adequate means for the population of adults with LD/dyslexia to maintain current 'identification', we end up with significant undercounts of adults with LD/dyslexia in data collection. For example:

- The National Adult Literacy Survey of 1993 found only 3% of adults having LD/dyslexia (based on self-identification).
- The annual report to Congress on the adult literacy system in the US shows a 1% rate of LD/dyslexia in persons seeking services in adult literacy programmes.

Public policy is developed in accordance with these figures. As there is no systematic study of adults with LD/dyslexia that can refute these figures, then these research and state reports determine the priorities that LD/dyslexia are given in public policy concerns.

The myth of success

The overwhelming evidence that is available to us today says that what we have been doing in schools and workplace training is not really working well for the LD/dyslexic population – even the 5% that is identified:

- LD/dyslexia students (the identified ones) drop out of high school at a rate twice to three times the rate of the general population.
- Students with LD/dyslexia enrol in college and post-secondary training programmes at one-tenth the rate of the general population.
- Studies show that persons with LD/dyslexia (both previously and newly identified) constitute at a minimum some 20% and perhaps as high as 60% of persons in welfare programmes.
- Numerous studies indicate that an extremely high percentage of persons in prison have LD/dyslexia, with estimates ranging as high as 80%.
- Some studies show that the LD/dyslexic population is very over-represented among runaway and homeless youths, in foster care, in juvenile justice, among school dropouts, among those involved in illegal drug use, and in divorce.

Some studies indicate that 70% of those in special education leave school with limited or no reading skills. This appears to be the case for all cohorts who have been through special education, dating back to the time that these records began in the mid-1970s.

Another indicator of success or lack of success of this population is college participation. Only about 5% of those identified as having LD/dyslexia in the US public schools and who received special education services go on to four-year colleges; less than 10% of those who enter college (or less than 0.5% of the total) received a four-year degree. (This compares to 25% of the general adult population in the US having a four-year degree.)

Legal intervention

There have been only limited (but successful) legal actions to protect the rights of persons with LD/dyslexia who are poor and on governmental assistance programmes. These actions have led to guidance from the US federal government on steps that need to be taken on behalf of persons with LD/dyslexia in state-supported job-training programmes.

As a result of these legal actions and some research studies it is now clear that there are strong indicators that a large percentage of those with LD/dyslexia are mixed extensively in with the 'failed populations' who are on welfare, in prisons, stuck without success in job training programmes or just getting by in some moderate to low-end employment situation. When we include these people in our 'pools of research' the number of 'successes' looks far smaller than previously indicated. In fact, almost all signs indicate that our efforts until now, in schools, and beyond, for the majority of persons with LD/dyslexia, have mostly failed.

Alternative perspectives

The crux of the problem is that in the research, and in interventions for adults, the issues that are addressed relate to LD/dyslexia from the perspective of children with reading problems, when we should be approaching issues from the perspective of adults with disabilities. Therefore we end up using the wrong intervention models for this population.

There are no data on successful intervention models for adults with disabilities if we define the issue as a disability issue, not an education or literacy issue. The way to develop success for this group, therefore, may be not to include the focus on 'reading skills only' or the focus on 'state support', but rather a 'disability-focused' approach.

If we look at disability success models, we see a consumer-based, independence model, not a teacher-based state-dependence model.

The success model is based on an informed consumer and self-empowerment.

The model stresses the following:

- acceptance of the disability;
- a focus on appropriate use of accommodations (adjustments);
- self-advocacy.

The model focuses on acceptance of differences and embracing of difference, rather than trying to 'fix themselves' to be just like everyone else. It is an ideology of self-pride, not pity.

This incorporation of thinking in a disability model requires us to stop thinking about learning disabilities as a literacy or reading issue, and one that only impacts on children in schools (again based on issues of qualification). We need to look at learning disabilities as a disability model with indicators and signs of the problem occurring early in life (slowness of development in speech and motor skills, and so forth) and the effects on the infant and child in early social interactions. The effects of these early developmental difficulties in social and in other areas continue through the life of the child into adulthood and into work, family and other settings.

The ideal system?

In late 1997, the US Department of Education, the National Institute for Literacy and the State of Maryland Department of Education convened a national expert panel to discuss the elements needed in an 'ideal system' for persons with LD/dyslexia involved in adult basic education programmes. The report developed by this meeting listed several ingredients for a successful approach to this population. Programmes need to be:

- *Consumer friendly:* culturally appropriate, adult centred, adult driven, sensitive to the complexity of adult lives.
- *Accountable:* outcome based.
- *Disability sensitive:* supportive of self-advocacy, supportive of reasonable accommodations.
- *Well funded:* adequately staffed, providing support services such as transportation, child care, educational supplies, diagnostic testing.

The report also stated that self-advocacy skills were among the most critical skills necessary for the adult in systems of all kinds, whether education, training, employment or financial assistance.

- In order to be well served, adult learners with learning disabilities must be equipped with knowledge about their disabilities and their manifestations, and have the documentation to show that they have the disability.
- They need to understand the laws and regulations concerning reasonable accommodations, and their right to have these accommodations in the workplace and in higher education.
- Adult learners need to know how to ask for what they want and to use accommodations as part of the general adult education process.
- These accommodations, and the ability to discuss them, can be key to success in transitioning through various phases of the learning experience.

These concepts of self-advocacy were seen by the national experts as the key to employment and education success for this population. The ability of people to explain to their employers what their limitations are, how they can be successfully accommodated and what if any costs are involved shows the potential employee to be knowledgeable, skilled and self-aware.

This is not a radical new approach. This model of self-awareness has long been a standard approach in vocational rehabilitation and other disability efforts in the US for all other disabilities. However, this disability model has not been used extensively by the programmes or organizations aimed at meeting the needs of adults with LD/dyslexia.

The use of this model helps to 'shift the power relationships' between the person with LD/dyslexia and programmes and work. For example, if an individual comes into the workplace and says, 'I learn differently', the employer is not legally required to provide any kind of accommodation. The individual coming in saying 'I have a disability' creates a situation requiring the employer to provide reasonable accommodations that would allow the employees with a disability to perform their job and to compete on a level playing field.

Disability laws are somewhat different in the US and UK, but in both countries:

- in special education, as a child, you receive attention and services if you *cannot* do the task based on the disability;
- in work and higher education, as adults, you receive protection from discrimination if you *can* do the task (with or without accommodations) despite the impact of the disability.

The approach to disabilities law concerning the workplace is almost 180 degrees opposite to the special education approach. When children transfer from special education to work, or higher education, they are often shocked to learn that 'things are not made easier' for them due to their disability. The schools have historically done little to prepare students with LD/dyslexia, or their parents, with knowledge of the laws of protection and also the ways and means of effective accommodation.

In addition, the schools (and sometimes parents) focus attention on the deficit, such as being unable to read, and focus very little on development of skills of the child through other means, such as learning to use books on tape. This historical approach has led to the individual with LD/dyslexia being unprepared for employment situations.

In the workplace, they need effective tools and accommodations so they can compete effectively. So much time is spent on 'remediation' of the disorders that the student often fails to gain the skills needed to use these tools. Furthermore, because students don't show progress in one area (learning to read) they are not allowed to take courses that would allow them to gain the skills. They therefore develop 'information deficit disorder', which prevents them from gaining and keeping jobs as effectively as their non-disabled peers.

The reforms of US education law in 1997 (Individuals with Disabilities Education Act, IDEA 97), in an effort to reduce the costs of special education and the paperwork involved, relaxed the requirements on schools to test children every 3 years for learning disabilities. As a result, it appears that there has been a marked decrease in testing in the public schools after age 14 or so. Unfortunately colleges, standardized testing organizations, and other groups require the documentation of disability to be no more than 3 years old. Many, if not most, students are leaving high schools with diagnostic test results that are far more then 3 years old, which may be acceptable for the school's special education requirements but not for any other system. Acquiring the proper test results outside of school is unaffordable for many. It appears that upwards of 90% of students with LD/dyslexia who are not going on to college lose their status as persons with a disability as they leave school.

A 'new' approach

Education and job training systems are preparing young adults to enter the workforce in a manner that is the opposite of what appears to be a successful model for persons with disabilities:

- The model of workforce success is based on a person who is self-aware, with the critical skills and knowledge needed for the job; who understands the laws on disabilities and is able to advocate for the right to accommodations and who possesses the proper documentation to show that they have a disability.
- The students coming into the workforce from school are not aware of what LD/dyslexia really is. They have not been trained in critical skills and knowledge other than in the area of reading. They are aware only of special education laws (if that) and have almost no knowledge of the other civil rights laws for persons with disabilities. They are usually unable to ask for the appropriate accommodations and are not in possession of documentation proving they have a disability.

The person with LD/dyslexia, knowing the facts about their disability potentially, could possibly avoid their 'fated' outcome of failure. It is possible that they can develop, within themselves, a sense of LD/dyslexia 'pride'. They could turn around the tendency to become 'fated to failure'.

Yet this concept of addressing LD as a disability is not present in most vocational training, adult literacy or employment services (Tomblin and Haring, 1999). Even when the concepts of disabilities are accepted, most of the interventions still remain, trying to teach how to read, rather than how to make the adult 'functional' in the adult world. Until we make this leap of understanding that we need to use 'disability' models for adults (and students) with LD/dyslexia, we will probably see the ongoing failure of this population.

This failure may not be noted well because much of the research in adults will continue to be biased to the more successful in college or those who have received extensive services. The failure, however, will still be evident in the ongoing chronic 'failures' of governmental programmes aimed at adult employment or literacy training, in welfare reform, in prison education and remediation efforts, and in fact in the broad national efforts to maintain economic competitiveness. Until the LD/dyslexia community moves itself towards acknowledging and supporting the 'broad middle of the curve', the adults who have not been identified or cannot prove they have the disability, the massive 'fated' failure of adults with LD/dyslexia will continue.

A new research paradigm

Throughout this chapter we have raised several points regarding how current and past research into the areas of adults with LD/dyslexia is flawed. The intervention models designed for adults based on these studies would consequently also seem to be mostly flawed, even if they appear to be successful for some adults with LD/dyslexia.

Recent NICHD research was and is far more inclusive, addressing many of the gender, race and class issues that so distorted other studies. Once the NICHD researchers included these non-white male populations, NICHD came to dramatic new conclusions on reading failure, LD/dyslexia, and about how to intervene in the reading deficits of children with LD/dyslexia. As noted, their research has had a major impact on federal law and teaching training in efforts to teach *all* children how to read, including the approximately 25% who come to school struggling, not ready or able to read, but who do not have a neurological impairment or disability. The success of these non-LD/dyslexia poor reading children in the NICHD studies has been remarkable, and almost universal – but less so for children with LD/dyslexia. However, this NICHD research does not address the needs of the cohorts of persons with LD/dyslexia who are currently adults, who are failing now, and who have mostly failed in the schools and need interventions now. There is a real societal need to 'leave no adult behind' when unsuccessful adults are increasingly impacting national budgets and economic productivity.

Addressing the needs of the adult population

Any research in this area of adults with LD/dyslexia should work in solid scientific models, as laid out by NICHD. These models have created the new professional paradigm on how educational research needs to be conducted. We need to ensure that adult research really follows the same paradigm.

Following these NICHD models, we cannot rely on self-report or even school identification for determining LD/dyslexia. Nor can we operate on the assumption that someone does not have LD/dyslexia based on some loose standard or measure of 'success'.

We have learned through the NICHD research that there are no gender, race or language 'deferments'. As Reid Lyon stated in Congressional testimony: 'Failure to learn to read adequately is much more likely among poor children, among nonwhite children, and among nonnative speakers of English.' Our research pools need to reflect that diversity and not continue the history of past inappropriate identification in the schools based on stereotyping minority and female populations.

Raising the issue of full-scale diagnosis is problematic because there are disagreements between schools and adult worlds, between countries and between diagnosticians, on what is an appropriate full-scale diagnostic process. Conflicts over proper diagnostic process have already filled several volumes and are not in the scope of this chapter. It is not our intention in this chapter to determine the outcome of the struggle about what tools to use or how nations define the issue but to suggest that strong guidelines be developed to which all future studies of adults with LD/dyslexia need to adhere.

The guidelines need to make sure that the diagnostic process:

- Uses 'adult models' (not child models). In the US the one most used for adults is the Vocational Rehabilitation (VR) testing model.
- Uses tools that have been normed and designed on and for adults, not children.
- Uses tools that take into account age, gender, class, race, language and educational background issues. (This is not to say that you cannot find that a minority-language-speaking person with a low level of education has learning disabilities. Quite the contrary, the tests used must be able to show that they have not eliminated persons from consideration for having learning disabilities, based on a language or education bias inherent in the testing model.)

In addition, the diagnostic process needs to look at the wide range of impact of learning disabilities, not just reading capacity. As expressed in the VR definition of learning disabilities, these areas include: attention, reasoning, processing, memory, communication, reading, writing, spelling, calculation, co-ordination, social competence and emotional maturity.

Conclusion

Future research must be based on questions that incorporate the understanding that those with learning disabilities *have* 'disabilities'. The research questions and approaches must always include disability models' intervention. We must modify Reid Lyon's research question of: 'Under what circumstances and conditions and using what types or combination of interventions and approaches can we positively impact the reading abilities of what types of child?' The modification for the adult with LD/dyslexia should be something like: 'Under what circumstances and conditions and using what types or combinations of instruction, accommodations including assistive technologies, and consumer training, can we increase the literacy, employment and social competency outcomes for adults with what type of impacts on their learning disabilities?'

This modification expands the needed elements in the research model beyond the academic, and the impacts of LD/dyslexia beyond just literacy. The question assumes consumer training as a key element. In addition it refines the term 'intervention' specifically to include accommodations and assistive technologies.

These modifications overtly state that research questions and models need to specifically include interventions designed for persons with disabilities, based in disability law.

It is clear from the research that the current models (prior to No Child Left Behind) for addressing these disabilities are failing dramatically almost all those with LD/dyslexia. This is especially clear if we include those who are not being identified in the school systems.

We need to develop research that can develop new, more holistic models for both children and adults that can accept 'disability' as a normal part of the life span, with no shame or stigma attached to disabilities; models that build in training on disability law and accommodations and include issues of interpersonal relationships and self-awareness as part of the general curriculum for children, teens and adults with LD/dyslexia in whatever programme they are involved.

Without these changes our research will continue to provide data and models that are biased and incomplete and the person with LD/dyslexia will continue to be fated to fail in employment and in life.

References

Reiff H, Ginsberg R, Gerber P (1997) Exceeding Expectations. Austin TX: ProEd.

Tomblin M, Haring KA (1999) Vocational training for students with learning disabilities: a qualitative investigation. Journal of Vocational Education and Training 51(3): 357–70.

Young G, Kim HJ, Gerber P (1999) Gender bias and learning disabilities: school age and long-term consequences for females. Learning Disabilities – A Multidisciplinary Journal 9(3): 107–14.

Further reading

American Council on Education (1995 through 2000) Who took the GED. Washington DC: ACE. See http://www.acenet.edu/calec/ged/.

Arrom, JO (1997) Latinos/Hispanics and Disability: An Annotated Resource Bibliography – 2. Learning and Language Disabilities and Mental Retardation. Chicago: Center for

Emergent Disabilities. See http://www.uic.edu/depts /idhd/ced/text/bibliography2txt. htm.

Brosnan, FL (1983) Overrepresentation of low-socioeconomic minority students in special education programs in California. Learning Disability Quarterly 6(4): 517-25.

Brown DS (2000) Learning a Living: A Guide to Planning Your Career and Finding a Job for People with Learning Disabilities, Attention Deficit Disorder and Dyslexia. Washington DC: Woodbine House.

Crawford V (2001) Embracing the Monster: Overcoming the Challenges of Hidden Disabilities. Baltimore MD: Paul H Brookes.

Fisher SE, DeFries JC (2002) Developmental dyslexia: genetic dissection of a complex cognitive trait. Neuroscience 3 (October): 767-83. See http://www.well.ox.ac.uk/~simon/dyslexia/nrn_dyslexia.pdf.

Gregg N, Hoy C, Gay AF (eds) (1996) Adults With Learning Disabilities: Theoretical and Practical Perspectives. New York: Guilford. See http://www.guilford.com/cgi-bin/cartscript.cgi?page=spase/gregg.htm&cart_id=.

Lander M, Hammons C (2001) Special but unequal: race and special education. Rethinking special education for the 21st century. In Finn CE, Rotherham AJ and Hokanson CR (eds) Rethinking Special Education for a New Century. Washington DC: Fordham Foundation. See http://www.edexcellence.net/library/special_ed/special_ed_ch5.pdf .

Patricia L, Travnikar B (2003) G Reid Lyon's views on rethinking learning disabilities: an introduction. The LDA Newsletter 1 (January). See http://www.earlyonmichigan.org/ld/articles/article03-01.htm.

Peterz KS (1999) The overrepresentation of black students in special education classrooms. Motion Magazine (May 31). See http://www.inmotionmagazine.com/peterz1.html.

Reid Lyon G (1998) Statement of Dr G Reid Lyon, Chief Child Development and Behavior Branch, National Institute of Child Health and Human Development, National Institutes of Health to the Committee on Labor and Human Resources Room 430 Senate Dirkson Building Washington, DC April 28, 1998. See http://www.readbygrade3.com/readbygrade3co/lyon.htm.

Ross-Kidder K (2003) Assessment for Adults with LD. See http://www.ldonline.org/ld_indepth/assessment/ld_ adhd_adult_assessment.html.

The Civil Rights Project (2002) Racial Inequity in Special Education. Boston: Civil Rights Project. See http://www.civilrightsproject.harvard.edu/research/specialed/IDEA_paper02.php.

The National Center of Workforce and Disability/Adult (2002) Review of State Plans for the Workforce Investment Act from a Disability Policy Framework. Boston MA: NCWD/A. See http://www.onestops.info/article.php?article_id=164&subcat_id=49.

United States Department of Education, Office of Educational Research and Improvement, ERIC Digest 189, Adults with Learning Disabilities. See http://www.ldonline.org/ld_indepth/adult/eric189.html.

United States National Institute For Literacy (NIFL), National Adult Literacy and Learning Disabilities Center (NALLD) (1999) Bridges to Practice: A Research-based Guide for Literacy Practitioners Serving Adults with Learning Disabilities. Washington DC: NIFL.

United States (1990) The Americans with Disabilities Act of 1990 Section 101, (9). See http://www.usdoj.gov/crt/ada/pubs/ada.txt.

United States Department of Education, Office of Special Education and Rehabilitative Services (OSERS) (1996-2002) Annual Reports to Congress. Washington DC. See http://www.ed.gov/about/reports/annual/osep/index.html.

United States National Institutes for Health, National Institute for Child and Human Development (NICHD), Keys to Successful Learning: A National Summit on Research in Learning Disabilities. Washington DC: NICHD. May 1999. See http://www. ldonline.org/ld_indepth/reading/ncld_summit99.html#why.

United States President's Commission on Excellence in Special Education (2002) A New Era: Revitalizing Special Education for Children and their Families. Washington DC: US Department of Education. See http://www.ed.gov/inits/commissionsboards/ whspecialeducation/reports/.

Warde BA (2001) Preliminary Findings Comparing Reading Characteristics of College Students with and without Learning Disabilities, (Florida Atlantic University). See http://www.bdainternationalconference.org/presentations/fri_s6_b_5.htm.

West T (2001) Dyslexic Talents and Nobel Prizes, Alexandria VA. See http://www.ldonline. org/ld_indepth/abilities/thomas_west_nobel.html.

Williams J (2001) Adaptations and Accommodations for Students with Disabilities. Washington DC: The National Information Center for Children and Youth with Disabilities. See http://www.nichcy.org/pubs/bibliog/bib15txt.htm.

For adult testing options and costs factors, see Assessment for Adults with LD at http://www.ldonline.org/ld_indepth/assessment/ld_adhd_adult_assessment.html.

For discussion of the discrepancy formula as a means for identifying individuals with LD/dyslexia, see Rethinking Learning Disabilities at http://www.edexcellence.net/ library/special_ed/index.html.

CHAPTER 12

Dyslexia – early identification and early intervention

MARGARET CROMBIE, DEBORAH KNIGHT, GAVIN REID

Introduction

For a number of years both early identification and early intervention have been seen as essential in the development of appropriate curricula and strategies for young children who may be at risk of failing in literacy tasks. This is not altogether surprising as conventional wisdom would lead one to believe that if any difficulty is evident then the earlier it is dealt with the better. Indeed research from both the US and the UK since the early 1980s has substantiated the benefits of early education in general and, more specifically, has valued the educational benefits of intensive intervention for those at risk of failure, particularly in language acquisition and literacy (Snow et al., 1998).

Yet, for some, early identification can be seen as an unfortunate step towards premature and unnecessary labelling. This may result in a dilemma for some policy makers on how best to proceed and the criteria that should be used for early identification and early intervention for children at risk of the failure generally associated with dyslexia. It is the view of the authors of this chapter that there should be no dilemma in using criteria for early identification and intervention.

It is suggested in this chapter that early intervention is the key and that 'identification' is essentially a component of that intervention. This means that the objective of early identification is not to label but to intervene, to monitor, and to ensure that the children's progress does not unexpectedly lag behind that of their peers. This is crucial as it is too easy to associate intervention with the label. Although we are focusing on early intervention in this chapter it is useful to note an observation from the adult sector in relation to identification and intervention. In the adult sector not only is the label necessary before intervention and support can be provided, but this requirement for a label is in fact backed by the legislation (see Chapter 11 of this volume). This can be discriminatory and detrimental to those who, for whatever reason, are not able to acquire the label, but may need the intervention. Young and Browning describe this population as the 'great middle' and suggest that this unidentified population, and therefore unsupported population, is far greater than one would imagine. They suggest that two-thirds of those with LD/dyslexia in the present school cohort in the US are not receiving the services they need in public schools because they have not been labelled and therefore do not qualify for the support of a special education programme. They suggest the same can be said for every cohort of students that has gone through school since the inception of special education (and before). If a child's achievement therefore does lag behind after intervention, then it might be appropriate at that time to consider a categorical label and specialized instruction. But intervention *should* come first and the intervention should not be based on the presence of a label but, in fact, on the identification of need. This need would almost certainly relate to the 'potential' risk of the child failing in literacy.

This chapter will therefore examine some issues relating both to early identification and intervention and provide examples from both sides of the Atlantic to support the notion of identifying the learning profile and the learning behaviour of those at risk of failure in literacy developments. Essentially, identification focuses on the barriers to literacy and these barriers may not only be the result of within-child factors. It can be beneficial to consider three factors in relation to these barriers – the learner, the task and the curriculum. Each of these can provide information on the identification of the difficulties and how these can be tackled. Therefore the principal element of difficulty for the child, for example, may be 'the task' and how 'the task' is presented. Intervention would therefore relate more to the principles of differentiation, rather than focusing on any cognitive difficulties experienced by the child. It is essential, especially in the early years, that learning is made as meaningful, and as child friendly, as possible for the learner and for that reason we need to consider a wider range of factors than 'within-child' factors.

Barriers to learning to read

As indicated above, the actual presenting and underlying behaviours that can be barriers to learning certainly need to be identified. It should be recognized, however, that although some of these barriers will be cognitive, some will involve factors relating to how the curriculum is presented, the expectations of the task, as well as the nature of the learning context.

The model proposed by Morton and Frith (1995) and Frith (2002) – the causal modelling framework – offers a model that highlights the range of areas that can be influenced by any specific learning difficulty, including dyslexia. These include neurological/genetic, cognitive, education/classroom and environmental factors. It is necessary therefore in any model of early identification and intervention to examine and focus on each of these factors. Only by doing this will all the barriers to learning and literacy development be noted.

Neurological and genetic factors

The fields of neurobiology and genetics have only begun to inform our understanding of dyslexia but there are a few things that we know. The brains of individuals with dyslexia look different and function differently from typical readers' brains. There is substantial behavioural and molecular genetic information to indicate that at least some reading abilities appear to be inherited and that certain patterns of inheritance result in dyslexia. Just as the cognitive and behavioural studies reveal that reading words involves a complex interaction of processing, sensory, phonological, orthographic, and semantic information, so do the neurobiological studies reveal that a sophisticated integration of a number of brain sub-systems are involved in reading words.

Behavioural genetics studies consistently indicate that dyslexia is heritable. What does it mean to inherit dyslexia? Is there a dyslexia gene? It is not likely that dyslexia *per se* is inherited but rather factors placing an individual at risk for dyslexia. Dyslexia is not an entity in itself. It is the manifestation of a range of cognitive 'weaknesses'. Miles (1983a) describes this pattern of difficulties and incorporates these in his Bangor Dyslexia Test (Miles, 1983b). Dyslexia is *not*, however, a name for the 'deficits'. It is a name for the way in which these deficits manifest themselves in different individuals. Thus an individual dyslexia gene would be difficult if not impossible to identify. Pennington (1999) makes a case that dyslexia is most likely inherited through multiple genes that increase one's susceptibility to dyslexia. In addition, Pennington and his colleagues have found heritability for normal variations in reading that are not clearly different from dyslexia. If these two observations are accurate, then dyslexia may be thought of as on a continuum. Genetics may make an individual susceptible to dyslexia with environmental factors determining the extent to which this predisposition is manifested.

Therefore, it can be too simplistic to propose that early identification which may suggest that a neurobiological approach is the most suitable for children with a genetic pre-disposition to dyslexia. As Sherman and Cowen (2003) highlight, the existence of a genetic pre-disposition to dyslexia does not necessarily mean that dyslexia will materialize. There are a considerable number of contextual and environmental variables that can influence the outcome of a child's developmental processes, making early intervention crucial. Environmental factors and the socio-cultural experiences of the child will therefore, quite inevitably, affect development. Education is a critically important environmental influence with the power to overcome some of the other influences and factors that can affect the child's learning development.

When a family history of dyslexia is present, it is crucial to carefully monitor a child's acquisition of literacy and intervene early should any difficulties arise.

Cognitive and linguistic factors

Early predictors of dyslexia are now well researched. They include factors such as phonological awareness (Snowling, 2001), letter–sound knowledge, verbal short-term memory, word finding, rapid naming, and non-word repetition. Other compounding factors may include early oral speech and language delay (Gallacher et al., 2000), balance (Nicolson and Fawcett, 1996), difficulty in maintaining rhythm (Avery and Ehrlich, 1987), and visual and/or auditory perceptual difficulties (Jordan, 2000; Singleton et al., 1996, 1997; Snowling and Stackhouse, 1996; Stackhouse and Wells, 1997; Stein, 2001). In the research literature, letter–sound knowledge and phonemic awareness emerge as the most potent predictors of early literacy achievement (Torgesen, 1997). These factors appear to predict early literacy difficulties, regardless of whether or not dyslexia is present (Stanovich, 1991). In addition, there is no research to support a differential response to treatment in children with diagnosed dyslexia compared to those who show phonological awareness difficulties but not dyslexia (Fletcher et al., 1998).

Education/classroom factors

In the US, an emphasis is currently being placed on use of an 'evidence-based curriculum' to teach all children – that is, use of the curricula and instructional methodologies that are supported by research. The National Reading Panel (NRP, 2000) reviewed the literature in five areas of literacy: phonemic awareness instruction, phonics instruction, fluency, vocabulary instruction, and text comprehension instruction. Currently, a considerable amount of school funding in the form of grants requires schools to adopt curricula and instructional methodology that are supported by the findings of the NRP. In addition, the schools must design a staff development component that develops teachers' skills and knowledge that are in line with the NRP findings. The goal is that students attending schools supported by these grants will receive instruction reflecting the best practices supported by research by well-trained teachers. The assumption is that children who attend schools receiving these grants will not have reading difficulties that are a result of inadequate instruction. Although the goal of providing adequate evidence-based instruction for all early learners is admirable, the reality eludes us. In an analysis of a national representative sample of 22,000 kindergarten children, Lee and Burkam (2002) found that children living in poverty in the US receive their early education in schools of lower quality than their peers with higher socio-economic status (SES). They examined quality in terms of student achievement, school resources, teacher qualifications, teacher attitudes, and neighbourhood and school conditions and found differences on all dimensions.

Environmental and socio-cultural factors

There are a number of environmental and socio-cultural factors that place children at risk for early reading difficulties, including race/ethnicity, family expectations, quality pre-school, home reading, computer use and television viewing (Lee and Burkam, 2002). English language learners (Snow et al., 1998) and speakers of dialects who are not readily able to imitate standard English (Scarborough et al., 2002) are also at risk of early difficulties in reading achievement. Although all of these factors explain variation in children's reading achievement, when income level is accounted for, the effects diminish substantially. In the final analysis, children living in low SES families are at considerably greater risk for reading difficulties. Poverty explains more variation in achievement than any other environmental factor. When children living in low-income families attend low-achieving schools, which is most often the case, the achievement gap widens (Lee and Burkam, 2002).

Children are at risk of reading difficulties for a number of different reasons. Regardless of the reason, children who struggle to acquire beginning reading skills tend to have difficulty with phonological awareness (Catts and Kamhi, 1999). Identifying very young children as dyslexic may have no instructional advantage. Indeed, as already mentioned, the attempt to provide a categorical label for young children may thwart attempts at early intervention. There may be an inclination to either only give those children with a categorical label the intervention, or provide a narrowly focused intervention concentrating only on those areas that can be described a characteristic of dyslexia. This may have an adverse effect as it may not fully provide for the holistic learning and emotional needs of the child.

Definitions of dyslexia

Definitions of learning disabilities (LD) in both Britain and the US, certainly in relation to the use of a label and the allocation of provision, have emphasized a discrepancy between achievement and ability as the hallmark characteristic of LD. In addition, definitions of LD have been largely definitions of exclusion, that is, defining what LD is not rather than what it is. In recent years, definitions of dyslexia that attempt to better define what dyslexia is have been adopted in both countries. Many of the definitions in use in the UK emphasize severe and persistent difficulty learning to read words in spite of adequate learning opportunities (BPS, 1999). The US definition states: 'These difficulties in single word decoding are often unexpected in relation to age and other cognitive and academic abilities' (Lyon, 1995). Both definitions suggest that the difficulties with reading are unexpected when compared to another attribute, whether that attribute be ability, age or instruction. These definitions reflect our improved understanding that dyslexia is a failure to learn to read because of difficulty in processing phonological elements of the language. Although there are other processing difficulties that are contenders in explaining reading difficulty, the definitions reflect the most extensively researched attribute, phonological processing.

One of the problems with these definitions is that they require repeated and persistent failure to learn to read words prior to even being referred for evaluation. One of the most serious disadvantages in such a model, often known as a wait-to-fail model, is the relatively late identification of children who need intervention in learning to read.

To accomplish the goal of early identification we must identify what predicts reading disability and be able to assess it early in the child's education. Many of the difficulties associated with low self-concept and 'learned helplessness' arise due to intervention being implemented at too late a stage in the student's education. Some have suggested (see Young and Browning in this volume) that this can lead to the spiral of disaffection that can account for many unidentified dyslexic people in the prison population, in unfulfilling occupations or even among those classified as unemployed.

Alternative approach to early identification

Delayed identification of children in need of intervention in reading words combined with the recognition that children at risk for reading difficulties, for reasons other than dyslexia, can benefit from the same early intervention, have resulted in attempts to design alternative methods of early identification and intervention.

Screening and monitoring progress

In the US, the gap between the researchers' construct of learning disability and the actual population of students identified as LD in the schools is considerable (Jenkins and O'Connor, 2002). One reason for this problem has been the lack of a clear definition of learning disabilities as well as the lack of instruments that identify children with LD. In the area of reading, progress has been made toward developing instruments that are more sensitive to identifying children in need of early intervention. These screening measures identify children at risk for reading difficulties rather than those children who are dyslexic. The dilemma of any screening instrument is over- or under-identification of children in need of intervention. One might argue that over-identification is preferable, particularly when no categorical label is applied. Nonetheless, limited resources necessitate that our instruments be as precise as possible. Over-identification is more prevalent in kindergarten than first grade (Vaughn and Fuchs, 2003). More kindergarten children than first-grade children who are identified as 'at risk' make adequate progress with no additional intervention outside the general education curriculum. Exposure to instruction does appear to influence the child's performance on screening instruments, indicating that monitoring a child's response-to-instruction may be a viable option for identifying both children at risk for reading difficulties and children with dyslexia (Jenkins and O'Connor, 2002).

Research suggests the combination of phonological awareness and letter knowledge accounts for 40% to 60% of the variance in reading achievement (Jenkins and O'Connor, 2002). Some researchers have attempted to offer a screening device that captures more of the variables believed to influence the development of early reading skills. In the UK, Weedon and Reid (2003) developed a screening tool – Special Needs Assessment Profile (SNAP) – which attempts to disentangle the overlapping conditions and characteristics that can contribute to the identification of specific learning difficulties, including dyslexia. SNAP has been developed for the 5–14 age range and through the use of diagnostic and teaching materials, including a CD-ROM and a dedicated Web site, provides criteria and information for teachers and parents that can help to look beyond the label and at the actual presenting behaviours. The insights that can be noted through the use of SNAP provide a practical analysis of the barriers to learning by mapping each child's own mix of difficulties on an overall matrix of learning, social and personal difficulties. From these clusters and patterns of weaknesses and strengths it is possible to identify the core features of a child's difficulties – visual, co-ordination, phonological, attentional or any of the other 15 key areas of difficulties targeted by SNAP. This matrix points the way forward for that individual child. Additionally the information sheet that it generates helps to strengthen home support. The rationale behind SNAP is that the diverse strands that can contribute to learning difficulties can be interrelated and the teacher can obtain an overview of these through identification of the actual characteristics and not through acknowledgement of the label.

In the US, several instruments designed to identify children who are at risk for reading difficulties have been developed – for example, Dynamic Indicators of Basic Early Literacy Skills (DIBELS), Phonological Awareness Literacy Screening (PALS): see Good and Kaminksi (2002) and Invernizzi, Meier and Juel (2003).

In addition, these measures are designed to monitor children's progress in early reading. The use of DIBELS has become especially widespread in the US as school systems attempt to design procedures to evaluate the effectiveness of the evidence-based instruction that they are implementing in their grant-funded projects. Knowing that children who are at risk for reading failure remain at risk of failure in reading and that the gap between grade-level reading and actual achievement increases over time, these instruments have been designed with the following two purposes in mind: *identification of children in need of early intervention* and *continuous monitoring of their progress.*

It is essential that the need to possess a label does not restrict or prejudice appropriate early intervention. SNAP, DIBELS and PALS were designed for precise identification of reading-related difficulties experienced in the learning context, regardless of their cause.

Response-to-intervention model

Although the development of instruments able to identify students in need of early intervention is promising, the issue of identifying those students with dyslexia who need intensive intervention still remains. Screening children on predictors of reading problems will identify children whose difficulties stem from environmental, educational and neurological causes. The predictors of early reading difficulties essentially remain the same, whether the cause of the difficulty is environmental or intrinsic. But some environmental factors such as opportunities to access books and an enriched language environment can influence this. The extent to which a differential treatment is necessary is not clear, but the assumption is that children with dyslexia, which is presumed to be of neurological origin, will need a more intensive, longer-term intervention. Children who are struggling to gain pre-literacy skills are not all the same, so will need to be grouped in a way which is empathetic to their difficulties, recognizing the symbiotic relationship between identification and intervention, and the part-circular nature of identify–plan–intervene–observe–monitor–plan–intervene (see Figure 12.1).

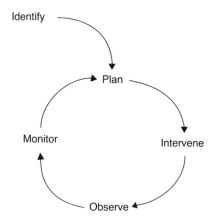

Figure 12.1 Model for intervention.

In the US, a 'response to intervention' (RTI) is one variation of the innovative models used in the UK, depicted in Figure 12.1. One variation of the RTI model involves a three-tier model. Level one consists of enhanced general education classroom instruction with validated instructional approaches. If children do not make adequate progress despite generally effective instruction, they receive level two assistance, which consists of more intense intervention in the general education setting but within small groups. Should a child continue to demonstrate inadequate progress, the child is placed in special education with intervention that increases in intensity and duration.

Vaughn and Fuchs (2003) identify the following advantages to an RTI model:

- children would be identified at risk rather than by deficit;
- identification of both at-risk and dyslexic students would occur earlier with this approach;
- gender and racial bias would be diminished as children would be identified on the basis of their performance on a measure monitoring progress;
- identification would be less dependent on teacher judgement;
- assessment would more effectively inform instruction than current eligibility models.

There are a number of prerequisites if an RTI approach is to work: the ability to model growth; accepted, evidence-based instructional approaches; the ability to ensure effective implementation of instructional approaches; and decision rules about what constitutes a failure to respond to intervention. Although the RTI model holds promise, a number of issues require further investigation. Which interventions are best for which children? Do we have validated instructional methods? What is an effective duration and intensity of intervention at each of the levels? What constitutes adequate growth? Are teachers adequately prepared to implement such a model?

In the US, the Individuals with Disabilities Education Act is in the process of re-authorization. An RTI approach is favoured by a number of legislators. At this point, despite acknowledged advantages of an RTI model, insufficient research exists to recommend its immediate, widespread implementation.

This overarching rationale of the RTI model can be noted in the underlying basis for the development and the implementation of a more formalized screening instrument in the UK – the Dyslexia Early Screening Test (Nicolson and Fawcett, 1996). Although this is a formal screening instrument and, as would be expected in a screening instrument for dyslexia, it considers aspects such as processing speed, co-ordination, balance, phonological awareness, working memory and fluency, the authors see it as part of a model consisting of screening, assessment and support. The rationale behind the development of this instrument is to provide objective information that would empower teachers to understand the difficulties and be able to relate the screening procedures to teaching objectives. In this way it can be seen as an initial step in the type of 'response-to-intervention' model described above. The dominant feature of the RTI model is however based on instruction and the child's response to the instruction, rather than a screening test.

Teacher observation and clinical judgement

Vaughn and Fuchs (2003) cite circumventing teacher judgement in the identification process as an advantage to the RTI model. Certainly, there will be bias in teacher judgement. Nonetheless, teachers have been shown to be effective judges of students' achievement (Perry and Meisels, 1996). One might notice that the US RTI model appears to consist of a cycle of identify, plan, intervene and monitor. Observation and teacher judgement do not appear to play a prominent role in the RTI model. In Scotland, one study (Crombie, 2002) used an observational screening programme to identify and provide intervention for nursery children from around the age of 4 years. This has proved effective not just for the children, but has informed the primary schools of children's needs and allowed them to prepare for any intervention programmes to be continued.

An observational framework from any early years/nursery curriculum can target the early signs of dyslexia. Most curricula will contain items that are readily observable in nursery. Specific dyslexia-sensitive items can be added along with early signs of any other specific difficulties to highlight children whose early needs are indicative of possible later problems that might be avoided through timely intervention. So if the curriculum involves physical exercise, add an item that looks at whether the pupil can balance on an upturned bench while at the same time counting to 10. An observational framework can then be made to identify the child who is showing early signs of what might be later literacy difficulties. Display the factors on a spreadsheet, and any children who show an early dyslexia profile can be identified without a need to label at this early stage.

Key Aspect: Communication and Language		
Children should learn to:	**Dates**	**Comments**
have fun with language and making stories		
find the right words for what s/he wishes to say		
be aware of alliteration -'Tim has trendy trainers'		
follow simple instructions in sequence		

Figure 12.2 Part of a profiling sheet, which can be used to record early signs of difficulty and help to plan appropriate intervention.

They may or may not receive a later formal identification, but early intervention will have ensured the child's later problems will be minimized. Policy and practice in the UK is, in most areas, moving towards earlier identification followed by appropriate intervention. The economic sense in all this is that later expensive teaching to try to remedy the situation will be avoided. Support is inevitably easier to implement in the nursery where there is a higher pupil–teacher ratio than in school.

Observational tools must tie in with the curriculum in kindergarten or nursery. Where there is a formal curriculum, this should be examined and may need to be enhanced to include dyslexia-sensitive items. Thus items on balance may need to be added to the content of the physical education programme. Ask children to balance on the spar of an upturned bench. When you have checked that they can do this, ask them to count to five or say an easy rhyme (or another verbal activity which they can otherwise do). Observe the children to see if they overbalance or if they can retain their balance. Observations on sequencing activities may be missing and should be added if they are not there already. Examples of sequencing activities in the early years could be doing up buttons, getting a very short story in the right order, sorting a series of story pictures (around three pictures), copying a series of movements when demonstrated (again around three). It is important to be aware of the difficulties the child has, but it is also important not to jump to conclusions prematurely, hence the importance of not labelling too early. Some children may be late developers and may still develop these skills. It is important however to put in intervention to tackle difficulties, and to observe what happens.

The role of parents

For many years now the involvement of parents has been seen as a key factor in the development of literacy skills in young children (Topping and Wolfendale, 1985). If early years programmes – both screening and intervention – are to be fully effective then parents need to be involved and feel that they are an important element in the process. At the same time many will feel it is too early in the child's educational career to involve parents and may not wish to cause unnecessary concern. However, as research has established, one of the main complaints of parents is often the lack of timely acknowledgement of problems (Nance-Dewar, 2000; Crombie, 2002).

The value of collaboration

Partnership with parents must be about more than paying lip service to parental concern. True partnership is about letting parents know about teachers' concerns so that all can act together in producing the best solutions. If the child turns out not to have later problems then all can congratulate themselves. They may never know whether it was the intervention that prevented failure. If the child has later problems, parents can feel reassured that difficulties have been minimized and problems of self-esteem will be lessened by a common understanding that there are reasons for the difficulties. It can be reassuring to recognize that these difficulties are not due to lack of effort, poor parenting or lack of appreciation of what it means to be dyslexic. School, pupils and parents are then working in harmony. Previous reluctance to acknowledge dyslexia early often resulted in acrimony and blame with no one gaining. In the previously mentioned Scottish study (Crombie, 2002) parents were all appreciative of efforts made to minimize difficulties, focus on strengths and identify intervention techniques.

Conclusion

Identification of needs, without premature labelling, is the key to promoting appropriate and constructive early identification and intervention criteria. This suggests a set of proactive procedures, but proactive in the intervention sense, not in the labelling sense. It is crucial that early identification and intervention be integrated and not seen as two separate sets of procedures. This is particularly important in the early years as the roles of teachers, other professionals and parents need to be co-ordinated as an essential component of policy and practice and not seen as a bolt-on in response to a 'failing child'.

One of the other factors to emerge in this chapter is the need to view the child as an individual and to intervene on that basis. This indeed is the rationale behind much of the screening work reported by Crombie (2002) and provides the overall strategy for observing the actual behaviours of the individual child in the learning context. In relation to dyslexia this of course carries a risk that the need to use the label will become redundant. While a label in the early years may be counterproductive, there is an obligation at some point to inform the child why he/she might be experiencing difficulties with aspects of the curriculum. A label, such as dyslexia, if fully understood, can be an asset to the student in developing an understanding of the difficulties experienced in learning and to the teacher in identifying a way forward for teaching. But for whatever reason it is crucial that identification and intervention are fully integrated in a proactive manner in early screening policy and practice.

References

Avery P, Ehrlich S (1987) Specific pronunciation problems. TESL-Talk 17: 81–116.
British Psychological Society (1999) Dyslexia, literacy and psychological assessment. Report by Working Party of the Division of Educational and Child Psychology. Leicester: British Psychological Society.
Catts HW, Kamhi AG (1999) Language and Reading Disabilities. Boston: Allyn & Bacon.

Crombie MA (2002) Dyslexia: The New Dawn – Policy, Practice, Provision and Management of Dyslexia from Pre-five into Primary. Doctoral thesis. Glasgow: Strathclyde University.

Fletcher JM, Francis DJ, Shaywitz SE, Lyon GR, Foorman BR, Stuebing KK, Shaywitz BA (1998) Intelligent testing and the discrepancy model for children with learning disabilities. Learning Disabilities Research and Practice 13: 186–203.

Frith U (1999) Paradoxes in the definition of dyslexia. Dyslexia 5: 192–214.

Frith U (2002) Resolving the paradoxes of dyslexia. In Reid G and Wearmouth J (eds) Dyslexia and Literacy, Theory and Practice. Chichester: Wiley, pp. 45–68.

Gallacher A, Frith U, Snowling MJ (2000) Precursors of literacy delay among children at genetic risk of dyslexia. Journal of Child Psychology and Psychiatry 41: 201–13.

Good RH, Kaminksi RA (eds) (2002) Dynamic Indicators of Basic Early Literacy Skills, 6th edn. Eugene OR: Institute for the Development of Educational Achievement.

Invernizzi M, Meier J, Juel C (2003) Phonological Awareness Literacy Screening. Charlottesville VA: The Rector and The Board of Visitors of the University of Virginia.

Lee VE, Burkam DT (2002) Inequality at the starting gate: social background differences in achievement as children begin school. Washington DC: Economic Policy Institute.

Jordan I (2000) Motive to magnify. Special Children 125: 29–30.

Jenkins JR, O'Connor RE (2002) Early identification and intervention for young children with reading/learning disabilities. In Bradley R, Danielson L and Hallahan DP (eds) Identification of Learning Disabilities: Research to Practice. Mahwah NJ: Erlbaum, pp. 99–149.

Lyon GR (1995) Toward a definition of dyslexia. Annals of Dyslexia 45: 3–27.

Miles TR (1983a) Dyslexia: The Pattern of Difficulties. London: Collins Educational.

Miles TR (1983b) Bangor Dyslexia Test. Cambridge: LDA.

Morton J, Frith U (1995) Causal modelling: a structural approach to developmental psychopathology. In Cicchetti D and Cohen DJ (eds) Manual of Developmental Psychopathology. New York: John Wiley & Sons, pp. 357–90.

Nance-Dewar S (2000) More SENs than money. Special Children 128: 14–16.

Nicolson R, Fawcett A (1996) The Dyslexia Early Screening Test Manual. London: The Psychological Corporation.

National Reading Panel (2000) Report of the National Reading Panel: Teaching Children to Read. Washington DC: National Institute of Child Health and Human Development.

Pennington BF (1999) Toward an integrated understanding of dyslexia: genetic, neurological, and cognitive mechanisms. Development and Psychology 11: 629–54.

Perry NE, Meisels SJ (1996) How accurate are teacher judgements of students' academic performance? See http://nces.ed.gov/pubsearch/pubsinfo.asp?pubid=9608.

Scarborough HS, Charity AH, Griffin D (2002) Is unfamiliarity with 'school English' (SE) related to reading achievement by African-American students? Presentation to the Society for the Scientific Study of Reading, June 2002, Chicago.

Sherman G, Cowen CD (2003) Neuroanatomy of dyslexia through the lens of cerebrodiversity. Perspectives 29(2): 9–13.

Singleton CH, Thomas KV, Leedale RC (1996, 1997). CoPS1 Cognitive Profiling System. Newark, Nottinghamshire: Chameleon Educational.

Snow CE, Burns SM, Griffin P (eds) (1998) Preventing Reading Difficulties in Young Children. Washington DC: National Academy Press.

Snowling MJ (2001) From language to reading and dyslexia. Dyslexia 7: 37–46.

Snowling MJ, Stackhouse J (1996) Dyslexia, Speech and Language. London: Whurr.

Stackhouse J, Wells B (1997) How do speech and language problems affect literacy development? In Hulme C and Snowling M (eds) Dyslexia: Biology, Cognition and Intervention. London: Whurr, pp. 182–211.

Stanovich KE (1991) Discrepancy definitions of reading disability: has intelligence led us astray? Reading Research Quarterly 26(1): 7–29.

Stein J (2001) The magnocellular theory of developmental dyslexia. Dyslexia 7: 12–36.

Topping K, Wolfendale S (eds) (1985) Parental Involvement in Children's Reading. London: Croom Helm.

Torgesen JK (1997) The prevention and remediation of reading difficulties: evaluating what we know from research. Journal of Academic Language Therapy 1: 11–47.

Vaughn S, Fuchs LS (2003) Redefining learning disabilities as inadequate response to instruction: the promise and the potential problems. Learning Disabilities Research and Practice 18: 137–46.

Weedon C, Reid G (2003) Special Needs Assessment Profile (SNAP): A Computer-aided Diagnostic Screening Instrument for 5–14 Age Range. London: Hodder & Stoughton.

PART THREE
PRACTICE

Introduction to Part Three

The two previous parts of this book were concerned with research and policy, but it is crucial that research and policy in some way point to practice. It is through practice that significant changes will be made to how children and adults with dyslexia are assessed and supported in whatever learning situation or challenge they face. Practice is multi-faceted and, for that reason, Part Three offers a range of approaches and perspectives on practice, both for children and for adults.

One of the significant developments in practice has been the uptake of the innovative dyslexia-friendly schools campaign, particularly in England and Wales, although its effects have been noted elsewhere. It is therefore fitting that this section of the book on practice begins with a chapter by Neil MacKay, who in fact was responsible for coining the phrase 'dyslexia-friendly schools', and developing dyslexia-friendly programmes that have now been disseminated throughout the country. MacKay makes the important point that 'the fine tuning needed to make schools dyslexia friendly has the potential to improve the learning of all pupils'. This, in fact, has been the basis of the development, and indeed the success, of the campaign. In this chapter MacKay perceives dyslexia as a specific learning 'difference' and provides a clear framework for schools that wish to be dyslexia friendly. This framework includes policy, training, responding to need and 'parents as partners'. MacKay shows how dyslexia-friendly schools can be both inclusive and empowering.

This point is developed in the following chapter by Johnson who questions the need for promoting a special category of 'dyslexia friendliness' but suggests that energies should be put into ensuring that teaching and learning is appropriate for all. Johnson provides a number of examples from pupils themselves that support his view. In his view 'dyslexia friendliness' does not go far enough and, although he accepts that the dyslexia-friendly initiatives and training have some excellent suggestions for practising teachers, he maintains that 'these are a necessary but far from sufficient basis from which to work.' He argues that the dyslexia-friendly school movement is currently too instrumental and more emphasis needs to be placed on the emotional development of pupils. Educational reformers, he suggests, often ignore the emotional dimensions of educational change and as a result reforms and initiatives fail because the classroom is essentially an emotional place.

In the following chapter Nicolson and Fawcett consider insights from the science of learning and look at how these can be applied to the processes of learning to read, and in particular how this applies to children with dyslexia. They describe the stages of scaffolding and provide a clear account of the cognitive processes involved in reading. They relate this to models of reading, and in particular to developing reading skills using 'articulation' and 'eye movements' in reading as examples. They provide some insights into the stages of learning complex skills including part/whole transfer and the importance of the zone of proximal development. They also describe aspects relating to the science of instruction and focus on the 'reading mountain'. This analogy highlights the challenges and obstacles children with dyslexia need to overcome in order to become competent readers. As they suggest, the 'sunlit pastures of pre-school play through the gentle but rockier slopes of letter learning . . . soon turns into quite a tough climb'. This chapter has many encouraging points for the teacher and contains insights into reading, learning and on mapping 'pathways to success'.

One of the well-recognized pathways is that of early intervention. Geoff Lindsay pursues this point in the chapter on baseline assessment and intervention. Lindsay accepts the potential limitations of early screening and argues for a move away from early identification by a screening measure and towards a systemic approach. Instruments that are used, therefore, should not be used in a one-off way but need to be seen as part of a wider strategy. 'Diagnosis' is more relevant to intervention but diagnosis need not lead to categorization of children. Lindsay also argues that diagnosis should complement and be used alongside teachers' observations.

Lindsay also discusses the development and implications of the Foundation Stage Profile, indicating that this type of scheme, which is to be uniformly implemented in England, should remove the variability and the inconsistencies noted in the adoption of some baseline assessment instruments.

The link between policy and practice in numeracy is developed in the chapter by Henderson and Chinn, particularly in relation to the National Numeracy Strategy. As the authors point out, although the National Numeracy Strategy was devised for pupils in England, the content is not fundamentally different from that of mathematics curricula in many other countries, and this chapter is therefore relevant to all countries. The authors discuss most of the key objectives in the numeracy strategy. In an excellent example of progression they detail these objectives from reception class to year 6. For example, one of the objectives in the reception year relates to the use of language to compare two numbers or quantities, such as more or less, greater or smaller, heavier or lighter. This often presents difficulties for children with dyslexia and, clearly, if this aspect is tackled in the reception year then the potential for successful outcomes in mathematics is much greater. The chapter contains an abundance of practical strategies in key areas such as familiarity with 3-D and 2-D shapes, understanding the concepts involved in subtraction and addition, learning multiplication tables, measurement and comparison of length, mass and capacity, calculation strategies, the use of fractions, symmetry and shapes, the use of decimal notation, understanding percentages and solving problems involving ratio and proportion. The chapter also focuses on the processes students engage in when learning and undertaking mathematics problems. These include procedures involving highlighting important words and numbers, selecting strategies, estimating answers, checking the question has been answered and that it answers the problem, and explaining to others the method chosen and why this method was selected. Understanding mathematics and being able to use strategies are important because, as the authors point out, 'once students begin to enjoy maths and find success their self-esteem will grow and this will reflect positively in all areas of their life'.

This chapter is followed by a chapter on the use of information and communication technology (ICT) to help children with dyslexia overcome barriers to literacy and learning at all levels — primary, secondary, higher education and working life. Like the previous chapter this aspect can have dramatic consequences for successful functioning in today's society. This chapter represents a collaborative effort involving practitioners from England, Scotland and Sweden, illustrating that ICT has no territorial boundaries. Sharing of knowledge and expertise in this way has been a significant feature of dyslexia research and practice in recent years. The authors suggest that, used appropriately and creatively, ICT can be a lifelong tool to help those with dyslexia overcome many barriers to learning. It can assist in reading and writing skills in school and at home and also in work environments. It can help restore dyslexic children's self-esteem, offer successful experiences and increase confidence. The chapter highlights a number of strategies and uses of ICT, such as in the planning, writing and recording of information, assessment of dyslexic difficulties, self-esteem, search skills, curriculum support, keyboarding and the use of ICT in examinations. The chapter also provides examples of appropriate software that can be used in different teaching situations. The authors make an important point when they suggest that ICT should not replace skilled and structured teaching, but it can provide an invaluable tool and support in the classroom, for both pupils and their teachers.

Intervention in ICT in relation to adults is described by looking at prevention, practice and compensation. There are many examples of strategies and software that can be appropriate for adults and students in higher education as well as an illustrative case study from the workplace. As the authors point out, we are living in an 'information society' and therefore people with dyslexia require 'tools' that will eliminate as many obstacles as possible and allow them to develop professionally and personally in their chosen occupations.

The final chapter both of Part Three and this book is by Pamela Deponio and, perhaps fittingly, focuses on the broader area of specific learning difficulties. As the author points out, there is considerable evidence for the co-existence of dyslexia with other specific difficulties and this co-existence often does not receive the attention it warrants, particularly in relation to identification and assessment. Deponio also suggests that the term 'specific learning difficulties' can no longer be used interchangeably with 'dyslexia', as it once was, because professionals now appreciate that there is a range of 'specific' learning difficulties, such as dyslexia, dyspraxia/developmental co-ordination difficulties, specific language impairment and the attention deficit disorders. Deponio offers suggestions in relation to assessment for the range of specific learning difficulties and the implications of the presence of overlapping 'indicators' of specific learning difficulties. The author makes a valuable point when saying that 'Despite the wealth of literature confirming the high likelihood of co-occurrence it would appear that schools do not always offer a holistic assessment of a child. Rather they are searching for a "condition".' It is important that professionals involved in all areas of practice take heed of the points highlighted in this chapter. Deponio provides a framework for the most frequently occurring difficulties, which can easily be incorporated into an observation schedule for a more comprehensive assessment. The chapter also highlights the importance of home–school links and of multi-professional collaboration. Deponio suggests that schools give careful consideration to the issue of policy with regard to specific learning difficulties and that a policy on dyslexia alone is not sufficient.

This chapter ends on an inspiring note by highlighting the positive and creative aspects that can be noted in children with dyslexia and other specific learning difficulties. Quoting from West, Deponio makes a point that needs to be recognized by all involved in the field and this provides a fitting conclusion to the book — 'Too often, the gift is not recognised and is regarded only as a problem.' It is crucial that all involved in the education and the development of children and adults with dyslexia recognize the 'gift' and help all use their abilities to overcome the barriers that confront them in learning and in life.

CHAPTER 13

The case for dyslexia-friendly schools

NEIL MACKAY

Introduction

More and more schools are aspiring to become dyslexia friendly, with the active and enthusiastic support of their local education authorities. The ideas and challenges launched by the British Dyslexia Association (BDA) dyslexia-friendly schools packs are striking a chord across the UK and beyond as teachers begin to realize that the fine tuning needed to make schools dyslexia friendly has the potential to improve the learning of all pupils. However, this initiative is not about special educational needs, nor is it necessarily the domain of special educational needs co-ordinators (SENCOs), unless they are already members of the school's senior management team. Becoming a dyslexia-friendly school requires a review of the implementation of major whole-school policies, especially teaching and learning, monitoring and assessment, differentiation and inclusion. The issue then becomes one of how these policies are monitored, evaluated and reviewed to ensure top-quality learning right across the range of ability and need.

Dyslexia-friendly schools – towards a working definition

For the purposes of the dyslexia-friendly schools initiative dyslexia will be defined as: 'a specific learning difference that may cause unexpected difficulties in the acquisition of certain skills.'

Accepting dyslexia as a specific learning difference rather than a difficulty conveys a realistic balance of opportunities and costs, strengths and weaknesses for the child, as do all the other learning styles and preferences. The 'straight-line thinking', typical of many mathematical logical learners, is vulnerable when creativity is required, whereas the eclectic style of linguistic learners may not yield results when step-by-step processing is required. So the notion of dyslexia as a specific learning difficulty is arguably unhelpful and wrong, certainly within the inclusive, classroom-based ethos of the dyslexia-friendly schools initiative. While there are undoubted areas of vulnerability, this is true of all learners and of all learning preferences. The skill of the teacher lies in achieving a balance between empowerment and challenge within clearly understood patterns of strength and weakness.

How does this difference manifest? Dyslexic learners are often imaginative and creative lateral thinkers who develop original solutions to problems. They may be skilful in design and construction, information technology and so forth, often seeming to 'know' how things work without reading instructions, manuals and so forth. One specific learning difference may be the ability to 'think in pictures', sometimes with original artistic talents and often with a strong visual preference in terms of information acquisition and processing. Some dyslexic children and adults seem to be able to run a test programme or sequence through in their mind in video and actually visualize what will happen when elements or parameters are changed. Many dyslexic learners are sociable and verbally able and may enjoy drama and sport. Typically they will demonstrate ability-appropriate interest in science, technology or current affairs often with a general knowledge to match. The specific difference enables some learners to be curious, eclectic and creative, identifying links and patterns unclear to others. Creating a big picture from apparently disparate bits is often another strength, as is the ability to form the 'whole' when some of the elements are missing or not quite appropriate.

Despite opportunities, there are inevitable costs associated with thinking in a dyslexic way, just as there are with all the other learning styles and preferences. The nature of the specific learning difference may cause problems acquiring basic literacy and numeracy skills, meaning that dyslexic children need to be taught in the way they learn. A particular priority is to recognize and compensate for possible problems with working memory, information processing and hearing the sounds and syllables in words. Dyslexic learners are particularly vulnerable when a pre-occupation with reading and spelling accuracy is allowed to detract from information processing and organizing thoughts on paper. When this happens the specific difference becomes a specific difficulty and a learning preference becoming a learning problem. Placing undue emphasis on accurate reading, writing, spelling and number work as a product rather than as a process is unhelpful, if not harmful.

The school that I would like

Imagine a school which recognizes that all children learn in different ways and in which teachers harness the power of learning styles and preferences to optimize teaching and learning. In this school teachers also recognize that many apparent learning difficulties can often be explained as learning differences that respond to changes in methods, materials and approaches.

Also many of the special educational needs that formerly occupied the attention of class/subject teachers and SENCOs are now seen as ordinary learning needs that are dealt with through the differentiated curriculum plan. As a result the school is writing far fewer individual education plans (IEPs): those that are written are of high quality, and are very carefully monitored and evaluated to actively direct and inform the way children are taught in mainstream settings.

The school is particularly aware of the needs of the growing numbers of non-traditional learners who do not function well in a didactic environment and who often think faster than they read, write, spell or do number work. Therefore there is a house style, evident in every classroom, in which children are required to explore ideas, concepts and strategies within the framework of their preferred learning styles. They are also actively encouraged to present evidence of their learning and understanding within these styles.

An interesting aspect of this school is the calm, confident way in which all children approach their leaning. Even the most vulnerable learners are set up to succeed because they are effectively working within their comfort zone for much of the time and operating from a secure platform of strength and competence. When challenged to move outside their comfort zone they are able to respond with confidence because of their platform of previous success. One consequence of this confidence and emotional security is the positive way in which all the children approach assessments – even some national assessments that seem to be carefully engineered to marginalize those who learn in non-traditional ways. Although this school is very successful in terms of results, it values this success less than it values the eclectic, confident and independent learners it is developing across the full range of ability and social, emotional and intellectual need.

This school is dyslexia friendly, without a doubt. However, it is also *learning friendly*, seeking to empower all pupils to be the best they can be. That is the incentive for becoming a dyslexia-friendly school.

The advantages are significant, with a positive 'opportunity cost'. However, it must be understood that the implementation of whole-school change needs to be the responsibility of someone who has the authority and support to drive the cycles of implementation, evaluation and review.

The development of dyslexia-friendly schools

The notion of dyslexia-friendly schools began in Hawarden High School, an 11–18 mixed comprehensive school in North Wales. At the request of Clwyd Local Education Authority (now Flintshire) a dyslexia resource was set up in the school, possibly one of the first to be so placed in the UK, and the most vulnerable dyslexic children in the authority were placed in the school. They received 5 hours of small-group specialist tuition and spent the rest of their time in mainstream classes. Whole-staff training was an obvious imperative because these children would be spending 20 hours each week with mainstream subject specialists and these would be the teachers at the front line of delivering a dyslexia-friendly comprehensive education. Training sessions were organized on dyslexia awareness, strategies for supporting spelling, reading and handwriting, information-processing techniques including mind mapping, and numeracy. These apparently discrete 'specialist' techniques gradually became custom and practice for many teachers and the BDA acknowledged that the school was a 'flagship provision for dyslexic children'. An unanticipated bonus was the developing success of the school in terms of examination results, especially with regard to the numbers of 16-year-olds leaving with 5 GCSE grades between A–G, arguably the real measure of comprehensive education.

Swansea Education Authority grasped the idea and developed it from a whole-school approach into a celebrated strategy across all schools in the authority. The well-documented successes included measurable increases in parental confidence, reduced referrals of cases to tribunal and a provision that became a byword for good practice across the UK.

However, individual schools across Wales and England were looking for more. What they seemed to be wanting was recognition of their achievements in meeting the needs of dyslexic children in mainstream settings. This was an interesting development because, perhaps for the first time, dyslexia was being seen as the responsibility of all teachers in a school, rather than as a discrete special needs issue. Working with the author and funded by Flintshire LEA, a group of SENCOs drew up the draft criteria for a dyslexia-friendly school. These criteria were challenging but achievable and were eventually to form the basis for many of the Dyslexia Friendly kite-marking initiatives being run by LEAs across the UK. Funding from the Welsh Dyslexia Project allowed SENCOs and advisory teachers from most LEAs in Wales to fine-tune and hone the criteria into a form that has since been accepted by the BDA as the basis for a national kite-marking scheme. Local education authorities in England have also been proactive, with Liverpool, Somerset and Staffordshire among others running well-established whole-school schemes.

The draft criteria fall into five discrete areas and are designed to be a balance of validation and challenge, validating existing good practice and challenging any less helpful current practice. A selection of criteria will be discussed below and a full list of the draft criteria will be found in the appendix.

The five key areas

- Policy – 'putting practice into policy'.
- Training – 'walking the talk'.
- Identification, assessment and monitoring – 'rigorous scrutiny and immediate intervention'.

- Responses to needs – 'walking the talk'.
- Parents as partners – 'completing the loop'.

Policy – 'putting practice into policy'

Policy is what a school actually does, rather than what is written down in documentation. Many successful schools find that whole-school good practice is often ahead of documented policy, and rightly so – someone launches a good idea, the school embraces it and policy will catch up in due course. However, the reverse is also true and it can be scary to audit actual practice, write it up as a policy statement and then see if it fits the ethos and aspirations of the school. For example, if a school does not actively require reading materials to be differentiated, it is pursuing a 'chalk face' policy of giving children work they cannot read and so is discriminating against weaker readers. While it is very unlikely that this discrimination is enshrined in print, it is policy because it is what is done.

A policy statement will define good practice in relation to dyslexia and will make it clear to all teachers exactly how this practice is to be delivered, monitored and evaluated, All whole-school policies, teaching and learning, monitoring and assessment, and so forth, will be guided and influenced by the main policy statement and clear guidelines will be available. In consequence a new teacher joining the school will be able to read the documentation and be absolutely clear about the ethos and house style. There is also a strong case for monitoring and evaluation at classroom level to be part of performance management, another decision that needs to be implemented at the highest level within the school.

Training – 'walking the talk'

The cornerstone of the training criteria is a trained teacher or a teacher in training in every school. This criterion has been fiercely debated because of implications for personnel, resources and funding. However, there is a strong view that a dyslexia-friendly school needs a properly qualified expert who can lead policy and practice. Also it is essential that this teacher is in a position to influence whole-school policy and ensure that it is translated into classroom-based action. The teacher with lead responsibility does not have to be the SENCO unless he or she is already in a position of authority in the school and has been given time to perform this additional role. Being dyslexia friendly is about the 20+ hours each week that a learner spends in mainstream classroom settings so, unless all teachers know how to make a difference and apply their knowledge, the process is doomed to fail.

Whole-school-awareness training for all contact staff is essential and schools will be required to keep a log of attendance at training events. A catch-up programme will also need to be in place for new staff – teachers, teaching/classroom assistants and so forth – when they join the school.

Evidence will also be required of training needs being identified and addressed on a regular basis.

Identification, assessment and monitoring – 'rigorous scrutiny and immediate intervention'

The criteria call for clearly defined and documented techniques for identifying the 'unexpected difficulties' in acquiring certain skills together with recommended classroom-based intervention strategies. 'Rigorous scrutiny and immediate intervention' are the watchwords. These perceptive and responsive strategies are part of a school's 'anticipatory duty' and are essential if dyslexic learners are to make ability-appropriate progress despite current weaknesses in basic skills.

A key attribute of a dyslexia-friendly school is the willingness to respond quickly to perceived needs without waiting for a formal assessment or 'diagnosis' in order to find a label. Making best use of available data will highlight the unexpected problems of a learner who is performing well in some areas but not in others and a speedy classroom-based response may be all that is required. When this does not work it can then be topped up by the investment of additional resources, perhaps in the form of school action and the writing of an IEP. There is a clear key difference between a traditional SEN approach and the proactive dyslexia-friendly response. Special educational need responses are often based on a child needing to fail for a period of time and being given a label before intervention can be arranged. The inclusive, dyslexia-friendly response comes from class teachers who are empowered to identify learning issues and respond appropriately in their day-to-day teaching.

Dyslexia-friendly strategies will need to be evident in everyday marking and assessment with the link between policy and practice being particularly transparent in this area. For example, many schools have a policy of target marking to highlight a small number of key elements for the learner to address. However, scrutiny of books can often reveal that some teachers continue to mark all errors – despite the existence of a policy that states otherwise. This is clearly unacceptable and needs to be addressed through performance management together with training linked to regular monitoring and evaluation. Once again, this type of response needs to be implemented at the highest management level within the school.

Responses to needs – 'walking the talk'

In a dyslexia-friendly classroom, currently weak basic skills will not be a barrier to ability-appropriate achievement. This is a key criterion and schools aspiring to a dyslexia-friendly kite mark will need to show exactly how learners are supported to be the best they can be, even though they may not be able to read it or write it just yet. Another important criterion is the opportunity for work to be presented and marked in a variety of forms – once again, concrete evidence will be required of policy being translated into observable practice. For example, while a paragraph is clear evidence of information processing, so is a mind map, a storyboard or a flow chart. Equally acceptable is information on strips of paper, which have been stuck into books. Here a classroom assistant or 'study buddy' may have written the information and the dyslexic learner has chosen the order in which it is to be presented. This is a whole-school teaching and learning issue that needs to be addressed as part of a co-ordinated management strategy and built into the school development plan.

Possibly the most controversial criterion is the provision of discrete, out-of-class opportunities for small-group/one-to-one support. This opportunity is seen as a key element of inclusion, which calls for mainstream opportunities without ever stipulating that all of the children must be in all of the classes for all of the time. Thomas Jefferson made the point perfectly when he said: 'There is nothing so unfair as the equal treatment of unequal children.'

In consequence a dyslexia-friendly school will be committed to the provision of out-of-classroom opportunities when needs dictate. For example, such provision would be appropriate when it would be emotionally damaging for a 10-year-old learner to address some early-years literacy and/or numeracy issues in front of peers. There is a clear balancing act between a child's right of access to the curriculum and the basic skill needs required in order for access to occur. This may result in value judgements being made about the relative merits of certain topics and the need to find more time to reinforce core basic skills. Schools that are committed to teaching the children rather than simply covering the curriculum will instinctively make the right choices and will be able to defend their decisions to the inspectorate. These schools are also likely to find that they have very strong parental support for the way learning is organized.

Parents as partners – 'completing the loop'

Dyslexia-friendly schools will enjoy the trust of parents and will be able to provide evidence of this trust in the form of written comments at review, letters of thanks/support and in the way the parents of dyslexic children are involved in the life of the school. A key element in establishing parental trust is the speed with which a school responds to concerns raised and the thoroughness with which dialogue is initiated and maintained.

A frequent question from class/subject teachers is: 'How do I respond when parents suggests that their child is dyslexic?' The short answer is that it would have been better if the conversation had been initiated by the school. A problem can occur when a teacher who does not have a specialist qualification in dyslexia rejects parental concerns with a dismissive 's/he is definitely not dyslexic!' This can be extremely damaging to the child and to relationships with the parent. A more appropriate response is to acknowledge that dyslexia might be an issue, to offer to seek further advice and, in the meantime, to agree to teach slightly differently and see if it works. There is an understandable fear that, when a school initiates the discussion, it will automatically require the investment of increasingly rare resources and a worry that it will 'open the floodgates'. This need not be the case, especially if the standard response is a commitment to:

- teach the child differently in the mainstream setting;
- offer helpful advice for the parents about how to help at home;
- set agreed improvement targets (with parent and child) and to monitor carefully over an agreed period of time;
- to report back on an agreed date.

If this response does open the floodgates then it means that the pressure has been building up for a while – better to deal with it now than wait for an inspection or a series of meetings with angry and frustrated parents.

If this approach works then it is likely that all will be well. However, if improvement targets are not met then it is clear that the school needs to take more action, perhaps in the form of directing a teaching assistant to support while the SENCO looks at available assessment data and perhaps does some diagnostic testing. Whether or not a decision is made to make special needs provision and to write an IEP, most parents are happy when the school responds positively to concerns and are willing to suspend their demands for statements and/or statutory assessments if they think that positive action is being taken.

The LEA response – a dyslexia-friendly kite mark?

There has been much debate about how best to co-ordinate a nationwide response to demands from schools and LEAs for a dyslexia-friendly kite mark. A significant number of LEAs in Wales and England and at least one LEA in Scotland have developed schemes that are rigorous and challenging. The issue now is how best to enshrine generic good practice while allowing the flexibility to reflect local and regional needs in some of the detail. Arguably it would be totally against all the principles of the dyslexia-friendly schools initiative to impose a 'one-size-fits-all' accreditation process.

Discussions with LEA officers suggest that the accreditation of dyslexia-friendly schools is taken extremely seriously and the process of monitoring, evaluating and assessing is done with rigour and consistency. Local education authorities and schools are particularly aware of the litigation culture and appreciate that the kite mark confers potential costs as well as opportunities; a school that is accredited as dyslexia friendly but that does not deliver is likely to find itself and the LEA answering some very hard questions, perhaps in tribunal and possibly even in the courts.

Local education authorities and schools are also aware of the need for a validating body to ensure consistency and quality control. Having considered and rejected a number of options it seems to be the view that the BDA itself is the most appropriate body, if it can establish a validation committee made up of representatives from participating LEAs. This approach eliminates a perceived weakness of many externally imposed inspection processes, which run the risk of being carried out by people who appear too far removed from the reality of the process they are inspecting. Of course an LEA-accredited system must be able to demonstrate impartiality, balance and rigour if it is to achieve credibility. If the kite-marking process is to succeed it needs to achieve a fine balance between validation, celebration and challenge within the pragmatic reality of reduced funding, ever-increasing pressures from central government and a dedicated workforce whose confidence is sometimes rather fragile.

The core values of a national kite-marking process would seem to include:

- a nationally agreed common core that allows room for local interpretation in agreed areas;
- a national validating panel to scrutinize applications and organize inspections and reviews of procedures;
- a transparent procedure for monitoring and evaluation, which is built in to existing systems rather than bolted on as an additional layer of administration;
- support for schools to achieve the criteria in terms of guidance and training, and so forth;
- quality control procedures between schools and between LEAs;
- agreed cycle of monitoring of participating LEAs;
- agreed intervention strategies when previously accredited schools fail to meet criteria.

Good practice in the classroom – 'the difference that makes a difference'

If dyslexia is accepted as being a specific learning difference it would seem sensible to teach through learning styles and preferences. More and more schools in the UK and beyond are identifying the preferred learning strategies of their pupils and making them the starting point for the preparation of units of work and individual lessons. This inclusive approach has the potential to enhance the learning of all children, from the gifted and talented to those with significant learning difficulties. One benefit of an eclectic learning styles approach is that many apparent learning difficulties may actually turn out to be learning differences that can be minimized or overcome by a change in approach.

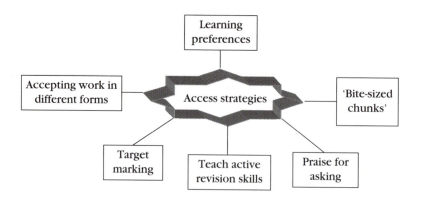

Figure 13.1 Putting policy into practice.

Many learners find it difficult to follow complicated instructions, especially those with specific learning differences like dyslexia, dyspraxia, Asperger's syndrome and children with special attentional requirements. One response is to develop a whole-school commitment to presenting instructions and information in 'bite-sized chunks' and to use positive language – telling children what to do rather than what not to do. For example, saying 'put your pen down' is more effective than 'stop fidgeting'.

Target marking, linked closely to lesson aims and objectives, encourages learners and supports the development of their self-esteem and emotional intelligence. The selection of two or three issues to be addressed is much more manageable and more likely to secure the desired changes. A whole-school commitment to the implementation of a target-marking policy, together with regular book trawls to assess what is going on, is very dyslexia friendly.

The willingness to accept work in different forms is a natural consequence of teaching through learning styles and preferences. It is inclusive to offer choice in the way information is presented for marking because this supports non-traditional learners to work with confidence and enthusiasm. End-of-unit assessments can also be fine-tuned to offer choice and learners who have successfully shown what they know through a preferred style seem much more able to adapt to more traditional techniques in national exams. From here it is a short step to invest some time in teaching active revision skills so that children know how to learn. This is particularly important for learners whose working memories are vulnerable. Active revision skills based on their learning preferences can overcome current limitations in working memory and transfer information to the long-term memory. Although this approach does take time, it may be a better long-term investment than some of the mentoring programmes currently in place to boost 'borderline' achievement. It is also much more inclusive as it empowers all children to develop their revision skills, not just a chosen few.

Putting it all together – 'the opportunities to balance the costs'

Dyslexia-friendly schools are effective schools

They demand excellence from pupils and staff alike and take positive steps to promote staff awareness and competence. Such schools tend to have a zero tolerance of failure and adopt best practice to ensure that all pupils learn. When learning is not happening the schools have the confidence to examine their practice and take action, even at the possible expense of leaving some of the more esoteric elements of the curriculum until very much later, if they are covered at all: 'covering the curriculum' is seen as much less important than teaching the child. This willingness to place the child's needs at the forefront of curriculum planning leads to flexible approaches to learning.

Dyslexia-friendly schools are proactive schools

The progress of all pupils is monitored and reviewed, and intervention organized when necessary. Whole-school targets are made explicit in the school development plan and are supported through carefully targeted INSET to empower teachers to deliver in the classroom. This constant drive to improve the achievements of all pupils is reflected in the way assessment and monitoring result in action

Dyslexia-friendly schools are empowering schools

These are schools in which everyone is important and all pupils are empowered to be the best they can be. A key strategy is the recognition and celebration of individual differences in learning styles.

Dyslexia-friendly schools are inclusive schools

Social, emotional and intellectual inclusion is a top priority in these schools and there is a focus on strengths and abilities rather than weaknesses and problems. Flexible approaches to marking and assessment ensure that currently weak basic skills are not a bar to ability-appropriate groupings.

Dyslexia-friendly schools are improving, 'value-added' schools

The drive for effectiveness on behalf of all pupils stems from an inclusive and proactive approach to the identification and fulfilment of all learning needs. This results in pupils who are confident, who understand and believe in their abilities and who are empowered to perform at ever-increasing levels of competence.

Taking it forward – 'more means different'

Most teachers are currently working as hard as they possibly can to meet the demands of the job. They are becomingly increasingly worried about children whose needs do not respond to traditional teaching methods and, quite understandably, the teachers find it impossible to find much time to do any more. This problem is exacerbated by performance targets that focus on narrowly defined groups of learners and that inevitably marginalize those outside the target boundaries. So the only way that schools and teachers can respond to demands for more is to do things differently, to work smarter rather than harder.

The dyslexia-friendly schools initiative has the potential to motivate and support schools to celebrate learning differences and to enhance the achievement of all. Fine-tuning of policy and practice is one of the keys to success, a fine-tuning which has received the support of teachers across the UK and beyond. The other key is recognizing dyslexia as a specific learning difference and accepting that, as Dr Harry Chasty used to say, 'if they don't learn the way we teach them, we must teach them the way they learn.'

Appendix: dyslexia-friendly schools initiative (draft)

Level 2 Master Checklist – Kite-mark Level

'ACTION' CHECKLIST

Check	Key requirements	Staff responsible	Date completed
	Organization of dyslexia-friendly schools INSET day Attendance of all contact staff (teachers, LSAs etc.) Attendance of governors Completion of audit Completion of action plan Submission of action plan		

AUDIT CHECKLIST

Check	Criteria	Staff responsible	Date completed
	1. POLICY – 'putting policy into practice and practice into policy'		
	1.1 Main policy contains statement defining good practice in relation to dyslexia		
	1.2 Good-practice statements present in all other whole-school-policy documents e.g. differentiation, inclusion, teaching and learning, assessment and monitoring, marking, homework partnership with parents		
	1.3 Good-practice statements present in all subject, year, key stage policies (as appropriate for school organization)		
	1.4 School governors formally involved in policy and practice amendments		
	2. TRAINING – 'How to walk the talk'		
	2.1 Record of all staff attending accredited INSET		
	2.2 'Catch-up' arrangements in place for absent/new staff – rolling programme		
	2.3 Additional training needs identified through CPD		
	2.4 Annual response to ongoing/changing training needs evident in school development plan		
	2.5 Trained teacher/teacher in training		
	3. IDENTIFICATION, ASSESSMENT AND MONITORING – 'rigorous scrutiny and immediate intervention'		
	3.1 Documented strategies to identify 'unexpected' issues relating to basic skill acquisition and development		
	3.2 Clearly defined classroom-based intervention strategies		
	3.3 Procedures in place for early assessment of needs		
	3.4 'Dyslexia-friendly' good practice evident in everyday assessments (e.g. marking, unit tests etc.)		
	3.5 Whole-school and classroom-based strategies in place for 'rigorous scrutiny and immediate intervention'		
	4. RESPONSES TO NEEDS – 'putting policy into practice'		
	4.1 Classroom management strategies in staff handbook		

AUDIT CHECKLIST (CONT.)

Check	Criteria	Staff responsible	Date completed
	4.2 Dyslexia-friendly good practice evident in all school policies		
	4.3 Dyslexia-friendly good practice evident in all classrooms – policy into practice		
	4.4 Pen portraits on all pupils with SpLD, to include individual teaching/learning strategies, available to all contact staff, including LSAs and supply teachers		
	4.5 Targets under regular review – classroom action when targets not met		
	4.6 Appropriate materials available and used by all contact staff		
	4.7 Dyslexia-friendly homework practice – differentiated homework tasks where appropriate		
	4.8 Work acceptable in a variety of forms – bullets, mind map, story board, flow chart etc.		
	4.9 Currently weak basic skills are not a barrier to ability-appropriate groups, sets and/or achievement		
	4.10 1:1/small-group opportunities available out of classroom as needs dictate		
	5. PARENTS AS PARTNERS – 'completing the loop'		
	5.1 Parental trust in the school		
	5.2 Speedy response to concerns/issues raised		
	5.3 Dyslexia-friendly communications – letters in plain English, pastel shades of paper etc.		
	5.4 Parents consulted re effective approaches and effectiveness of approaches		
	5.5 Parents know of and understand the complaints procedure		

CHAPTER 14

Dyslexia-friendly school policy and practice

MIKE JOHNSON

Introduction

> Policy is the product, whether written (laws, reports, regulations), stated or enacted (e.g. pedagogical practice), of the outcomes of political states of play in various arenas. In these arenas there are struggles between contenders of competing objectives, either about objectives or how to achieve them: in these struggles discourse is deployed as tactic and theory. (Fultcher, 1989: 11-12)

In the current enthusiasm for making almost everything 'dyslexia friendly' it is useful to be reminded by Fultcher that policies are created by negotiation and are usually responses to perceived inequities or the resolution of dilemmas. You may like to think for a moment about the term 'dyslexia friendly'. Medicalization of a learning difficulty has been conceded (after a period of insistence on the term 'specific learning difficulty'). The Department for Education and Skills (DfES) resisted the concept when drawing up its standards and it was the Special Educational Needs and Disability Act backed by the Disability Rights Commission that declared dyslexia to be a disability in the legal sense and therefore having protection from discrimination under that Act. We thus accept 'disabled status' as it strengthens our case for insisting on the use of a 'rights' discourse. The Salamanca Declaration stated that:

- every child has a fundamental right to education, and must be given the opportunity to achieve and maintain an acceptable level of learning;
- every child has unique characteristics, interests, abilities and learning needs;
- education systems should be designed, and educational programmes implemented, to take into account the wide diversity of these characteristics and needs;
- those with special educational needs must have access to regular schools, which should accommodate them within a child-centred pedagogy capable of meeting these needs;

- regular schools with this inclusive orientation are the most effective means of combating discriminatory attitudes, creating welcoming communities, building an inclusive society and achieving education for all. Moreover, they provide an effective education to the majority of children and improve the efficiency and ultimately the cost-effectiveness of the entire education system.

Article 2 of the EU Convention on Human Rights states:

> No person shall be denied the right to education. In the exercise of any function which it assumes in relation to education and to teaching, the State shall respect the right of parents to ensure such education and teaching in conformity with their own religious and philosophical convictions.

Article 14 states:

> The enjoyment of the rights and freedoms set forth in this convention shall be secured without discrimination on any ground such as sex, race, colour, language, religion, political or other opinion, national or social origin, association with a national minority, property, birth or other status.

These had proved of little force but we could now take our place with other 'proper' disabilities!

Dyslexia friendly?

I wish to examine what the 'dyslexia-friendly' movement has meant in practice. At the outset, let me be clear, as was Ofsted (1999), that where schools give appropriate consideration to the needs of their pupils with dyslexia the positive effects are widespread. However, I also want to be clear that a price has had to be paid and we should be prepared to continue the discourse until pupils with dyslexia are seen as a constituent part of the majority not a separate and coherent disabled minority. In Johnson (2001) I made the point that for the DfES:

> mainstream education is seen to be a 'given', in the mathematical sense. The question relates to whether pupils with SEN will fit into it, not how the system needs to alter. The same 'reversed thinking' can be seen in relation to speaking of 'extra resources' for pupils with SEN, not what is their fair share of all existing resources.

This brings us to consider the term 'friendly'. A nice, soft term that, when we consider what pupils say, turns out to be rather apt. However, recognize its reciprocity. Is it meant to convey 'as your friend I wish to do whatever I can to help you, please tell me what this is', or 'by making these "allowances" for you I am performing a friendly act and expect you to be friendly towards me also which means not making any more demands'?

Neil MacKay claims to have coined the term in the early 1990s during work developing the concept and principles at Hawarden School in North Wales (MacKay, 2001). This consisted, in the main, of specialist provision, called a 'resource', which delivered five hours a week of teaching in groups of three by a 'very experienced and highly qualified dyslexia specialist'. This price was National Curriculum disapplication from Welsh and French. This is an interesting choice. MacKay makes the point that 'It is essential that all contact staff are aware of the needs of dyslexic pupils in general and the Dyslexia Resource pupils in particular.' He goes on to say that strong leadership and whole-school approaches to SEN in general are also essential, that staff development must be valued and all children seen as important regardless of ability or need. 'Failure to aspire to such a culture risks alienating a significant proportion of the school population and their parents.' He does not detail who these might be.

At the other end of the Principality the City and County of Swansea were involved in a classical Fultcherian policy development. Under local government reorganization they had inherited the highest percentage statements for dyslexia in any LEA and had the fewest qualified teachers to deal with them. They had large numbers of angry parents and frustrated and disillusioned teachers. Deliberately deploying 'discourse' as a vehicle through public meetings and other consultations and working groups they produced a new approach centring on four key elements:

- working in partnership with parents and voluntary organizations, the production of clear expectations and good practice guidelines, accepted by parents and schools;
- awareness raising and continuing professional development for staff;
- provision of BDA accredited training for at least one teacher in most, if not all, schools;
- specialist support for schools to ensure quality improvement and appropriate provision.

Other LEAs are now following suit and there have been numerous articles detailing the development and use of 'dyslexia-friendly resource packs'.

Policy and practice

The policy approach by the government through the National Literacy Strategy has been somewhat different. Initially developed in 1997 by a committee of experts and implemented in 1998 it took a mixed phonic and 'look–say' approach to literacy within the very structured literacy hour. Fortunately, a committee on which the BDA was represented monitored the results and so the impact on pupils with dyslexia stayed in focus. The first response was to produce the Additional Literacy Strategy materials (DfES,

1999) and then to strengthen the phonics element through 'progression in phonics' (DfES, 2000). At the same time the BDA was asked to investigate how pupils with mild to moderate dyslexia could be taught in mainstream schools. In collaboration with Manchester Metropolitan University, a two-year project resulted in the publication of MTSR (Johnson, Phillips and Peer, 1999), a package that consisted of a multi-sensory literacy programme for use with groups of up to six pupils and deliverable by a teaching assistant under the direction of a qualified teacher. A range of methods of working with pupils with dyslexia was evaluated and a list of recommended 'Wave 3' methods was published, of which MTSR was one (DfES, 2003: 3). As this chapter was in preparation, the DfES held a seminar to look at how the National Literacy Strategy (NLS) could improve the teaching of phonics. Brooks (2003) reported on the papers presented and the discussions at the seminar. One of the significant recommendations from the 'dyslexia-friendly' point of view was 'Make it clear that, within the 100 most frequent words, only those that are irregular should be taught as sight words' (Brooks 2003: 24).

Examining the current situation with regard to SEN generally the Audit Commission reported some interesting findings (Audit Commission, 2002). The first was that 'In England, there are no common definitions of need, so while LEA may hold detailed information on the needs of pupils, this cannot be aggregated' (paragraph 13). In other words, we do not know what is going on! The position is different in Scotland and Wales and specific learning difficulties make up 16% of the statements in each. The only larger group is the somewhat amorphous category of 'moderate learning difficulty' (MLD) at 34% and 33% respectively. They also pick out factors influencing identification of and provision for pupils with special educational needs (SEN). Amongst these is type of need (paragraph 22) where if the difficulty is not susceptible to medical tests, 'Differing professionals may reach different conclusions.' Another is family circumstances (paragraphs 28–30), where

> Children from disadvantaged backgrounds are relatively less likely to be identified as having SEN given their needs profile as a group. Conversely, our research with parents suggests that those with the knowledge, resources and confidence to challenge staff in schools and LEA are more likely to get their child's needs assessed and secure a more generous package of provision.

This finding is similar to that of Bowie (2003: 1) reporting an Abel Foundation study claiming that 'Poor children in the US are less likely to be identified as dyslexic are an early age and get the help they need to overcome their reading difficulties than children in middle-class families.' Under 'school related factors' (paragraph 31) they comment 'The proportion of pupils with Statements varies five-fold between LEA in England and Wales.' They also report major variation between the primary and secondary phases of education: 'In England 15% of primary schools have 3% or more of pupils with Statements compared with 36% in secondary schools. And in Wales 27% of primary schools have 3% or more of pupils with Statements compared with 55% of secondary schools' (paragraph 31). As the dyslexia-friendly movement started in Wales this is somewhat puzzling. Accepting that some of this variation is due to macro variables such as criteria, policy decisions and so forth, the note significantly adds: 'However, it also reflects varying attitudes and practice' (paragraph 32).

Unfortunately, a report by the BDA on a dyslexia-friendly schools audit produced some less than encouraging results. When asked about routine screening some schools replied, 'Children have to be referred to the educational psychologist who has limited time' and 'The SENCO would like to know when she would have time to screen the whole school.' When asked about INSET a significant number of replies commented that they needed all their INSET days to keep up with government initiatives. Out of 473 schools, 333 reported that they had no staff with additional qualifications in the area of dyslexia; only 66 reported staff with a BDA-accredited qualification and a further 84 had staff that had done a short course. Sixty-seven per cent of schools had never had an INSET day on dyslexia (BDA, 2001).

It would seem that policy and practice are somewhat different and that in Fultcher's 'struggles between contenders of competing objectives' dyslexia is not exactly winning. Whilst it may be desirable to follow the 'profession-alized' policy of having an appropriately qualified teacher as a resource in every school and early identification of pupils' difficulties, it is simply not happening. Even the Special Educational Needs and Disability Act (SENDA) is unlikely to have much effect as it also relies on 'parents with the knowledge, resources and confidence to challenge staff in schools and LEA'.

Pedagogical considerations

However, there are some useful indications of a more dyslexia-friendly school environment from other work in the inclusion area. Norwich and Lewis have made a significant contribution in their rejection of a qualitative difference between 'mainstream' and 'SEN' pedagogies:

> [Our evidence] rejects distinctive teaching strategies and accepts that there are common pedagogic principles which are relevant to the unique differences between all pupils, including those designated SEN. However, this position is qualified by some recognition of the need for more intensive and focussed teaching for those with SEN. (Norwich and Lewis, 1999: 324)

The words 'focussed' and 'intensive' characterize much of the teaching rated highly by Ofsted inspectors. Norwich and Lewis (1999) quote Connor (1994) and Veluntino (1987) as suggesting that for pupils with dyslexia these terms mean bottom-up approaches to phonics and phonemic awareness, greater structure and attention to detail, continuous assessment, record-keeping and overlearning. None of these requirements would seem to put unreasonable demands on teachers given a positive, inclusive attitude. However, it is important to stress that the words 'focussed' and 'intensive' are active. What needs to be addressed are the 'unique differences' between pupils.

A final quotation from Lewis and Norwich (2000: 41) gives an insight into how this might best happen:

> Pupils with specific learning difficulties also generally require more practice than other pupils and practice that is well designed. They need, like other pupils, to be actively engaged in managing their learning, though they tend to have difficulties in applying learning and performance strategies. However, evidence has shown that such pupils can be taught to use and apply such strategies.

Teachers' and pupils' understandings and attitudes

Regan and Woods (2000) surveyed 36 teachers in six focus groups in an attempt to discover more about their understanding of dyslexia and how educational psychologists might best support them in teaching pupils with dyslexia. Their findings suggest that teachers see a difference between a 'dyslexic' child and a 'poor reader'. Most explanations of the latter relate to poor home backgrounds or learning more slowly in other areas. Definitions of dyslexia still related to some notion of a discrepancy between ability and reading attainment. The extensive body of evidence showing how questionable this is does not seem to have reached classroom level. They did, however, recognize that, 'some children seemed to have an understanding of language which was beyond their ability to decode written words' (Regan and Woods, 2000: 345). Pupils with dyslexia were linked with other pupils thought to have SEN by the fact that their difficulties persisted and they showed 'lack of progress'. This is an example of the problem pointed to earlier in the Reason statement. It shows that a clear 'within-pupil' model is held. This is summed up in quotations from teachers: 'Would it be correct to say that once everything's in place for a dyslexic reader their ability in reading can accelerate, rather than the poor reader who will go on plodding?' (Regan and Woods, 2000: 340). 'We need to know which particular thing the child is finding difficult and why . . . a very detailed analysis of what the problem is' (Regan and Woods, 2000: 341). And perhaps, most revealingly, '[A psychologist is] the person to pass the buck to, the person who'll carry the responsibility . . . It's very useful' (Regan and Woods, 2000: 342).

Kerr (2001: 82) noted in a survey into attitudes towards and beliefs about dyslexia amongst teachers doubt, uncertainty and confusion and considerable misgiving as a consequence: 'A marked degree of learned helplessness was apparently induced in respondents when faced with a student with dyslexia. Tuition was greatly simplified and expectations lowered.' Given the lack of INSET in the area as demonstrated earlier (BDA, 2001) and that only one university (MMU) has an element in its ITT course strong enough to give its graduates accredited teacher status from the BDA [ATS (ITT)] this is hardly surprising. We thus need to examine the effects of this teacher apprehension on attainment.

Neil Humphrey has examined the importance of the role of teachers and peers on the self-esteem of pupils with dyslexia (Humphrey, 2002; Humphrey and Mullins, 2002). In Humphrey (2003) he summarizes those findings and develops ideas relating to practical implications. His previous research showed that:

> Dyslexia produced marked effects on the self-concept and self-esteem of the children. This was more apparent in those children attending mainstream schools. Children with dyslexia felt isolated and excluded in their schools, and up to half were regularly bullied or teased. (Humphrey 2003: 130)

He reports some disturbing statements by both pupils and teachers:

> They shout at you for not doing work.

> I had a supply teacher who wouldn't help me – I just feel invisible.

> Well, I mean, it's just one of those things that has been conjured up by pushy parents for their thick or lazy children, quite often both.

No one is trying to claim that this represents the generality of teacher attitudes. However, given the frequency with which pupils report negative perceptions of teacher support it may be only an extreme statement of many teachers' reactions to their own perceived helplessness.

Success and failure

These findings are made more disturbing in the light of work relating to the reasons why pupils believe they succeed or fail. Fredrickson and Jacobs (2001) refer to Borkowski (1988), who suggested that the achievement of children with dyslexia was influenced by whom they felt had control over their learning. They also refer to Halmhuber and Paris (1993) who reported that the more pupils felt they were in control of their learning the more likely they were to attain well. In their own study they discovered that 'Children with dyslexia were found to have significantly lowered perceived scholastic competence than their normally achieving peers.' However, 'They did not experience significantly lower self-worth' (Fredrickson and Jacobs, 2001: 412). In other words they felt OK as people but had learnt that they were no good at schoolwork! They also found that those pupils with dyslexia felt far less in control of their learning than other pupils.

Humphrey and Mullins (2002) looked at whom they felt had this control. They asked pupils aged between 8 and 15 years why they thought they succeeded or failed in their schoolwork. Dyslexic pupils believed that their success or failure was due to the quality of their teachers rather than their own efforts. They believed that if one was good at reading one could be considered intelligent and that hardworking people were also intelligent. This suggests sensitivity to teaching style and teachers' comments, as both will be associated with likelihood of success.

> Successful pupils with dyslexia were significantly more likely to attribute their (schoolwork) outcomes to teacher quality, an external factor. Thus situations of success do not reinforce positive self-referential information, since pupils with dyslexia do not equate success with ability or effort. (Humphrey and Mullins, 2002: 201)

It looks as though they thought of themselves as good, hard-working pupils who did well when teachers were good at their job!

Humphrey (2003) went on to look at the role of peers. Unfortunately he reports: 'In the research I conducted peers were a source of low self-concept and self-esteem; in particular the problems of bullying and teasing were a recurrent theme.' The protection of pupils is a major professional responsibility for teachers and schools. There is a wealth of material relating to how bullying can be prevented and dealt with. The results seem less than satisfactory for pupils with dyslexia. An interesting sidelight on the issue comes from the work of Blatchford et al. (2003). They looked at the effects of class size in relation to social and behavioural adjustment to school. At first sight the results were not hopeful with regard to dyslexia friendliness. They concluded that, 'Children in large classes are more distracted from work and more often off-task. The unexpected result [was that] small classes may lead to less social and more aggressive relations between children' (Blatchford et al., 2003: 15–16). However, they do go on to point out that,

> Although we have seen that children engaged in more off-task behaviours, at the same time they engaged in more on-task-related behaviours with their peers. If children by being less able to get their teacher's attention, then turn to their peers then this may be a distracting influence and not productive. On the other hand using peers as sources of information may be a valuable context for learning. (Blatchford et al., 2003: 31)

A different conceptualization?

Our argument is starting to build into a dyslexia-friendly classroom being a friendly, co-operative classroom generally. One is reminded of that now somewhat passé concept, 'school ethos'. Unfortunately, the idea sits poorly with the current unedifying drive for personal attainment and greater and greater emphasis on differentiating amongst the top grades. However, Humphrey (2003) presents a most useful set of suggestions based on emotional support approaches involving both teachers and peers. He suggests that this support comes from counselling-based approaches, mediation, befriending and listening. However, he admits that 'Teaching is an increasingly busy and stressful occupation and the recommendations in this article may not sit easily with the hectic schedule of the modern practitioner' (Humphrey, 2003: 135).

Kozharskaya and Olson (1999) propose another different and interesting approach again based on Rogerian/humanistic principles. They suggest that 'Information learning takes place in the emotional channels and leads its way from emotions to cognitions. In order to be a success a teacher should learn to work with both his and his pupils' [sic] emotional manifestations as with special content' (Kozharskaya and Olson, 1999: 63).

Westwood (2003) also puts significant emphasis on the affective domain. He cites Driscoll (2000) as commenting that, 'teachers believe that lack of motivation is the underlying reason that students avoid class work, refuse to become fully engaged in a learning task, fail to complete work they could easily do, or are willing to complete a task only for some extrinsic reward it may bring.'

He goes on to quote Galloway et al. (1998) as arguing that motivation 'Can be seen as the product of an interaction between pupils and the varying situations in which they find themselves at school.' Echoing both Humphrey and Fredrickson earlier, Westwood (2003: 12) states that: 'Students' past causal inferences about their own successes and failures are major determinants of future motivation and achievement.'

He goes on to postulate a downward spiral where children's learning problems have a negative impact on teachers' attitudes and motivation that can, in turn, be conveyed all too easily to their students.

> The everyday actions of teachers . . . may add to students' own perceptions of being incompetent in school. Even unintentional cues from teachers – such as providing simplified materials, easier tasks, too much praise, too much help – may cause students to believe that they are lacking in ability, or that teachers believe them to be so. (Westwood, 2003: 13)

Eysenck (1995) provides a cognitive psychological basis for these observations when he suggests that an anxious person is unable to concentrate and that distractibility may well come as much from internal stimuli such as worry and self-concerns as from external threats. Furthermore, 'the worry associated with anxiety reduces processing efficiency because it uses up valuable resources of the working memory system' (Eysenck, 1995: 458).

Dyson and Skidmore (2002) believe that the only way out of this apparent impasse is to recognize it as a dilemma and therefore not susceptible to resolution within the terms of the current debate. They propose a model for specific learning difficulties provision founded on a distinctive conceptualization of the subject (Figure 14.1).

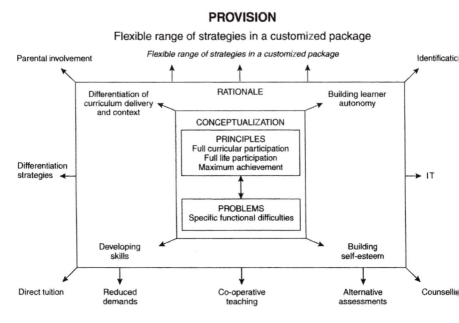

Figure 14.1 A possible model of an approach to specific learning difficulties provision.

In essence, the model moves from a conceptualization of dyslexia in terms of deficits and weaknesses to one in which, 'there is a discrepancy between what a pupil can do and understand and what s/he can show s/he can do and understand. The aetiology and diagnosis of weaknesses are seen as less important than their impact on participation and achievement'. Working with this model means that teachers can feel much more confident as the child's difficulties have not been 'professionalized'. It is their everyday effects that concern the teacher and they can take advice as to how those particular effects may be approached. It also means that the first person they should approach is the child.

For Dyson and Skidmore (2002: 180-1) there should be four aims that provision should fulfil: differentiation, developing skills, building learner autonomy and building self-esteem. They suggest that the notions of 'differentiation' and 'developing skills' are 'established' in work with pupils with either SEN or specific learning difficulties (SpLD) in most schools. (Even if it is in principle rather than in practice.) However:

Building autonomy and building self-esteem, on the other hand, mark a crucial boundary between rationales for provision and those for learning support. ... The building of autonomy and self-esteem are not the desirable – but optional – extras they may perhaps have been in Learning Support, but are absolutely central to effective responses to specific learning difficulties. (Dyson and Skidmore, 2002: 181)

Recognizing the uniqueness of each pupil's response to difficulties implies seeking individualized approaches capitalizing on pupils' strengths and circumventing their weaknesses. It also implies enabling the pupil to take ownership of effective approaches so that they can both act upon them and convey them to others. However, few researchers have actually asked pupils for their views in a systematic fashion.

Thompson and Chinn (2001) asked a group of adolescents attending a mathematics and dyslexia summer school what hindered learning:

- 'Teachers who go too fast and expect too much. Being expected to produce the same amount of work [as non-dyslexic pupils] in a given time.'
- 'Teachers who don't stick to the point.'
- 'Teachers who know I'm dyslexic but don't help me enough. Being patronized.'
- 'Too much copying off the board and/or dictating notes. Rubbing work off the board too soon.'
- 'Having test results read out loud. People who make fun of me or who are sarcastic.'
- 'Being told off when I'm asking a friend for help.'
- 'Not being allowed to use my lap-top in lessons.'
- 'Confusing "dyslexic" with "stupidity". Lack of empathy for dyslexia.'
- 'Being made to read aloud in class.'

What helped was:

- 'Help being given discretely (and quietly) to individuals.'
- 'Being given more time.'
- 'Handouts with summaries of work.'
- 'Marking work in dark colours, tidily. Praise!'
- 'Working in smaller groups.'
- 'Trained teachers. Awareness of dyslexic difficulties. Teachers who care.'
- 'Grades that show individual improvement.'
- 'Marking that is clear and helpful.'
- 'Catch-up exercises.'
- 'Work judged for content not spelling.'

The pupils' views

In April 2003 Manchester Metropolitan University, in partnership with the BDA, was awarded a DfES SEN In-service Fund grant to develop a course for newly and recently qualified teachers to enable them to teach in 'dyslexia-friendly' classrooms. The BDA has a network of local associations, each of which is composed mainly of parents of children with dyslexia. It also has a dedicated Internet forum for the exchange of information and experiences between parents, teachers and others with an interest in the area. A message was posted on the forum asking for volunteers to complete a questionnaire to help with the project and a similar request was made in a mailing to all local associations. We were amazed by the response as the request was made in the last week of the school summer term. Not only were questionnaires completed promptly and fully but also many respondents took the opportunity to write other comments at length. Overall 138 useable questionnaires were available for analysis, 52 from pupils aged up to 10 years and 66 from pupils aged 11 years upwards.

As they had dyslexia, probably quite severely, the pupils were encouraged to fill in the questionnaires with the help of their parents but to respond in their own words. They were asked always to think about teachers, classes and schools in their own experience and finally to offer advice to teachers to make things better for dyslexic pupils. The results for primary and secondary pupils were similar but with some interesting differences.

For primary pupils, a teacher they could learn easily from would 'Make it clear exactly what she wants us to do.' This should be taken slowly. 'Show us, don't just tell.' 'Give us time to listen.' The use of pictures and structural materials makes it easier to understand. A significant number of pupils said it was easier if the teacher was enthusiastic. After this pupils liked to be able to ask questions and to have teachers check that they were doing the right thing. Effective teachers gave help if you 'got stuck' and were patient if you needed things repeated. Finally teachers should be nice, should not shout if pupils made mistakes, should be patient with mistakes and should create a peaceful environment in the classroom.

It is interesting that these personal characteristics were all seen as more important than the provision of support materials. When mentioned, good support materials included putting and leaving instructions and spellings on a large white board or personal 'crib sheet', putting homework instructions on tape, allowing oral or taped responses, and so forth.

A number of pupils mentioned the importance of the teacher making eye contact with them when giving instructions and/or being prepared to work on a one-to-one basis. The effectiveness of small classes and small groups was also mentioned. However, the overall impression is quite clear – pupils with dyslexia need teachers who are clear and concise, pleasant with their classes and prepared to recognize that not everyone understands the first time.

Teachers it was difficult to learn from gave too many instructions too fast, didn't check if pupils understood and didn't allow them to ask questions. Time was important too. Pupils not only wanted time to think about and understand instructions - they also needed time to do their work, particularly if it involved writing. Ineffective teachers 'Rush you - they tell you off if you don't get enough done.' 'They don't let you think long enough before making you start work.' 'Say you have a time limit for something and you want to make it a good piece of work and then you have to finish it off badly by saying something like, "Happily ever after!"'

For a third of the pupils the main complaint was shouting and they were clear about its effects on their learning: 'They shout all the time for no apparent reason' as one pupil succinctly put it. 'Getting into a stress when I get something wrong' resulted in disruption of their ability to think. 'When she shouts a lot it makes it hard to think, you can't concentrate.' 'If I get told off it sticks in my head and I can't concentrate on my work.' The second complaint was being shown up in front of the class: 'Like being asked aloud in class how many correct in my spelling test.' 'Ask you to do things that they know you will fail at.' 'One teacher told the whole class I wasn't doing very well and I felt embarrassed and really couldn't think.' This ties in neatly with our earlier quotation from Eysenck (1995).

One in five complained about work on the board and displays generally. These included not being able to see the board, teacher writing on the board and then rubbing it out too soon or standing in front of it and one teacher who 'Put the number line at the back of the class and then told me off if I turned round to look at it!'

When asked what subject they found most difficult because of their dyslexia three subjects were identified by a significant number of pupils - English (60%), mathematics (22%) and science (18%). The reasons, unsurprisingly, related to literacy - writing, spelling and reading being mentioned in that order. When asked which subjects were affected least, three subjects were mentioned by significant numbers of pupils but similar numbers mentioned a range of other subjects. Art was the least affected (40%) with perhaps surprisingly mathematics next (30%). Pupils seem to differentiate between the mathematics itself, with which they found they could readily cope, and the reading and writing associated with it. Physical education (22%) was the third subject mentioned. There then followed science, music, design and technology, music and games, each being mentioned by six to eight pupils. The main reasons were given as 'no writing' (36%), they felt they were 'good at it' (20%) or that it was a practical, hands-on subject (14%). This emphasis on the demands that the actual teaching process makes rather than the conceptual nature of the discipline is even clearer in the responses from pupils at secondary schools where specialist teaching throws it into greater relief.

We then asked about their feelings. What were the three worst effects on school life generally of having dyslexia? Nearly one third of the responses related to feeling stupid or different and/or not knowing as much as the others. Some of this is brought about by thoughtlessness:

> You have to ask for spellings all the time if you want to get them right and the teacher writes them on the board which makes the rest of the class think how stupid I am.

> Not being given credit for being as intelligent as others just because I have difficulty in speed of writing and spelling.

> I am never picked to do cool things because I can't read or remember things like everyone else.

The second effect was not being able to write either easily or properly and the problem of working slowly; therefore work, particularly homework, 'taking ages'.

Finally we asked: 'If you were able to tell all teachers something about how to teach pupils with dyslexia, what would you say?'

There was a clear consensus amongst the pupils. More than eight out of 10 said that teachers should explain better in the first place, and then check whether pupils had understood. They should be prepared to repeat instructions and explanations. 'Talk plainly, clearly and to the child.' 'Watch over my shoulder every so often and write spellings in the margin.' 'Concentrate on what the person is saying without thinking about what you are going to have for dinner or who's fighting over there. They are having a hard time telling the teacher because they are embarrassed.' 'They should explain what you have to do as many times as needed – twice the same way before maybe a different approach.'

This was then followed by almost as great consensus (7/10) that teachers should not shout, and that they should be patient and give more time. In other words once instructions and so forth have been understood they should trust pupils to be involved in their work and accept mistakes as genuine attempts at learning. As one of them said in answer to an earlier question, 'don't get into a stress when I get something wrong'.

Overall, it is clear that these pupils have no difficulty recognizing the learning environment in which they can succeed. It is interesting that the underlying theme is the environment rather than any specific techniques or special methodology. They want calmness and security, the feeling that teachers might actually like them and are enthusiastic about their subject, quiet recognition of their difference and the provision of low-key differentiation and support.

As one would expect, there were clear similarities between the responses of pupils at primary and secondary schools, but there were also some significant and interesting differences. There were 67 useable questionnaires from pupils in secondary schools yielding 195 codeable responses. There were far fewer 'no answer' codes than with the primary pupils. Nearly half of the responses to the question asking for the characteristics of teachers from whom dyslexic students learned easily related to being understanding, ready to spend time helping, explaining things carefully, and proactively checking, repeating instructions and explanations and being ready to answer questions.

Next came the use of handouts, writing instructions clearly and carefully on the board (preferably a white board) and ensuring that students had a homework diary. Only after these crucial elements have been provided do they mention making lessons fun and practical, giving time to think and write and encouraging and rewarding good attempts.

Typical responses were:

Explain, then ask if I understood. If not, explain with pictures, etc. But if I do understand then don't overdo it so that it becomes boring.

Good teachers aren't ignorant and unsociable people. They can notice when you are having problems and they don't dismiss you by ignoring you and your questions.

A good teacher writes things down clearly and just writes and teaches the basic information without rambling on about other things.

When I am stuck I know I can put my hand up and not get shouted at for not listening. The teacher smiles at me and then explains it again, doing at least two examples with me.

Two categories of teachers who were difficult to learn from emerged – teachers who don't give you enough time and teachers who make you copy from the board, an overhead transparency (OHT) or a book. 'Feeling rushed' is probably a very good indicator that all is not right with the teaching/ learning process rather than a direct cause in itself. Again, resorting to the very ineffective method of just getting pupils to copy down information is a feature of poor teaching generally. This is confirmed by the next most frequent category, 'talks too much or too fast.' Taking these categories together they cover a third of all the responses. The next complaints were, 'can't control the class', 'shouts all the time', 'puts you down' and 'doesn't explain'.

The curricular subjects difficult to learn were: English (mentioned by over half the pupils), mathematics, modern foreign languages (MFL), science and humanities each mentioned by about one in three. The reasons given related to curriculum delivery rather than content or process. Overemphasis on grammar, spelling and punctuation was the main complaint, followed by the need for writing or having to take dictation, too much reading or having to remember facts or formulae. The only actual criticism of a subject was directed at MFL, 'I can't spell in English so spelling in French and Spanish is madness.' 'I find it hard to spell and I don't understand tenses and punctuation. I can barely understand English so French is worse.'

Interestingly some students disclaimed any problems: 'In secondary school I do not find any subject too difficult – I like a challenge. In primary school however I found Maths hard. This is probably because we (the class and I) were forced to do many timed tests (mainly mental arithmetic) approximately four times a week.'

This both validates our earlier comment about teaching methods rather than subject matter and suggests that current primary school methods may need rethinking for some pupils. Another student said, 'none, because all teachers were well informed by the SENCO and IEPs'. One summed up the whole issue succinctly with the reply, 'maths, because he is not a good teacher!'

The 'top' subjects that were 'easy to learn' were art followed by physical education – no surprise there. However mathematics, science, humanities and design and technology posed few problems if teachers demanded 'no writing', presented their subject in a 'practical' way or did not emphasize spelling. There were also comments relating to enjoying the subject, it being made interesting by good teachers, appropriate support or that they themselves were prepared to work hard. A significant number of respondents mentioned all these factors. Typical comments were:

> I like them [sic] subjects.
>
> I have a real interest in them and that overrides my dyslexia.
>
> We have good teachers and Science and History you can think through.
>
> My dyslexia helps me to think in a different way.

The majority of pupils said that the main effect of dyslexia on school life generally was that they couldn't read, write or spell easily. ('Ask a silly question' was an expression that came to mind on reflection!) 'Being different' followed, then 'people don't understand you', 'work taking a long time to complete' and bullying in one form or another. The two interpersonal categories are somewhat worrying. Nearly 40% of our respondents claimed that their dyslexia affected either how they felt about themselves or how others treated them. Judging by the overall quality and cogency of their replies, these pupils and students were well integrated with good self-awareness. They were being made to feel different, sometimes aggressively, in their school situation. In other words their classrooms were not inclusive in the sense that the principles of 'universal design' were not being applied. Typical responses in this area were:

> People can do things I can't. They can understand things more easily.
>
> Being embarrassed to keep asking for help – going to the special needs group.
>
> When you are in need of help people explain things to you as if you are stupid.
>
> Being made to feel stupid in front of my friends.
>
> Teachers saying, 'Children like you ...'

Letting down my parents (but dad is dyslexic too).

Being followed around by a teaching assistant.

Finally we asked what they would tell teachers about how to teach. The replies consolidated and affirmed what had gone before. Over half wanted teachers to 'understand' them and 'be discreet' in the way they gave support and made modifications. This was followed by requests to explain better in the first place and recognize the need to check understanding and repeat, if necessary, without having to be asked. A quarter felt that giving more time for both explanations and completion of work was helpful. Finally, a fifth mentioned 'encouragement'.

This all builds up to a picture which suggests that enhancing the achievements of pupils with dyslexia does not make unreasonable demands on teachers at either primary or secondary phases of education. It is the way they go about their teaching and organizing classrooms that is seen as either facilitating or frustrating. The key comes in understanding how each pupil thinks and feels.

Conclusion

Overall, the comments from the pupils indicate that dyslexia-friendly environments are those that would benefit all pupils. This echoes the findings of Ofsted (1999: paragraph 22): 'The teaching strategies devised for those pupils with specific learning difficulties were often used effectively with other pupils who had more generalised learning difficulties.'

The principles of universal design might be applied with good effect: 'A more efficient way to provide student access is to consider the range of user abilities at the design stage of the curriculum and incorporate accommodations at that point. This "built-in" access for a range of users, those with and without disabilities, is the underlying principle of universal design' (Orkwis, 1999).

This chapter points up the importance of recognizing the vulnerability of pupils with dyslexia. Both our work and that of others indicates a reliance on their teachers not only to ensure that they understand but also that they feel safe emotionally. In terms of the curriculum delivery methods suggested by the pupils these are congruent with Guilford's 'structure of intellect model' relating to the cognitive processes underlying intelligence (Guilford, 1967; Meeker, 1969). This highlighted the importance of sensory input buffers, types and content of memory, operations performed on memory contents and mode and type of response required.

This latter is given increased importance when one considers the effects of anxiety on performance. Eysenck (1995) argues that there are very important links between anxiety and attention due to the fact that the main functional value of anxiety is that it facilitates the detection of environmental threat. This means that in an anxiety-producing situation pupils may attend more to the things producing threats and become distracted from the educational task by them. You will remember that they referred to teachers 'getting in a stress' as preventing them from thinking.

Most importantly, none of what the pupils saw as important in any way conflicts with good educational practice for all pupils. However, maintaining that practice in the face of difficulties the teacher does not understand is taxing. A small piece of teacher research carried out in the area of autistic spectrum disorder indicates the power of understanding. Asking her colleagues what had been the main impact of her school-based in-service education and training on the nature of autistic spectrum disorders she received the reply 'We are now much more patient as we can understand what is going on in their minds.'

Clearly, teachers and others concerned with the education and support of pupils with semantic–pragmatic language disorder need specialist knowledge, skills and understandings. There are many excellent guides to classroom principles, practices and techniques at varying levels of detail and practicality. The BDA publish their own materials and the Report on the Dyslexia Friendly Initiative Training (MacKay, 2002) has some excellent suggestions from practising teachers. However, our thesis is that these are a necessary but far from sufficient basis from which to work. Pupils need to believe that the general competence they feel within themselves as individuals is recognized by teachers who are ready and willing to help them display this competence in the artificial world of the school and classroom. There are many examples of highly gifted people in all walks of life who have only been able to demonstrate their strengths when released from the confines of the school system. As one of them, Jackie Stewart, told the last BDA International Conference, unless you have had to fight the prejudice, misunderstanding and bullying from both pupils and teachers personally, 'You will never know what it feels like.' We have an obligation, whatever the pressures from targets, league tables and the like, to deal effectively with Dyson's two additional principles. However, we would not want to suggest in any way that teachers in general are either unfeeling or unwilling. What we do suggest is that the dyslexia-friendly school movement is currently too instrumental.

Fullan and Hargreaves (1992) argued, long before schools and teachers became submerged in an 'alphabet soup' of initiatives, that if educational reformers ignored the emotional dimensions of educational change they would fail because the classroom is an emotional place and therefore classroom improvements must engage teachers' hearts as well as their minds. They warn that if we lose this focus then we will end up with changes that are calculative and managerial, owned by the professional not the pupils.

References

Audit Commission (2002) Special Educational Needs: A Mainstream Issue. London: Audit Commission

Blatchford P, Edmonds S, Martin C (2003) Class size, pupil attentiveness and peer relations. British Journal of Educational Psychology 73: 15–36.

Bowie L (2003) Report: poor children's dyslexia less likely to be treated. The Baltimore Sun, 8 March.

British Dyslexia Association (2001) Dyslexia Friendly Schools Audit. Reading: BDA.

Brooks G (2003) Sound Sense: the Phonics Element of the National Literacy Strategy. London: DfES.

Department for Education and Skills (1999) Additional Literacy Support Materials. Nottingham: DfES.

Department for Education and Skills (2000) Phonics – Progression in Phonics for Whole Class Teaching. Nottingham: DfES Publications.

Department for Education and Skills (2003) Targeting Support: Choosing and Implementing Interventions for Children with Significant Literacy Difficulties. London: DfES.

Dyson A, Skidmore D (2002) Contradictory models: the dilemma of specific learning difficulties. In Wearmouth J, Soler J, Reid R (eds) Addressing Difficulties in Literacy Development. London: Open University Press, pp.174–88.

Eysenck M (1995) Cognitive Psychology: A Student's Handbook. Hove: Lawrence Erlbaum.

Fredrickson N, Jacobs S (2001) Controllability attributions for academic performance and the perceived scholastic competence, global self-worth and achievement of children with dyslexia. School Psychology International 22(4): 401–16.

Fullan M, Hargreaves A (eds) (1992) What's Worth Fighting for in your School? Working Together for Improvement. Buckingham: Open University Press.

Fultcher G (1989) Disabling Policies? London: Falmer.

Galloway D, Rogers C, Armstrong D, Leo E (1998) Motivating the Difficult to Teach. London: Longman.

Guilford JP (1967) The Nature of Human Intelligence. New York: McGraw Hill.

Humphrey N (2002) Teacher and pupil ratings of self-esteem in developmental dyslexia. British Journal of Special Education 29(1): 29–36.

Humphrey N (2003) Facilitating a positive sense of self in pupils with dyslexia: the role of teachers and peers. Support for Learning 18(3): 130–6.

Humphrey N, Mullins P (2002) Personal constructs and attribution of academic success and failure. British Journal of Special Education 29(4): 196–203.

Johnson M (2001) Inclusion: the challenges. In Peer L and Reid G (2001) (eds) Dyslexia – Successful Inclusion in the Secondary School. London: David Fulton Publishers.

Johnson M, Phillips S, Peer L (1999) A Multi Sensory Teaching System for Reading. Manchester: Manchester Metropolitan University.

Kerr H (2001) Learned helplessness and dyslexia: a carts and horse issue? Reading 35(2): 82–5.

Kozharskaya V, Olson V (1999) Personality training for SEN teachers. In Van der Wolf K, Sayer J (eds) Opening Schools to All. Leuven: Garant, Chapter 6.

Lewis A, Norwich B (2000) Mapping a Pedagogy for Special Educational Needs. Exeter: School of Education, University of Exeter.

MacKay N (2001) Achieving the dyslexia friendly school. Paper delivered at the 5th BDA International Conference, May.

MacKay N (2002) Report on the Dyslexia Friendly Initiative Training. Bangor: Welsh Dyslexia Project/Prosiect Dyslecsia Cymru.

Meeker MN (1969) The Structure of Intellect. Columbus OH: Merrill.

Norwich B, Lewis A (1999) Mapping a pedagogy for special educational needs. British Educational Research Journal 27(3): 313–29.

Ofsted (1999) Pupils with Specific Learning Difficulties in Mainstream Schools. London: Ofsted.

Orkwis R (1999) Curriculum Access and Universal Design for Learning. Reston VA: ERIC Clearing House on Disabilities and Gifted Education.

Regan T, Woods K (2000) Teachers' understanding of dyslexia: implications for educational psychology practice. Educational Psychology in Practice 16(3): 333–47.

Thompson M, Chinn S (2001) Good practice in the secondary school. In Fawcett AJ (ed.) Dyslexia Theory and Practice. London: Whurr, pp. 281–97.

Westwood P (2003) Commonsense Methods for Children with Special Educational Needs. London: Routledge.

CHAPTER 15

Learning from the science of learning: implications for the classroom

RODERICK I NICOLSON, ANGELA J FAWCETT

Overview

We consider insights from the science of learning to the processes of learning to read. We identify a number of issues that appear to us to be crucial in optimizing the reading process and note that a surprisingly high percentage of them have been overlooked in current approaches to reading instruction. Finally, we consider how these insights might be used when considering how to help dyslexic children learn to read. We hope that these analyses will point us towards achieving Harry Chasty's goal of 'teaching dyslexic children the way they learn'.

Introduction

A few months ago the parent of a dyslexic child said to us: 'They always say that you should help dyslexic children exploit their strengths. Johnny hates phonics and is terrible at hearing the sounds. I read words without using phonics – why put Johnny through this purgatory? Surely there must be a better way for a dyslexic child to learn to read.'

The simple answer to this question is of course that no one can move straight to adult-style skilled reading – it is necessary to go through a series of stages. Each stage 'scaffolds' the next stage. For a child learning to ride a bike, this scaffolding might take the form of stabilizers. In fact the stabilizers teach the child some of the wrong skills (they encourage the child to lean the wrong way), but the benefits in terms of confidence outweigh the disadvantages. Similar scaffolding is needed for acquisition of any complex skill. For instance, an expert reader will perceive a whole word at a time, but this does not mean that the 'whole-word' method is the appropriate method of learning to read. The necessary scaffolding (which allows one to attack a word one has not learned already) is to learn the 'letter-by-letter' blending approach. Phonological skills underpin these processes (Adams. 1990).

However, the more we think about this issue, the more concerned we become as to whether this really is the only way to learn to read. We address these issues in the remainder of the chapter. We start by outlining why current approaches to helping children learn to read make use of the phonological route. Next we consider skilled reading – the eventual target for any reading instruction. Thirdly, we note that is surprising that the science of reading instruction appears not to be aware of the more general science of learning, and we present a number of well-established findings that have direct relevance to reading. Finally, we attempt to pull all these strands together by developing the analogy of learning to read in terms of climbing a mountain massif. It is premature to suggest that we can find a better way up the reading mountain for dyslexic children. Nonetheless, we consider that the advent of new technology and old theoretical concepts gives us the necessary tools to try.

A digression to cognitive analyses of reading

Before we consider the approaches to learning to read it may be valuable to outline an influential cognitive analysis of the processes involved. Figure 15.1 gives an indication of the possible brain mechanisms underlying reading, and is derived loosely from the 'dual-route' model (see, for example, Coltheart et al., 1977). Before children learn to read they have already learned to understand and reproduce speech with familiar (route 1a) and unfamiliar words (route 1b). For reading, there are the two routes: 2a and 2b. Route 2b is known as the sub-lexical route and shows how, with an unfamiliar word, it is possible to break the word down into its components (sub-lexical means parts of the word), pronounce the word, and then use one's ability to understand spoken words (route 1a) to identify what the word means. More normally in skilled reading, the lexical route (route 2a) is used, in which a written word is perceived as a whole. This, of course, bypasses the need for re-entry to the system via the auditory routes.

Models of learning to read

A child starting to learn to read will normally have a number of the necessary sub-skills in place. First, she will understand the language and know the spoken version of the words use. Second, she will be able to move her eyes to fixate words on the page. Third she will (normally) have some idea of what Marie Clay calls 'concepts about print' (Clay, 1993) and perhaps some knowledge that her own name is constructed from a set of letters. In short, the pathways indicated as routes 1a and 1b in Figure 15.1 will be in place, as will the speech output route. The child proceeds to exploit these skills, and by a process of 'bricolage' (Piaget and Inhelder, 1958) uses these skills as building blocks in the development of reading skill.

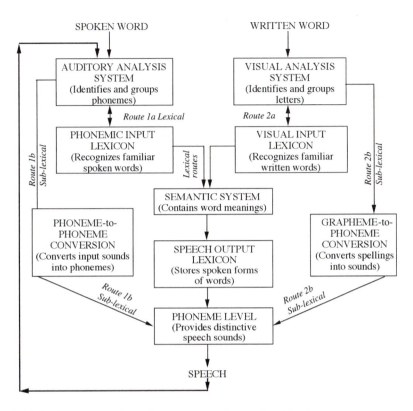

Figure 15.1 Different routes in understanding spoken and written language.

There is no space here to provide a detailed account of the various theories of learning to read. An early and justly influential model (Frith, 1985) involves three main stages:

(i)   In the initial *'logographic'* stage children learn to read a few words as *gestalten* (as a single unit, a sight word) – route 2a in Figure 15.1.

(ii) The next stage is the *alphabetic stage*, in which they learn the skills for decoding a word into single letters, which can then be combined into the appropriate sound using grapheme–phoneme conversion rules – route 2b in Figure 15.1.

(iii) Finally, there is the *orthographic stage*, in which the child need not break down the word into single letters but need only break it down into a few orthographically standard chunks (letter sequences) which may be spoken via letter-sequence to syllable-sound rules. Orthography refers to the rules of written English, including the use of prefixes, suffixes and morphemes – a variant on route 2a, but requiring blending and perhaps also reanalysis via speech output and route 1a.

For example, in the logographic stage, children learn words such as 'the', their own names, and words from their reading books (for example, Sam, fat, pig and so forth) by sight, maybe not even knowing the sounds of the individual letters making up the word. In order to get started, everyone has to have a basic vocabulary of sight words, and many reading schemes attempt to build up a sight vocabulary of around 50 words by frequent repetition. Soon, however, it becomes necessary to learn the alphabetic principles – ways of reading a word that one does not already know. Here the traditional approach is to teach the single letter shapes (graphemes) and their sounds (phonemes), and to get the child to read them aloud one at a time: 'cat' to /c/ /a/ /t/, and then to blend the series of phonemes (cuh – ah – tuh) into a single sound /cat/. This involves considerable mental gymnastics!

More recent approaches (such as Goswami and Bryant, 1990) suggest that it is easier for the child to concentrate on the 'onset' and 'rime' of words. The onset of a syllable is the set of consonants before the first vowel (the onset of 'cat' is 'c'; the onset of 'train' is 'tr'), and the rime is the rest of the syllable ('at' and 'ain' respectively). The advantage of using onsets and rimes is that one can learn rimes separately (for example, by focusing on the word family 'at' – 'bat', 'cat', 'fat', 'hat', 'mat', and so forth), and for simple words it is then easier to blend the resulting phonemes: /c/ and /at/ go to /cat/ etc. These simple alphabetic principles do not scale up well to longer words, for which the principles of orthography are needed. Frith suggests that in the orthographic stage, children (and adults) are able to analyse words 'into orthographic units without phonological conversion', by recognizing strings of letters that 'can be used to create by recombination an almost unlimited number of words'. In other words, children move from a letter-by-letter approach to a letter-string-by-letter-string approach. The latter is clearly much more efficient, and could also account for our ability to develop the sub-lexical route in the dual-route models above. Finally (although not discussed by Frith), adult readers might well develop an essentially logographic approach, in which their sight vocabulary might well expand to include almost all their reading vocabulary – that is, back to route 2a. Frith also discusses spelling. She notes the surprising fact that some children are able to spell some words that they cannot read. Presumably the word in question (typically a simple word such as 'mat') is not in their logographic reading vocabulary, but can be constructed using alphabetic principles. This suggests that spelling (rather than reading) might be the causal skill underpinning the acquisition of the alphabetic stage. This led to the development of her 'six-step' model for reading and spelling in which spelling scaffolds the acquisition of alphabetic reading whereas reading scaffolds the acquisition of orthographic spelling.

Goswami and Bryant's causal model

On the basis of subsequent research, Goswami and Bryant (1990) argue that rather than progressing through a series of stages, much of a child's development involves just becoming better at strategies that the child used right from the start. Furthermore, they consider it is more fruitful to look for causes for progression between stages rather than merely describing each stage, and identified three hypothetical causal factors that facilitate progress.

- Pre-school phonological skills (such as rhyme and alliteration) provide the initial word-attack skills and inference strategies that underlie the apparent transition from the logographic stage to the alphabetic stage, and provide the basis for categorizing words by orthographic features (especially rime), as discussed above in Frith's model.
- The learning of the alphabetic script provides the basis for the skill of analysing the sounds of a word into phonemes that underlies the ability to spell words alphabetically. For instance, knowing that 'cat' is spelled 'c' 'a' 't' helps the child to analyse the sound /cat/ into its constituent phonemes /c/, /a/ and /t/. This skill only later transfers to the analogous reading skill, and at this stage reading and spelling are relatively independent skills.
- Reading and spelling skills come together to provide mutual support for learning the many orthographic components of language. Later on in reading development, knowledge of orthographic rules – such as 'ize' is pronounced with a long 'i', 'ate' is pronounced with a long 'a' and so on – allow children to reason by analogy how to pronounce 'ite', 'ile', 'ate' words, and consequently, by analogy, the entire set of 'silent e' pronunciation rules, thereby significantly enhancing the coverage of their orthographic rules. Goswami (1993) has further developed the idea of the use of analogies.

A significant advantage of the Goswami/Bryant theory is that it does attempt to model not only what the stages are but also what the causal factors are in allowing a child to move from one stage to the next. Their theory therefore goes beyond mere description towards a pedagogical theory. The Goswami/Bryant theory provides an important integration of developmental and pedagogical approaches to reading. However, we argue below that for completeness it needs to be augmented with a considerable range of skills that have received little attention in the reading development literature.

In order to address this issue we need to take a step back, and consider the target – skilled reading.

Skilled reading

A comfortable rate for continuous speaking aloud is around four words per second – 240 words per minute. An average skilled reader will probably read many millions of words per year, at a rate of around 300 words per minute (significantly faster than she can speak them out loud). She will also understand them as she reads, and will remember their gist. She will also be able to read out a passage in an intelligible and interesting fashion, with appropriate prosody and intonation.

Think for a moment what is entailed by the skill of reading aloud. Try reading the following passage to a friend – ask them to note any word on which you falter:

> Modern reading research starts with the major contribution of Huey (1908). His analysis, added to by theoretical concepts such as practice and reinforcement, formed the cornerstone of reading teaching for half a century and more. It was only when the winds of change hit education in the 1960s that colourless green ideas hedgehog. More recently, Adams (1990) provides a spirited defence of the central role of phonological skills in learning to read.

With any luck, you faltered round about 'that' in 'that colourless green ideas hedgehog'. This indicates that you have (with your eyes but not your voice) read on for the rest of the phrase from 'that' and realized that the rest of the phrase is nonsense. You might then go back to check it, and so on. This is an indication of the 'eye–voice span'. In order to be able to read with prosody, one needs to know how a phrase turns out before starting to read it. Hence one's eyes have to be ahead of one's voice. This is a well-established finding (established using objective methods such as eye movement monitors rather than the one we tried above).

Now consider the implications of this finding. A well-known technique in cognitive psychology is that of 'articulatory suppression'. This involves asking the subject to speak out loud some sequence such as 'the, the, the' or '1, 2, 3, 4, 5' continually. This is known to prevent the conversion of visual (graphemic) information to its phonemic (external or internal speech) form. Reading words aloud at a reasonable speaking rate is therefore a relatively taxing form of articulatory suppression. Three implications follow:

- those items in the eye–voice span ahead of the voice must have been read entirely visually, without phonemic translation (if you don't believe this, try reading while saying 'the the the' continuously – most readers can do this quite easily);
- skilled readers are therefore capable of using a non-phonemic route for reading;
- readers who have to sub-articulate the word they are reading will not be able to read aloud fluently.

Hence

- two of the cornerstones of skilled reading are the ability to read without sub-articulating (see also Simmonds, 1981) and the ability to synchronize one's eyes with one's voice such that the eyes and voice work on different words.

It remains a great puzzle to us why these two obvious points have not generated a great deal of research. There is of course some information about eye movements in reading, but nothing in the literature about how these eye movements develop as a function of reading skill. There is nothing that we can trace on the gradual elimination of articulation from the reading process. We will outline some thoughts on these issues.

Eye movements and reading

Most of the work on eye movements and reading derives from eye-tracking devices used with relatively skilled readers. During reading, the eyes engage in saccadic movements, in which they jump abruptly from one point of fixation (typically the middle of a word) to the next point of fixation (typically the next word, or maybe two or three words further on). Usually, the eye jumps roughly every 200 ms (five times per second) from one fixation to the next. A jump is called a saccade, and it is generally considered that information is extracted from the text only when the eye is at rest (in practice this is not a serious limitation because saccades are very brief, say 10–20 ms in duration. A representative 'standard' trace is shown in Figure 15.2. Notice the relatively consistent 'staircase' pattern of eye movements, fixating pretty much every word in turn (with the occasional regression). It is worth emphasizing that there are major differences between individuals in these patterns. Probably as few as 10% of skilled readers have such consistent movements, and there is even greater variability in intermediate or beginning readers!

Articulation and reading

Given traditional reading approaches, children are taught to articulate each letter independently, and then to use the (fading) auditory trace as the stimulus for blending /c/ /a/ /t/, that's /cat/. This corresponds to route 2b then route 1a in Figure 1. Modern onset-rime phonics approaches use a similar approach /c/ + /at/ that's /cat/.

At some stage the word reading probably becomes either whole-word or whole-syllable, but still with overt articulation. This allows the articulated phonemes to enter the 'phonological loop' where they can be further analysed. Next, the child finds it is not necessary to use overt articulation but can use 'inner speech', thereby gaining access to the phonological loop more directly (and saving vital processing time). Finally presumably the need for inner speech is avoided altogether, and some purely visual processing takes place. The procedure has become 'internalized' with direct access from the graphemic code to the semantic lexical entry.

Having set the scene in terms of current models of reading, and noted that skilled reading is a complex skill that involves much more than just linguistic and phonological processing, it is now time to consider whether the general theories of learning complex skills have anything to contribute to the theories of reading instruction.

The figure on the right shows the trace over time of fixations made by the reader while she is reading three lines starting:

'As society has become progressively more complex, psychology has'

These traces are very hard to follow, so it is usually more informative to change them into a chart of fixation times and locations, calculated from the trace, as shown below.

The notation indicates that the reader makes her first fixation on the 'c' of 'society' (1). Her eyes rest there for 234 ms, then saccade (essentially instantaneously) to the middle of 'has', then the middle of the next word, then early in 'progressively', the middle of 'more', then overshoot somewhat to the comma after 'complex'. This results in regression (indicated in the code by a |) by a couple of letters (7) followed by standard saccades to the middle of the succeeding words.

The saccade to the start of the next line (10) does not go quite far enough, resulting in another regression (11).

Overall, the reader is showing the standard 'staircase' pattern (imagine the chart turned on its side!) of steady steps moving consistently across the page.

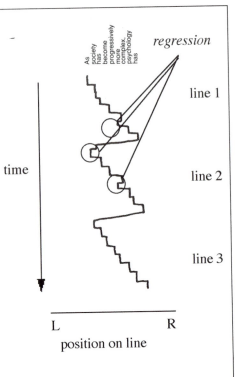

As	society	has	become	progressively	more	complex,	psychology	has
	•	•	•	•	•	• •	•	•
	1	2	3	4		5	| 6	8	9
							7		
	234	310	188	216		242	188 144	177	159

assumed	an	increasingly	important	role	in	solving	human	problems
• •		•	•	• •		• •	•
| 10		12	13	14 15		| 16	18
11						17	
244 206		317	229	269 196		277 144	202

Figure 15.2 The staircase pattern of fixations while reading a passage.
Acknowledgement: Redrawn from Table 2 (p. 115) and Figure 1 (p. 116) in Rayner (1986).

The varied forms of learning

In a contribution to Nicolson and Fawcett (2001) we outlined the different forms of learning that normally blend together to provide the unrivalled learning capability of the human brain. We outlined the process by which the brain 'self-organizes' to exploit the consistencies in its environment (taking the example of why a 6-month-old infant's brain is able to distinguish all the human language sounds, whereas 3 months later it has specialized on the language that surrounds it, giving it advantages in its own language environment (at the cost of losing important abilities in other languages); 'declarative skill' acquisition, where one is told (or reads) how to do something ('knowledge that'); 'skill proceduralization' where one moves from 'knowledge that' to 'knowledge how' (one actually performs the task); 'skill tuning' where through extended practice the skill becomes more and more efficient to the extent that many of the subskills take place automatically; how world-class skills take a long time to acquire (the 1,000-hour rule) and often require a number of stages, with plateaux with relatively little progress occurring between stages. We went on to outline our studies that suggested that dyslexic children reduced automaticity not just for reading but also for a range of 'primitive skills' (including balance) that normally occur without the need for conscious monitoring. This led on to our analogy that being dyslexic was a bit like driving in a foreign country - one can do it, but at the expense of the need for continual conscious monitoring leading to greater stress, faster tiring, and greater susceptibility to interference. We also presented data on skill learning that demonstrated that dyslexic children suffer from difficulties in the speed at which they manage to blend two subskills together to create a more complex skill. Finally we reported an experiment that suggested that dyslexic children show abnormal performance on one of the fundamental building blocks of skill - the process of classical conditioning of the eye-blink response. In this section we go back to basics, and outline what is known from the science of learning

Learning simple skills

Psychologists (Fitts and Posner, 1967) suggest that one can distinguish three stages in learning a 'simple' motor skill such as typing. The early or 'cognitive' stage involves initially understanding what the task is about and what to attend to, and then using one's general skills in making the first efforts to carry it out. For typing this involves noting the location of the key for each letter. The intermediate or 'associative' stage involves working out a method for actually doing the task - in this case pressing the appropriate key with the appropriate finger. Here performance is initially slow and error prone. Nonetheless, the task is done. With further practice performance becomes faster and errors are eliminated. The late or 'autonomous' stage occurs after extensive practice and involves the escape from the need to attend consciously to the task - it has become automatic. At this stage one often loses conscious awareness of how the task is done.

If one starts the task properly (using all 10 fingers, not looking at the keys), the transition between the stages is probably relatively smooth, requiring merely extensive practice. If one starts in an unsystematic manner, one will learn bad habits that need to be 'unlearned' if one wishes to achieve fluency. In general it is considerably harder to unlearn skills than to learn them. Essentially, learning the skill has become one of learning a complex skill (see below) rather than a simple skill.

Controlled and automatic processing

The above analysis highlights one of the fundamental distinctions (Schneider and Shiffrin, 1977) in cognitive psychology – that between controlled processing, which requires attentional control, uses up working memory capacity and is often serial, and automatic processing, which, once learned in long-term memory, operates independently of the subject's control and uses no working memory resources. Controlled processing is relatively easy to set up, and is easy to modify and use in novel situations. It is used to facilitate long-term learning of all kinds (including automatization). Automatic processing doesn't require attention (although it may attract it if the training is appropriate – for instance, if we are trained to respond on hearing our name called, as are most children, then we will automatically hear our name and turn round even if we were not consciously attending to that conversation). Automatic processing is acquired through consistent mapping – that is, the same response is always made to the same stimulus. Stimuli can acquire the ability to attract attention and initiate responses automatically, immediately and independent of other memory loads. By contrast, if the link between stimulus and response is variable (varied mapping), then automatic processing is not learned.

Reading (and spelling) English provides classic cases of this varied mapping. At different times, in different words, the same sound or sound combination are spelled differently, and the same letter combination read differently. This variability seriously impedes the development of automaticity, accounting for the difficulties in learning to read and spell English.

In earlier work (Nicolson and Fawcett, 1990) we have argued that for some reason dyslexic children have greater than usual difficulty in making skills automatic. Therefore, even with simple skills, dyslexic children have to consciously monitor their performance whereas non-dyslexic children are able to perform the skill without thinking. Their skills are more automatic, less easily disrupted, faster and less error-prone.

Learning complex skills

Typically, when learning a complex skill, one starts learning, plays around a bit, improves, then diminishing returns set in, and however hard one tries, one does not seem to perform any better. One has reached a 'performance plateau'. Many of us stop at that stage and do something more rewarding. However, given the right support, it is sometimes possible to move onward from the plateau and up to a new, higher level of performance. Ericsson (for example, Ericsson and Charness, 1994) suggests that to get to world-class performance in any skill at least four stages of progress (with plateaux between stages) may be identified (Figure 15.3). In phase 1 practice takes the form of play. Most people never get beyond this stage, but those who are going to progress then typically are taught how to perform the skill better. There is rapid improvement to begin with, but then diminishing returns set in, with each hour of practice leading to smaller and smaller amounts of progress. If the person wishes to proceed, it is then necessary to get a coach, an expert, to give further individual training. It is rare to get to final stage 3 performance without around 1,000 hours' practice. To improve yet further one would need a 'star coach' according to Ericsson.

The key point we wish to bring out is that, unless there is a specific intervention, there is only a certain amount of progress made. To get off the plateau and move towards a further learning peak, it may be necessary to 'unlearn' some of the skills as preparation for learning new ones. One needs to climb down from the false peak to find the route towards the true peak.

Part-whole transfer

Most everyday skills, such as reading, or tennis, or car driving are complex, in that the complete skill depends upon a range of sub-skills. It is clear that, for fluent performance of the complete skill, the sub-skills should be automatized, but one important question is whether each sub-skill should be automatized individually, in isolation (which is easier), or whether all the sub-skills need to be automatized in the context of performing the complete skill. Shea and Morgan (1979) provided a clear answer to this issue. Essentially the

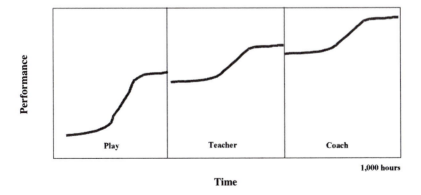

Figure 15.3. Stages in learning complex skills.

answer is that it is important *not* to train the sub-skills purely in isolation. If this happens there is a danger that the automatic method that the subject develops for the sub-skill might require some resources that are needed for performance of one of the other sub-skills, and so, when one attempts to blend the sub-skills into the complete skill, there is interference between the sub-skills, preventing the complete skill from being performed efficiently. Therefore, in order to make sure that this interference will not arise it is important to interleave sessions of the complete skill with automatization training on the sub-skills, so that the sub-skills are learned in a compatible fashion. This issue is known as 'part–whole' task training.

The zone of proximal development

One of the limitations of the above approaches is that, although they give general principles for support, they do not help a teacher decide how to help a particular child. Perhaps the closest educationally feasible approaches to this problem are those provided by Vygotsky (1934/1962) and Bruner (1981). Vygotsky's insight was that there is a great difference at any stage in learning between what one can achieve unaided and by coaching. He suggested that at any moment there are some skills/knowledge that are attainable from the learner's current knowledge, and some that are not. He described the set of skills which are currently attainable (given coaching) as the 'zone of proximal development' (ZPD), and suggested that the art of effective teaching was to make sure that at all times the learner was presented with tasks within the ZPD – always give achievable challenges. It was Bruner who introduced the term 'scaffolding' – if a concept/skill is not within the ZPD, we can introduce some halfway house, some related skill which helps the learner climb towards the target skill.

Natural learning

Papert (1980) caused something of a revolution in educational theory when he confronted the issue of how to help children learn mathematics. His answer was very different from that of Ericsson. Consider skills in which we are all expert – skills like walking and speaking, seeing and listening. These, in fact, require a high degree of skill, and take a long time for children to learn. Children do receive thousands of hours' practice at talking and walking, but they are mostly self-taught. The world provides the learning environment! Papert advocated wholesale changes in education, putting forward the telling analogy of ski evolutif. Thirty years ago, beginning skiers were just given standard skis. Because the skis are long and cumbersome, it was necessary to teach the beginners a method of controlling them – the snowplough and the snowplough turn. Once the skiers became more expert, they were then able to learn the parallel-turn method. To do this, they had to unlearn the snowplough turn, and learning to ski well was therefore a slow, expensive and frustrating business. The revolution occurred when it was noticed that children with short skis just seemed to learn the parallel turn naturally, without bothering with the snowplough. Ski evolutif, in which beginners were issued with short skis and taught parallel turns from the start, was born. Learning to ski is now simple and natural. How do children learn to speak French? The best way is to live in France, to be immersed in the culture and the language. Surely the same thing would be true for mathematics. What we need is a 'Maths Land' where mathematical principles are all around us. Papert designed the computer language Logo for children to use, together with a programmable 'turtle', which could be programmed to travel forwards, backwards, left and right, so that they could experiment and learn from their mistakes. He reasoned that this would give children the 'natural' learning environment, so that they would discover mathematical ideas for themselves.

It is worth noting that many of our everyday skills, such as walking upright, talking and using our hands, are in fact truly most impressive. Although it is now routine for a computer program to beat all but the very best chess players, there are no robots that can walk as well as a three-year-old, never mind talk as well as a five-year-old. Furthermore, skills are relative. Only four centuries ago, scholars who were able to read and write were treated with reverence. For most children whose home provides a 'Book Land', learning to read becomes a fairly natural (but lengthy) process.

Fluency and the real-time constraint on skill

Action is at the heart of learning, and timing is at the heart of action. Synchrony of the order of milliseconds is required for the irreversible linking of two synapses in the brain via long-term potentiation; muscular sequences synchronized within centiseconds are needed for fluent speech; reactions within deciseconds are required if prey are to be caught or predators avoided. In terms of understanding speech, we seem to have a 'phonological loop' of about 2 s. If we are able to compress speech sounds into this time we can process them, if not they are at least partially forgotten. The real-time constraint on action is that it must take place within the necessary time window. When walking, our adjustment to upcoming uneven ground must take place before our foot hits the ground – the eye–foot span! When playing sport we must play the stroke before the ball is past; when listening we must process the words before they fade from the phonological loop; when reading we must be able to process a whole word (or later, a whole phrase) before the phonological components fade. Visually, we must be able to 'decode' the word before our eyes saccade to the next fixation.

Think back to our analogy of learning to ride a bike. It's actually much easier to ride fast than slow, because the bike is less stable at slow speeds. Above a certain speed, the bike rider 'takes off' and everything becomes easier (and exciting). We believe that for reading, take-off speed is when one can read a whole sentence in the time one's working memory is able to store the components – about two seconds. There is a danger that phonological processing provides the 'stabilizers' that make it harder to reach take-off speed. The importance of fluency has been overlooked in many approaches to reading, which appear to assume that speed of processing is irrelevant to reading ability. This is not only false but deeply misleading.

Motivation

Motivation holds the key to most human learning. It is common to distinguish between intrinsic motivation, in which the topic is interesting in its own right, and extrinsic motivation, in which the motivation derives from some external source (for example, a teaching requirement). Sometimes a change in focus can have marked effects upon motivation. If the learner has a personal interest in a topic ('ownership'), motivation and success follow naturally. By contrast, if the learner cannot perceive the point of a topic, it is very difficult to make much headway. A related concept, which is also relevant to type of learning, is that of locus of control. Studies (for example, Rotter, 1975) have shown that learners who perceive themselves to be in control of their learning situation tend to cope better than those who see themselves as 'pawns' in the teaching machine. Furthermore, studies of failure (such as Holt, 1984) have often revealed a vicious circle in which, following repeated failures, a learner either adopts a passive learning strategy, or maybe some coping strategy which downplays learning at the expense of some more attainable goal (sport, disruption, truancy and so forth).

There is also the concept of fun. Children (and adults) learn better if they are enjoying themselves. We fear that this critical insight seems to have been lost in most walks of life. If learning can be made fun, people will try harder, concentrate better, come back for more, and generally do better all round.

Dangers afflicting approaches to reading

We have outlined some of the important issues in learning. Before turning to analyses of the processes of learning to read it is valuable to name and shame some of the more common mistakes made within the reading research community. These mistakes are of course not specific to reading research but also apply, to a greater or lesser extent, to almost any area of scientific endeavour.

Egocentricity

This takes several guises. Perhaps the most insidious aspect is that researchers are normally adult and fluent readers. It is particularly difficult once one has acquired fluency in a skill to be able to intuit quite what processes young beginners are going through when learning. Our brains have changed irreversibly. It is as though we have to guide the learning readers over the rough terrain of the reading mountain, but we must stay at the summit and peer down at the beginners toiling far below.

Overspecialization

Given the rate of increase in academic knowledge, there is an irresistible trend towards individual researchers specializing more and more – often at the expense of knowing more and more about less and less. A serious risk is that this specialization is accompanied by an increasingly myopic view of the field in question. The focus of reading research on language-related issues, to the detriment of research into other, probably equally important, characteristics, such as learning, fluency, eye movements and motivation, seems to us to be a paradigm case of such overspecialization.

The QWERTY phenomenon

It is natural in any area where standardization is a requirement for initial approaches to become entrenched, even if they are not optimal. This tendency even has a name – the QWERTY phenomenon – after the hegemony of that initial keyboard layout. The QWERTY keyboard was designed to ensure that common letter pairings were well separated to minimize the danger of the keys (which were of course on long metal holders which swung out to physically stamp the inked letter shape on the page) sticking together. This design feature is of course irrelevant in today's world. Indeed, there is clear evidence that the QWERTY keyboard seriously inhibits typing by schoolchildren (for example, Nicolson and Gardner, 1985). Nonetheless, because the QWERTY industry is fully established (think of the trained secretaries) the inertia of the system prevents change.

The current approach to the teaching of reading is one solution to the problem. It is not much changed from that advocated by Huey (1908). It certainly works for most children. There is, however, solid evidence that most approaches, if applied systematically, also work pretty much as effectively. Throughout the 1990s the US government commissioned studies designed to establish once and for all that phonics-based reading instruction was more effective than alternative methods. The results, published in the report of the National Reading Panel (NICHD, 2000), indicated that alternative methods were in fact pretty much as effective. More important, it is clearly established that the approach does not work for a significant proportion of the population – probably as many as 10% have intractable problems with the approach, and up to 30% fail to benefit from the approach for a variety of reasons.

Consider the changes in lifestyle and technology that have taken place over the past century, and even the past five years. Schoolchildren routinely send text messages where spelling is unimportant and, in any case, are scaffolded by predictive text systems that are well in advance of cutting-edge research a decade ago. Computers can use good 'text to speech' routines to 'speak' anything on the screen. There are now more than adequate speech recognition systems, which, when trained for a specific voice, have 99%+ accuracy. Where is the research aimed at harnessing new technology to facilitate learning to read?

One size fits all

We have already highlighted the fact that too many children fail to learn to read. One size does not fit all for learners, especially not for dyslexic learners. There is no need to labour this point in a book for a dyslexia conference.

However, an equally important fact is that one size does not fit all for teachers. However good the prescribed programme of reading support, a good teacher will be able to adapt it to the interests, needs and environment of their particular children, class, school and environment – and should be encouraged to do so. The issues of ownership, motivation and fun apply just as much to the teachers as to their pupils.

Mistaking means for ends

In any area of science it is common to lose focus on the important issues. As part of the research endeavour to understand how the cognitive system works, a technique is introduced to study, say, memory. Difficulties in interpreting the results of the technique emerge, and an industry is then created to investigate the technique. Years pass, many research papers are written, but nothing much is decided. In the meantime, the superordinate goal, investigating cognitive function, is forgotten. To an extent this reflects the need to concentrate on potentially soluble problems, and to an extent it reflects the need for specialization in science. Nonetheless, it reflects a concentration on investigating the means to an end rather than the end itself. If confronted with a brick wall it is surely more appropriate to look for a way round, rather than undertake a painstaking analysis of its construction.

Phonics instruction is a means to the end of learning to read. It is a method of bootstrapping the reading of novel words by concentrating on the individual letters in a word and their sounds. It would appear from, say, the UK National Literacy Strategy that the understanding of phonics and language has become an end in itself.

Building on sand

In skill learning it is necessary to have a range of sub-skills in place before the skills can be acquired efficiently. Sub-skills include meta-cognitive skills such as ability to concentrate and readiness to learn as well as the specific prerequisites such as linguistic/articulatory competence. If these skills are not in place at the start of learning, learning will be much less effective and may even be seriously flawed because the sub-skills are incompletely learned. This is one of the dangers of starting the learning process at too young an age.

Towards a science of reading instruction

The reading mountain

As a reception class teacher, one's task is to take a group of children and help them make progress up the reading mountain. Unfortunately, once a skill is acquired one can no longer imagine what it is like not to have the skill. Therefore, as a teacher one is confined to the summit and has to peer down to see how they're doing. The mountain is actually more like a massif than a single peak, with a range of foothills – the phonological foothills, the fluency marshes and the eye movement crags, all of them connected, and all leading towards the reading peak. Much of the massif is poorly mapped, and there is consistent mist, making it difficult to see what is happening much of the time.

The usual approach to the massif is well trodden, from the sunlit pastures of pre-school play through the gentle but rockier slopes of letter learning, but soon this turns into quite a tough climb. Most children emerge, perhaps a bit bruised and footsore, at the formidable corrie where marsh blocks the path to the side and towering cliffs block the way ahead. Some intrepid children clamber up the cliff without even looking back, and run happily on the slopes of the reading mountain. Most, however, follow the paved trail that leads towards the phonological foothills. For most, this is a boring but relatively straightforward route and in due course they arrive at the peak of the first hill. Those with good balance can make their way along the up-and-down ridge walk back towards the reading massif. They emerge after a few scrambles at a point higher than the initial impasse, and start climbing the central massif again. The way is not at all clearly mapped but most children seem to make their way slowly through the fluency marshes and the eye-control crags and eventually emerge on the sunlit uplands near the reading summit. The particularly intrepid ones may, in fact, pursue the path further, moving into the snow-capped rapid-reading range but that is a different story.

The problems for the teacher (group leader) are first that she is peering down from the heights and so at best she has only a limited view of the terrain. Second, the massif is covered in mist most of the time. From time to time the mist clears, and she is able to see how the party is faring – some well ahead, most roped together in the middle, some standing forlornly, confronted by a raging stream as their classmates move off into the distance, some limping back towards home . . . She is able to shout instructions, suggest paths, implore them to use the map, flashlight, rope or compass in their rucksacks, but can't come down to them. However much help she tries to give, it's a difficult task and many of the party can't keep up with the group. At the end of the year she passes on the task to the next teacher, who inherits a motley bunch, still toiling in the foothills. Some teachers prefer to use the mountain hut on top of the phonological hills. It's easier to keep track of the children as they toil upwards towards the hut, but the route toward the reading peak is harder to see.

A fanciful and completely inadequate analogy, of course. However, we hope it does bring to life some of the major concepts.

Fun and motivation (or lack thereof) are represented implicitly via the description of trudging up arduous and dull paths (as opposed to the pleasant sunny lower slopes), with the main pleasure being the occasional opening up of a distant vista, or the realization on looking back how far one has come. The difficulty of learning complex skills (and later partially unlearning) is introduced via the concept of the 'Grand Old Duke of York' ridge walk, where one has to relinquish height that one so painfully gained in order to progress. Indeed, it is often very much harder to descend a ridge than to ascend it. The idea that there might be a range of viable routes is implicit in the description of the mountain range. Taking the area round that dyslexia-friendly town of Bangor, there are about seven major routes up Snowdon, all with very different characteristics. Perhaps if one started elsewhere the route might be better suited to those with poor balance. Scaffolding comes in almost literally. Can we throw a bridge across the ravine, cut handholds into the cliff? Fluency is not well represented, and the interplay between phonology, sight vocabulary, eye movements and fluency is not that good either. We try to get that across via the idea of having to be high enough on all three or four ridges in order to be able to cut across to the summit.

Phonics and dyslexia

Finally, let us return to the issue with which we started this chapter. The parent of the dyslexic child questioned whether it is necessary to scaffold the reading process via a skill that dyslexic children find supremely difficult – phonics. We have now marshalled the necessary information and analyses to attempt a preliminary answer. Our answer to this is twofold: at present and in future.

Given the current teaching processes that intertwine the learning of reading and spelling, there seems little alternative to teaching phonics. Phonics is a requirement for sub-lexical processing, and in particular the alphabetic principle. However, the current extended focus on phonics alone has become an end in itself, rather than a means to the end of learning to read fluently. Explicit phonological analyses should be seen as scaffolding that assists the learner to read novel words and to move to the orthographic phase. Unfortunately, letter-by-letter word building, and even syllable-by-syllable word building, is slow – too slow to give the fluency necessary to enable the reader to capture a phrase or sentence within the time available in working memory. There is a real danger that over-teaching phonics leads to this scaffolding becoming more and more permanent, an edifice that the learner has to lump around long after it should have been left behind. Explicit instruction needs to be introduced so that, after the appropriate point, reliance on phonological scaffolding is gradually reduced until the reader is able to read words visually, without phonological recoding. It may be that articulatory suppression – requiring children to read while articulating 'the, the, the' – will have the desired effect. In other words, we need to find a route through the phonological foothills that does not explore them thoroughly, does not climb to the top merely to descend the ridge to the col leading back to the reading mountain, but winds up the shoulder of the foothills to the col without investing more time and effort than needed for the true end of getting back on course.

Looking to future developments, we have to say the outcome is not clear. It may well be that there are other starting places in learning to read. There is a clear case for a comprehensive re-evaluation of early learning materials from the viewpoint of the learning theory issues that we have outlined above – fun, success, consistency, fluency, scaffolding. Above all, we need to try to pinpoint methods for identifying and rescuing children who are clearly failing given the current approach.

The path forward

Let us now consider the issues from the perspective of the 'dyslexia eco-system' (Nicolson, 2002). Here we argued that many of the major 'players' in reading and dyslexia – parents, children, teachers, schools, government, educationalists, researchers, representative bodies – may appear to have different (and sometimes opposing) day-to-day perspectives, but share the long-term goal 'to develop significantly improved support for dyslexic infants, children and adults in an effective but cost-effective fashion'. Here we outline how, from each perspective, we might make progress towards this goal.

In terms of the mountain analogy, the goal would become that of finding a range of good routes up the reading massif, and smoothing out these routes so that all children can follow at least one route. There is a range of tasks involved: mapping out the massif properly, so that the fluency marshes and the eye-movement crags are better understood, as is their relationship with the main peak and the phonological foothills; to map out the major impasses on these routes, and to develop means of overcoming them; mapping out the various foothills with the intention of finding a 'contour' path that ascends to the col in between the phonological foothills and the massif without climbing up and down the phonological ridge; to improve methods of finding out where everyone is on the mountain; to improve the 'mountain rescue' service; to predict which route will be best for each child; and how to make the mountain walk more enjoyable.

We hope it is clear that there is scope for all players to make significant contributions in this endeavour. We outline a few obvious strategic directions.

The governments should be keen to provide the funds for the necessary integrative, joined-up, research. Given that the cumulative additional cost to the educational system of a child with special educational needs from 7–16 years old is around £50,000 (Crowther et al., 1998), it is clear that there is great scope for substantial savings given a more effective system. The major need is for the 'helicopter view' instead of the rather myopic approach taken to date.

Researchers and teachers can collaborate to identify the major sticking points on each of the different ascents, and to develop the necessary tools and scaffolding that allow children to overcome or avoid these impasses.

There is growing (but still disputed) evidence that at least some dyslexic children benefit from non-reading support aimed at eliminating problems that make it especially hard for them to learn to read. These complementary approaches include dietary improvements, use of tinted lenses, elimination of primitive reflexes and use of exercise treatments. An analysis of these approaches is beyond the scope of this chapter. See Fawcett (2002) for a review. However, in terms of our analogy, one can see them as, for example, trying to equip the climbers with better footgear, so that, whichever path they are on, they will climb more easily and safely.

We consider that it is time to harness new technology to address these issues. As noted earlier, computer-based methods have the potential to transform the learning opportunities. Now routine but vital, the Internet provides the opportunity for centralized dissemination of appropriate materials, and sophisticated testing and diagnostic procedures. Synthesized speech, predictive spelling, voice to text . . . the possibilities are immense and yet barely explored. Perhaps most novel is that it seems likely that affordable eye-tracking devices may be available shortly. Such technology allows the development of seamlessly integrated fluency, eye movement and reading-support programmes.

In order to support dyslexic children better we need to explore a range of ascent routes, and a range of diagnostic procedures that predict which route will be best for each child. It may even be that for dyslexic children a route that dissociates the traditional scaffolding of reading by spelling will prove the most effective. This is an empirical matter, rather than an issue of dogma.

Overall, therefore, these are exciting times. In the past decade outstanding progress has been made in mapping out the phonological foothills. If, in the next decade, by working together, we are able to make equal progress on the uncharted landscapes of the reading massif, we are confident that we will be able to meet the dreams of Seymour Papert and Harry Chasty, by finding methods of 'read evolutif' that dyslexic children can use to learn to read in the way they learn best.

Acknowledgment

We gratefully acknowledge the comments of Rebecca Brookes on a draft of this chapter.

References

Adams MJ (1990) Beginning to Read: Thinking and Learning about Print. Cambridge MA MIT Press.

Bruner JS (1981) The social context of language acquisition. Language and Communication 1: 155-78.

Clay M.M. (1993). An Observation Study of Early Literacy Achievement. Auckland NZ: Heinemann.

Coltheart M, Davelaar E, Jonasson JT, Besner D (1977) Access to the internal lexicon. Attention and Performance VI. London: Academic Press, pp. 535-55.

Crowther D, Dyson A, Millward A (1998) Costs and Outcomes for Pupils with Moderate Learning Difficulties in Special and Mainstream Schools (RR89). London: DfEE.

Ericsson KA, Charness N (1994) Expert performance: its structure and acquisition. American Psychologist 49: 725-47.

Fawcett AJ (2002) Evaluating therapies excluding traditional reading and phonological based therapies. DfES: London. See http://www.dfes.gov.uk/sen/documents/ACF429C.htm.

Fitts PM, Posner MI (1967) Human Performance. Belmont CA: Brooks-Cole.

Goswami UC, Bryant PE (1990) Phonological skills and learning to read. Hove: Erlbaum.

Holt J (1984) How Children Fail. Harmondsworth: Penguin Books.

Huey EB (1908) The Psychology and Pedagogy of Reading. New York: Macmillan.

NICHD (2000) Report of the National Reading Panel: Teaching Children to Read. Washington DC: National Institute for Child Health and Human Development.

Nicolson RI (2002) The dyslexia ecosystem. Dyslexia: An International Journal of Research and Practice 8: 55-66.

Nicolson RI, Fawcett AJ (1990) Automaticity: a new framework for dyslexia research? Cognition 35: 159-82.

Nicolson RI, Fawcett AJ (2001) Dyslexia as a learning disability. In Fawcett AJ (ed.) Dyslexia: Theory and Good Practice. London: Whurr, pp. 141-59.

Nicolson RI, Gardner PH (1985) The QWERTY keyboard hampers schoolchildren. British Journal of Psychology 76: 525-31.

Papert S (1980) Mindstorms: Children, Computers and Powerful Ideas. New York: Basic Books.

Piaget, J. and Inhelder, B. (1958), The Growth of Logical Thinking from Childhood to Adolescence. New York: Basic Books.

Rayner K (1986) Eye movements and the perceptual span: evidence for dyslexic typology. In Pavlidis G, Fisher DF (eds) Dyslexia, Its Neuropsychology and Treatment. Chichester: Wiley, pp. 111-30.

Rotter J (1975) Some problems and misconceptions relating to the construct of internal versus external control of reinforcement. Journal of Consulting and Clinical Psychology 43: 56-67.

Schneider W, Shiffrin RM (1977) Controlled and automatic human information processing I: detection, search and attention. Psychological Review 84: 1-66.

Shea JB, Morgan RL (1979) Contextual interference effects on the acquisition, retention, and transfer of a motor skill. Journal of Experimental Psychology: Human Learning and Memory 5: 179-87.

Simmonds DAD (1981) Reading and Articulatory Suppression. Unpublished PhD thesis, University of Cambridge, Cambridge UK.

Vygotsky LS (1934, trans. 1962) Thought and Language. Cambridge MA: MIT Press.

CHAPTER 16

Baseline assessment and the early identification of dyslexia

GEOFF LINDSAY

The early identification of developmental difficulties has long been a focus of interest among researchers and practitioners. It is not difficult to understand why. Surely if we can identify developing problems in their early stages we should be better able to prevent or at least ameliorate their continuation. The origin of this line of thinking is in medical science where early screening for some developmental difficulties is simple to carry out, highly accurate and has clear-cut implications for action.

Unfortunately the situation with psycho-educational developmental factors is not so straightforward. Indeed, the position within medical science is also frequently problematic, with relatively few conditions allowing as high a level of success for early screening as, say, the identification of phenylketonuria (Hall, 1996). The approach to developmental difficulties within paediatrics has changed emphasis in recognition of the complex nature of the range of difficulties children experience in their early years, and the lack of appropriate early identification measures providing rigorous, accurate and helpful information in the case of many areas of problems. Indeed, this change in emphasis is exemplified by the change in title of the handbooks produced by the British Paediatric Association (now Royal College of Paediatrics and Child Health) from *Child Surveillance Handbook* first and second editions (Hall et al., 1994) to the third edition's *Health for All Children* (Hall, 1996).

Mild and moderate psycho-educational difficulties have proven to be difficult to identify at an early stage. By 'early' in this context is meant either at a time when abilities develop normally, or even at a time prior to this when the purpose is to identify children 'at risk' of later problems. For example, screening of 7- to 8-year-olds was reasonably common in the 1970s in the UK, primarily to identify children with reading difficulties, but as the Bullock Committee argued, this resulted in children being offered help after 2 to 3 years or more of failure to develop this key skill (Department of Education and Science, 1975).

During the 1960s in the US, and the 1970s in the UK, there was some interest in trying to develop effective instruments and procedures to identify children 'at risk'. The target concern was typically literacy, and reading in particular. However, as I have previously argued, these attempts were not successful (see, for example, Lindsay, 1974, 1995; Lindsay and Wedell, 1982). The critique of attempts at such early screening focused on the failure to achieve appropriate levels of sensitivity and specificity. While many children with difficulties at, say, 5 years did go on to have later literacy problems, this was also true of others who passed the screening assessment (false negatives). On the other hand, the screening instruments available also missed children who appeared to have problems at an early stage but later were found to be developing normally (false positives).

The degree to which any screening instrument balances these 'misses' compared with the 'hits' (those who fail the screen and have later problems, or pass and develop normally) is a key factor in determining the usefulness of such a screening procedure for early identification. Misclassification may lead either to failure to modify educational input for children who would benefit or to making inappropriate changes to normal education for children for whom this would be necessary.

As a result of these limitations I have long argued for a move away from early identification by a screening measure to a systemic approach. This includes the use of instruments, but as part of a wider strategy. For example, the assessment tool would not be used to 'diagnose' but rather to aid the teacher's structuring of their observations and assessment of a child and their hypothesis formulation, and then to provide initial information for intervention (Lindsay, 1995).

During the 1980s and 1990s in the UK, schools and local education authorities (LEAs) developed a range of approaches to this issue. Some focused more on developing instruments whereas others took a more systemic approach. During the 1990s the government became interested in this issue and, after a consultation exercise, instituted a statutory programme of 'baseline assessment' (Schools Curriculum and Assessment Authority, 1996, 1997). This policy acknowledged the range of schemes already in existence – and schools' and LEAs' reluctance to have a new national scheme imposed – and set in place a statutory framework that allowed 91 different schemes to be accredited (Lindsay, 2000). Some schemes had been subject to research and development programmes that allowed examination of their technical qualities and usefulness (see, for example, Infant Index and Baseline – PLUS: Desforges and Lindsay 1995, 1998; Savage and Carless, in press; Wandworth: Strand, 1999; PIPS: Tymms et al., 2000). Unfortunately, these schemes (Infant Index and Baseline – PLUS, Wandworth and PIPS) were in a minority. The Qualifications and Curriculum Authority, which had replaced SCAA, tried to address this by developing and evaluating its own scales (for example, Caspall et al., 1997; SCAA, 1996, 1997). Many LEAs then took up the SCAA scales but a number made various modifications, so reducing comparability and losing the reference with the research undertaken on the original SCAA scales.

By 1998, therefore, a plethora of instruments had been developed, by LEAs in the main, but there were also a small number of commercially produced instruments. This was the situation when the statutory system of baseline assessment came into operation.

Statutory baseline assessment

The present chapter is concerned with early identification of developmental difficulties, and literacy difficulties in particular. It is necessary to stress, however, that this was not the only, or even the main, impetus behind the government's statutory scheme. The Education Act 1997 states that

'a baseline assessment scheme' means a scheme designed to enable pupils at a mainstream primary school to be assessed for the purpose of assisting the future planning of their education and the measurement of their future educational achievement.

To understand the sub-text it is necessary to appreciate the content and emphasis in the earlier SCAA consultation document (see Lindsay, 2000, and Lindsay and Desforges, 1998, for reviews). Inspection of these documents makes it clear that the other and, it is argued here, the main driver was the attempt to introduce a means of judging 'value-added' performance. That is, the difference made by schools to the performance of pupils, for example at the end of key stage 1, given the children's developmental levels at entry.

Two quite separate rationales were therefore underlying the statutory baseline assessment programme. One was essentially pedagogical in origin, aiming to identify children's strengths and weaknesses and thereby help teachers adapt their teaching appropriately. The use of baseline assessment for the early identification of special educational needs (SEN) sits squarely within this rationale. The second rationale was managerial and concerned with accountability of schools, teachers and LEAs. This was part of the broader policy objective to improve standards, characterized by target setting for expected achievements and league tables to report results and identify 'winners' and 'losers'.

The statutory baseline assessment programme, therefore, had two distinct intellectual origins. Nevertheless, it was an open question as to how it would operate. Would this, the first statutory programme of school entry assessment in England (Wales and Scotland had comparable but different initiatives running at this time), produce an effective system of early identification of children with SEN despite its complex origin and despite the earlier research which had questioned the usefulness of instruments for use with children of about this age?

In 2000, Ann Lewis and I were commissioned by the Qualifications and Curriculum Authority (QCA) to evaluate the national arrangements (Lindsay and Lewis, 2003). We carried out a large-scale stratified survey of schools with 5-year-old children, including special schools (N = 982); we visited 46 schools where we interviewed headteachers, reception teachers and parents, and interviewed a sample of LEA assessment officers and educational psychologists with responsibility for the schemes. (Full details of the study may be found in Lindsay et al., 2000).

The study confirmed that 91 different schemes were in operation. Many were variants of the QCA scales. The most popular was PIPS (16.4% of schools), Signposts (Birmingham LEA, 6.6%) and Flying Start (Durham LEA, 5.5%). Many schemes were used only by schools in the LEA in which they were developed.

In the present chapter I shall focus on issues arising from the research that pertain specifically to the early identification of children with SEN, and particularly those with literacy difficulties.

Use of schemes for early identification

About three-quarters of schools reported using baseline assessment for the identification of SEN (47.0%) 'a great deal'; 25.4% 'quite often'. However, a larger number reported using baseline assessment for the initial assessment of children (70.2%; 16.9%). This discrepancy is interesting, and illuminated by the interviews. Many reception teachers stressed that they were not seeking to identify whether a child has SEN at this early stage. They described their focus as assessing *all* children in order to set targets and also to arrange groupings of children for teaching. These teachers were concerned that the first half-term was too early to be sure a child 'had' SEN. Indeed, they were even less keen on using baseline assessment to allocate children to the SEN Code of Practice stages of assessment (only 28.3% reported doing this 'a great deal', 20.1% 'quite often'). These results were further illuminated by the teachers' reports of the level of satisfaction with a range of aspects of their particular scheme. About two-thirds overall were satisfied with the use of their baseline assessment with children with SEN (28.8% 'very'; 37.3% 'moderately').

Hence, although early identification was a common use for baseline assessment, and its use with children with SEN was considered helpful, teachers were tending to avoid its use as a 'diagnostic' tool, leading to categorization of children. Rather, they saw it as an aid, providing useful information to add to other data. Also, and importantly, they used this information to plan and intervene.

Consistency of practice

Screening programmes need to be carried out at specific times if developmental age is a key factor. In the case of baseline assessment, teachers were allowed a window of 7 weeks in which to complete the procedure for their class. This may appear a short period, but the research identified an interesting variation in practice. As shown in Figure 16.1, schools adopted the complete range of possible practice with respect to when they started and completed the procedure over this 7-week first half-term. Indeed, some schools were outside the permitted period.

An issue for early identification is the comparability of results. For example, common items included writing own name, sound recognition and identification of letter sounds. All three of these skills are likely to be taught in this first half-term. Depending on when the assessment was undertaken, a child's score could vary significantly from week 1 to week 7, resulting in comparability being compromised by a decision regarding timing.

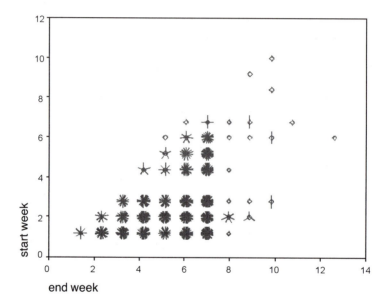

Note: density of petals represents number of schools.

Figure 16.1 Comparison of start and end weeks for baseline assessment: schools' responses (N = 982).

Comparability of schemes

As noted above, 91 different schemes were in operation. The accreditation criteria included a requirement that an acceptable scheme should include items that addressed language, literacy, mathematics and personal and social development. The schools generally confirmed that their scheme did in fact comply with this requirement, but many also reported that their scheme included other domains. In fact, 14 different domains were identified by schools, ranging from 11.2% identifying spirituality and 12.6% health factors to 96% identifying mathematical skills. Also included were concentration (64.3%), motivation for learning (46.5%) and physical development (42.5%). This variation raises questions about comprehensiveness, comparability and specificity. A broad assessment is useful in order to gain a comprehensive view of a child's development. For example, motor skills may not be identified as a cause for concern if baseline assessment comprised only the four specified domains. On the other hand, variation in breadth of assessments will introduce different meanings for the instrument. One may be focused specifically on the four domains while another may include motor skills. These two will have different operational relationships with, for example, reading. Hence, variation in content will reduce comparability of results of different baseline assessment instruments. This will be particularly problematic if different schools use different schemes (as happened in a number of LEAs), or if a child moves school/LEA.

We explored this question of comparability in more depth in a subsequent analysis of 42 of the schemes that had been sent to us (Lindsay et al., in press). The main weighting of the language and literacy components was 48% (SD 13%) but with a range from 24% to 75%. Assessment of a child's development using baseline assessment would therefore have many different implications depending on the scheme. One with 75% language and literacy content may be expected to be more sensitive to literacy difficulties than one with just 24%.

We then explored more specific aspects of the literacy domain, the writing element, and finally the more specific ability to write own name. At each level substantial variability was found. For example, reading varied between 3% and 51% of the literacy component (mean 21%, SD 12%). Twenty-one different descriptors were found within the 42 schemes concerned with writing name from 'makes marks to represent own name' (N = 1), through the most common 'independently writes own name spelt correctly, initial letter upper case remainder lower case' (N = 22) to 'can write some words to communicate meaning which need not be spelt correctly, and their own name' (N = 2).

Again, this wide variation has strength in providing discrimination in a developing skill, but this potential benefit is illusory as any one scheme only comprised a small number of these descriptors. On the other hand, this range reveals, again, a substantial lack of comparability between scales.

Baseline assessment – conclusions

Baseline assessment as a statutory requirement for school entry assessment of children aged 4 to 5 years has generally been welcomed by teachers. They have also used it to contribute to identifying children's needs and determining the appropriate teaching requirements. However, in terms of a national scheme for early identification of psycho-educational difficulties at school entry, baseline assessment has not been successful. To be fair, however, this was not its main aim. Rather, the pedagogic aims identified above were more general than identifying SEN. Also, QCA guidance required that an accredited scheme should include 'how the scheme *links with* [emphasis added] identification of children with special needs and more able children' (QCA, 1998a: Parts 2, 3).

A subsequent report from the QCA was commissioned because the then Secretary of State (David Blunkett) was reported to have been surprised at the relatively low proportion of schools using baseline assessment for identifying children with SEN (Lindsay, 2001). In addition to reviewing the findings of the national evaluation, I was asked to review the use of schemes for the identification of dyslexia. In fact, this was not a specific aim of baseline assessment. Dyslexia was not distinguished from literacy difficulties. Two alternative approaches were considered: the Dyslexia Early Screening Test (Nicolson and Fawcett, 1996) and the CoPS (Singleton et al., 1997) as exemplars of a more focused approach. It is not possible to do justice to these scales in the present chapter (see Lindsay, 2001) but their differences from the typical baseline assessment schemes are clear. Each is focused on literacy and is specifically grounded in a perspective on the nature of dyslexia. Each, therefore, may be considered to be theory driven, albeit the theoretical bases are not identical, whereas baseline assessments are typically non-theoretical. For example, the Infant Index (Desforges and Lindsay, 1995) was deliberately developed on the basis of the characteristics of children that teachers considered were important at age 5 years if the child were to be developing normally at 7 years.

Baseline assessment, therefore, cannot be used for early identification of children who have, or may have, literacy difficulties, whether these be considered dyslexia or an alternative variation. But does this matter? Much of what is in this review of baseline assessment may be seen as negative. On the positive side, however, the evidence suggests teachers are using measures to gain information to structure their understanding of children, and thereby direct their teaching. I have long argued that early identification should be a systemic matter, with any screening instrument *contributing* to teachers' competence, and not as a diagnostic tool. What is not acceptable, however, is for poorly or non-evaluated instruments to be used, which may produce data whose reliability and validity is at best unknown, and at worse unacceptable.

As we develop further our understanding of children's literacy difficulties, the trajectories their development takes and the target skills and correlates that can be usefully assessed, we may improve our ability to teach. This is a more demanding task but one that is more realistic than seeking to develop an instrument or scheme to identify dyslexia at an early stage. Dyslexia is itself multi-faceted and a contested concept. Research demonstrates trends and correlations, but also substantial discontinuities and developmental trajectories, and large numbers of 'misses' in predictive studies.

Foundation Stage Profile

The government has now changed the system within England from a statutory baseline assessment scheme at school entry to one at the end of foundation stage – that is, the end of the reception year (QCA and DfES, 2003). The guidance stresses the same approach as advocated here, one that is assessment-based teaching rather than a seeking of diagnoses or categorizations.

The Foundation Stage Profile (FSP) has been developed by the QCA to address several of the issues raised in our evaluation of the national baseline assessment scheme. It is a single scheme requiring all state schools across England to complete a profile on every child unless there is a sound case otherwise. This removes the problem of variability and non-comparability. It has also been developed by the National Foundation for Educational Research in collaboration with Birmingham LEA. It is hoped that this should produce an instrument whose psychometric properties have been examined and are satisfactory.

The FSP will also be completed on each child at the same time, improving comparability. A final assessment is required, to be made in the summer term, providing a summary of the child's development at that stage. However, the guidance advises that the FSP may also be used over the year, building up a profile of development. This approach also addresses concerns raised in our report.

The FSP is broader in scope than the expectations for baseline assessment, with six areas of learning: personal, social and emotional development; communication, language and literacy; mathematical development; knowledge and understanding of the world; physical development; and creative development. Each area has between one and four sub-areas, each of which has a nine-point scale making 13 scales in all. It is based upon observation, a method generally favoured by teachers, because it has a greater face validity and is also more practical. However, this raises questions of reliability of measurement. Training and subsequent moderation procedures are required to optimize consistency across teachers. Hutchin (2003) has produced a useful book for teachers on using the FSP to supplement the extensive guidance in the FSP handbook (QCA and DfES, 2003).

It is too early to judge the usefulness of the new approach, on any dimension, including whether it will indeed be used over time to assess change. If this does not occur, but it is used only at the end of reception, the opportunities grasped by teachers who used baseline assessment to guide teaching will be lost.

With regard to the assessment of literacy, only four out of 13 scales address literacy *per se*: language for communication and thinking, linking sounds and letters, reading, and writing, each with a nine-point scale. Hence, the literacy component comprises a minority of the FSP. It is important to remember, therefore, that the FSP can only provide a general indicator of justified concern, or of a child's literacy development. More specific and detailed assessments will be required to explore further any child with progress that is causing concern. Of course this is no different from the baseline assessment it replaced.

However, to end this chapter on a positive note, it is to be hoped that the new FSP will be used to aid teachers to identify children's needs, by alerting them to the need for modified teaching, and in some cases, more detailed assessment. The FSP is only a rough guide but its use by *all* teachers on children over their crucially important first year of schooling provides a platform from which to continue to develop and use more refined assessments, teaching based upon children's needs, and more effective levels between teachers, outside professionals such as educational psychologists and speech and language therapists, and parents.

References

Caspall L, Sainsbury M, Crapper A (1997) Trials of Baseline Assessment Scales: Report 3. Slough: NFER.

Department of Education and Science (1975) A Language for Life. London: HMSO.

Desforges M, Lindsay G (1995) The Infant Index. London: Hodder & Stoughton.

Desforges M, Lindsay G (1998) Baseline-Plus. London: EDEXCEL.

Hall DMB (1996) Health for All Children, 3rd edn. Oxford: Oxford University Press.

Hall D, Hill P, Elliman D (1994) The Child Surveillance Handbook, 2nd edn. Oxford: Radcliffe Medical Press.

Hutchin V (2003) Observing and Assessing for the Foundation Stage Profile. London: Hodder & Stoughton.

Lindsay G (1974) Screening for Children with Special Needs. London: Croom Helm.

Lindsay G (1995) Early identification of special educational needs. In Lunt I and Norwich B (eds) Psychology and Education for Special Needs. Aldershot: Arena/Ashgate, pp. 7–24.

Lindsay G (2000) Baseline assessment: how can it help? In Daniels H (ed.) Special Education Reformed: Beyond Rhetoric? London: Falmer Press, pp. 123–37.

Lindsay G (2001) Baseline Assessment, Special Needs and Dyslexia. Coventry: University of Warwick, CEDAR.

Lindsay G, Desforges M (1998) Baseline Assessment: Practice, Problems and Possibilities. London: David Fulton.

Lindsay G, Lewis A (2003) An evaluation of the use of accredited baseline assessment schemes in England. British Educational Research Journal 29(2): 149–67.

Lindsay G, Lewis A, Phillips E (2000) Evaluation of Accredited Baseline Assessment Schemes 1999/2000. Coventry: CEDAR, University of Warwick.

Lindsay G, Martineau E, Lewis A (in press) The consistency of baseline assessment schemes as measures of early literacy. Journal of Research in Reading.

Lindsay G, Wedell K (1982) The early identification of educational 'at risk' children (revisited). Journal of Learning Disabilities 15: 212–17.

Nicolson RI, Fawcett AJ (1996) The Dyslexia Early Screening Test. London: Psychological Corporation.

Qualifications and Curriculum Authority and Department for Education and Skills (2003) Foundation Stage Profile Handbook. Sudbury: QCA Publications.

Savage R, Carless S (in press) Predicting curriculum and test performance at age 7 years from pupil background, baseline skills and phonological awareness at age 5 years. British Journal of Educational Psychology.

School Curriculum and Assessment Authority (1996) Baseline Assessment: Draft Proposals. London: SCAA.

School Curriculum and Assessment Authority (1997) Target Setting and Benchmarking in Schools: Consultation Paper. London: SCAA.

Singleton CH, Thomas KV, Leedale RC (1997) CoPS 1 Cognitive Profiling System: Windows Edition. Beverley: Lucid Research Limited.

Strand S (1999) Ethnic group, sex and economic disadvantage: associations with pupils' educational progress from baseline to the end of Key Stage 1. British Educational Research Journal 25(2): 179–202.

Tymms P, Merrell C, Henderson B (2000) Baseline assessment and progress during the first three years at school. Educational Research and Evaluation 6(2): 105–29.

CHAPTER 17

Dyslexic pupils and the key objectives of the National Numeracy Strategy

ANNE HENDERSON, STEVE CHINN

Objectives of the Strategy

Although the National Numeracy Strategy (NNS) was devised for pupils in England, the content is not fundamentally different from that of mathematics curricula in many other countries. The structure and level of detail in the NNS is unusual in the history of English education and the scheme consequently imparts a degree of uniformity in schools across the country. Pupils have always had to deal with the objectives set by teachers, schools and local authorities. Government is now setting these objectives. The objectives are not negotiable and they will create a sub-population of pupils with specific learning difficulties, which are partly a consequence of defined objectives.

The key objectives of the National Numeracy Strategy define the backbone of the programme. They define what the programme expects of pupils. What we have done in this chapter is to look at these objectives, to consider some of the ramifications, and to suggest where the expectations these objectives imply may be challenging for dyslexic learners.

The consequence of failing to meet expectations is often a sense of failure and helplessness that may create a barrier to learning that even the most carefully designed programme cannot address in later years.

For the sake of the length of this chapter we have not addressed every objective. For the same reason we have only addressed the primary curriculum, but then this is where the foundations of success and failure are built.

The primary stages

Reception

Say and use the number names in order in familiar circumstances.

This requires a memory for sequential verbal information. There is no logic in the language or in the symbols (unlike Roman numerals, for example). This is an early example of the inconsistencies of the English language creating learning difficulties.

During their early years children learn to count, recognize and say numbers, connecting them to a specific number of objects. Parents are encouraged to involve their children in everyday activities to help reinforce the numbers. If children are dyslexic then the vocabulary involved may be too complex and too irregular for them to follow. Their short-term memory may be faulty so that they cannot match up the correct word to the specific number of objects and they will keep failing. So even before they come to school there may be the start of a loss of self-confidence. In the reception classroom just saying and using the number names in order will take them much longer than their peers. A great deal of multi-sensory teaching with specific help to assist in this important task is vital at this stage

Use language such as more or less, greater or smaller, heavier or lighter, to compare two numbers or quantities.

Language is, inevitably, already a significant component in numeracy, although one may be tempted to think of numeracy as a subject with lower language content.

Children almost always are familiar with counting songs, for example 'Ten green bottles hanging on a wall', so will sing the numbers quite happily. It is not always clear whether they realize that the numbers are decreasing in size. So when asked which number or quantity is bigger, smaller, heavier or lighter this language component may confuse those children for whom the order of number is not firmly established.

Find one more or one less than a number from 1 to 10.

This is a key skill but requires an ability to reverse a sequence. Often a dyslexic pupil will find that reversal significantly more problematic than a teacher might anticipate.

Initially when working with small children we use objects that they can easily manipulate. We talk about taking one away or adding one on until they become used to these words. Even at this young age pupils understand the meaning of a 'take-away' meal, so it is important to point out the disparity in meaning when it applies to mathematics. When the language is slightly altered so that we are talking of one more or one less, children who think that this is a completely different task because the words are different will experience a time delay before they understand this. Teachers need to give time for this important skill to develop. Some children find it difficult to start any procedure in mid-sequence and need to start at the beginning each time.

Talk about, recognize and recreate simple patterns.

This is a key skill for mathematics but the ability to generalize and recognize similarities may need much more directed learning than might be expected.

All pupils have their own learning style, which means that they will understand and recognize patterns in different ways. Some will have excellent visualization techniques, so teachers will need to give them a quiet time for them to absorb patterns before speech is used to describe them. Other pupils will require time to play with objects to recognize patterns, while there may be pupils who prefer to talk about patterns, describe them in their own words and then recreate them. A multi-sensory approach will help all pupils by acknowledging the range of thinking and learning styles that will be present in any class.

Year 1

Count reliably at least 20 objects.

Pupils will need to have the basic skill of one-to-one correspondence but the ability to chunk or sub-divide the counted objects, say into groups of five, will aid number sense and relationships. This is not always a skill that develops by osmosis.

Our counting system becomes rather confusing after 10 for those pupils who have some difficulty with language. Eleven to 15 are particularly difficult so pupils will need to make good connections with these numbers. The Kumon maths magnetic number box is really helpful in allowing pupils to see how the numbers are progressing. The big magnetic buttons numbers are grouped by colour from 1 to 10 and 11 to 20 and they are placed in groups of five so that the order is easy to see.

Other counting activities will help to develop the pupils' understanding of the links between numbers; for example, demonstrating the playing card pattern of dots. Knowing that 9 is 1 less than 10 and that 4 is 2 + 2 and that 10

1	2	3	4	5
6	7	8	9	10
11	12	13	14	15
16	17	18	19	20

Figure 17.1 Kumon mathematics magnetic number box.

is 2×5 are key skills for mental arithmetic and other topics, such as percentages.

Count on and back in ones from any small number, and in tens from and back to zero.

Often dyslexic pupils will have difficulty in picking up a number in mid-sequence. As with many of the difficulties highlighted in this chapter, this problem will not be unique to just the dyslexic pupils.

Counting on can be difficult when sequences and number words are difficult but most pupils are able to master this skill eventually. However, counting backwards is particularly difficult for dyslexic pupils and often their dyslexia may be identified by their problems with this skill. The ability to reverse a sequence is an important skill for mathematics learning.

Know by heart all pairs of numbers with a total of 10.

Although we acknowledge the importance of knowing a core of basic facts and information, we also acknowledge the difficulties dyslexics have with memory and retrieval of mathematical facts. There is a clash of objective and the characteristics of the pupil.

Although knowing by heart all pairs of numbers up to 10 really helps with many mathematical calculations, many of our pupils were still struggling with its mastery in their teens. If great emphasis is placed on acquiring this skill then pupils who find it difficult begin to lose confidence and start to experience fear of mathematics. It is also important to let pupils pass by this difficulty and experience other areas of mathematics. Obviously, if this is not addressed at an early age pupils are turned off mathematics and their sense of failure is exacerbated. Numicon Maths is a new multi-sensory approach to teaching young children number skills and is particularly good for teaching number bonds to 10.

Use everyday language to describe features of familiar 3-D and 2-D shapes.

This requires spatial awareness. Representation of 3-D with a 2-D drawing, language skills, but it can be an area of strength and success for some pupils.

It is important for pupils to know the correct words of 2-D and 3-D shapes but many of these are multi-syllabic words that are difficult to read, say and understand. A poor short-term memory means that the long names may be forgotten and then familiar properties may be connected to the wrong shape. Once these are mastered the visual strength of the dyslexic enables many of them to really become excellent with dealing with shapes.

Year 2

Count, read, write and order whole numbers to at least 100; know what each digit represents (including zero as a place holder).

Place value is a highly sophisticated concept. The fact that we use it in everyday life does not detract from that statement. Teen numbers cause considerable language confusion. Zero is very abstract. There are directional inconsistencies. This is a topic that needs careful use of good manipulatives to build a secure understanding.

The Numeracy Strategy has introduced a great deal of concrete material into the mathematics classroom; this is most beneficial for dyslexic pupils struggling with mathematics. Place-value cards, number lines and number squares all help with knowing numbers to 100. There is still much language used to describe these numbers which if done too quickly can throw pupils into confusion. It is essential that extra time be allowed for students to understand the counting system at this early age. Money is invaluable in helping with place value as well as giving pupils a vital life skill. If pupils are encouraged to do mathematics at home with their parents, playing games to help with understanding numbers, they are able to gain important skills. The computer plus calculators all help to give confidence if they are used appropriately.

Understand that subtraction is the inverse of addition; state the subtraction corresponding to a given addition and vice versa.

This is another vital skill if pupils are to learn flexibility in number work and to relate facts and to learn methods to compensate for poor recall abilities.

The words themselves are not easy to remember so pupils need time and extra help in connecting the symbol to the appropriate word: once they have visual clues, discussing connections is made easier. Directional problems can make this difficult for pupils to grasp (Chinn and Ashcroft, 1998; Henderson et al., 2003; Chinn, 2004).

Know by heart facts for the 2 and 10 multiplication tables.

Ten is the easier pattern, with the answers following from the vocabulary of the question. Not so for 2, but most pupils can learn to count in 2s, just not always reliably – look out for close answers, such as '7 + 2 = 12'. It is important to see 2s as evens.

Singing and counting in 2s and 10s can make this a pleasurable task especially if it is reinforced visually with a number chart with the appropriate numbers coloured in. Doubling and halving are skills in which many dyslexics excel.

Estimate, measure and compare lengths, masses and capacities, using standard units; suggest suitable units and equipment for such measurements.

Again, this is a topic where familiarity may lead to an underestimation of the difficulty of the concept. Mass is difficult, as is capacity, because there are interfering parameters, for example 'ton of feathers' or different shapes for pint glasses.

Many pupils who struggle in mathematics are afraid to estimate because they are afraid to use similar rounded-off numbers in case they make a mistake. To measure they need to be good with a ruler, knowing where to start and how to read the measurement accurately; dyspraxic pupils struggle with this. The words and abbreviations of length, mass and capacity may cause extra problems. These pupils need to be given appropriate assistance and much hands-on experience in acquiring these skills – prompt cards using lots of colour that they can keep in their pencil cases are most helpful.

Choose and use appropriate operations and efficient calculation strategies to solve problems, explaining how the problems were solved.

This introduces the all-important problem-solving skills, taking the pupil beyond recall and rote; but what defines 'appropriate'? It should be appropriate to the learner as well as the problem. This comment applies equally to 'efficient'.

The complexity of mathematical language often means that pupils may struggle reading the words and then not understand what is required of them. They need to have the opportunity to discuss the meaning of the problem before they think of a plan of action. If they record in colour the mathematical symbols they are going to use first, they will have a starting point from which they can move forward. Some pupils like to think of the answer and then move back from there to the question and then devise a plan of action. Allow them to do this. Once again there is a need to respond to the range of learning styles in the class.

Year 3

Count on or back in 10s or 100s from any two- or three-digit number.

Dyslexics may well find this move from the familiar and secure 10, 20, 30, 40 to the less familiar 11, 21, 31, 41, 51, a disproportionately difficult extension of process.

Pupils often begin to struggle a great deal when they reach this stage of the curriculum and gradually start to lose confidence. For many this may well be when their difficulties are highlighted as the place value plus complex and sequential procedures all play their part to make the mathematics hard to understand. The National Numeracy Strategy encourages teachers to allow a variety of different methods, which enables the dyslexic who may be a different thinker to work through in his own way.

Recognize unit fractions such as 1/2, 1/3, 1/4, 1/10 and use them to find fractions of shapes and numbers.

It is difficult for many pupils, dyslexic or non-dyslexic, to understand fractions. One of the reasons may be their relative complexity in that they consist of two digits and a hidden division sign. Also, the normal rules of addition and subtraction do not apply to both digits in the fraction. For example, 1/3 + 1/3 = 2/3: the 3s are not added. Fractions are a classic example of my colleague Richard Ashcroft's observation that 'Maths is easy, it's the writing it down that's hard.' This objective could almost earn a whole chapter to itself!

In our joint experience it is hard to recall even one pupil who was happy doing fractions! It also seems that this could be an international experience. Pupils not only struggle with reading a fractional part accurately – they also struggle to understand what it means. They may understand a half or a quarter when it relates to a pie but when it is connected to an amount of money then the calculation often stops there. Fractions could be one of those topics that is introduced too early, and in doing so much with fractions in the primary school it often means that pupils are frightened of them for the rest of their school years.

Know by heart all addition and subtraction facts for each number to 20. Know by heart the 2, 5 and 10 multiplication facts.

The order and progression of knowing the + and – facts compared to the × facts suggests that the expectation is that the + and – facts are easier to learn. As a straight comparison of two rote-learning tasks this is not so. If the facts are set out in a square then both involve 121 facts. As a pure rote-learning task, then, both require the recall of 121 answers. What makes the two tasks different is that the strategies for compensating for poor recall skills in addition and subtraction are simple counting strategies. For the multiplication and division facts, working out what you cannot recall can be much more involved.

It may be of interest that the addition facts are always linked to the subtraction facts. There is not yet a link between multiplication and division facts even though the next objective does require that link.

So many of my pupils have struggled 'knowing by heart' anything to do with mathematics that I wonder if it is necessary to do this before one can become good in maths. Once again it is essential to teach these facts slowly, make simple connections, use multi-sensory materials and focus on visual strengths in order to reinforce these basic facts. If pupils can be taught strategies to help them with quick recall then they often are able to succeed. Recent research is beginning to confirm what we, as teachers, have believed for many years (see Chinn, 1999).

Use units of time and know the relationships between them (second, minute, hour, day, week, month, year).

Time introduces many challenging new ideas. There is a vocabulary. There is language – for example we say 'quarter past six' and write 6:15. There is base 12, base 60, seven days in a week (and the seven times table is the hardest challenge of all the tables). Clock faces have multiple scales. Time is a difficult topic and needs very careful teaching if pupils are not to take the 'opt out, no involvement' strategy of self-preservation.

The digital clock has enabled dyslexic pupils to be able to read the time, but not necessarily understand or quantify it. The analogue clock face still presents a problem, as pupils have to understand clockwise and anti-clockwise directions. They need to be able to count in fives and connect the numbers 1 to 12 with this. 'Past' and 'to' times are additional problems.

Identify right angles.

Angles are a very different topic and challenge some established concepts. For example, the length of the two lines that construct the right angle is immaterial to the size of the angle.

The word right has many different meanings and often pupils find it difficult to apply the correct one to the problem. We often use the word 'right' to mean 'yes' so it is easy to see why pupils struggle. Using a protractor to measure can cause complications because of the directional problem and knowing just where to start.

Identify lines of symmetry in simple shapes and recognize shapes with no lines of symmetry.

This topic moves away from number and gives some pupils a chance to succeed. Despite this advantage, there will be other pupils for whom this topic provides an enormous challenge. For example, many pupils forget what lines of symmetry are and so are unable to identify them.

Year 4

Use symbols correctly, including less than (<), greater than (>) and equals (=).

As pupils move up through the years numeracy becomes more and more about symbols. There are mnemonics to help them remember which < > is which. But the use of multi-sensory materials may well become less acceptable to the pupil in terms of self-image in front of peers. Yet the ideas are more abstract and need to be rooted in secure and robust images.

Once again the direction problem shows because pupils cannot remember which side of the symbol indicates 'less than'. A good wall chart clearly showing these symbols is helpful as are prompt cards using colour plus some good examples.

Round any positive integer less than 1,000 to the nearest 10 or 100.

This is a surprisingly difficult skill for literal, formulaic and insecure (unwilling to take a risk) learners. These learners find it hard to interrelate numbers, seeing each number as an isolated unique number. Suitable materials to give a visual image are the empty number line and empty number squares.

'Round', 'positive integer', 'less than' and 'to the nearest' are words and phrases that seem to confuse many pupils, giving them problems putting the exercise into its proper context. This confusion is exacerbated by the fact that they have to consider whether a number is less than 5, is 5 or is greater than 5, before any action can be taken.

Recognize simple fractions that are several parts of a whole, and mixed numbers; recognize the equivalence of simple fractions.

Equivalent fractions are an enigma. They can be seen as an everyday example of maths as with a half being represented by 1/2 or half a pound (£) 50/100 or half a kilogram 500/1000 or half an hour 30/60. All these are precise and accurate images of a half. We also use a 'half' more colloquially as in 'half a pizza' or 'half a slice of cake' or 'half a tick', which was used to suggest a short period of time. Unless these inputs are managed carefully then equivalent fractions will not be understood. There is an additional problem in the flexibility of these equivalent fractions. We usually write three as 3, but a half can be written in an infinite number of ways. Ultimately they can be reduced or simplified to 1/2, but then the pupil needs to know multiplication and division facts to achieve the simplification.

Fractions again cause enormous problems but equivalent ones for some pupils are a nightmare. The fraction key on the calculator may be helpful for some but they need to be shown how to use it properly.

Use known number facts and place value to add and subtract mentally, including any pair of two-digit whole numbers.

There are a number of skills that are needed to perform these calculations. These include good short-term and working memories, an ability to recall basic facts quickly and accurately and a general ability to process numbers quickly. So simple to say and yet so devastating for the learners who do not possess these skills.

Pupils who struggle with mathematics need to be told clearly that no one can see inside their heads, which in effect means that they can use any method they like to solve problems mentally. Encouraging pupils to use their visualization strengths is important so that they can devise strategies that enable them to reach a correct answer. If they have to do this exercise in a mental test with perhaps 10 questions, tell them to try to answer one question correctly before trying to do all 10 quickly and not reaching one correct answer.

The culture of speed in doing mathematics problems is not beneficial to any pupil whose processing skills are slow (but possibly accurate).

Carry out column additions.

Column additions are a good example of the need to encourage the use of flexible methods. They can be done by 'casting out 10s' or with '10 tallies' or by combinations of two or more numbers. 'Casting out 10s' revisits number bonds for 10 and gives another reason to remember these key facts. The 10 tallies acknowledge that some pupils have problems with short-term memory and basic facts (see Chinn, 1999).

The correct kind of paper, squared, lined or plain, helps individuals set out their work correctly so that the spatial organization aspects of this task become simple. Occasionally pupils need to have some sort of visual clue to remind them of where to start.

Know by heart facts for the 2, 3, 4, 5 and 10 multiplication tables.

The requirement to know these vital facts by heart is a recurring theme. Despite this the National Numeracy Strategy does suggest some alternative ways of accessing facts, for example doubling the facts about multiplying twos to obtain the facts about multiplying fours. Learning strategies for accessing these facts can also help develop a stronger sense of numbers and number operations

Once again, pupils need to develop strategies that will enable them to have access to these facts as 'knowing by heart' is almost impossible. Finger tables have helped thousands of pupils to cope with this skill (see Henderson, 1989).

Quickly derive division facts corresponding to the 2, 3, 4, 5 and 10 multiplication tables.

Learning the inverse facts is even more challenging. If pupils struggling with mathematics are told to do any activity at speed it only exacerbates the difficulties.

Year 5

Multiply and divide any positive integer up to 10,000 by 10 or 100 and understand the effect.

This truly is a key objective, but it is not certain that all pupils will 'understand the effect'. Whilst purists, quite rightly, insist that the numbers 'move' to change place values, many pupils and adults use the theory of relative motion and move the decimal point. Using the decimal point like a 'bouncing ball' to multiply and divide has been successful with many pupils! There are many adults who would not even begin to start to do this task. The directional problems of dyslexic learners show clearly here. The 'Smile' computer program 'Tenners' was found to be most helpful for many pupils.

Use decimal notation for tenths and hundredths.

Any mathematics teacher will tell you that if decimal numbers are preceded by a £ sign, they become much easier for pupils. The move from £13.50 + £5 to 13.50 + 5 often shows the inability to transfer knowledge from one setting to another. If this observation is extrapolated to other areas of mathematics then we might challenge the efficacy of allowing pupils to make too many of their own generalizations.

The place-value cards plus a very large red plastic decimal point have been found to be useful whilst teaching this skill. Recording such work needs careful supervision in order to reinforce the fact that columns must be straight.

Calculate mentally a difference such as 8006 – 2993.

As with column addition, there are several effective ways to tackle this computation, depending on the pupil's thinking style, skills with basic facts and procedures, and short-term and working memory. Just what happens will depend on the ethos and management of the classroom.

The number line proved to be a most helpful tool to show how to do this calculation. Visualizing the number line as a fat 3-D line seemed also to be helpful so that pertinent numbers could be identified and used in reaching an answer.

Know by heart all multiplication facts up to 10 × 10.

The multiplication facts have been the subject of a cumulative set of objectives, which, for some pupils, will be building into a cumulative sense of failure and frustration. Again classroom management of the included dyslexic pupil will be a critical factor affecting the learner now and for the future. Being 'dyslexia friendly' means a pervasive and proactive awareness of the areas of potential difficulty by all teachers in all subjects. There are no exceptions; self-esteem and self-image are always under threat.

One of my (AH) students, when he was 16 years of age, said that he thought that his troubles in mathematics had started when he was required to remember all the times tables. He failed abysmally with this task and that seemed to have a knock-on effect throughout the whole of his mathematics education.

Carry out long multiplication of a two-digit integer by a two-digit integer.

This objective illustrates the principle of setting firm foundations and developing robust learning. If the right manipulative/image has been used to develop learning then this objective follows on a progression of learning objectives. A suitable image is the two-dimensional/area model.

Long multiplication seems to put fear into the hearts of many pupils! However, with the Numeracy Strategy a variety of methods are now permissible and pupils are usually able to find one that they can use to reach a correct answer. However, when teaching pupils who are struggling in mathematics it may be advisable not to make them listen to six different methods to do this task during one lesson.

Recognize parallel and perpendicular lines, and properties of rectangles.

There is less dependence on number skills and knowledge here, so it may be an area of strength for some pupils, but the level of language is demanding.

The method that is used to identify parallel lines needs to be discussed with dyslexic pupils as they do not always realize what the marks mean and possibly will ignore them. The same applies to the lines indicating a right angle.

Understand area measured in square centimetres (cm^2); understand and use the formula in words 'length × breadth' for the area of a rectangle.

Later the pupil will use 1/2 base × height for the area of a rectangle. It is likely that this formula will be derived from the area of a rectangle where the vocabulary is length and breadth! Insecure learners, including learners with specific learning difficulties, do not like such inconsistencies. In addition area now becomes a number problem. Pupils need to be taught how to connect the length of a line with the actual line by using colour. Many pupils will become involved in the calculation then forget which length is which and the whole calculation will fail because of disorganization initially.

Use all four operations to solve simple word problems involving numbers and quantities, including time, explaining methods and reasoning.

There are a lot of factors hidden in this objective. The opportunity to solve problems can allow some pupils to show their true abilities in mathematics. Word problems are rarely 'simple' for many varied reasons, including vocabulary. Some pupils can explain their methods but others find it difficult to explain their intuitive thoughts on paper.

This objective involves:

- reading the question accurately;
- highlighting important words and numbers;
- deciding how the problem can be solved;
- choosing a strategy;
- deciding which mathematical operations will be used;
- estimating an answer;
- working out the answer;
- checking against the estimate;
- checking that it answers the problem;
- explaining to others the method chosen and why.

As shown, there are many steps in finding a solution to the problem and all of them will take the dyslexic pupil a considerable time and at each step there are hurdles to overcome. For more information on problem solving see Henderson et al. (2003).

Year 6

Reduce a fraction to its simplest form by cancelling common factors.

Pupils have to know those common factors. There are some simple rules for identifying some of these factors for those who have been unable to memorize these facts.

Another principle is illustrated here: the learner does not have to be perfect in all his knowledge and skills. It may not be possible or feasible to completely eradicate a difficulty, but it may be possible to reduce its effects on learning and keep the pupil's motivation alive.

The majority of my pupils ignored the cancelling down as they found that they may have started with the correct number but made so many mistakes that it all went wrong. Opting out of the problem means the pupil is not involved in the learning task.

Understand percentage as the number of parts in every 100, and find simple percentages of whole-number quantities.

Once pupils realize that percentages are the same throughout the world they are happy to use them. The concept of percentages should be related to decimals and fractions. The principle of interrelating ideas and facts can be vital for some pupils.

Highlighting the interrelationships between numbers is an effective way of dealing with many percentages – for example, obtaining 5% by halving 10% and combining the two to make 15%. Connecting up other facts about percentages can be helpful.

- To find 10% divide by 10;
- to find 20% divide by 10 and multiply by 2;
- to find 30% divide by 10 and multiply by 3;
- to find 40% divide by 10 and multiply by 4;
- to find 50% divide by 10 and multiply by 5;
- to find 60% divide by 10 and multiply by 6;
- to find 70% divide by 10 and multiply by 7;
- to find 80% divide by 10 and multiply by 8;
- to find 90% divide by 10 and multiply by 9.

Eventually pupils will work out easier methods but connections will be made in a positive way.

Solve simple problems involving ratio and proportion.

Sometimes the speed culture of mathematics does not encourage thoughtful evaluation of problems. Proportion is another facet of fractions and so difficulties may transfer on. The developmental structure of numeracy does lead to difficulties becoming developmental. The words and language here cause some difficulties.

Some hints for proportion:

- Use the correct words and many examples.
- Have a strip pattern where one in every three strips is shaded. (This helps with equivalent fractions.)
- Use a longer strip with the same pattern. (The children discover that 1 in every 3 is shaded regardless of the whole.)

Some hints for ratio:

- Ratio is a comparison between two numbers.
- Divide a strip of paper into 3 equal parts. Colour I part red. The ratio of the red part to the other parts is 1 to 3.
- Divide a circle into 8 equal slices, colour 5 slices blue. The ratio of the blue slices to the other slices is 5 to 8.
- The symbol : is introduced later. It replaces the word 'to' when writing a ratio.

Instead of writing 1 to 3 we write 1:3 and read it as 1 to 3.

Use a protractor to measure acute and obtuse angles to the nearest degree.

This can be a separate skill, not part of that developmental structure of number, but there will still be the potential for procedural errors. It will be helpful if the pupils get the procedure correct from the start, so that they do not have to unlearn any incorrect actions.

Here is another principle. Intervention may not just be about teaching how to 'do it right', but about teaching how not to 'do it wrong'.

The protractor has to be read accurately and in the correct direction. Pupils need to be shown where to begin and how to read off the circular scale. Make notes on how to do this and practise extensively with a variety of examples.

Calculate the perimeter and area of simple compound shapes that can be split into rectangles.

Later, when the numbers are replaced by letters in algebra, some pupils may fare much better at this topic, which is, yet again, numerical.

Tackle the language issue by talking about the prefix 'peri' meaning 'around' so that the pupil will understand the word. Draw a little man walking the perimeter. Discuss the simple shapes that can be found and how to find their area. Discuss the units of measure – dyslexic pupils often forget about the importance of recording accurately and lose vital marks because of their inaccuracies.

Read and plot co-ordinates in all four quadrants.

This can be another topic where pupils can avoid some of the number manipulation that creates problems for them. It is also a topic where it is easy to underestimate the seemingly slight increase of difficulty in dealing with negative co-ordinates. However, if pupils are introduced early enough to the four quadrants they are able to plot points. The Smile program 'Tessellations and Symmetry' is most helpful with regard to this exercise.

Summary

Thomas West (1991) said that, for some dyslexic students, 'easy' things in mathematics are hard and 'hard' things can be easy. It is essential when dealing with students who have a learning difficulty in mathematics that we remember West's words and allow these students to work with students of all abilities and not just those who struggle in maths. We must give them the tools to tackle problems in an optimistic way that enables them to be successful. Multi-sensory teaching coupled with the right approach to match learning styles should make the maths classroom a 'fun' place to be. Once students begin to enjoy maths and find success their self-esteem will grow and this will reflect positively in all areas of their life.

References

Chinn SJ (1999) What to Do When You Can't Add and Subtract? Baldock: Egon.

Chinn SJ (2004) The Trouble with Maths. In press.

Chinn SJ, Ashcroft JR (1998) Maths for Dyslexics: A Teaching Handbook, 2nd edn. London: Whurr Publishers.

Henderson A (1989) Maths and Dyslexics. Llandudno: St Davids College.

Henderson A, Came F, Brough M (2003) Working with Dyscalculia. Marlborough: Learning Works.

West T (1991) In the Mind's Eye. New York: Prometheus Books.

CHAPTER 18

Using information and communication technology (ICT) to help dyslexic children and adults

VICTORIA CRIVELLI, MOIRA THOMSON, BODIL ANDERSSON

Primary years

Introduction

Since the 1990s information and communication technology (ICT) has had a great influence on all of our lives and especially on those of children. For children at primary school in the UK the use of the computer in the classroom is now a regular part of the school day, either as curriculum entitlement or an opportunity to increase their ICT skills and capability. Used appropriately and creatively it can also be a lifelong tool to support those with dyslexia and to help overcome many barriers to learning. It can assist in reading and writing skills not only in education but also at home and in work environments.

What makes ICT so effective for dyslexic learners?

An increasing number of computer programs have features that meet many of the needs of dyslexic learners and ameliorate their difficulties. This can be especially effective in the primary years when literacy skills are being learned daily.

Computers can create a patient, non-judgemental environment for children. Speech-supported programs offer opportunities for recall and repeating when sequential, auditory or visual memory needs support. Programs offer auditory and visual interactions, the opportunity for users to have a 'dry run' at an activity, self-correct errors and control the pace of their learning.

Information and communication technology can support written work which is so often onerous and frustrating for dyslexics. Planning, organizing, writing, spelling, editing and presentation can be assisted in such a way that users feel more able to express their intended content and demonstrate their true ability. Programs and tools can offer real independence for many children who depend on adult or peer help in literacy activities.

Many young children with dyslexia have good self-esteem on entering school but this can deteriorate rapidly as the demand for reading and writing increases. Information and communication technology can help restore their self-esteem, offer successful experiences and increase confidence.

Being asked to use ICT does not single out those experiencing difficulties as different, unlike many support activities. Children usually associate ICT with making learning fun.

Selecting software for dyslexics

All literacy programs, however visually attractive, need to be fully speech supported to avoid frustration or misunderstanding. Pictures or graphics need to be identified too, to avoid confusion. For example, young children need to be sure they are being asked to find the initial sound for *cap* and not *hat*.

Programs need to be easy to navigate, to have on-screen help and uncluttered screens. Children need to know exactly what to do and where to focus on the screen.

It is especially useful if programs have additional options for both pupil and teacher – for example, options offering a choice of formats, such as font style, size and background colour or opportunities for listening again. Record-keeping and pupil-tracking options are useful both for teacher and pupil, when appropriate. Pupils like to know when they are doing well and many programs can produce evidence of their success.

Some programs are generic tools to assist reading or writing tasks. Others will be more skill-specific to support newly learned skills, increase ability and offer practice in such areas as sequential memory (*Mastering Memory* (CALSC)), learning high-frequency words (*Wordshark 3* (Whitespace), *Catch Up CD* (REM)), or skills in phonics, spelling and punctuation (*Wordshark 3*, *Starspell V2* (Fisher Marriott), *Punctuate* (Xavier)). These programs should be used as part of a structured literacy programme.

Some programs will help with literacy skills across the curriculum allowing dyslexics the same opportunities as their peers to explore topics of interest. Mathematics programs (*Intellimaths* (Inclusive Technology), *Numbershark 3* (Whitespace)) with speech support can be helpful and reassuring.

The use of headphones in most cases is essential. They ensure discreet support, aid concentration and reduce any distraction for other pupils.

Supporting literacy skills

Early years

Many pupils at foundation level enter school with dyslexic difficulties undiagnosed. However, the use of ICT and all the benefits listed earlier will help compensate where there are difficulties. Boys, in particular, show grea interest in using ICT as it suits their preferred learning style.

There are many programs available to help with early and pre-readin; skills. Listening, sequencing, memory, following instructions, matching, earl vocabulary, rhyming skills, stories, rhymes and phonological awareness cai all be practised independently and repeated with a minimum of adult hel; (*Tizzy's Toybox, Izzy's Island, Sound Stories* (Sherston), *Spider in th Kitchen* series (Inclusive Technology), *Rhymes* (Xavier), *Multisensor Literacy Games* (REM), *Earobics* (Don Johnston)).

It is essential that the programs are used selectively as part of a planne¢ progression and that responses are observed and monitored.

The use of a smaller mouse or a tracker ball may help young users initiall It is often at this early age that key indicators of dyslexia can be observec Information and communication technology can also help in th¢ identification of dyslexia at this level with discreet, timed assessmeɴ programs (CoPS baseline, *Rapid Dyslexia Screening* (Lucid)) offerin₂ detailed profiles of strengths and weaknesses that can support furthe observations and assessments. This can be a preferred way of assessing young child in a relaxed environment.

The Literacy Strategy for most of the UK at key stage 1 and 2, which ᵢ operative in most schools, incorporates text-level work (involving strategie for reading and writing passages), word-level work (focusing mainly on higɪ frequency vocabulary and phonic skills) and sentence-level work (focusin₂ on grammar and punctuation). Many pupils benefit from the structure¢ progression.

Pupils with dyslexia will usually find the pace too fast and will need mor time to learn the skills and strategies to help overcome any difficulties. The will need targeted support using a variety of multi-sensory and kinaestheti¢ approaches.

The use of ICT can support this, at class and individual level. Th increasing use of interactive whiteboards to model skills and good practic provides opportunities for greater participation by dyslexic pupils.

Phonics and high-frequency words (HFW)

Teaching of key phonic skills is designed to occur before the child is 8 year old in the current literacy strategy. Dyslexics need extra time and practic with these important skills.

There are several excellent programs that can support the learning o₁ phonics and HFW – *Wordshark 3* (Whitespace), *Catch Up CD1 and .* (REM), *Starpell v2.2* (Fisher Marriott), *Sounds Great 1 and 2* (Kingscourt, *Sounds and Rhymes* (Xavier), *Multi Sensory Literacy Games* (REM). The provide a fun and motivating way to learn skills that otherwise could becom tedious and dull. Such programs also offer another vital resource for teachers and parents looking to increase the variety of activities to consolidate such skills.

Many programs keep detailed progress records and can be set up to meet precise individual needs both in content and activity. Records will help to inform progress, thus avoiding the need for unnecessary and often stressful tests.

Reading

Talking books are a boon to many dyslexic children. Unlike tape recorders they can ensure that the text is seen and heard simultaneously, word by word in early-years texts (*Wellington Square* (Granada), *Oxford Reading Tree* (Sherston), *Spinout Stories* (REM), *Clicker 4 books – Planet Wobble, Daisy* (Crick)) and phrase by phrase in later texts (*Start To Finish* (Don Johnston)). Talking books offer the user the opportunity to enjoy a story, read independently in a reassuring and supported environment, increase fluency, accuracy and aid expression. Texts similar to those of their peers can be shared.

Many texts come with additional on-screen activities to support literacy skills, such as phonics, spelling and comprehension. Some talking books are purely for pleasure with interactive screens or animations to explore. Some offer both (*Mattie Mole* (Sherston)).

Several programs (*Find Out and Write About* (Crick), *Spin Out Stories* (REM)) offer non-fiction texts to support curriculum topics or create activities to use with any text (*texThing* (Topologika), *Cloze Pro* (Crick), *All My Words* (Crick)).

Text-to-speech software, such as *Penfriend* (Penfriend Ltd), will enable children to access any text, including those on the WWW. A low-tech solution, such as dropping text files into a talking word processor (*Textease* (Granada), *Write Out Loud* (Don Johnston)) can be just as effective and will ensure the dyslexic child can hear as well as see text.

Planning, writing and recording

The task of writing becomes the most dominant for many children in their primary years as it requires so many skills to be used simultaneously. Information and communication technology can help ameliorate many of the difficulties and support the user in a variety of ways.

There is often a notable change in attitude together with an increase in the quantity and quality of written work, when dyslexic children use ICT programs that help. Such programs enable them to demonstrate their true ability and use of vocabulary.

Talking word processors can offer users the opportunity to hear what they are writing as they type. Many will read tool bars, spell checkers and on-screen word banks within the word processor. Other programs, such as *Penfriend*, are designed to work in tandem with standard word processors, enabling them to speak. There are dedicated on-screen word banks, such as *Clicker 4* (Crick), which allow both speech and pictorial support on screen.

The use of a digital camera to support writing is a powerful tool for dyslexic pupils. It can help with sequencing, memory and storyboarding. It can prompt the most reluctant writer. It is especially effective when young children are involved in taking the pictures. The photographs can be used as graphics to support writing as well as being used with an on-screen word bank such as *Clicker 4*.

Many dyslexic pupils find predictive ICT programs with speech powerful tools to use with any word processor or application where typed text is required. With a single keystroke pupils can be offered a choice of words on-screen, to enter into their text. Predictors save typing time and aid spelling. Predictive software, such as *Penfriend* (Penfriend Ltd) and *Co Writer 4000* (Don Johnston) can support individual needs and curriculum topics.

Word processing removes the laborious task of copying out written drafts. It enables users to produce legible, well-presented text every time. For younger users this is hugely motivating. The simplest of typed texts can be enlarged and formatted to a high standard. The use of graphics and borders is always a welcome addition to the finished texts. Dyslexic pupils may prefer to add their own designs and pictures to the final printed copy and they often excel in this.

There are some useful programs that support the planning, organizing and drafting process that is often a particular barrier for dyslexics. Some, such as *Kidspiration* (REM), offer a visual concept map approach that will convert to linear text. Others, such as *Draft Builder* (Don Johnston), offer a more linear stepped approach. Both can set up templates or writing frames to scaffold the task, with spoken prompts or notes.

Whilst the importance of handwriting must not be overlooked, many dyslexic children will opt to use ICT as their preferred way of recording, especially if their typing speed and keyboard efficiency progress.

Where writing and recording is the predominant difficulty, a portable writing aid is a practical solution and will continue to be used at secondary school. Examples include *Dreamwriter 500* (Dreamwriter Solutions Ltd), *Alphasmart 3000* (Alphasmart Inc.) and *Calcuscribe* (Inclusive Technology). The use of a hand-held spell checker, particularly those models that interpret phonic attempts, such as *Literacy Wordbank* (Franklin), can offer a 'low-tech' solution to support spelling.

The opportunity to encourage and teach good keyboard awareness and typing skills is often disregarded in primary years. Single-finger or one-hand typing can be difficult to change. Simple programs should be introduced early on to embed correct posture and practice. Examples are *First Keys to Literacy* (REM), *Speedy Keys* (Granada), *Type to Learn* and *Magi Type* (REM).

As with all learning tools and strategies, those involving ICT need to be monitored and reviewed on a regular basis. It is important that the programs continue to meet learning needs and any ICT tools and applications are introduced as the pupils' capability and knowledge progress. This is particularly important in the transitional period leading up to high school. Sufficient time must be devoted to preparation and training in any new ICT to be used. Specialist advice may need to be sought at this point.

Schools need to liaise carefully so the provision is well anticipated and pupil stress is minimized at such an important phase.

Whilst the emphasis of this chapter is on supporting literacy skills, using ICT can be equally beneficial in other areas of the curriculum where literacy skills are required. Mathematics programs with speech can reassure the use of correct numerals for instance. Spreadsheets, diagrams and tables can be created and modified easily on screen, whereas paper-based tasks may often present difficulties.

In summary, ICT cannot replace skilled and structured teaching but can provide an invaluable tool and support in the classroom both to pupils and their teachers. Teachers must not underestimate the importance that ICT can have for dyslexics or how it will continue to support them in the future. It is the teachers' responsibility to ensure that all of their pupils receive their ICT entitlement and increase their ICT skills. With their dyslexic pupils they will also need to seek advice in matching individual need to the best and most appropriate ICT where possible, to maximize these pupils' true potential.

Brief case studies to illustrate use of ICT as an appropriate support

Pupil A

Six years old (Y1) with suspected dyslexic difficulties. Knows many HFW but has difficulties with specific consonant and medial vowel sounds, using consonant–vowel–consonant (CVC) blending and simple rhyming skills. *Sounds Great* (Kingscourt) story-plus-activity-and-assessment CDs and *Sounds and Rhymes* (Xavier) activities and games with pupil tracking provide opportunities for independent practice and reinforcement.

Pupil B

Eight years old (Y3), recently identified as dyslexic. Loves books but finds it frustrating to read texts independently. He knows some HFW and finds CVC blends difficult. His school uses *Oxford Reading Tree* (ORT) and he has used accompanying CDs (Sherston) to enjoy stories at an appropriate interest level but the activities are too difficult. He is using *Clicker 4 Planet Wobble* stories (Crick), which are visually similar to ORT, but content and activities are appropriate. He is starting to use *Clicker* for writing tasks following success with *Planet Wobble* writing activities. He is also using *Wordshark 3* to practise high-frequency work and CVC words as part of individualized education plan targets.

Pupil C

At 10 years old (Y6) he is an able, articulate dyslexic whose reading is progressing well but for whom writing tasks are causing frustration. He has used *Clicker 4* successfully but wants more choice of words and regular access to a word processor for longer writing tasks. He uses a *Literacy Wordbank* (Franklin) to help with spellings and is now using an *Alphasmart 3000* with *Co Writer 4000* predictor to assist with word processing. These are also used in the local high school.

Pupil D

Nine years old (Y5/6). The pupil is in a mixed age class but is finding reading especially non-fiction, difficult for topic work, and is also experiencing difficulty with writing and recording.

The pupil uses *Clicker 4* (Crick) to support writing and the *Find Out and Write About* series for *Solar System* and *Ancient Greeks*. In addition, the teacher has also introduced talking books on computer from the *Start to Finish* series (Don Johnston) to offer further non-fiction titles to read. From the same series the pupil is also enjoying reading abridged texts of classic novels included in the year 5 and 6 curriculum, enabling him to partake in book discussions with his peers.

Secondary school

It is difficult to make any comment on ICT support for dyslexics that will still be valid for even a short time after it is written. The rate at which new hardware and software is becoming available – for both the assessment of dyslexic difficulties and to support dyslexic learners – makes it virtually impossible to keep up to date.

Assessment of dyslexic difficulties

Recently developed software, such as *CoPS, LASS* and *LADS* (Lucid Research Ltd) and *Dyscalculia Screener* (Butterworth), used in conjunction with other forms of detection, such as BDA checklists and DST (Fawcett and Nicolson 1996), now makes it possible to screen for dyslexic indicators from as early a age 4 up to adulthood. At the secondary school stage identification of dyslexia may be difficult because non-specialist teachers must recognize indicators and make appropriate referrals before the assessment process can begin. Use of ICT at the start of this process is non-threatening for many pupils who are already comfortable with computer use – and the software itself can indicate the direction that further assessment might take.

Self-esteem

The use of ICT can increase the dyslexic learner's independence. Some dyslexic learners have great difficulty in moving information from short-term memory to long-term memory. Memory failure is frustrating and may be humiliating, especially for those of secondary school age, and may contribute to low self-esteem leading to a failure to engage with some aspects of the curriculum. The use of ICT can re-motivate learners, boost their self-confidence and encourage them to develop strategies to compensate for their difficulties. It can enhance access to the curriculum, providing extra support in areas where difficulties are experienced without frequent requests for help and support. Some dyslexics may retain information more easily when more than two senses are involved in the learning process. The use of ICT involving visual, auditory and kinaesthetic memory with sound prompts and spoken feedback is likely to be of great value to them not only in the quality of language processing and mastery of subject-specific concepts but also in improved self-esteem and reduction of fatigue.

Supporting reading and writing

Writing is a frustrating experience when writers are unable to begin to write down the words they wish to use to express themselves. With the use of specialized software packages (see Nisbet et al., 1999: Chapter 12) dyslexics are able to keep up with their peers in subject classrooms and produce a standard of work that more closely reflects subject knowledge and ability than does handwritten work. As speech recognition software such as *Dragon Naturally Speaking* (Scansoft) and *Via Voice* (IBM) becomes more readily available for laptop computers, dyslexics will gain even more independence and improve the quality of written work at the same time.

Reading

There is an increasing range of software (*Word Shark* (White Space Ltd), *Starspell* (Fisher Marriott), *Sounds & Rhymes* (Xavier)) available, designed to improve the basic reading skills of dyslexic learners. These may take the form of flash cards, games or reading comprehension exercises. Many are similar to text-based reading programs but an advantage of ICT-based reading is that its use means that dyslexic pupils do not have to persist with reading interventions at which they have already experienced failure. They also have the advantage of being multi-sensory programs. For example, *Earobics* (Cognitive Concepts) strengthens reading, spelling and comprehension – so that individuals may use strengths in one area, perhaps visual processing, to compensate for weaknesses in another, such as auditory–verbal processing as well as involving physical processes that may help with memory difficulties.

It is very difficult for readers who lack fluency, or whose decoding is such a struggle that they cannot remember what they have just 'read', to enjoy fiction. In the past, audiotaped books have been used to give such pupils access to literature. Now ICT can make books available on CD-ROM (such as Don Johnston's *Start to Finish* books) and online. Developing literacy skills are supported by software, such as *Kurzweil 3000* (Kurzweil Education Systems), which will read whole books aloud, and interactive packages that respond to prompts by the reader, all of which require only minimal intervention, so increasing the independence of the dyslexic reader.

Writing

The tasks of choosing and sequencing words, spelling them correctly and writing them neatly may be so daunting to some dyslexics that they will produce only short, scrappy pieces of written work that in no way reflect their ability or their understanding of subject content and concepts. Using a word processor frees them to concentrate on the content of writing and gives them the opportunity to become more organized. Spell checkers applied after the writing is completed allow the flow of writing to progress without being interrupted by the difficulties presented by inability to spell appropriate vocabulary – *Word Bar* (Crick) allows the teacher to suggest appropriate vocabulary that sits on screen while the pupil is writing – and enables the dyslexic, finally, to demonstrate subject knowledge and ability more appropriately. Written work may be easily edited and re-sequenced without the need to write it all over again and the dyslexic may then be given help and guidance appropriate to ability shown in the content rather than the teacher's attention being focused on the quality of written language.

It is important to match the use of ICT to the specific needs of the individual. Not all dyslexics may be able to make effective use of laptop computers. However, many dyslexics who have not been able to write easily find their powers of expression unlocked when given a laptop. However, a spell checker or predictive lexicon – such as *Co-Writer* (Don Johnston) or *Text Help* (Lorien) – may be of little use to someone who cannot read the words brought up. Fortunately, software is increasingly available that removes this problem by reading aloud spelling suggestions.

Search skills

Most dyslexics experience great frustration when they need to use dictionaries and other reference books as the sheer volume of text on the printed page often makes it impossible for them to find anything. Many dictionaries and encyclopaedias are now available online or on CD-ROMs, often with speech output – for example *World Book* (IBM) – which reduces the need for sophisticated reading skills. These aids still require some reading/spelling skills, but it is possible for the dyslexic to concentrate on the use of key words and use these to search for information. Access to the Internet may be virtually impossible for dyslexics because of reading and spelling difficulties, but use of *Kurzweil 3000* software makes it possible for them to 'read the Web' and opens up the 'information highway' to dyslexics for whom this was previously closed.

Curriculum support

Many dyslexics need substantially greater amounts of practice in structured activities to help them achieve the literacy skills which others master apparently effortlessly. There are now many interesting and varied didactic software programs available that allow dyslexics to spend the necessary time on tasks in a more enjoyable learning environment that does not lead to the same degree of fatigue as using printed text and notebooks. Many of these programs are designed to give frequent, positive feedback to the user, which generates improved self-esteem due to success. Interactive, integrated learning systems, such as the *Successmaker* (RM Systems) and *PLATO* (Plato Learning Inc.) learning packages, are computer-based resources covering mathematics, reading, writing and spelling with the option of including other subject areas. Each pupil has an individualized programme of work, which is continually updated, based on ability, rate of progress and prior knowledge. Dyslexic learners do not feel threatened by the computer and find it an endlessly patient teacher. This is also true of bilingual dyslexic learners (Peer and Reid, 2000) who are faced with not only acquiring speech and understanding of an additional language (which they often manage exceptionally well) but also with acquiring literacy in the new language. If learners experience a dyslexic difficulty in acquiring literacy in another language it is likely that software packages that support monolinguistic dyslexic learners will be of equal or greater help to them.

Keyboarding

Appropriate training in the use of ICT must be given and individuals should be assessed carefully on keyboard use. Some dyslexics will benefit from the use of a touch-typing tutor, such as *Type to Learn* or *Magictype* or *Type for Fun* (Sunburst), whereas others may 'hunt and peck' with one finger – which may still be faster, and will certainly be more legible, than their handwriting.

There are a number of laptop computers (including Alphasmart remote keyboards, suitable for use in school) available now, which means that it is possible to match individuals to the most appropriate type of machine. As dyslexics need adult support most at the editing stage of word processing this can be done at a mutually convenient time and the pupil does not have to wait for teacher attention in order to complete written work.

There are several software packages suitable for dyslexics including predictive, adaptive lexicons – such as *CoWriter* (Don Johnston) and *Text Help* (Lorien) – and word-processing packages – *Write Out Loud* (Don Johnston) and *TextEase* (Granada) – with many easy-to-use features, including speech feedback of text and several editing icons, which reduce the amount of reading needed to edit text. Both types of program can be used together, combining the lexicon offering correctly spelled words and the speech output, which will read these words to the user. Many dyslexics find that this combination slows down their writing but, if they persevere, the benefits may outweigh the problems. Adding programs designed to help with writing structure, such as *Draft Builder* (Don Johnston) and *Star Think* (Fisher Marriott), to these enables dyslexic writers to connect the whole writing process. For example *Draft Builder* can be used to give a simple structure to writing; the draft is then transferred to *Write Out Loud* for re-drafting. *Co-writer* can be integrated with both of these to help with sentence structure and spelling.

Independence

The aspect of current ICT use that will give the greatest independence in learning to all dyslexics may be that of speech recognition (SR) software such as *Dragon Naturally Speaking* (Scansoft) and *Via Voice* (IBM). It is possible, with training, to dictate, edit, move and format text and data directly into any application. Text-to-speech features provide immediate feedback. Not only does the use of this software dramatically improve self-confidence in dyslexics but it also gives them a level of independence in their learning that they have never before achieved. It also reduces the need for someone to read, scribe and transcribe for dyslexics. There is growing awareness in schools of the potential of SR to increase access to the curriculum for dyslexic pupils. However, approaches and success with SR vary widely. Some dyslexics use SR routinely as their main means of writing and recording work whereas others have found it difficult to implement with any success at all. (Introducing Speech Recognition in Schools, a CALL Centre Project funded by the Scottish Executive Education Department Special Educational Needs Innovation Grants Programme, aims to investigate how the introduction and use of SR by pupils with special educational needs can be made to work.)

Use of ICT in examinations

Use of word-processing packages by dyslexics in examinations is now fairly common practice but this does require considerable prior learning – for example, developing fast, accurate keyboarding skills and trying out a range of software packages in order to find the combination that suits an individual

Schools must then negotiate the use of the chosen package with the examination board concerned and ensure that hardware and software are available to the individual for all assessments. A natural development from such arrangements is the introduction of electronic examination papers. These have already been introduced at some universities for some subjects, and some researchers (such as Paul Nisbet, University of Edinburgh CALL Centre – for the Scottish Qualifications Authority) are currently investigating possibilities for other examinations.

Limiting factors

Developments in ICT may clearly lead to increased independence for dyslexic learners at the secondary school stage, and enable them to improve reading, writing and search skills using new materials and methods instead of continuing with approaches in which they have already failed. However, the introduction of ICT support requires considerable resources. This includes hardware such as laptop computers allocated to individuals, a wide range of software and time for training dyslexic learners in the use of these. Equally important is the need for the training of school staff in the use of ICT so that they may then pass on expertise to their dyslexic pupils. All of this will cost a great deal of money and, unless placed high on a priority list, this may not be readily available. Dyslexics moving on to higher education will be expected to produce work using ICT, but the specialized training they may need will not be easily accessible at this level, so it will fall to the secondary school to ensure that dyslexic pupils leave with the required ICT skills already in place. Not an easy task either for dyslexic learners or the teachers who help them acquire skills and develop strategies for coping with their difference.

Higher education and working life

This section of the chapter will discuss the benefits of ICT for dyslexic students in higher education and people in working life. It will also highlight general aspects of compensatory ICT as opposed to use of 'drill-and-practice' software. Appreciating that the BDA conference addresses an international audience, it will present the general conditions for societal support and funding for dyslexic children as well as adults in need of ICT in Sweden. It will begin with a few words about the concept of dyslexia in Sweden, since this forms a basis for all other discussions. It is important to appreciate the different conditions present in different countries, where the view of dyslexia is often related to general disability policy.

The Swedish dyslexia situation

In Sweden, various professional groups are involved in the dyslexia field. There is no Swedish legislation governing the right to make a dyslexia

diagnosis. This varies according to circumstances. The National Board o
Health and Welfare supervises Swedish medical care and is in charge of th
Swedish translation of the ICD-10, which is the classification system in use i
Swedish hospitals. Within the hospitals, speech and language pathologist
usually carry out the assessments. Within the unemployment servic
psychologists do this. Sweden does not have a professional group equivalen
to the UK's educational psychologists. In schools, the prevailing situation i
to have either a trained special education teacher or a school psychologis
carry out the assessment. Many psychologists rely on the DSM IV fo
diagnosis, this being the other major international classification systen
besides the ICD-10. Team assessments are often recommended
acknowledging the complex and multi-dimensional nature of readin,
problems.

An extensive project, managed by professor Mats Myrberg of Th
Stockholm Institute of Education, has recently been carried out. Sweden's 2
PhDs presently active in the reading field (representing psychology
linguistics, medicine and pedagogics) have been interviewed regarding thei
view on reading disabilities, dyslexia, prevention and intervention. It turn
out that most of them would agree in principle with the definition suggeste
by the IDA (www.interdys.org) where a phonological deficit is viewed as th
core problem in dyslexia. About 100 'expert teachers' have also bee
interviewed for the same purpose. However, we must distinguish betwee
diagnoses and disabilities. From society's point of view disability and nee
should be the key to support and intervention, not diagnosis. Not onl
dyslexia causes a reading disability. Our task must be to find the reason wh
each individual is failing, discover his or her strengths and suggest trainin
and support designed to fit individual needs.

In Sweden, there are no government ICT grants to help people wit
reading disabilities. Each school has to produce a plan of action for a chil
with special needs, but when it comes to ICT rights the situation i
complicated. Schools normally have no money for ICT in the form o
personal aids for students. To have access to a personal computer wit
suitable software, people need to turn to the technical aids offices connecte
to the hospitals. Presently, these rely on legislation dating from 1984, i
which the groups that should be allowed technical aids are listed. Th
problem is that the reading disabled group is not mentioned at all, whic
leaves room for arbitrariness. In practice, it is virtually impossible to receiv
ICT support through the community. A new governmental investigation is o
its way and should be ready early in 2004. Understandably, people wit
reading disabilities are hoping for better opportunities. Today, parents o
dyslexic children and basically all private persons have a tough time applyin
for funding to obtain a computer and technology. In Sweden, universit
students receive a loan to support their university studies – Sweden does no

have a fee-based system. University students with a dyslexia certificate can have access to ICT for use within the university through the handicap officer at the university, but for personal ICT use university students must also apply for funding. The chances are normally good for dyslexics in working life to obtain ICT to overcome a work handicap caused by reading problems.

Practice versus compensation

Dr Christer Jacobson of Växjö university, Sweden, has presented a model (Jacobson, 2000) of the way we approach dyslexia that makes a good framework for our continued discussions about the adults' situation.

According to Jacobson, three main types of intervention can be recognized: prevention, practice and compensation (see Table 18.1).

Table 18.1 Main types of intervention

Prevention	Practice	Compensation
Linguistic awareness training, building self-esteem and motivation.	Improving skills, manually and through ICT ('drill-and-practice' software).	1. Internal compensation (coping strategies). 2. External compensation: a) ICT tools; b) attitudes in the environment.

In Sweden, the emphasis until the late 1990s has clearly been placed on prevention and practice. Methods of prevention are practised in most pre-schools and Sweden has a variety of drill-and-practice software, the dominant program for many years being a toolkit called *Lexia* (produced by Stiftelsen Stora Sköndal, Olle Gunnilstam and Martti Mårtens), which is well known and widespread.

In recent years, an increasing volume of literature regarding compensation aspects of ICT has been published in Sweden (Föhrer and Magnusson, 2003). The concept of compensation in Jacobson's model becomes much more than just a question of technology. In fact, a Swedish study (Svensson et al., 2002) has hinted that the most important factor in an ICT effort is the attitude of the teachers – and attitude is usually a product of knowledge. In other words: if the key people around a student find using computers 'unfair', or if the key teachers have insufficient knowledge and understanding of compensatory software, then the student may not be able to use ICT as efficiently as possible. What this means is that ICT efforts in schools must include plenty of teacher training, otherwise it may be a waste of money and time. In order to arouse enthusiasm teachers need to be confident. And as the child with dyslexia grows up, the more important the matter of compensation becomes.

Students in higher education

Being a student is tough, as it is even without dyslexia. Time pressure is ever present. Extensive spelling courses or other drill-and-practice activities are often an unrealistic vision. The challenge for us is to find the 'retaining wall' that gives the dyslexic student a chance to study on equal terms as the other students.

Most of the ICT tools mentioned in Moira Thomson's previous section on ICT at secondary school will also be relevant in higher education and in working life. As Thomson points out, dyslexics moving on to higher education will be expected to produce work using ICT. It is therefore important that the student has sufficient skills to handle ICT and, if not, is given the opportunity to learn. It is crucial that ICT is integrated with concrete tasks. It is also important that students have access to the *specific* tools needed to facilitate their individual study situations, with *individual* settings. No dyslexic students will have exactly the same needs.

The ultimate goal for using ICT in higher education must be student independence. Although it is pleasant to have helpful people around you, students will have to manage on their own, and may prefer to do so.

Some of the most important compensatory strategies and ICT tools for higher-education students are the following:

● prolonged examination time;
● oral examinations;
● note-taking assistance during lectures;
● digital audiobased note takers;
● talking books (digital books or tapes);
● text-to-speech strategies to enable students to proofread their own manuscripts and for reading emails and articles by others;
● efficient Web search methods that allow poor spelling;
● efficient spell checkers.

In Sweden, the state-governed Talking Books Library (www.tpb.se/english/) offers more than 70,000 titles as talking books. Anyone who finds reading difficult can borrow a talking book from a normal library – no certificates are needed. A dyslexic student is allowed to have all course literature on tape/DAISY.

An area of special interest for dyslexics in higher education is information access on the Web, as students are bound to search for information and present it in papers and essays. Even today, most Web pages will not allow poor spelling, which means many dyslexics are excluded from the information society in many respects. Which search engines understand that 'shopen' could mean 'Chopin', the composer? Not many! A Swedish company called Oribi Ltd (www.oribi.se) has developed a search method that does allow severe spelling errors. This function, used by the Web-based Swedish National Encyclopaedia, has become highly appreciated by students – and others.

People in working life

In working life a reading disability becomes a particular handicap. The demand on people's literacy level has increased tremendously over the last few years and not only dyslexics are having a tough time trying to keep up with 'the information society', where written language in digital format is the dominant means of communication. The pace of working life does not allow you to spend a lot of time dwelling upon spelling when creating an email, or to spend hours going through an A4 page of text. Dyslexics therefore need tools that will eliminate as many obstacles as possible and allow them to bloom in whatever their professional field might be. The case study below serves as a good example of this.

Case study: Nils, 49, self-employed businessman

Nils (assumed name) was a successful self-employed businessman, running his own company in a highly specialized field for more than 20 years. Severely dyslexic, he had managed to create a career using his entrepreneur skills without having to read and write at all. His wife, also employed by his company, took care of all business paperwork. Nils's work included lots of travelling, adapting physical environments and supervising. After an accident involving his arm he could no longer perform these tasks and had to look for other opportunities. The Social Insurance Office suggested he leave his business to become a taxi driver, an idea that Nils did not like at all. Certainly, doing this would have been a waste of skills.

Nils was assessed by a speech and language therapist who, together with a company dealing with workplace computer adaptations, helped recommend suitable software. In order to do this the team had to understand in depth what Nils' job situation was like. What tasks could be transferred to a computer? What had to be taken care of by someone else? What were Nils's weaknesses and strengths? Initially, Nils was somewhat hesitant towards using a computer, but gradually, he began to see new possibilities. Parallel to trying out suitable ICT for Nils' new tasks, he was offered a 1:1 course with the speech and language therapist. This was to overcome Nils's agony and doubts about being a reading and writing person through practising in a safe setting. As a second step, Nils was trained in his own environment to use his ICT equipment in real work situations. His equipment consisted of the following parts:

- laptop;
- mobile phone with Internet connection;
- digital camera (rather than describing workplace environments verbally, Nils would email a digital photo to his colleagues on site);
- spell checker developed especially for dyslexics ('Stava Rätt');
- a digital dictionary which allowed spelling errors ('Svenska Ordboken');
- text-to-speech software ('Vital').

Nils also had special furniture and computer accessories, recommended by an occupational physiotherapist.

Today, Nils communicates using email like anybody else, only he reads incoming emails with his ears and checks his outgoing emails both with text-to-speech and by spell checking. He has hired a couple of people who have been taught by Nils to do the manual work he used to do himself. Now Nils, dyslexic, takes care of business supervision.

Workplace adaptations are about matching needs with technology in a carefully defined work environment, which normally requires smooth teamwork between different specialists.

References

Blamires M (1999) Enabling Technology for Inclusion. London: Sage Publications.

Butterworth B (2003) Dyscalculia Screener. London: NFER-Nelson.

Crivelli V (2001) Write to Read with ICT. Wakefield: SEN Marketing.

Crivelli V, Lannen C (2001) ICT Across the Curriculum. In Peer L and Reid G (eds) (2001) Dyslexia – Successful Inclusion in the Secondary School. London: David Fulton in association with BDA, pp. 218–29.

Dimitriada Y (2000) Using information and communication technology (ICT) to support bilingual dyslexic learners. In Peer L and Reid G (eds) (2000) Multilingualism, Literacy and Dyslexia – A Challenge for Educators. London: David Fulton, pp. 102–10.

Dougan M, Turner G (1993) Information technology and specific learning difficulties. In Reid G (ed.) Specific Learning Difficulties (Dyslexia) Perspectives on Practice. Edinburgh: Moray House, pp. 154–67.

Fawcett A (ed.) (2001) Dyslexia, Theory and Good Practice. London: Whurr.

Fawcett A, Nicolson RI (1996) Dyslexia Screening Test (DST). London: The Psychological Corporation, Harcourt Brace & Co.

Föhrer U, Magnusson E (2003) Läsa och skriva fast man inte kan. [Reading and Writing Without Being Able To.] Lund: Studentlitteratur.

Horne JK, Singleton CH, Thomas CV (1999) LASS Secondary Assessment System. Beverley: Lucid Research Ltd.

Jacobson C (2000) Kompensatoriska åtgärder vid läs- och skrivsvårigheter. [Comp-ensatory intervention for reading and writing disabilities.] www.fmls.nu/sprakaloss/ Kompjacob.htm.

Kaufman C, Whiting B (2002) Parents' Guide To Using Computers. Reading: BDA.

Keates A (2000) Dyslexia and Information and Communications Technology. London: Fulton.

Nisbet P, Poon P (1998) Special Access Technology. Edinburgh: CALL Centre, University of Edinburgh.

Nisbet P, Spooner R, Arthur E, Whittaker P (1999) Supportive Writing Technology. Edinburgh: CALL Centre, University of Edinburgh.

Ott P (1997) How to Detect and Manage Dyslexia. A Reference and Resource Manual. Oxford: Heinemann Educational.

Peer L (1996) Winning with Dyslexia – A Guide for Secondary Schools. Reading: BDA.

Peer L, Reid G (eds) (2000) Multilingualism, Literacy and Dyslexia. London: David Fulton.

Peer L, Reid G (eds) (2001) Dyslexia – Successful Inclusion in the Secondary School. London: David Fulton in association with BDA.

Singleton CH (1996) Computerised Screening for Dyslexia. In Reid G (ed.) (1996) Dimensions of Dyslexia. Vol. 1. Edinburgh: Moray House, pp. 111–24.
Singleton CH, Thomas KV, Horne JK (2001) Lucid Adult Dyslexia Screening (LADS). Beverley: Lucid Research Ltd.
Snowling MJ (2000) Dyslexia, 2nd edn. Oxford: Blackwell.
Stansfield J (1998) Communicating in Writing. Reading: BDA.
Stansfield J (2001) Catch 'em Young. Reading: BDA.
Svensson I, Jacobson J, Björkman R, Sandell A (2002) Kan man ha kompensatoriska hjälpmedel för yngre skolbarn? (Can Young Pupils Benefit from Using Compensatory ICT?) www.fmls.nu/sprakaloss/jacobssonhjalpmedel.htm.

Video references

Dyslexia – A Framework of Support. In Dodds D and Thomson, M (1999) Dyslexia – A Framework of Support – An In-service Training Pack for Secondary Teachers. Edinburgh: City of Edinburgh Council Education Department.
IT Works (1997) Edinburgh: CALL Centre, University of Edinburgh.
Portable Writing Aids (1996) CALL Centre, University of Edinburgh.

Resources/Software

Reading/spelling software

Cloze Pro/Planet Wobble. (Crick.)
Dyspel. (Sally Systems Ltd.)
Earobics. (Cognitive Concepts.)
Find It, fix It. (4mation.)
Gamz Player. (Gamz Literacy Resources.)
Kurzweil 3000. Scans print, reads text aloud, reads the Web. Links to writing software. (Kurzweil Education Systems.)
Screen reader. (textHELP!)
Spin Out Stories. (4mation.)
Starspell 2.2. (Fisher Marriott.)
Start to Finish Books. (Don Johnston.)
Study Wiz. (Inclusive Technology.)
Superspell. (4mation.)
Wordshark. (White Space.)

Writing software (including text-to-speech software)

Clicker 4/Word Bar (Vocabulary Toolbox). (Crick.)
CoWriter/ Write Out Loud. (Don Johnston.)
Draft Builder. (Don Johnston.)
Inclusive Writer. (Inclusive Technology.)
Inspiration/ Kidspiration. (Inspirations Software.)
Read & Write/Wordsmith. (textHELP!)
Speak Out. (Sensory Software.)
Star Think. (Fisher Marriott.)
TextEase. (Softease Ltd.)

Type & Talk. (textHELP!)
Writer's Toolkit. (Learning & Teaching Scotland.)

Integrated learning software

PLATO. (Plato Learning Inc.)
SuccessMaker. (R.M. Systems)

Maths/number software

Interactive Calculator. (Inclusive Technology.)
Maths Circus. (4mation.)
Maths Mania. (Topological Software.)
Numbershark. (White Space.)

Study/search skills

Wordswork. (Alphabetics.)
World Book Encyclopedia. (IBM.)

Speech recognition

Dragon Naturally Speaking. (Scansoft.)
Via Voice. (IBM.)

Keyboarding

Expert Typing. (Microprose.)
KAZ Typing Tutor (also available in SmartAplet for Alphasmart 3000). (KAZ.)
Magictype. (Magictype Ltd.)
Touch Type. (Iota Software.)
Typing for Fun/ Type to Learn. (Sunburst.)

CHAPTER 19

The co-occurrence of specific learning difficulties: implications for identification and assessment

PAMELA DEPONIO

Specific learning difficulties

'Specific learning difficulties' was once considered to be a term that could be used interchangeably with 'dyslexia' (Pumfrey and Reason, 1992). Since the mid-1990s, however, professionals have begun to appreciate that there would appear to be a range of 'specific' learning difficulties, the most commonly recognized, and those discussed in this chapter, being dyslexia, dyspraxia/developmental co-ordination difficulties, specific language impairment and the attention deficit disorders. The term 'specific learning difficulties' has therefore taken on a wider meaning. Macintyre and Deponio (2003) have defined it as 'an umbrella term which indicates that children display discrepancies across their learning, exhibiting areas of high competence alongside areas of significant difficulty.'

Much progress has been made in recent years in the identification, assessment and support of children described as having specific learning difficulties. Although many parents would claim that much is still to be accomplished, there is no question that more and more children are benefiting from early identification, empathic teaching and the availability of specific interventions if required. The British Dyslexia Association has worked closely with successive governments to raise awareness within schools, and publications have facilitated staff development in this area (BBC2, 2001). Dyspraxia has also been recognized as a specific learning difficulty with the Scottish Executive Education Department's guidelines now distributed to every primary school in Scotland (SEED, 2001). Attention deficit disorder (ADD) and attention deficit hyperactivity disorder (ADHD) have made their controversial impact on our thinking and teachers are now aware of the existence of these as specific difficulties even if opinions on

323

their management remain divided. It is also recognized that some childrei experience a specific difficulty with language and the term 'specific languag impairment' (SLI) has become the accepted terminology for a range o specific language problems. Teachers have begun to enhance thei understanding of the range of specific difficulties, despite the confusing an constantly changing terminology employed. Literature offering sucl understanding and ideas for support strategies is abundant and sells rapidly!

The overlap of indicators

Paradoxically, the increasing ability to recognize and support specifi learning difficulties has brought its own problems. One of the key difficultie is that a label cannot be applied until a specific difficulty is identified and thi means there needs to be some agreement on the list of indicators. Scrutiny o such lists for dyslexia, dyspraxia, ADHD and SLI, however, reveals man* commonalities. As an example, some of the accepted pre/early schoo indicators of dyslexia are 'difficulty dressing', 'poor hand control' an('clumsy'. These indicators are also to be found in a checklist for dyspraxia This begs the question whether a child who meets many of the criteria fo dyslexia, including those that are common to dyspraxia, is dyslexic, o perhaps this can be interpreted as co-existing dyslexia/dyspraxia?

Research at the neurological level has been facilitated by the developmen of positron emission tomography (PET) and magnetic resonance imaging (MRI scans. Such research demonstrates that brains develop and information i; processed in different ways. It is considered that children with specific learnin; difficulties are examples of children who process information in a differen manner. Since many children who seem to experience this 'processin; difference' also exhibit areas of great strength and ability it is important t(investigate and consider this phenomenon. In consideration of this, th(difficulties that children displayed were noted and attempts were made t(cluster these difficulties, and subsequently attach a label, for example dyslexi: or dyspraxia. Identification of each specific learning difficulty has always beei problematic, perhaps because we have attempted to match children to thes(identified clusters of difficulties but, as teachers and parents know all well most children refuse to be compartmentalized!

Kaplan et al. (2001) suggests that children with specific learning difficultie: may be displaying variable manifestations of one underlying impairment rathei than discrete conditions and suggests the term 'atypical brain development would better describe specific difficulties and encourage professionals t(assess more widely. A brief look at common factors in the occurrence o specific learning difficulties supports Kaplan's view. It is generally acceptec that there is a high heritability factor with dyslexia (Gilger et al., 1991) dyspraxia (www.dyspraxiafoundation.org.uk/dyspraxia-information), SL.

(Bishop et al., 1995) and ADHD (Hinshaw, 1994). Also, a ratio of four to one boys to girls is consistently suggested for all four difficulties, although many would disagree.

It is well accepted that dyslexia cannot be confirmed by adding up the number of ticks achieved on a checklist and the case study outline below reveals the dangers of an incomplete assessment.

> 'D' was recognized as experiencing difficulty in acquiring age-appropriate skills in his primary school, although teachers were aware of a high level of general knowledge and areas of particular strength. Midway through his primary career a 'concerned' learning support teacher referred him to an occupational therapist as aspects of dyspraxia had been observed. Following assessment, he was considered not to be dyspraxic. He continued to experience difficulties in the upper primary and was referred to an educational psychologist as his poor literacy skills indicated possible dyslexic difficulties. The subsequent report suggested that he was not dyslexic. During his second year at secondary school, attention and behavioural problems became the main focus of his difficulties and the probability of ADHD led to a psychiatric referral. Again, assessment confirmed no particular condition.

Therefore, throughout his years at school, teachers had consistently observed difficulties in learning but no one had been able to offer a definite 'diagnosis' of any specific learning difficulty. The fact that 'D' had not achieved sufficient ticks in any one box had denied the recognition of the serious learning difficulties experienced and had resulted in his teachers not having a suitable explanation or understanding of his range of difficulties. Funding for appropriate support and resources had also been denied but, more importantly, 'D' remained confused and frustrated by the difficulties he experienced.

Despite the wealth of literature confirming the high likelihood of co-occurrence it would appear that schools do not always offer a holistic assessment of a child. Rather they are searching for a 'condition'. This chapter encourages professionals to be aware of the possibility of the co-occurrence of specific learning difficulties and to consider the whole child rather than attempt to match specific behaviours to a set of indicators under a particular heading. If a child is assessed as dyslexic, schools are now able to offer appropriate support. If, however, there is co-occurring dyspraxia, which is not identified, the child may not benefit from the most appropriate intervention and support.

Co-morbidity or co-occurrence?

Developmental paediatricians are well aware of the complex and interwoven developmental syndromes which may occur within a child. Keen (2001) depicts the possible co-occurrence as a 'neurodevelopmental blossom' (see Figure 19.1).

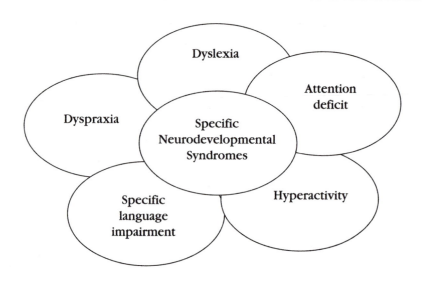

Figure 19.1 Specific neurodevelopmental blossom (adapted from Keen, 2001).

Once again terminology becomes problematic. Those with a medical background refer to the 'co-morbidity' of diseases and this term has also been used in education when referring to the possible existence of more than one neurodevelopmental syndrome. Knivsberg et al. (1999) have considered this term, citing the definition of co-morbidity in Stedman's medical dictionary as 'the simultaneous occurrence of two or more unrelated conditions or disorders.' They question whether 'co-morbid' specific learning difficulties are, in fact, unrelated. Kaplan et al. (2001) also challenge the use of the term, preferring the phrase 'atypical brain development' (ABD), which they suggest is the underlying impairment affecting children with most developmental problems and propose that ABD manifests itself with variable syndromes.

Clearly a more appropriate term needs to be employed when referring to the co-existence of two or more specific difficulties within a child. For the purposes of this chapter the term 'co-occurrence' will be used. The following literature review suggests that in the case of specific learning difficulties, co-occurrence is related. Duane (2002), when discussing specific learning difficulties, says emphatically that co-morbidity is not by chance.

Dyslexia/dyspraxia co-occurrence

The relationship between dyslexia and motor skills is well documented by researchers (Dewey et al., 2000; Fawcett and Nicolson, 1995; Kaplan et al., 1998; Nicolson and Fawcett, 1999; Portwood, 1999; Wolff et al., 1990). Kaplan's research (1998) has suggested that around 50% of children with dyslexia have features of dyspraxia whilst Portwood (1999) has suggested that 40% to 45% of children with dyspraxia have co-occurring dyslexia, ADHD or ASD (autistic spectrum disorder). Nicolson and Fawcett (1999) have investigated the role of the cerebellum and suggest that dyslexic children have cerebellum impairment. They suggest that such impairment would result in balance impairment and motor skills impairment, both indicators of dyspraxia. Stein (2001) also suggests a relationship between dyslexia and dyspraxia, considering that both may result from impaired development of magnocellular neurones in the brain. Richardson (2002) proposes that dyslexia, dyspraxia and ADHD are linked by a common disorder of fatty acid metabolism leading to a deficiency in unsaturated fatty acids considered necessary for the development and functioning of the brain.

Dyslexia/ADHD co-occurrence

Perhaps the greatest body of evidence of co-occurrence is in the relationship of dyslexia with ADHD. Wilcutt and Pennington (2000) found that individuals with a reading disability (dyslexia) are more likely than individuals without a reading disability to meet criteria for ADHD. Interestingly, research by Smith et al. (2001) on linkage analysis has reported linkage of both dyslexia and ADHD to the short arm of chromosome 6. Cantwell and Baker (1991) report that 63% of children with learning disorders in a particular study had 'co-morbid' ADD. George Hynd (editor of the *Journal of Learning Disabilities*) suggests that around 50% of children with dyslexia will also have ADHD (Hynd, 2002). A study conducted to investigate the co-occurrence of ADHD in a sample of reading disabled (dyslexic) children revealed co-occurrence in around one fifth of cases (Gilger et al., 1992).

Dyslexia/specific language impairment (SLI)

The relationship between dyslexia and SLI has also been considered by researchers. Goulandris et al. (2000) consider some findings and select Catts (1996) and Stackhouse and Wells (2000) who suggest that dyslexia and SLI exist on a continuum of language disorder. In such a case dyslexia would be regarded as a form of language impairment affecting only the phonological system or as a residual problem that remains should language difficulties be resolved. They also consider the views of Snowling et al. (2000) who suggest that children with SLI who have phonological difficulties are clearly at risk of dyslexia. Snowling (2000) further suggests that children with SLI who have good semantic skills may compensate for their phonological deficits and exhibit the typical dyslexic profile of better reading com-prehension than word-level decoding. Snowling, in a further study (2001), states that children with significant reading impairments at 8 years showed a pattern of oral speech and language delay in the pre-school years. This delay, however, is not reported in the early school years and is therefore less likely to be considered a specific language impairment, which would be unlikely to be resolved so early. McArthur and Bishop (2001), in their review of the literature, report that many researchers have suggested overlaps between dyslexia and SLI (Anderson et al., 1993; Habib, 2000; McArthur et al., 2000). Tallal et al. (1997) suggest there is a broad overlap and believe that as many as 8% of all children are language impaired and of this 8% more than 85% exhibit indicators of dyslexia. They suggest that the majority of children with oral language deficits at a pre-school level will have reading deficits in the early years of school.

The variation in the percentage overlap suggested by the above researchers is not important. What is important is the fact that research consistently demonstrates that a percentage of pupils displaying discrepancies in their learning and performance do not meet the criteria for only one specific learning difficulty. Examination of indicators of dyslexia common to other specific difficulties demonstrates how difficult it can be to reach an appropriate 'diagnosis'.

Commonalities

Accepted indicators of specific learning difficulties reveal some that may be described as 'core' to a particular difficulty and some that may be considered to be 'common' to other difficulties. It is the commonalities that lead to confusion when attempting to understand a difficulty. Whilst it is accepted that indicators of each specific difficulty vary according to which list is consulted, an attempt has been made in Figures 19.2, 19.3 and 19.4 to illustrate 'core' and 'common' indicators. It is important that these figures are regarded only as illustrations. Figure 19.2 is an attempt to demonstrate the core and common indicators between dyslexia and dyspraxia. Figure 19.3 attempts to illustrate core and common indicators between dyslexia and ADHD. Figure 19.4 attempts to display core and common indicators between dyslexia and specific language impairment.

Implications for identification and assessment

The way in which specific learning difficulties are conceptualized can depend on which particular area of the literature is consulted and the perceptions of the author. Assessment is not a simple process yet schools are becoming increasingly adept at recognizing individual specific learning difficulties. They are, however, faced with dilemmas. Should screening for a specific learning difficulty be automatic? If so, what procedure should be used? If a school routinely screens for dyslexia must it also routinely screen for dyspraxia? If routine screening is not undertaken is the onus on the class teacher to identify problems too great? Are we at risk of again not identifying

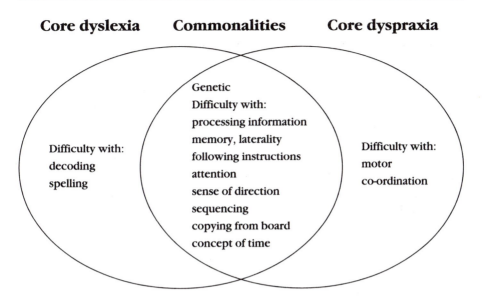

Figure 19.2 Dyslexia/dyspraxia: core and common indicators.

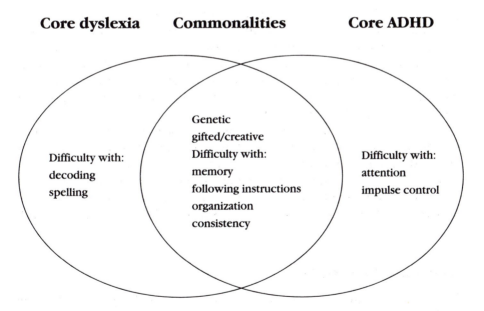

Figure 19.3 Dyslexia/ADHD: core and common indicators.

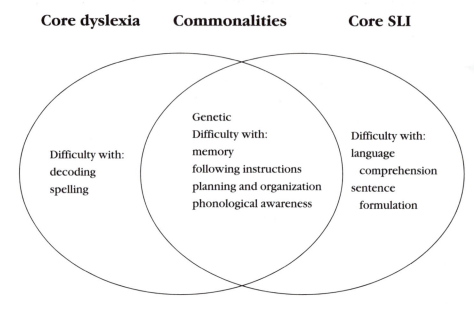

Core dyslexia   **Commonalities**   **Core SLI**

Figure 19.4 Dyslexia/SLI: core and common indicators.

problems until the child has 'failed?' Many schools do routinely test for dyslexia. However, if the results do not suggest dyslexia there may be a danger that this possibility will not be considered in the future since the child has 'had the test'! The literature suggests that if a specific difficulty is identified and further difficulties are not investigated then that assessment is incomplete. Failure to assess the whole child may lead to inappropriate or incomplete support being offered.

Changing conceptualization and terminology add to the confusion when attempting to identify difficulties that lie on a continuum, have no universally agreed definition and where no one assessment tool confirms existence. Yet it is a school's duty to identify difficulties and a child's right that appropriate accommodations be offered in an inclusive context. It would therefore seem important that the assessment process ensures a holistic assessment of each child.

Assessment process

How, then, might a school identify children with specific learning difficulties? No one test confirms the existence, therefore schools need to consider a process of assessment. Many education authorities are now augmenting the baseline assessment used in the first term of school or are supplementing with a wider assessment later in the school year. When considering the structure of such assessments it might be helpful to examine the commonalities between dyslexia and other specific learning difficulties demonstrated in Figures 19.2, 19.3 and 19.4. From these figures it is possible to extrapolate the most frequently occurring difficulties, namely:

- attention/concentration;
- short-term/working memory;
- inconsistency in performance;
- difficulty following instructions;
- planning, organizing and sequencing;
- phonological awareness;
- language difficulties;
- literacy difficulties;
- concept of time;
- confused laterality.

(See Macintyre and Deponio, 2003, for further discussion on this.) Many of the above points could be incorporated into an observation schedule that would form part of the more comprehensive early primary assessment. In this way difficulties across a wider spectrum would be highlighted. Curricular achievement should also be monitored with particular attention paid to progress in reading and discrepancies across the curriculum noted again as a possible indicator. Any evidence of demotivation in a child may be taken as an indication of a mismatch between the child and either the curriculum on offer or the way the child is expected to access the curriculum. Liaison between home and school is also an important part of the assessment process, with parental concerns noted and investigated. Thus a variety of assessment approaches is likely to result in a more holistic assessment.

Levine (1994) suggests a complete assessment and he cautions that difficulties are not always revealed by tests. He offers, as an example, the skill of copying from the board, noting that no test assesses this all-too-frequently required skill but observation by a teacher can reveal the extent of difficulty a child may encounter in undertaking such a task. Brown (2003) also advises that tests do not reveal the whole picture and observes that many pupils perform well when individual sub-tests of a battery are administered or when individual sub-skills are assessed. He suggests, however, that many pupils who have specific learning difficulties have an impairment of the executive functions, which are necessary to synthesize these sub-skills.

Policy and support

Whatever difficulties are experienced, it is the school's task to define them, to identify the strengths and motivational aspects, to inform planning, and to counsel both child and parent/carer, who must both feel confident of the school's understanding and support. A description of a child's difficulty or difficulties is also necessary to inform teaching. In the case of co-occurring difficulties it is likely that a more comprehensive consideration of abilities and difficulties will result in a more complete profile of a child. Given a full and appropriate assessment profile, targets may then be planned within either the general class plans or through individualized plans with school and home in collaboration. The most appropriate way of achieving these targets may require focused teaching, specific interventions, overlearning, differentiation or the use of accommodations to offer a more appropriate learning experience.

It is important therefore that schools give careful consideration to the issue of policy with regard to specific learning difficulties. Schools benefit from appropriate policy and guidelines to help teachers with aspects of identification, assessment and the support of pupils with specific learning difficulties. Clearly a policy on dyslexia is not sufficient. However, the value of separate policies addressing each specific learning difficulty must also be questioned. Yet the difficulties encountered by children with specific difficulties must be understood and their strengths must be harnessed to compensate for difficulties. Serious consideration must therefore be given to policy and guidelines which support teachers to support pupils. Continuing professional development for teachers and focused attention to all specific learning difficulties in our teacher education establishments is essential to increase understanding and shape future policy.

As researchers pursue their attempts to make links between the syndromes, schools must be prepared to accept the high likelihood of co-occurrence or to conceptualize specific difficulties more as Kaplan's atypical brain development (Kaplan et al., 1998). They must ensure that policy offers a holistic assessment of a child rather than an identification of one particular syndrome. The consequences of lack of assessment or incomplete assessment are well accepted and easily recognized. The child whose difficulties are neither understood nor appreciated is confused and uncertain, with self-esteem and academic progress subsequently affected. Research by Brown (2003) reports that a study of 103 adults with ADHD and an IQ of 120+ revealed that 42% dropped out of tertiary education and that 40% were unemployed. He cautions that children with co-occurring specific difficulties are at high risk because they often do not receive a complete assessment or treatment, suggesting that often only the most severe difficulty is treated. The consequences of a lack of understanding are far reaching.

Pause for thought

Research continues into this fascinating field. Are we dealing with discrete conditions, co-occurring conditions, causal factors or an atypical brain development? The race is on to establish the cause(s). If the reason for our quest is to offer what is considered 'appropriate' remediation, perhaps educators are misguided. Whilst the benefits of a perceptual motor programme to a child with dyspraxia or intervention by a speech and language therapist for a child with a specific language impairment cannot be questioned, we must ensure that we do not simply offer interventions to enable a child to 'fit in' with the existing curriculum of a school. Schools have many aims and objectives, the acquisition of literacy being one of the most important. Reading is a necessary skill, which, if taught in an appropriate manner, need not be overly problematic for dyslexic children. However, spelling and writing remain problematic for those not at the 'mild' end of the continuum. We must question our constant attempts to instil structures and sequence in a brain that has other attributes. Schools must be careful not to overtrain the left brain at the possible expense of the right. Children with dyslexia would appear to be most at risk of this counterproductive intervention. West (1997) suggests that dyslexia is nature's way of providing a range of brains, the dyslexic brain complementing the more linear, language-based non-dyslexic brain. This difference appears to result in right brain strengths and abilities in early life and, for many, subsequent 'entrapreneurship' in later life (BBC2, 2003). Successful dyslexics abound, but how many are successful despite their education rather than because of it?

> [T]he complex traits referred to as 'learning difficulties' or 'dyslexia' may be in part the outward manifestation of the relative strength of a different mode of thought, one that is available to everyone to one degree or another, but one that few children (and adults) find difficult to suppress. Too often, the gift is not recognised and is regarded only as a problem. (West, 1997)

References

Anderson KC, Brown CP, Tallal P (1993) Developmental language disorders: evidence for a basic processing deficit. Current Opinion in Neurology and Neurosurgery 6: 98-106.

BBC2 (2001) Teaching Today. Staff Development Pack. Dyslexia in the Primary School.

BBC2 (2003) Mind of a Millionaire. Broadcast Tuesday 7 October.

Bishop DVM, North T, Donlan C (1995) Genetic basis of specific language impairment: evidence from a twin study. Developmental Medicine and Child Neurology 37: 56-71.

Brown T (2003) ADHD Intelligence and Executive Functions. Paper presented at 'See the Bigger Picture', Mindfield Conference, Edinburgh International Conference Centre, 2-3 April 2003.

Cantwell DP, Baker L (1991) Association between attention deficit hyperactivity disorder and learning disorders. Journal of Learning Disabilities 24(2): 88-95.

Catts HW (1996) Defining dyslexia as a developmental language disorder: an expanded view. Topics in Language Disorders 16(2): 14-29.

Dewey D, Wilson BN, Crawford SG, Kaplan BJ (2000) Co-morbidity of developmental co-ordination disorder with ADHD and reading disability. Journal of the International Neuropsychological Society 6: 152.

Duane D (2002) Dyslexia ADHD and Non Verbal Learning Disorders. Paper presented at Policy on Dyslexia conference, Uppsala University, Uppsala, Sweden, 14-16 August 2002.

Fawcett AJ, Nicolson RI (1995) Persistent deficits in motor skills of children with dyslexia. Journal of Motor Behaviour 27: 235-50.

Gilger JW, Pennington BF, De Fries JC (1991) Risk for reading disability as a function of parental history in three family studies. Reading and Writing 3: 204-18.

Gilger JW, Pennington BF, De Fries JC (1992) A twin study of the etiology of co-morbidity: attention deficit-hyperactivity disorder and dyslexia. Journal of the American Academy of Child and Adolescent Psychiatry 31: 343-8.

Goulandris N, Snowling M, Walker I (2000) Is dyslexia a form of specific language impairment? A comparison of dyslexic and language impaired children as adolescents. Annals of Dyslexia 50: 103-20.

Habib M (2000) The neurobiological basis of developmental dyslexia: an overview and working hypothesis. Brain 123: 2373-99.

Hinshaw S (1994) Attention Deficit Disorders and Hyperactivity in Children. Thousand Oaks CA: Sage.

Hynd G (2002) Neurobiological Basis of Dyslexia: Implications for Diagnosing Subtypes of Dyslexia and ADHD. Paper presented at Policy on Dyslexia conference, Uppsala University, Uppsala, Sweden, 14-16 August 2002.

Kaplan B (1998) Developmental coordination disorders – how do you define what it is and what it is not? Paper presented at the Novartis Foundation Meeting, October 1998.

Kaplan B, Dewey DM, Crawford SG, Wilson BN (2001) The term co-morbidity is of questionable value in reference to developmental disorders: data and theory. Journal of Learning Disabilities 34(6): 555-65.

Kaplan B, Wilson BN, Dewey DM, Crawford SG (1998) DCD may not be a discrete disorder. Human Movement Science 17: 471-90.

Keen D (2001) Specific neurodevelopmental disorders. Paper presented at the Conference on the Needs of Children with Specific Developmental Difficulties, Bishop Auckland, England, February 2001.

Knivsberg A, Reichelt K, Nodland M (1999) Co-morbidity or coexistence between dyslexia and attention deficit hyperactivity disorder. British Journal of Special Education 26(1): 42-7.

Levine M (1994) Educational Care. Cambridge MA: Educators Publishing Service.

McArthur GM, Bishop DVM (2001) Auditory perceptual processing in people with reading and oral language impairments: current issues and recommendations. Dyslexia 7: 150-70.

McArthur GM, Hogben JH, Edwards VT, Mengler ED (2000) On the 'specifics' of specific reading disability and specific language impairment. Journal of Child Psychology and Psychiatry and Allied Disciplines 41: 869-74.

Macintyre C, Deponio P (2003) Identifying and Supporting Children with Specific Learning Difficulties – Looking Beyond the Label to Assess the Whole Child. London: Routledge Falmer.

Nicolson RI, Fawcett AJ (1999) Developmental dyslexia: the role of the cerebellum. Dyslexia 5: 155-77.

Portwood MM (1999) Developmental Dyspraxia – Identification and Intervention. London: David Fulton.

Pumfrey P, Reason R (1992) Specific Learning Difficulties (Dyslexia), Challenges and Responses. Windsor: Routledge.

Richardson AJ (2002) Dyslexia, Dyspraxia and ADHD – Can Nutrition Help? Dyslexia Research Trust, www.dyslexic.org.uk.

Scottish Executive Education Department (2001) Understanding and Supporting Children affected by Dyspraxia DCD in Early Years. Edinburgh: SEED.

Smith SD, Willcutt E, Pennington BF, Deffenbacher K, Hoover D, Baker M, Moyziz R, Smollen A, Olson RK, De Fries JC (2001) Investigations of the co-morbidity of dyslexia and ADHD through linkage analyses. Paper presented at the Fifth British Dyslexia Conference, 18–21 April 2001.

Snowling M (2000) Language and literacy skills. Who is at risk and why? In Bishop DVM and Leonard LC (eds) Speech and Language Impairments: from Research to Practice. Hove: Psychology Press.

Snowling M (2001) From language to reading and dyslexia. Dyslexia 7: 37–46.

Snowling M, Bishop DVM, Stothard SE (2000) Is pre-school language impairment a risk factor for dyslexia in adolescence? Journal of Child Psychology and Psychiatry 41: 587–600.

Stackhouse J, Wells B (2000) Children's speech and literacy difficulties. In Goulandris N, Snowling M and Walker I (eds) Is Dyslexia a Form of Specific Language Impairment? A Comparison of Dyslexic and Language Impaired Children as Adolescents. Annals of Dyslexia vol 50. Baltimore, USA: International Dyslexia Association, p. 104.

Stein J (2001) The magnocellular theory of developmental dyslexia. Dyslexia 7: 12–36.

Tallal P, Allard L, Miller S, Curtis S (1997) Academic outcomes of language impaired children. In Hume C and Snowling M (eds) Dyslexia: Biology, Cognition and Intervention. London: Whurr, pp. 167–81.

West TG (1997) In The Mind's Eye. New York: Prometheus Books.

Wilcutt EG, Pennington BF (2000) Co-morbidity of reading disability and attention-deficit/hyperactivity disorder: differences by gender and subtype. Journal of Learning Disabilities 33(2): 170–91.

Wolff PH, Michel CF, Ovrut M (1990) Rate and timing precision of motor co-ordination in developmental dyslexia. American Psychological Association Inc 26(3): 349–59.

Index

accessibility strategies, 155

accurate reading in context (ARC), 122–123, 125

active revision skills, 232–233

addition, National Numeracy Strategy, 289, 291, 292, 294, 296–297

Additional Literacy Strategy, 239

additional support needs (ASN), 11

advocacy, 186–187, 195–196, 197

alphabet, knowledge of the, 143

alphabetic stage, learning to read, 259, 260, 265

American English, 93, 94

American Eugenics Society, 76

America Reads programme, 166–167

analogies, 261

anterior fusiform gyrus, 92

anxiety, 245, 253

apprentice model of training, 121

Arabic, 140, 141

area, National Numeracy Strategy, 299

articulation and reading, 263

articulatory suppression, 262, 275

assessment process

co-occurrence of specific learning difficulties, 328–331

English as an additional language, 135–138

information and communication technology, 310

Ireland, Republic of, 10–11

multi-lingualism, 13, 14, 135–138

see also baseline assessment; brain-based assessment; early identification and early intervention

Assisted Support for Learning legislation (Scotland), 8

association studies, 81, 82–83

associative stage, learning simple skills, 265

at-risk groups

early identification, 208, 209

English as an additional language, 143, 144

flexible mapping, 65–68

attention

cerebellum, 38

flexible mapping, 68

future research, 8

attention deficit disorder (ADD), 41, 323

attention deficit hyperactivity disorder (ADHD), 323

cerebellum, 38, 41

co-occurrence of specific learning difficulties, 327, 328, 329, 332

genetic issues, 80, 83, 325

atypical brain development (ABD), 324, 326, 332–333

auditory discrimination in depth (ADD), 123–124

auditory processing, 37

auditory support, 62

autistic spectrum disorder (ASD), 327

autoimmune problems, 80, 83–85

automatic processing, 266

automatization

cerebellum, 27–28, 38

flexible mapping, 49, 52, 56, 69

lesson plans, 108

varied forms of learning, 266, 267–268